REPORTING AND EDITING IN JOURNALISM

Dedicated to

DR. JAI NARAIN SHARMA
Professor of the Panjab University

My Mentor

&

Utkarsh, the little Angel

Contents

PART 2
EDITING

Foreword

Communication is like our nervous system. Society became civilized, more cultured and mankind made tremendous progress in gaining knowledge and undertaking pioneering role in all spheres of human activities, only because of communication. Journalism as a spirit has become formidable mass media force; the government activities are overseen by it through its prying eye, for pointing out errors of omission and commission on the part of those in authority. All deviations from the policy and norms of behaviour are reported and, in fact, policy itself is sometimes influenced by it. It does influence public opinion and generates open debate and public discussion on subject or topic.

The champions of individual liberty have created ideas to firmly establish democracy; this spirit has permeated the world and has in fact taken the earth planet by storm. It is in the dawn of such beckoning that Journalism evolved as the formidable Fourth Estate to take charge and appeal to the conscience.

Political thinkers and social scientists are unanimous in stating that all the actions of government must be transparent and all information about governance be furnished correctly to the public as a matter of their inalienable right. James Silk Buckingham went boldly to the extent that the government should be subject to control by the press. The monarchies in the medieval period did not digest the idea of permitting the Journalists to speak or write against the kings and kings' servants. They unleashed terror upon those who dared; many early journalists, fired with the spirit of being watch-dogs of society, were made to suffer all kinds of harassment and humiliation including imprisonment. Despite that kind of repression, some of the gentlemen continued championing the cause of individual liberty. They established the fundamental truth that real Journalism, as a mission, required courage of a soldier, curiosity of a cat, vitality of a child, sniffing of a dog, apart from perseverance, initiative, drive and all good qualities of dedicated public servant.

Dr. K.C. Sharma, the first of the two authors of this book, is one of the core faculty members at Swami Vivekananda School of Management who was earlier Director there at the time of starting the College. He has been also one of the senior-most Professors at Bhartiya Vidya Bhavan's Dayanand College of Communication and Management, having officiated there as Vice-Principal and Principal. The book has been written in a simple language and in own style which is instantly descriptively gripping. It will be a proud and populár edition in libraries and with teachers and students of Journalism and Mass Communication.

The co-author, Mrs. Anupama Sharma Pathak, is Associate Professor of English. She teaches English and Communication at Government Post-Graduate Degree College, Nalagarh (H.P.). She is an M.A. (English), M.Phil. (English), doing Ph.D. in English (being at final stage of submission of thesis), M.A. (Mass Communication), B.Ed. and is also Bachelor of Journalism and Mass Communication.

I welcome this book by Dr. K.C. Sharma and Mrs. Anupama Sharma Pathak and feel myself privileged to write a short foreword to his work. Besides, it was a rewarding experience to go through the manuscript of this book. Dr. Sharma is a senior and respected scholar and popular teacher. He has been ably assisted by Mrs. Anupama S. Pathak, a writer in her own right. I fondly hope that they will continue their pursuits further in their chosen field of interest which indeed would be welcome and necessary contribution to the knowledge world.

PROF. JAI NARAIN SHARMA
Professtor and Hon. Director
Gandhi Bhavan, Panjab University
Chandigarh

Preface

Journalism has firmly established its status as an art, science and profession. In fact, it is profession of love for the humanity and has bedrock of courage and adventure. Apart from the courage of a soldier, curiosity of a cat, vitality of a child, it requires the vision of an ascetic, missionary zeal and subordinating personal goals to the welfare of the human race, irrespective of class, creed, religion, region or nation. It is indeed an exceptionally demanding profession as it requires traits of initiative and drive, steadfastness in the basic values, perseverance and whole-hearted commitment; and these are found in genuinely pioneering, exploring and creative people, they alone can be called as the trailblazers who commit their energies to direct all their activities to build the future of their dreams. Their mission serves the foundation of evolving democracy where the children of God comprising the society will one day enjoy the complete freedom, unfettered liberty, unrestricted right to information and above all, demanding the working of people's agency—the government—with absolute transparency and accountability. The profession of Journalism demands commitment to truth, fortified with facts and facts only, overcoming challenges.

Journalists are classified into various groups based on the type of duties performed. There are reporters who gather news from their beats and write stories. There are sub-editors under the charge of a Chief Sub-editor who function in the newspaper office and there are editorial writers, feature writers, columnists, sports specialists, photo journalists and other experts.

They man desks according to the beats allotted to them. The sub-editors edit the material passed on to them by the News Editor who collects it from the reporters and gets from the freelancers and News Agencies. Some material reaches from the corporate sector and government in the form of Press Notes, Press Releases and background papers of various meetings, seminars, conferences and Press statements. Sometimes, when authorities do not listen or care, complainants approach with their grievances in writing.

The present book is designed to give full possible picture of what process is followed in reporting and editing in a newspaper organisation. The book is meant for any keen reader, particularly the beginners in the career of journalism and, teaching and student community. The readers will find all connected material to understand and make themselves fully aware of the reporting techniques and editing responsibilities along with the nuts and bolts of the professional activities. A chapter on glossaries and another on oft-quoted statements of celebrated editors/journalists have been included and these add to the value of the book. We entertain the hope that the book will be found useful not only by those connected with the media but also to others as communication is a subject that interests every one.

DR. K.C. SHARMA
ANUPAMA SHARMA PATHAK

Acknowledgements

Idea generates enthusiasm and that spurs one to action—activity and energy, through to sense of satisfaction, called achievement; the top agenda is to innovate and create, for the posterity if it does not fructify fully in this short span of life. That is what moved us from the passive state to the vibrant activity in the library, at home, in the company of friends and professionals. To take proper route and study relevant literature and scan operating environment, it required expert guidance and proper direction, which we received from our mentor, Professor (Dr.) Jai Narain Sharma of the Panjab University, Chandigarh. We bow and prostrate in profound reverence to 'his exalted self'.

We express our thanks to Dr. (Miss) Ashu Pasricha, Reader at the Panjab University for her ideas, guidance and encouragement and in going through the manuscript with the keenness of a critic. We welcome her feedback and frank opinion shared spontaneously.

There are many others who were frank and forthright in sharing their valuable views. Among them, we like to mention the names of Mrs. Vandana Korpal, Chief Sub-editor, *The Tribune*, Chandigarh; Mrs. Sharda Rana, Senior Reporter, *Dainik Tribune*, Chandigarh; Mr. Kanwar Sandhu, Resident Editor (now moved elsewhere), *The Hindustan Times*; Mr. Vipin Pubby, Resident Editor, *Indian Express*, Panchkula (Haryana). They were sources of information and encouragement throughout our work.

We can not forget the help extended to us, more particularly in editing work, by Anjana Sharma who is M.A. (English) and M.Phil. (Education) and has teaching experience of 20 years in the teaching of English and liaison with the media. We thank her for her suggestions and unstinted periodic help.

We thank Mrs. Vidya Sharma, wife of the first author (Dr. K.C. Sharma) who, though with indifferent health, never complained if we failed to socialize with relatives and friends. She handled all of them single-handed and relieved us also of the other numerous usual duties. We are grateful to her for bearing with us with solitude and sense of sacrifice.

Last but not the least, we thank Abhmanyu, Kushagr and Mrikula, students, who helped on computer whenever we found any difficulty.

DR. K.C. SHARMA
ANUPAMA SHARMA PATHAK

PART I

NEWS REPORTING

CHAPTER

1

The Concept of News

INTRODUCTION

There is no gainsaying the fact that News is one of the most known commodities in today's world. Any one who understands a language and has access to mass media recognizes it. The concept of news is possibly as old as the human civilization is. It must have been in existence even before the beginning of the era of mass media. It is not surprising that one may find relics of a primitive system in remote tribal areas where people exchange local news during weekly markets in informal manner just by talking to one another. This practice is found in all societies and in the context of India, in all corners of the country.

It is generally observed when two friends meet after lapse of some time, they exchange information, which can be called personal news. Letters written to friends and relatives carry what can unhesitatingly be described as news by them. This kind of information exchange or sharing of information is continuing since early days of human society in one form or the other.

All of us will agree that death makes news. When a person dies of a disease or in an accident, it makes news. The importance of this news is relative: it has importance to others, other than those related to the affected persons, commensurate with the *importance of the person* and/or deadliness of the disease.

We can illustrate this by taking a good example. Mrs. Indira Gandhi, India's Prime Minister, was assassinated in 1984. It was big news. If she had died of a heart attack or in an accident, even then it would have been big news. That news was important because of the importance of Mrs. Gandhi. Other factors were there, but the biggest news value of that event was the person involved.

We can see that there is another angle to the news. If a person dies in a road accident in Chennai, it will be news in Chennai, but if he dies of AIDS in a Chennai hospital, it will become news of not only national but of international significance. Note that in this case, the importance of news is because of the *deadly and incurable disease.*

It is indisputably true that even ordinary death of an ordinary old man will make news at least for those who know him and more so to those related to him. The news may not appear in a newspaper but it will be news to some people. Considering the foregoing, we can say that the concept of news in human society is as old as recognition of death as an event and its communication by any means to those whom the event would affect. We have witnessed that there have been revolutions in transport and communication, which have led to various changes in significance and reach of the news but the basic concept remains the same.

In the considered opinion of not only the authorities on the subject of journalism but also of philosophers, it can be inferred that the concept of news may even be older than the concept of God. Since even today, we do not have a universally agreed definition of God; there is no definition of news either on which everybody agrees.

While exploring the human history, some facts which incidentally emerge are like this. Before the advent of newspapers (print media) and electronic media, ushering in the modern era, news was communicated by word of mouth.

People in power communicated public announcements to the people by engaging services of various kinds of drummers. Even now, such announcements dominate the news coverage in the newspapers, radio and television in almost all countries of the world irrespective of what methodology and ideology they follow. It is worthy of mention that *radio and television stations become the first targets in military coups or civil revolutions.* Also, those who snatch power from the old regime, make usė of these print and electronic drummers for their first announcements of triumph.

The concept is very old but the word 'news' is relatively of recent origin. It has not yet been defined with finality. In English, it appeared as 'newes', in 1423, "newyes" in 1485 and revolved to "newes" in 1523. It was only after 1550 that it became "news", and even in 1622, there was Butler's Weekly Newes in London while in 1685, we had such sentences as "The amazing newes of Charles at once was spread".

It is said that the four letters of the word 'news' have been described as representing the four directions—North, East, West and South. News can come from any or all of these directions. As we see every day, all events do not make news. Only important and interesting events (interesting to the readers/viewers) make news. Further, an event itself is not news; it becomes news when its accounts are available. It is precisely this factor, which made it possible for Bhagalpur Jail blinding incident to make news, that, too, several weeks after the event had taken place. Similarly, the activities of Coomar Narain and Ram Swaroop were going on for quite some time before they made news, that is, "when" *the account* became available.

We know what history means. It is also an account of important events. It relates mainly to the past. News is current; in a way, current history. Truly, to-day's newspapers will be source material for historians of tomorrow as today's historians consult newspapers of yester years in the archives. What is happening or occurring today may go down in history as an account, but surely its account which media gives now is news.

It is true, therefore, if new facts about an event of historical significance are brought out today then those facts will make news. What Richard Nixon wrote about the Indo-Pak war of 1971 made news for more than a decade later. Vijaya Laxmi Pandit's account of the relationship of her brother, Jawaharlal Nehru, with Edwina Mountbatten appeared a few years back in news columns throughout the world.

Not only events or occurrences but also *opinions make news*. Opinion of Prime Minister, Rajiv Gandhi, about arms race in the world made news. The opinion of the man in the street about the budget makes news for other newspapers. Coverage of the Indian Prime Minister's visit in the media of the country regarding foreign country visited made news in India. What the Pakistani press is publishing about an event in India may be news for the Indian press. What the US press wrote about the *Bhopal Gas Leak Tragedy* was news for Indian newspapers. The Bhopal High Court decision indicting the Company came as late as after 26 years, and the punishments are an apology. This decision has made news for a number of days and may come up again and again.

NEWS DEFINED

It is the *account of an event*, not the event itself. Professional news gatherers judge the potential interest and/or importance of an event before deciding whether to render an account of it, thus making it news. Understanding of the nature of news can not be made simple by adding such words as "timely", "concise", "accurate" or the like to definitions, as all such adjectives require explanations, which differ with the editors or the circumstances. Nothing is news until it is *reported*, no matter when it occurred. Nor is its nature changed by analysis of its effect on those who learn of it, regardless of whether the response is immediate or delayed.

The dutiful Reporter does not ask himself what the potential use of effect of his information will be. He also does not bother himself to know how many "gatekeepers" will handle it. His sole duty is to concentrate on discovering rather ferreting out the truth.

According to James Lewis, "although the press and its concepts of news value differ considerably from country to country, there are still common factors that attract readers to news. Four of them are: locality and nearness of an event; the people involved in it; unusualness, and human interest".

Keeping the varying situations in mind, as stated above, we can attempt a definition of news: *"News is an account of a recent event or opinion which is important or interesting".*

Importance and Interest are the two factors that present unlimited variety and thus explain why an event is newsworthy for one newspaper or broadcasting station and not for many other newspapers and radio or TV networks: why one news item becomes world news while another may be fit for only a local daily (edition).

News Value

Having discussed the matter in the foregoing paragraphs, we can say that importance and interest are often described as news values. However, these represent the sum total of news values or intrinsic characteristics that distinguish news from non-news.

News Sense

Identifying and measuring these values is usually called news sense. It is commonly believed that reporters identify news by intuition. But this intuition, which should be called news sense, develops in newsmen who sub-consciously learn how to measure news values. Avoiding making things simple, we can also say that experience develops the trait in all reporters, some times slowly.

Change

Change is a basic news value. If nothing happens, there will be no change. However, the world is not static. Every moment things are different from as they were the moment before. The bigger the change and the more the people affected by this change the more important it is from the news point of view.

Conflict

Actual conflicts and even the danger of conflicts make news as they tend to bring about major change. All wars and threats leading to wars have proven record of newsworthiness. Conflicts of smaller dimensions like group or personal conflicts resulting in crimes, strike and demonstrations, etc. also make news.

Even conflicting ideas and resulting debates make news. Tension and suspense, which are often associated with conflicts, are also regarded as having news values.

Disaster

It is tragedy or calamity of large dimension. Therefore, be it a result of natural calamity like an earthquake or a volcano eruption or be it a man made event like the Bhopal Gas Leak Tragedy or the Kanishka crash, disasters always makes news. It is also true of disasters of lesser dimensions like boat tragedies, small acts of sabotage resulting in loss of life or property or both.

Progress

We see that progress has also news worthiness, as it is the positive result of efforts made by enterprising individuals or concertedly in an institution/group in society. It improves quality of life. Shining successes emerge frequently through routine struggles of life. It is common knowledge that from laboratories and after years of hard work there emerge new devices, new inventions and new remedies. All this and its various dimensions make news.

Consequences

The immediate and/or long-term consequence of an event also makes news. The more people it affects by the event happened/happening the greater the consequence. Not only that, even fear of consequences of an event also makes news. It is true that the possible consequences of a nuclear war make news and all efforts to avert it and failures or successes in that direction make news. The Indo-US Nuclear Deal (123 Agreement) has been making news for quite some time now.

Consequence also serves as measure of conflicts, disaster and progress. The greater the consequence, the more the news value.

Cause

Like consequence, the cause of a newsworthy event also makes news. Every event has consequences so has its causes also. The cause of a hotel fire may be known immediately. It will make news. If it is not known, all efforts to find out the cause and possible interpretations will make news. Similarly, various theories and interpretations of Punjab crisis (Sacha Sauda cases) will keep on making news from time to time.

Eminence and Prominence

Involvement of eminent personalities in an event adds to its news value and it is directly proportional to the prominence of the person. Thus, if an eminent scholar says something on a problem, it will have news value while the same remarks made by an ordinary person may go unnoticed.

When Mulk Raj Anand fainted while speaking at Lucknow, it became national news. If this would have happened to a less known figure, the importance of that event would have been reduced to that order.

Prominence is, many a time, built up by media. Media had a major role in bringing Jarnail Singh Bindranwale, Charles Sobhraj, Billa and Ranga and Rajnarain into prominence. Then whatever they said or did, even if it did not have any other news value, got into newspapers just because of their prominence. People were interested in them because they were familiar persons. A big chunk of news in media is about those who are known in public.

The following are also called the 'Elements of News':

Timeliness

It is also a basic news value as old news is no news. In a highly competitive world of journalism, every medium tries to be first with the news. News is a highly perishable commodity and, therefore, every medium tries to give the latest available news to score over the other.

Proximity

News is meant for human beings. It is said that the prime concern of a man is himself, then he is interested in his neighbourhood. If other things are equal, proximity becomes key news value. A traffic jam in Mumbai may be news there but may not find a place in a Delhi newspaper. If the Prime Minister is visiting Chennai, his activities will get more space in the Chennai edition of *Indian Express* as compared to its Chandigarh Edition.

Novelty

If a dog bites a man, it is not news, but if a man bites a dog, it is news. This old newspaper saying recognizes the news value of the unusual novelty.

Human Interest

Almost everything in news concerns human beings, but this particular news value is the emotional context of the news event. Anything that appeals to everybody, shares human experience and has news value. Human interest is the element with which the reader identifies anything familiar that stirs his feelings. Crime stories often have a human-interest angle that makes them readable.

Human interest content of stories is higher when ordinary persons are involved in extraordinary situations like an adventure, a disaster, a tragedy or a triumph. Human interest is also involved when it depicts *extraordinary persons in ordinary situations*.

An event may have many or all of these news values and, taken together, these values determine which news story is more important than the other; which should be printed or broadcast and which should be left out or put on hold.

The Ethics of Journalism

In considering a possible life work, any young person with an adequate social conscience asks himself, "How much of my soul would I have to sell"? As regards journalism, he wants clarification of the accusations he has heard that the media are owned and run by conservative or reactionary businessmen whose interest is profit-making rather than public service. He also needs clarification on the accusations that news and editorial policy are influenced too much by advertisers and powerful pressure groups. He is also seeking answers to the accusations that the individual reporter, to survive, must suppress, exaggerate, sensationalize and distort the news which he often gathers by means of dishonest practices, unjustly invading the privacy and betraying the confidence of those with whom he deals.

The Reporters' Prerogatives

Journalists are human beings; they are selfish at times, some of them may even be greedy. Therefore, flat denial of these and similar charges is impossible. Bad journalistic practices do exit in some places and it may not be much solace to know that a review of history reveals that the worst offenders ultimately succumb. We must avoid making sweeping statements in favour of Journalists.

Newspaper Policy

It is true that newspapers and other journalistic media are big business enterprises, which means they are owned and operated by wealthy persons whose natural and sincere outlook is generally conservative. Many of these publishers deserve more credit than they receive for their efforts to prevent their personal bias from distorting the fairness of basic news coverage.

Newspapers are not instructed nor expected to fake or commit hoaxes. Only a few reporters occasionally engage in picture stealing or misrepresent themselves as policemen, etc. Most of them on almost all the occasions fail to give their readers more "inside dope" because they don't possess it themselves. On the other hand, newspapers have expended huge sums of money, involving great expenditures of time and energy, to expose corruption or to verify or discover facts in the public interest.

Invasion of Privacy

Privacy is the intimate aspect of one's living. It is sacrosanct because of the world-view on life as a result of naturalist philosophers defining concept of individual as a unique and independent entity with full freedom of thought, action and deed. Still, no legal or judicial clarification has ever been made regarding the extent to which any person possesses a right to privacy. The fact generally accepted is that anyone who courts public attention, as the politician or entertainer, sacrifices much or most of his privacy. Witnesses to accidents, crimes and the like lose it temporarily through no fault of their own. Very few persons like gossip about themselves but fewer still fail to enjoy it when it involves someone else. Many newspapers suppress the names of juvenile first offenders, relatives of persons unfavourably in the news like innocent victims of rape and other offences and the like. Such policies are determined at the journalistic summit and should be made clear to all news gatherers. Editors deplore this matter, as do all others, and brand it as insensitivity and stupidity on the part of the news gatherers.

An example cited to show lack of common sense by television reporters was the question, "How did you feel?", Asked of a father who had just seen a jet plane with his daughter aboard break into flames and crash.

Reportorial Decision-making

The same is true as regards many other ethical or policy matters, as whether to play up or down an outbreak of interracial violence, sensationalism in the handling of news of sex or crime, the details or even the facts of suicide, identification as to race, nationality or religion and the like.

A troublesome decision which the reporter sometimes has to make for himself is whether to listen to "off-record" statements, that is, whether to receive information in confidence. Sometimes, by promising not to quote a news source, he can obtain facts which the public has a right to know, or he may get tips which he can follow up without implicating the tipster. At other times, however, he may find that he has allowed himself to be "conned" into suppressing something. It is difficult to set a rule which applies to all situations. One thing is certain, however, once given, a promise must be kept. Many journalists have gone to jail for refusal to betray a confidential news source.

Freedom of Press

Many pioneers in the field of journalism had undergone

hard times, including imprisonment and deportation and banishment when they persisted in demanding freedom of the press. Public interest is at the core of journalism and, therefore, anything that the idealist ranks of journalism can contribute to the improvement of the role of the news media is in the public interest.

The credo of the *Chicago Tribune* suggests what the profession involves:

> "The newspaper is an institution developed by modern civilization to present the news of the day, to foster commerce and industry, to inform and lead public opinion, and to furnish that check upon government which no constitution has ever been able to provide".

No newsman in America can do better than to attempt to live up to the code of the American Society of Newspaper Editors adopted in April 1923, which is as follows:

> "The primary function of newspaper is to communicate to the human race what its members do, feel and think. Journalism, therefore, demands of its practitioners the widest range of intelligence, of knowledge, and of experience, as well as natural and trained powers of observations and reasoning. Indissolubly linked to these are the obligations as philosopher, teacher and interpreter. Efforts have been put in towards finding some means of codifying sound practices and just aspirations of journalism; these are based on the following canons:
>
> (1) *Responsibility:* The right of a newspaper to attract and hold readers' attention to what is published is restricted by nothing but consideration of public welfare. Since inception, journalism is taken as mission and, therefore, public welfare or public interest is supreme in this profession. So, the use of a newspaper makes of the share of public attention it gains serves to determine its sense of responsibility, which it shares with every member of its staff with

emphasis that journalism is a trust. A journalist who uses his power for any selfish or otherwise unworthy purpose is faithless to the high trust, which the general public reposes in the persons connected with journalism.

(2) *Freedom of the Press:* Taking cue from the right of individual liberty, freedom of the press is to be guarded as a vital right of mankind. It is the unquestionable right to discuss whatever is not explicitly forbidden by law, including the wisdom of any restrictive statute. There is no comprehensive law in India which defines and guarantees 'Freedom of Press' exclusively. The Constitution of India guarantees to the citizens of India several fundamental rights, the most relevant to the Press is the right to every citizen is the right to expression and speech vide Article 19(1). This freedom can be exercised by the Journalists (say the Reporters) as citizens, subject to reasonable restrictions in the interest of security of State or for maintaining foreign relations, etc. under Article 19(2).

(3) *Independence:* There are no obligations on the press except that of fidelity to the public interest and that is vital.

(a) Promotion of any private interest contrary to the general welfare, for whatever reason, is not compatible with honest journalism. So called news communication from private sources should not be published without public notice of their source or else substantiation of their claims to value as news, both in form and substance.

(b) Partisanship in editorial comment, which knowingly departs from the truth, does violence to the best spirit of Journalism. In the news columns, bias is subversive of a fundamental principle of the profession.

(4) *Accuracy, Sincerity, Truthfulness:* Power of the pen is well known. Therefore, good faith with the readers is the foundation of all journalism worthy of the name.

(a) It is due to every consideration of good faith that a newspaper is constrained to be truthful. It can not get excuse for lack of thoroughness or accuracy within its control, or failure to have command of these essential qualities.

(b) As headlines disclose the central idea or summarise contents of news, these should be fully warranted by the contents of the articles, which they surmount. They should tell the story without sensation, exaggeration nor mislead.

(5) *Impartiality:* Newspapers establish sound practices. These practices make clear distinction between news reports and expressions of opinion. News reports should be free from opinion or bias of any kind. However, this rule does not apply to the so-called special articles, which are unmistakably devoted to advocacy or characterized by a signature authorizing the writer's own conclusions and interpretations.

(6) *Fair Play:* A newspaper should not publish unofficial charges affecting reputation or moral character without opportunity given to the accused to be heard. Right practice demands the giving of such opportunity in all cases of serious accusation outside judicial proceedings.

(a) Privacy is sacred. Therefore, a newspaper should not invade private rights or feelings without sure warrant of public right as distinguished from public curiosity.

(b) Newspaper takes upon it as its privilege as well as the duty to make prompt and complete correction of its own serious mistakes of fact or opinion, whatever their origin.

(7) *Decency:* A newspaper can be convicted of insincerity

> if while professing high moral purposes, it supports base conduct, such as are to be found in details of crime and vice, publication of which is not demonstrably for the general good. Journalism lacks authority to enforce its canons. Still, it can but express the hope that deliberate pandering to vicious instincts will not be done; it will encounter effective public disapproval or yield to the influence of a preponderant professional.

REQUIREMENTS TO BE A JOURNALIST

Time was when it used to be said that a journalist is born, not made, that you could not push a man through a journalism school. Gandhi never saw the inside of a journalism school. Neither did Bal Gangadhar Tilak, nor did a score of distinguished editors since James Augusts Hicky who brought out the first full-fledged printed newspaper in India, the Bengal Gazetee, on 29 January 1780. Yet, they were men who brought much honour to the profession.

But those were different times. It was sufficient, then, for any one with a sense of mission, to declare him a journalist, buy or hire a printing press and bring out a journal. Today, however, things are quite different, more complicated. And while, no doubt some are born journalists, they would be even better if they attended a course in journalism.

This fact, indeed, was recognized as early as in 1920 by none other than Dr. Annie Besant, founder of the National University at Adyar (in Chennai, then called Madras). The University was launched by her under the auspices of the Theosophical Society of India. Its first Chancellor was Rabindra Nath Tagore. Dr. Besant was the Pro-Chancellor and Sir C.P. Ramaswamy Iyer, Vice-Chancellor. The National Open University, as it was named then, had courses in arts, science and commerce. The subject of journalism was added to the Arts Faculty and was part of the English Department. Dr. James H. Cousins was the Head of the Department of English and Journalism. The subjects taught were History of Journalism, Press Laws, Editorial Practice and Newspaper

Administration. Although the Degree Course was closed down at the end of five years yet it is interesting to note that the importance of adequate training had been recognized as long ago as 1920 and that among the first teachers of journalism were such men of note as N.S. Rama Rao, C.S. Trilokesar, Yadunath Sarkar, and Seshagiri Rao.

We may, therefore, concede for the moment that, to be a good journalist, it is important to receive adequate and obviously the right kind of training. But here we may enter a caveat; not everyone who aspires to be a journalist necessarily becomes one merely by receiving a diploma.

A journalist should be full of energy, must be able to get at the truth; if necessary, by hustling, though these are but partial answers. More things go into the making of a journalist than mere energy or the drive to do a job. Yet, there is much sense in what Leo Reston once said in a talk to the Columbia School of Journalism:

> "I am a strong advocate of education and specialized training for newspapermen. Yet on the Washington staff of the *New York Times*, we have men with multiple degrees from universities and other men who did not complete their higher education for one reason or other. . . . Both do well. In going over their records, I am struck by the fact that all of them have this one great quality—vitality, drive, aliveness—call it what you will.

It occurs to me, therefore, that the most thorough education and the finest training in some specialty are of no avail to make a newspaperman outstanding unless he also had the necessary vitality to get on with the job".

S. Sadanand, founder editor of the *Free Press Journal* fits Reston's description of a Journalist. Sadanand never went to college and yet all those who knew him would concede that he was a great journalist. He was a man of tremendous vitality and what Reston called "aliveness" and "drive". And what he was, he sought in others. The point about such a man is that, while he may not have come to this profession with a university degree, he would have energy and initiative to provide himself with the kind of education needed to be a good and successful journalist. In the old days, men with the necessary drive got themselves jobs as journalists and educated themselves as they went along. They were largely self-taught men. Today, however, with competition being what it is for the few openings available to aspiring men and women, the wise among them would acquire the necessary pre-education before applying for a post.

The student of journalism must have, to start with, a good degree whether it is in the arts, sciences or commerce. This presumes that he can write grammatically and is familiar with the structure of a sentence. It is advisable that a student who had graduated in a non-English medium take a special course in English to get the utmost benefit from studies in journalism imparted in that language.

This does not mean that, a student, not proficient in English, can not benefit from a course in journalism. The essentials of journalism hold good whether the future journalist works for English or an Indian language newspaper. Accuracy, honesty and sensitivity to news are universal assets. In the absence of journalism courses in the Indian languages, there is only one way in which an aspirant can learn his trade, and that is by attending courses in the English language.

Journalists deal in facts, but facts are expressed in words, whether they are in English, Hindi, Marathi, Malayalam or Tamil. A journalist who is not proficient in the language of his choice cannot possibly hope to make an impact on his readers.

This leads to the issue of proficiency not just in open language but several languages. The more languages one knows, the more one's chances of landing a job, especially these days when states in India vie with one another to conduct their business in the regional languages. The journalist who is conversant with a foreign language such as French, German, Russian or Arabic stands a better chance of being selected for posts abroad than one who knows only English. It is fashionable to say that journalism is a profession like law or medicine or engineering. A profession it is, but, at the same time, it is a craft that has to be learnt. And more so to the publisher journalist who is ignorant of the principles of business management. Sadanand was a great journalist but a poor business manager and, in the end, was a sad failure. He would have been better journalist if he were a better business manager. Successful journalism is not necessarily good journalism but good journalism needs to be successful journalism as well. The primary purpose of a journalist is to communicate and a journal that does not sell is a journal that fails in its primary purpose. To say, therefore, that journalism is a lofty profession and not a trade or a craft is a bit of snobbery that one can usefully do without.

A professional is a man who has had training in his particular field. An individual is not allowed to practice medicine unless he is certified by a duly recognized medical school. Lawyers, Chartered Accountants and, in some countries, even "barbers" and "beauticians" have to acquire a certificate that recognizes their competence. It would be in the fitness of things, therefore, if newspapermen, too, acquire adequate recognition of their professional talent from their compeers. However, in the absence of institutional recognition, a journalist in India acquires professional respectability by the very fact of being on a journal's payroll. The belief, obviously, is that if a person is on the payroll, he must be competent.

In the circumstances, the only way to distinguish a processional from an amateur is to find out whether the person is actively employed on a full-time basis by a newspaper or journal. If he is, he literally qualifies himself to be known as a professional. The freelance journalist is the one who is not regularly employed but is a frequent contributor to a newspaper.

The Random House Dictionary of the English language defines a free-lancer as a person who works as a writer, designer, performer, etc., but not on a regular salary basis for any one employer, organization or the like. The description or definition obviously stems from the fact that in the middle ages, military adventurers, often of knightly rank, offered their mercenary services to whoever paid them best. Their lances were, so to speak, available to the highest bidder.

The term is now applicable to writers, designers, *et. al.* who sell their work to whoever offers them the best terms.

They may be amateurs or professionals who have retired but whose work is deemed worthy of acceptance. Among the best-known free-lancers, surely, is Ruskin Bond, the short-story writer who contributes widely and is considered a success.

Free-lancing, however, is not an easy way to make a living, especially in India where magazines and journals are not known to be good paymasters.

Free lancing for a beginner is a precarious way to make a living. A person willing to free lance must either be willing to live on a subsistence level or have sufficient financial means to stay alive without having to depend on income from writing. Many free-lancers have regular jobs that guarantee them their bread and butter. Jagjit Singh, the distinguished science writer, was a railway administrator.

Only a few writers can expect to launch a successful full-time career in free lancing until they are thoroughly competent and well-known. Too often, competence is not enough; they must be recognized as competent. The recognition factor, in the case of free-lancers is just as important as the competence factor.

You will not, from your first week, in office be writing stories which make politicians humble and governments shaking. It will be a long time before you get a 'by line'. The only way up is hard. Hard work and merit will first have to be proved. You may be writing good essay in school but that is no guarantee that you will make a good journalist.

CHAPTER

2

Reporter : Interface with Environment and Society

QUALIFICATIONS, FUNCTIONS, ROLES, RESPONSIBILITIES, QUALITIES

Reportorial Qualifications

Myth: there is the myth that newspapermen are born and not made. Joseph Pulitzer, patriarch of the old New York World, and founder of the Pulitzer School of Journalism at Columbia University, said years ago in this regard as follows:

> "The only position that occurs to me that a man in our Republic can successfully fill by the simple fact of birth is that of an idiot. Is there any position for which a man does not demand and receive training—training at home, training in schools and colleges, training by master craftsmen, or training through bitter experience—through the burns that make the child dread the fire, through blunders costly to the aspirant?".

There have been exceptions, too. The "born editor" who has succeeded greatly without special preparation is simply a man with unusual ability and aptitude for his chosen profession, with great power of concentration and sustained effort. Even in his case, might it not be an advantage to have a system of instruction that would give him the same results at a saving of much time and labour.

In the not too distant past, a committee on schools of journalism of the American Society of Newspaper Editors, reported:

> "We want the departments of journalism to turn out men capable of appraising the changed and new world, which will be their tomorrow. We want these boys, of course. They will start at the bottom capable of rising to the posts of great newspaper power, equipped to wield that power intelligently. In other words, we wish them, while they are collecting police news and reporting banquets, to carry the mental equipment which, rightly directed, will one day invest them with editorial control. Each graduate ought to have in the knapsack of his mind the baton of the editor and the publisher; in just the same way a soldier keeps the baton of the Field Marshal with him. This society knows it is far more vital to the welfare of mankind that the men who make its journals of public opinion be culturally superior than it is that the surgeon or corporation lawyer be a man of manifold intellectual attainments".

Training in Journalism

We observe that too many college freshmen think that training for journalism consists primarily in learning how to write. Unfortunately, there is no such thing as 'just writing', in journalism or any other field. William Shakespeare is immortal, not because of vocabulary or style but because of greatness of thought. He had an incomparable knowledge of history, psychology, geography, philosophy and many other fields. He and other masters of past centuries are read today because they had something extraordinarily worthwhile to say.

Subject-matter of Journalism

The subject matter of journalism includes all that is taught in courses in political science, history, economics, sociology, chemistry, physics and other subjects, too numerous to mention. The student who recognizes this fact in his fresh man year has a big advantage. By the time he takes his first journalism course in, he will have more than the average liberal arts student's superficial interest in and knowledge of the contents of the innumerable textbooks he will have studied. He should have his head and files full of information on which to rely when he starts wandering on and off the campus in quest of news. It is the purpose of his journalism courses to make his textbook knowledge come alive, to show him how to utilize it in understanding and interpreting the contemporary scene. Through experience in hiring both liberal arts and journalism school graduates, editors have learned that a so-called "broad background" of general courses is not in itself adequate preparation for newspaper reporting. The journalist deals mostly with news related to the subject matter of courses in the different social sciences. Therefore, the student who discovers he has little or no interest in political science, economics and sociology should take stock to determine whether he really is wise to aspire to a career in journalism.

TRAITS IN REPORTERS CONSIDERED VALUABLE

Without any exaggeration, it is factually and harshly true that the young person who should be encouraged to go into journalism is the one who wants very badly to spend his adulthood saying or writing worthwhile things. It is also equally true that his chances of success may be judged by the extent to which at an early age he becomes interested in the world of affairs. Needless to say, there is no sense aspiring to a newspaper career unless one finds newspaper reading pleasurable; as a youth, the more cosmopolitan the interest the better for heralding such career.

There are unlimited interests for the 'would be' journalist in this complex global society. Still, among the courses which relate to the kind of news the future journalist will cover are the ones in criminology, urban sociology, labour problems, public finance, taxation, political parties, population problems, state and local government and others in the field of sociology, politics science and economics. Taking them is the comparatively "easy" way to learn what any successful journalist must know the "hard" way is on the job. There is no easy substitute for 'hands on' practice.

There is no distinct stock of traits for a journalist. Most of the personality traits usually listed valuable for the journalist are the ones which would be equally essential for success in most other professional fields—intelligence, friendliness, reliability, imagination, ingenuity, nerve, speed, accuracy, courage, endurance, ability to organize one's activities, perseverance, mental alertness, honesty, punctuality, cheerfulness, the power of observation, shrewdness, enterprise, optimism, humour, adaptability, initiative, emotional balance, and the like.

If there is any clue to be discovered in childhood by which to estimate journalistic capacity, it probably would be in the extent to which the boy or girl demonstrates curiosity and skepticism; a news gatherer's stock in trade is his ability to keep on asking questions until he has exhausted all angles of an assignment. The youngster who wears out his parents by his querulousness may be worth encouraging as a potentially great journalist.

ABILITY TO RECOGNISE POSSIBILITY OF NEWS

The first usually listed qualification among the special qualifications, which a news gatherer needs is a *"nose for news"*, which means the ability to recognize the news possibilities of an item of information. It involves:

(1) The ability to recognize that the information can be made of interest to readers.

(2) The ability to recognize clues which may be very casual but which may lead to the discovery of important news.

(3) The ability and capability to recognize the relative importance of a number of facts concerning the same general subject.

(4) The ability and capability to recognize the possibility of other news related to the particular information at hand.

An Apocryphal Anecdote

The following possible apocryphal anecdote is told of Deems Taylor when he first became music critic for the *New York Times*. It is said that he had arrived at the premier of an opera only to learn that the prima Dona had taken poison in her hotel room and the programme had, therefore, been cancelled. Taylor later attained eminence. Therefore, it is hard to believe that he went home and to bed. He was awakened in the middle of the night by an outraged editor. The latter told him that every other paper in town had the suicide story on page one. Taylor had murmured, "Well, there was no opera performance to write about, so what else could I do but go home?"

Another anecdote, possibly factious, is that a reporter was assigned to cover a speech, which an important man was to deliver. The Reporter was asked to follow the speech with the advance copy in his hand to see if the speaker deviated at all from the manuscript. As per usual practice, the speech had, meanwhile, been written up and its publication awaited only the confirmation of its actual delivery. The reporter, however, strolled back and presented himself before the editor. He (Reporter) reported that the speaker had cast aside the manuscript, prepared earlier, and had talked extemporaneously. He also said that it had been impossible to follow the speaker by means of the copy, which he had in his possession. The reporter, however, had failed to take a single note on the speaker's impromptu remarks.

From these "classic" examples, it is clear that common sense is indispensable for the reporter. In these days of public relations counsel and press releases, it is often difficult to see the news sources. It is advisable that the reporter must ask question after question to draw out whomever he gets opportunity to interview, to learn about the less obvious but important phases of the subject at hand. Differently put, *he must be inquisitive, perceptive and healthfully skeptical.*

To collect facts to report a story "in-depth", a reporter must be constantly "on his toes", as the expression goes. He has to think and think and think, and he has to ask and ask and ask. Good reporting consists in getting all the pertinent facts and then some more facts or information. Otherwise, the story will not be complete and may be misleading because some of the important elements might have been left out. The reporter who learns to do a thorough job of delving deep into all the potential angles of a simple "straight" news story is surely obtaining valuable training for interpretative reporting.

"Smelling a rat" is also an attribute of the straight news reporter. It is so for the interpretative reporter. For example, a reporter, noting that average school attendance in the elementary grades had gone up, still investigated the matter and came up with a surprise article on the successful use of cold sheets and other sickness preventatives.

This "smelling a rat" attitude should be the most valuable attribute of any kind of researcher—journalist or academic. The truth-seeking reporter explores every possible avenue for information.

The editor and the publisher of a newspaper are responsible for whatever is printed in it. There is no exaggeration in this statement. In some papers, the editor and publisher is the same person. The editor is also proprietor and manager in many Indian newspapers.

However, situation is different where the editor and the publisher are different persons. The editor looks after the editorial content that is anything except advertising. The advertising manager is in place to look after the advertising. There are other officials like the publisher, general manager or managing editor or executive director to look after the management of the paper.

There are a number of assistant editors who assist the editor in looking after editorial and feature pages. The News Editor looks after the news content of the paper. He is available for guidance, which is available, unsought, and voluntary, to a number of sub-editors and reporters. All the assistant editors, reporters and sub-editors work as a team.

As in higher level assignments in management in corporate entities, a journalist enters the profession of journalism and is placed under study to observe the nitty gritty and skills of the missionary profession. In India, too, the entry into the profession of journalism in normally as a trainee journalist who is later absorbed as a reporter or a sub-editor, called staffer.

All of us know that the job of a reporter is to gather news and write it for his organization. Sub-editor makes it fit to print. As newspaper is run both as business and mission, the entire organisation is tuned towards marketing. Therefore, news stories have to be suitably packaged to be attractive and interesting. The sub-editor is, therefore, assisted by artists, designers and skilled printers. While the reporters go out to their respective beats, the sub-editors work at the 'desk' where all the news that comes, is selected, edited, each news story is given a suitable headline and its place in the newspaper is decided.

Career Path

Reporters have a clear career path to go up the hierarchical ladder. They can become senior reporters, correspondents, senior correspondents, special correspondents and foreign correspondents. Sub-editors are promoted to the positions of senior sub-editor, chief sub-editor, deputy news editor and news editor. But the basic job of a reporter remains news gathering and filing the report or "copy" to the news desk. Similarly, the basic job of the sub-editor also remains the same to "sub" copy to make it fit to print which includes collecting, selecting, arranging, reducing, framing, translating and adapting for publication according to the importance of the story. Sub-editor is also called copy editor as what he edits is called copy. Whatever is filed by reporters, special correspondents, etc. is copy for him. Whatever comes to the news desk from wire services (news agencies like PTI and UNI) is also copy although it is technically called creed

Although reporting and editing are separate and independent activities yet reporting and editing sides are not water-tight compartments. Reporters and sub-editors can swap places. In many newspapers, it is a routine. A sub-editor is sent on a reporting assignment many a time. He is also asked to write news items from the handouts that land up in the newspaper office from various government departments, business organisations and voluntary associations when the reporters are away on routine or special assignments.

Academic Push-up

The celebrated theorists and writers on Journalism had foreseen that there would probably always be exceptions to what has so far been discussed. The prophesy made by them is fast coming true. The current trends indicate that future journalists will be college trained. Most of the degree-holders at present go to schools of journalism. Among them, the proportion of those with masters' and other higher degrees is also increasing. While those who are ambitious to specialize ultimately in particular fields should do so, but the majority should, in my humble opinion, strive for a thorough and well-rounded background in the social sciences: political science, sociology and economics in particular, and in literature, psychology, anthropology and philosophy in general. A student of Journalism should try to get in courses in public finance, criminology and labour problems among others as these are the areas fast emerging as affecting human life profoundly. The courses in History give him perspective and psychology enables him to come closer to understanding both individual and crowd behaviour: behaviour in fact response to environmental stimuli.

Advance Courses in Journalism

There are and should be advanced courses in journalism, in which the student should expect to learn how to utilize the background and theoretical knowledge acquired all over the rest of the campus, in reporting and interpreting the contemporary scene. On being placed on assignments, he observes to his surprise and pleasure "theory becoming action". Learning some philosophy, he will be better placed to comprehend and evaluate the immediate incident in terms of the general and eternal.

I strongly feel rather I am confident that the graduate of the school of journalism is fortunate where he learns practical side of his job. The first job enables him to write as well as report. I suggest thorough preliminary journalistic training, which should include some contact with politics and government as well as the fine run of general assignments—meetings, speeches, obituaries, accidents, interviews, routine business, society and similar news. My opinion is to get a stint of "under study" with an experienced Reporter for observing the nuances of the profession by self-study. After a few years of such varied experience, the beginner (pup-reporter as he/she is called) is able to start thinking about settling down to specialize.

Importance of Possessing Occupational Aids

The one in the journalistic profession should have the ability to use a typewriter as well as use shorthand; it is essential. As observed, when it often is necessary to interview news sources in the company of other reporters or to attend news conferences at which only a few get opportunity to ask questions, a verbatim record of what transpires is often valuable. He can also take down the testimony in court or proceeding at the committee hearings in shorthand; both at in-house or before Press Council sub-committee. In view of this utility, more and more news gatherers who specialize in such kind of work are learning it to their advantage.

Still, there are cases of those who have not cared to do so. They usually develop their own system of short of longhand. They may know some of the commercialized systems which are based primarily upon abbreviations for common syllables and combinations of letters. The reporter who develops his own system uses abbreviations for frequently used words and phrases. For instance, "2" is used for "to", "too", and "two", and "c" for "see", "u" for "you", "r" for "are", etc. The reporter can use simplified spelling in note taking if not in actual copy and can make use of such common abbreviations as "rr" for "railroad", "inc" for "incomplete", etc. He may even use foreign words which are shorter than English, as the French "selon" instead of "according to". Instead of "capital punishment" he may write down "cp" and instead of "labour union" he may write "lu". Still used by some old timers is the Phillips Telegraphic Code patented in the late 19th century by the Associated Press Official. Typical code abbreviations are lgr for "legislature," bd for "board", sap for "soon as possible", cn for "constitution", itxd for "intoxicated", etc. There are several similar systems all using abbreviations, including Zinman Rapid Writing and Streamline.

Tape Recorder

Tape recorders today are in widespread use by magazine and freelance in which they are circulated. These are valuable but not quite dependable as there can be technical snag or in unruly/aggressive assemblies which might turn into mob due to sudden frayed tempers.

Interpretation of News

It is becoming a realization that interpretation is required here and there in almost every story. There are certain stories that are basically the result of interpretation of events, circumstances or various kinds of data available from different sources. Such stories are called interpretative stories.

Knowledge of Subject

For reporting of this kind, the reporter should have a strong background of the subject. He should not forget checking all sources of information before writing such a story. If there is any doubt regarding facts, it is better not to do a story than to give a wrong interpretation based on half truths. It is truly said that a wrong interpretation is worse than no interpretation.

Opinion

This kind of reporting offers a reporter the opportunity to give his opinion in news columns. But one should avoid editiorialing news stories. Attempts in the interpretative story should be to use logic and background knowledge; conscious effort should be made to keep personal bias away from the report.

There is no bar to one's expression of opinion based on analysis of facts but distortion of facts to suit one's bias should be avoided. An interpretative reporter should always have an open mind. He may have a hypothesis to begin with, but if the facts do not support it, he should never try to mould facts to do his story.

Qualities of Reporter

Every person wants to excel in his assignments. So, to be a good reporter or a good sub-editor what one needs is common sense and command over language. These two requirements in fact summarize the qualities, which all newsmen should have as other qualities flow from these two, and the basic human values.

It is customary to describe desired qualities of a reporter and sub-editor separately, but as both of them deal with the same commodity called news, and their basic job is to communicate effectively, many of these qualities have to be common.

He must possess, among other things, the courage of a soldier, the curiosity of a cat, perseverance of historical character, King Bruce of Scotland, drive and constant movement (like the vitality of a child), nose for news (smelling power of that of a pup/dog), good health (good leg work demands it), innovativeness to formulate strategies and creativity of that of an entrepreneur, etc.

News Sense

It is the basic quality of newsmen. Every reporter has to have news sense or nose for news to distinguish news from non-news. He should be able to compare various news values and decide where to begin his story and should not miss important details.

News sense is essential for a sub-editor also. He is the first reader of a reporter's copy, and if the reporter has made a mistake, he has to correct it. A bad copy may have the most important element of the story buried in the fourth paragraph. It will be left to the sub-editor's nose for news to bring that to the first paragraph.

Clarity

A reporter should have clarity of mind and expression. A person who is confused himself cannot tell a story to others. Only clarity of mind is not enough unless it is accompanied by clarity of expression. Without clarity of expression, clarity of mind has no meaning.

After the reporter has done his job, the sub-editor is the judge of clarity of the copy. A good sub-editor will never allow a copy escape him unless the meaning is crystal clear. He has every right to make life miserable for a reporter who is not clear and does not write in simple language.

Objectivity

Objectivity is the soul of journalism. Therefore, both reporter and sub-editor should aim at objectivity while dealing with a story. They should not allow their personal bias or ideas to creep into a story. They should not take sides but try to cover all the different viewpoints to achieve balance in the story.

Accuracy

As a matter of habit, a reporter should strive for accuracy. He should check and re-check his facts until he is satisfied that he has them accurate. In this respect, he should not take any chance as accuracy is directly proportional to the credibility of a reporter and his newspaper.

The main role of a sub-editor is to check for accuracy. It is particularly important when background is involved. In the case of dates and names, the reporter may rely on his memory but the sub-editor must check them from reference material available in the newspaper office. When there is a doubt, he should leave it out—this is the golden rule of journalism. It is better not to say a thing than to say it wrong.

Alertness

A reporter should always be alert while dealing with his subjects. Many major news breaks in the past were possible because of alertness of reporters. Scoops don't walk into newspaper offices; alert reporters catch them in the air and pursue.

A sub-editor has to be alert while working on news desk. Lack of alertness of a sub-editor can be seen by readers in the morning for he will be leaving mistakes uncorrected, for everybody to see.

Speed

In today's world, speed matters everywhere; people expect jet speed. A person who cannot work fast cannot be a good reporter. While maintaining all other desirable qualities, a reporter should strive to work faster. He should think fast, decide fast and write or type fast for he has to meet deadlines or may have to go for another assignment.

Speed is of great consequence in the profession. A sub-editor also has to work with speed. He cannot sit with a copy for long. He has to do swiftly whatever is required of him for a lot more copy is waiting for him.

Slow person at the desk is just unwanted because he/she halts the work of others, particularly of integration. Therefore, a slow sub-editor is a curse at the news desk and is treated with contempt. Such people are misfits in the profession.

Calmness (balanced mind, emotional balance, adaptability)

Maintaining balance, calm, sense of achievement, loyalty to the readers and organisation are the qualities, which must be imbibed, emulated and sustained. Reporters and sub-editors often work in trying situations and difficult circumstances. They have to remain calm and composed in most exciting and tragic circumstances. In many situations, they have to be calm devoid of hysterical actions or utterances and apply appropriate mental and physical effort to write or edit the story.

We all agree that reporters and sub-editors are human beings. They have emotions but they have to stifle them in the face of disturbing influences. They have to develop resistance to excitability. Being in the field, reporters face many such occasions when they have to control their emotions.

Adaptability is a necessary virtue in reporters and sub-editors. Therefore, the sub-editors should develop a temperament to work under pressure of deadlines. They should not lose their cool if they are behind the clock for calm mind can work faster.

Curiosity

Curiosity of a cat is invaluable possession of a sub-editor

and reporter. It generates creativity and brings innovation to the job. Therefore, reporters and sub-editors should have an unsatiable curiosity. For reporters, it is useful in developing lust for facts that may lead to better stories. This characteristic will keep on improving a sub-editor for with every passing day a curious sub-editor will have a better background to do his job the next day. Reporters and sub-editors should read as much as possible to constantly improve their awareness level.

Scepticism

Doubting Thomas to begin with became St. Thomas in reality and realized truth with acceptable facts. Like him, the sub-editor and reporter must develop the desirable attitude of brainstorming self to find answers and facts for each story. Therefore, it is another necessary quality, which a reporter and a sub-editor should cultivate. They should not take anything for granted. They should have an unwavering posture of doubt until faced with undeniable proof.

Vigilance is yet another virtue of reporter and sub-editor. Reporters should be *more vigilant* for many forces constantly try to use them, and through them their paper. Many people try to plant on reporters a wrong story for their own ends. Many a time, reporters fall into such traps in good faith. They should have enough scepticism to avoid such plots.

The world is full of selfish and crafty men and organisations. Sub-editors should, therefore, also be careful since some clever politicians, public relations men and product advertisers keep on trying to take them for a ride. They should not allow anything to go in news columns that should actually go as an advertisement. They should not fail to check even the reporters' copy for such foul play.

Punctuality

It is a good habit in personal life as well as in professional life. For reporters, it is a must. If they are not punctual, they may miss something for which they may have to depend on secondary sources. It is always better to be punctual and then wait than reach late and ask others. A rival may misinform you or hide some important information.

At the desk, too, punctuality pays. If a sub-editor is punctual, he will be treated with respect by his co-workers. If he happens to be late, he will irritate them and spoil the working atmosphere. Besides, he may have to face the problem of piled up backlog of copy, which he will have to clear under the pressure of the deadline.

Patience

It is the quality, which helps a reporter in a big way for many a time rather almost daily: for he has to test his patience. It denotes the voluntary self-control or restraint that helps one to endure waiting, provocation, injustice, suffering or any of the unpleasant vicissitudes of time and life. It is not unusual that most of the time a reporter waits for someone or something and patience gives him the willingness to wait without becoming disgruntled or anxious. Many a time, he has to tolerate other people's shortcomings and remain unperturbed by someone else's tardy actions or other quirks.

Patience helps also the sub-editors as they work long hours in trying conditions. As things do not reach in the condition they want, they have unavoidably to put up with many annoying situations everyday *vis-a-vis* reporters, proof readers or printers.

Imagination

It is the art and craft to add springs to the story for swings and uniqueness.This basic mental faculty helps reporters in writing better stories that retain the readers' interest. For a sub-editor, this creative faculty is very useful as he can add sparkle to somebody or subject-matter of someone else and make it lively and colourful like a butterfly. It is common knowledge that imaginative headlines attract the reader and improve the quality of a newspaper. After all, it is the age of packaging! News stories are also packaged to make them attractive, interesting and gripping.

Farsightedness

Looking into the future with imagination is the recipe, which adds flavour and unique or memorable taste to the mental palate. It is, therefore, but natural that an intelligent envisioning of the future helps newsmen in general. The quality helps them in identifying processes and people who will be important in future, reporters can watch such processes and cultivate people who may become important news sources in the future.

There is truth in the assertion that it helps reporters and sub-editors in determining the importance of an event. This significant quality of reporter with foresight can think ahead and prepare for eventualities. With a little forethought, sub-editors, too, can plan their work to avoid tension and it results in better functioning of the desk bringing in the desired efficiency.

Self-Discipline

All of us are aware of the importance of self-discipline. One can achieve a degree of proficiency in sub-editing or reporting by systematic effort and self-control. Judged from this angle, self-discipline suggests dedication and firm commitment, apart from other traits or qualities/attributes. Self-discipline helps in journalism as in any other field of activity.

Integrity

It is the core of one's character. It is a virtue in itself and implies undeviating honesty and strict adherence to a stern code of ethics. This human quality is important for journalists. It is more important for reporters for they are more likely to be exposed to temptations as compared to sub-editors.

Fearlessness and Frankness

Swami Vivekanand said, 'fear not for fear is death and fearlessness is life". These qualities help reporters in asking unpleasant questions and taking professional risk to ferret out truth. No body gives the reporter a story on a platter. The reporter will have to probe, question, authenticate and exercise his skill of deduction to get a good story by separating the grain from the chaff.

Tactfulness

A reporter should be tactful. He should have the ability to

handle sensitive people and situations gracefully without causing hurt or arousing angry feelings. He should be considerate of others and should be careful not to embarrass, upset or offend them. A Reporter should have flexible approach, dynamism and sociable personality and should have a nature that tastefully realizes variety of experiences. He should have an understanding of human nature, behaviour and emotions. This will help him in developing contacts that are very essential for news gathering.

Initiative

A reporter has necessarily to be self-starter. As he works in the field, he should have an outgoing nature with initiative and drive. These qualities will help him get acquainted with news sources and get stories from them. A meek, retiring or shy person is not fit for reporting. He may be good at his desk. Reporters need a fair amount of assertiveness and aggressiveness to be successful in their profession and go up the career path.

Mobility

A great amount of leg work is involved in journalistic work in the world of realm. A reporter should, therefore, be mobile. He should display an attitude to enjoy moving around and should not hesitate travelling distances to get stories when required. He should go to his news sources as often as possible for such constant contacts help him get news. A mobile reporter is seldom caught napping when a major story breaks.

Diligence

It is a necessary attribute of the personality of a journalist. Reporters and sub-editors should be diligent. Their jobs require painstaking exertion of intense care and effort, alertness and dedication to the task and wary watchfulness. They have to build capacity to be able to make extremely fine distinctions while writing or editing copy. A sub-editor should aim at and insist on perfection. He should love his job; he can make or mar the newspaper.

All the qualities described in the preceding paragraphs are basically qualities of good and efficient human beings.

Those persons who possess these qualities make good and efficient sub-editors and reporters. All other things being equal, reporters need additional qualities to deal effectively with all sorts of people they meet in the field. Sub-editors should have better command over language as they improve what reporters write.

Regarding training in the past, there were no courses in Journalism. Annie Besant was the first person in India to start a course in Journalism in National University, established under the umbrella of Theosophical Society of India, as part of Arts Faculty. Similarly, there was no provision of training. Now, most of the Institutions and Universities require their students of Journalism and Mass Communication to undergo six to eight weeks training in a newspaper of repute for gaining practical experience.

CHAPTER

3

The News Story

The assortment of news items that appear in newspapers are also called news stories. In literature, stories are mostly fiction and may not have their bases in actual events, but a news story is always based on facts of occurrence, happening or event. History is also based on facts but it deals with things or events of the past while news stories are based hundred per cent on current events. Further, a news story is normally written in inverted pyramid style, that is, the most important facts come first followed by other facts in order of their impact, consequence or significance.

The inverted pyramid style has evolved in journalism over the years. It helps the readers who don't have enough time to read the lead or intro and not the whole story. It also helps sub-editors who can easily discard as much of the story from the tail without affecting its readability.

NEWS STORY STRUCTURE

Let us have a look at a typical news story:

Islam on One Side and Western Values on Other, which

appears in bold type is the head line. It is put at the head of the story and gives an idea to the newspaper reader about the subject of the story.

Moradabad, October 24 (PTI): Moradabad is the source place of news story and October 24 is the date line. It tells the reader the place and the date of the news story. (PTI) is the credit line. The newspaper has published this story, which was supplied by news agency Press Trust of India and by putting (PTI), the paper acknowledges the source of the story and this gives the credit to the news agency.

Sometimes, the name of the reporter or correspondent appears below the headline with a 'By' or 'From'. For example, the notation, "From Vidya Sharma" or "By Kanwar Sandhu" is the 'by line'.

The first paragraph of the story is called intro or lead. In the above example, "The Off-White curtain cuts right through his living room. . . , " is the intro.

The rest of the story is called "body of the story". Intro gives the most important information, which is contained in the story and, therefore, it is the most crucial part. It should contain highest quantum of news value. A good intro is pre-requisite of a good story. The proverb "well begun is half done"—goes very well in this case. You really do half of the work on a news story if you write a good intro. The body of the story will automatically follow in the inverted pyramid style.

ELEMENTS OF NEWS STORY

We can ask questions and find answers to six basic questions popularly known as the five Ws and one H. The five Ws are—What, When and Where, Who, Why and How.

There was a time when journalists were supposed to answer all the questions in the intro and that too in 28 words, later increased to 35 words and then to 48 words. However, they slowly found it unnecessary restriction and discovered that it resulted in over-crowding of the opening paragraph and loss of clarity, which at times confused and irritated the reader.

News Agencies Pool of Non-aligned countries has recently published a stylebook on this subject. The book says that "Basically a news story must answer the three Ws"—What, Why and When. As a rule, the answers to these should find place in the opening paragraph. The three other questions could be Who, Where and How but they do not necessarily arise in all stories. Except 'where'; they themselves form the cardinal points of a story, answers to them can usually be accommodated in the later paragraphs.

There is thus no hard and fast rule about these Ws and H and their inclusion in the intro or lead. A news story may not necessarily have answers to all of them but all these questions should be asked to identify the basic elements of a news story. Then, on consideration of the news value, the most important element should come in the intro.

An intro may be in reply to one, more than one or all of these questions, but there should be no compromise on clarity of expression. The acid test is: if a reader has to look over a sentence a second time to understand it, then it cannot make a good intro or lead.

A test for elements of news and their proper order could be provided with four letters from 'NEWS' as keys:

N for newsworthiness—does the story contain news values?

E for emphasis—does the intro contain the most important and interesting fact?

W for the five Ws and the H—do their answers exist in the story?

S for sources of information—does the story identify or imply the source where it is necessary?

Types of Intros or Leads

Society and business have become quite complex. Therefore, the Newsmen deal with a very wide range of subjects and everybody has his own way of presenting things: style is the man. Therefore, there are innumerable ways of writing intros and leads. This variety is obvious to everybody who reads newspapers carefully. It will occur to him that the same news story is presented in different ways in different newspapers, while the same paper presents its different stories in different ways. Any two reporters working on the same story will write it differently because of personality differences, and this explains the reason for variety.

Journalists and readers alike can classify intros or leads in various ways depending on different criteria. Based on the number of incidents involved, the intro could be simple or complex.

(i) Simple Lead involves a single incident. Even if the event may have several different incidents, the intro takes account of a single incident. Simple lead is very common in newspapers and should normally be favoured as it is easy to write it clearly. For a complex event like police action in the Golden Temple in 1984, the *Indian Express*, Chandigarh, gave a simple lead.

Hindustan Times, October 26.

COMING, school to brush up soft skills

Dale Carnegie Training has tied up with Walchand PeopleFirst to open a finishing school

Dale Carnegie Training, which has taught business skills to more than eight million professionals worldwide, said on Monday that it would open its first school in India to make graduates "employable".

(ii) Complex lead is one, which involves more than one incident in the intro. Journalists normally find its use when they have to club together similar or related incidents into one news story. As it is normally long and at times confusing, the writers must remain careful with this kind of intro, sometimes un-escapable to them.

Based on grammar of the sentence, intros can be classified into several categories:

- Substantive clause intro
- Conditional clause intro
- Present participle intro
- Past participle intro
- Prepositional phrase intro
- Infinitive phrase intro

Intros or leads can also be classified *according to the elements of the news (five Ws and H)* that dominate in the lead:

- Who lead
- What lead
- Where lead
- When lead
- Why lead
- How lead

Another classification is possible on the bases of *variety of presentation* in the intro.

Astonisher

This intro is of moderate length, from twenty five to thirty five words, and tries to arrest the reader's attention by presenting the unexpected but not of world rocking importance.

Question Lead

This lead fits with unusual or routine stories, which need an informal tone as well as with those stories that deal with matters of universal interest. Examples are :

(i) The dry climate of the region compels the people to wage a continuous struggle against the vagaries of nature.

(ii) Entrepreneurship springs out of adversity, the study says.

Indirect Quotation

Instead of using the speaker's actual words, the reporter can say in his or her own words what the speaker said. It is must to give credit to the speaker in the intro. This variety of intro gives more information compared to direct quotation.

Contrast Lead

It attracts the attention of the readers by comparing extremes. Example: Floods in Rajasthan desert.

Direct Address Lead

This intro makes the writer speak directly to the reader on an interesting subject or on the one with a universal appeal.

Descriptive Lead

It is also known as situation or picture lead. It tries to paint a word picture of an interesting person, place or thing to help create mood in the reader for the story.

Parody Lead

This intro attempts to play on words, using widely known proverbs, quotations, song titles, currently popular sayings, book titles and other expressions to help establish immediate identity with the reader (poor imitation, though) and to bring a bit of sparkle to what otherwise might have been a routine story.

One-two-three/one-two-three-four lead

It is rarely used now. It is, however, useful in giving the salient points of an important programme or putting forth important budget provisions of the Finance Bill. In this kind of intro, a general statement is followed by various important points with numbers (1), (2), (3), (4) or letters (a), (b), (c), (d) and so on.

Staccato Intro

It consists of short clipped words, phrases, sentences, sometimes separated by dots or dashes. It is casually descriptive and should not be used if the facts of the story do not justify it.

> Mid night ...an Old Yamuna Bridge ..... a scream .... a shot ..... a splash . . . a second shot .... a splash.
> This morning Delhi police recovered bodies of a couple...

Miscellaneous: Freak Lead

This type of intro has a novel approach in sentence structure and presentation, in order to catch the reader's attention.

Almost all or many of the above leads actually present summarized news stories and, therefore, they can be described as summary leads.

With interpretative news stories becoming more and more prominent in Journalism, *interpretative* leads are also becoming common in newspapers.

As per widely prevailing practice, Interpretative leads do not normally quote any body and begin with a statement from the writer of the story. The interpretative lead gives the assessment of the reporter or special correspondent based on facts of the situation. Here is an example:

The News Story

Mohali Odi: Punjab Cops Once Bitten Twice Shy (Headline in HT dated October 24, 2007)

Aseem Bassi and Manish Tiwari, October 24, Amritsar/ Chandigarh

The Body of the News Story

> *Cricket Mania* may excite fans but it is giving Punjab Police the jitters. Citing security reasons, the Intelligence has recommended granting of visas to a limited number of Pakistan fans for the India-Pakistan ODI at Mohali on November 8.

After a communiqué from the Union Home Ministry, regarding the issuance of visas to Pakistani fans who would be coming to watch the Mohali game, the State's Home Department had suggested about 5'000 visas for Pak nationals.

After writing the intro, the body of the story will follow in the logical sequential order, following the principles of inverted pyramid style.

Mention of the source in the lead is inescapable, when the news point is controversial or, in any case, not indisputable. However, where the fact is unchallengeable, the opening paragraph may give the straight news, bearing the source for mention in the next as in the above story.

It is worth noting that in such cases, one should avoid starting the next paragraph with: "This was announced (or stated) here today by ...." Such a sentence just after lead arrests the momentum of the story. The second paragraph can cover the next important point of the story straightaway, bringing in the source of the story in an easy manner, so that the flow of the story is smooth.

Skillful Journalists know it by experience that in the body of the story, choice of apt words is essential to ensure precision and better readability. The body should be concise and shorn of all verbiage. It should take notice of all material points concerning the news event, appropriately elaborate them or background them, where necessary, but should not be burdened with dispensable details.

Language of News

The language of news story should be simple and familiar for the average reader to understand without difficulty. Observe the KISS principle which says thus: Keep it simple and short. Simple and direct sentences are more effective than long, winding ones. The simple style is also easy to translate if copy is used in some sister publication in a different language. In the multi-language societies as India has, this is of a significant advantage.

It is not enough to collect news. It is must to put the stories across to the readers. Meaning must be unmistakable and it should be succinct. Readers do not generally have enough time and newspapers do not have space for elaborate reiteration. An ordinary man should remain in focus, he/she should be able to understand each word, and every sentence must be clear. There must not be any abstractions.

Some people are proud of writing long sentences with many dependent clauses, with subjunctive and conditional, with exclamations and interjections, quotations, allusions, metaphors, long images, Latin terminology, etc. They presume that the reader has enough time, old classical education and has not to work for his living.

One must always kept in mind that a sentence is more likely to be clear if it is short, communicates one thought or closely related ides. The length of sentences with too many ides is not the cause of the disease but it is often a clear symptom. Where the ides in a sentence are complex they cannot intelligibly be presented in subsidiary clauses separated by a mere comma. A full stop in such cases proves a great help to clarity.

The tendency of prefixing of a subsidiary clause with one or more ideas in advance of the main idea often produces a long confusing sentence. Opening a sentence with a subsidiary clause has special difficulties for the reader if the two ideas go in different directions. The sentence carrying the most important thought should receive immediate identity of its own.

This should not lead us to say that newspaper should use only simple sentences. Economy of space as well as rhythm requires use of all kinds of sentences. For example, it may be wasteful to introduce a complete subject and make effort to predict for each idea. A subordinate clause in a complex sentence can express in better way precisely and economically many times than a series of simple sentences or compound sentences joined by 'and', 'but', etc. The long and short of the story is—have something to say to the readership and say it as clearly as you can.

It is essential to avoid unfamiliar words and jargons (expressions peculiar to various fields of special knowledge) as far as possible. The choice should fall on words that are simple and elegant. If it is not possible to avoid unfamiliar words, explain them in simple language.

Subjects like law, medicine, biology, etc. use Latin and Greek expressions and some of these expressions have become part of the English vocabulary through usage. If these are readily understood, they may be used without any explanation, but if the Latin or Greek expressions have a popular English equivalent that should be preferred.

The point is relevant also in other cases. These expressions, if used, should be accompanied by an interpretation or an explanation for the benefit of the lay reader. There is no respectful place for using such expressions for mere fashionable presentations. The use of foreign expressions should be avoided; profanities or obscene or vulgar language should be very eschewed. Good journalism demands that they should be cut out even from direct quotations. Slang, though not in such bad taste as obscenities, should also likewise be avoided, even in the portions quoted. It sounds good sense to avoid colloquialism except in quoted tests.

Active Voice should get preference in journalistic writings. Sentences in the passive voice have a deadening effect. Vigorous, economic writing requires a preference for sentences in the active voice. One should always prefer "The directors will meet next week" to "A meeting will be held by the directors next week".

Official reports are full of the passive voice. In official circles, it was always felt necessary. If this style is adopted, the journalist may convert into active voice unless statements are to be quoted necessarily for credibility and assigned focus or emphasis. In official releases, the language is polluted by viscous verbiage; meaning is clouded by vague abstraction, euphemism, concealed identity and heavy words weighing the mind down. It does not rain, in officialese, but precipitation is experienced.

However, in certain circumstances the passive voice is useful, especially where the deed is more significant than the doer. "A general strike has been called for tomorrow by . . . to protest against . . ." is better than: "The . . . has called a general strike for tomorrow in protest against . . .", because strike is of great consequence in this story.

It is important to identify all names in the copy properly as far as possible. Where the subject of a copy has multiple identifications, that is, if he or she can be identified in more than one ways, the most pertinent among them should be identified. As a rule, the office or position of consequence he or she currently holds should be mentioned in the first instance, the others being suitably mentioned in later parts of the copy. Where the subject does not hold any office currently, he or she would have to be identified by the former office or refer to the current position.

Note that adjectives and epithets (descriptive terms) retain their significance only when used in proper context and sparingly, chosen carefully and used aptly. They add colour to a news story and improve its quality. On the other hand, they can mar a story wen used needlessly or without careful thought. It is important further that, in view of objectivity, no adjective or any other expression that smacks of bias, involves a value judgement or personal preference should be used. Use the language carefully to avoid any value judgement when it is not intended. For example, while reporting police firing, one can say, "the police had to open fire . . . 'or' . . . was forced to open fire". The correct way to give a factual narration is, "The police opened fire". However, when a minister or an official states that the police had to open fire, it may be reported as such with attribution.

Quotations should not be over-used and must be restricted to more telling portions. Sometimes, a couple of words within quotation marks are more effective than a whole sentence. It should be remembered that excessive use of quotations can have potential of spoiling a copy.

In the matter of reporting statements or speeches, the safest verb is "said". There is no harm if it appears repeatedly in a copy. In appropriate circumstances, an occasional change from "said" should be considered. Verbs that substitute "said" are: observed, remarked, stated, averred, declared, affirmed, pointed out, told, informed, opined, confirmed, admitted, accepted, conferred alleged, denied, rejected, repudiated, refuted, argued, contended, alleged, denied, rejected, repudiated, refuted, argued, disclosed, revealed.

"Remarked" may be used with any ordinary statement, but "observed" and "stated" may be used only where there is really an observation or a statement. They are not to be treated as normal variants of "said".

"Averred" is in legalistic use and it is better to steer clear of it. "Declared" is acceptable subject to the condition that the person making the concerned declaration is competent to do so. "Declared" must be backed by the strength of authority, not in an absolute sense but in relation to the concerned statement.

"Affirmed" has an element of "firmness" in it and is stronger than "said". "Asserted" is stronger still. The use of these verbs, if at all, should be restricted.

"Opined" sounds pedantic and, therefore, should not be used except as part of a quoted passage.

"Told" and "informed" cannot stand by themselves. "told" or "informed"—whom? It could be like "told newsmen or a conference or informed parliament"; it would be correct, but not as, "Mr. . . . told that . . ."

"Pointed out" may be used only in relation to a universally accepted proposition or an incontrovertible fact, and not in relation to a matter on which views differ, or are likely to differ. Since it is not always easy to determine what is a universally accepted proposition, the use of "pointed out" is best avoided.

"Accepted", "refuted" and "confessed" should also be avoided, "Admitted" is admissible in the coverage of court proceedings.

The words, "denied", "rejected", and "repudiated" may be selected on the basis of how strong a denial or contradiction is. "Argued" and "contended" should be used when a serious contention is involved and not when a mere opinion is expressed.

"Alleged" can be used with reference to a statement, which contains an allegation or a charge. "Revealed" should be avoided altogether. "Disclosed" can be used when the person has the competence to make the disclosure.

Sentences should assert. The reader does not want to be told what is not, he should be told what is. As a general rule, newsmen should strive to express even a negative thing in a positive form. For example, "the project was not successful", should be written as "the project failed". Likewise, "they did not pay attention to the complaint", should be written as, "They ignored the complaint".

No sentence should contain unnecessary words and no paragraph should have any superfluous sentence. There should be the right words in the right order. Adjectives and adverbs should be used only when they add to precision and economy of a sentence.

Redundancies or meaningless modifiers should find no place in news copy. No word should have a parasite consuming space and debasing language. An accident is either unique or it is not. It cannot be "rather unique". It is like being "rather pregnant". In "widow of the late Mr. . . . " words "the late" are redundant since "widow" presupposes that the husband is no more. One should not write "at 9 a.m. in the morning". It should be either "a.m." or "morning".

Remember that repetition is always needless. At times, it becomes irritating. A peculiar journalistic problem is repetition of source. It has crept into Indian journalism through Associated Press (AP) news agency copy. Once the report has identified the source of the information, there is no need to keep paradising it. Only if identity is in doubt should it be repeated.

Grammar of the language is very important. It applies to newsmen as it applies to others. On finer points of usage, the style book of the newspaper or news agency should be adhered to. Many newspapers have not developed stylebooks; they can make use of Press Trust of India Style Book with modification to suit their specific requirements.

CHAPTER

4

News Gathering (Sources of News)

From where do the newsmen get news? What are the sources of news? These are the questions that a layman generally asks. With changes being brought about by developments in the fields of science and technology through inventions and discoveries and thereby in the activities of human beings, particularly in business and education, and in equal measure, and not less important, in the field of technology, there are changes taking fast everywhere. Sources of news are, therefore, innumerable, provided one has nose for news. He can get news while walking on the road or even casually talking to people. On occasions, news comes to the newspaper office without any effort just because it is a newspaper and the sender wants it to be known, for which no other regular and recognized medium is available with credibility, and under deadlines. All in all, a lot of effort also goes into gathering news.

Far too many rather the innumerable sources of news can be classified into various categories depending on the criteria applied for such classification. There is no fixed source, which is proper for all kinds of stories. A particular source, however highly placed, may be relevant for one kind of story but very irrelevant for another kind. Therefore, this makes it necessary to determine in each case the appropriate source or sources of news. As per practice, legal requirement or not, the source should always be named in the stories to lend credibility and transparency, except in special circumstances.

Sources can be considered hard or weak. A source is hard when the facts of a report come from the horse's mouth, and they are thereby ascribed to the concerned person or persons by name. Consider the government policies, for example, and you find that the prime minister or other ministers, top officials of the concerned ministries or departments, etc. are the hard sources. Now consider those matters that do not fall within the purview of their own functioning and you find beyond doubt that they are not the sources hard enough for news relating to those matters; these sources are weak sources. Equally hard are official press releases and the briefings made by the "spokesman" even if not identified by name.

There are occasions when the names of the sources are not given because of certain reasons but the same are authentic enough to be considered as hard source. In those cases, the following phrases are used to indicate authenticity.

Phrases like "It is authoritatively learnt" mean that the source is as good as official. Likewise, "According to knowledgeable or informed sources" means that the source is not official but has access to official information.

Take the phrase, "According to a source (or quarter) close to X". It would mean that information may be taken as if it is coming from X.

Very often, more particularly in diplomatic matters, an official spokesman discloses an authentic piece of information on the clear understanding that it would released without attribution. In other words, on what is called "understood basis". The press publishes it with narration, "it is understood" or ". . . is understood to be", etc.

There are situations when a general opinion within a particular group with a wide base is to be given, the practice followed is to quote "circle" for example, political circles, trade circles, social circles, etc. Such souring can relate to reactions, comments, responses, expectations, etc. but these do not constitute hard news sources. These are taken weak sources.

Other phrases used that constitute weak sourcing are: "It is learnt", "it is believed", "it is stated", "it is gathered", "it is reliably learnt", or "according to reliable sources," "according to political observers" or "according to political circles".

We can classify sources as government sources and non-government sources. Government sources include legislative, executive, and judiciary and institutions attached to them Non-government sources include political parties, voluntary and other non-government institutions and members of public.

NEWS AGENCIES

Granted that news-gathering work is the job of the reporters but all the news that is printed in a newspaper is not gathered only by its reporters, correspondents and special correspondents. Still, some news stories come from them and some from retainers or stingers who are not on the regular staff but send news to the paper as and when they get it under an understanding.

We observe that the main source of news for a newspaper is news agencies, also called wire services. We find their credit lines PTI, UNI, Reuter, AP, AFP, TASS, etc. with the dateline of the story or in the end. In some papers, these credit lines appear after "intro" such as, reports PTI.

All the wire services have large network of teleprinter circuits for connecting hundreds of cities and towns from where their reporters gather news. They then process it before delivering to newspapers who subscribe for the news, delivered in their newsrooms at a teleprinter receiver set.

India now has two large news agencies or wire services, PTI (Press Trust of India) and UNI (United News of India). Both of them have a language wing, Univarta (of UNI) and BHASHA (of PTI). Earlier, there were two other multilingual wire services with Hindi as base language, Hindustan Samachar and Samachar Bharti. During the internal emergency declared in 1975, all the four were merged by Congress government under Mrs. Indira Gandhi into one that was named "Samachar". Later, the status quo ante was restored and thus the four agencies again revived by the Janata Party Government. However, because of poor management and inadequate support from the press (subscribers), the two language agencies Hindustan Samachar and Samachar Bharti collapsed. Although not yet liquidated, they are dead for all practical purposes.

We should clearly understand that News agencies and News Agents are two different entities. Therefore, do not confuse News Agencies with newspaper agents, which are also called news Agents. While a News Agent sells newspapers and periodicals, News Agencies gather news, process it for its news value and transmit to the Newspaper subscribers for price on regular basis. Similarly, a name such as Central News Agency, can also be confusing. It may not be a news agency but only a newsagent, supplying newspapers and magazines to homes or made available at their show rooms.

It is now clear that News agencies or wire services do not sell newspapers but they collect and sell news to newspapers. They also have reporters, sub-editors, news editors, special correspondents and foreign correspondents. News agency desk in the News Agency processes copy received from own reporters and foreign news agencies not for printing but for creeding to newspapers on their teleprinter network. News agency copy is also called creed in the newspaper news room.

MONITORING OF RADIO STATIONS AND TV STATIONS

The above sources apart, namely reporting staff and the wire services, monitoring of radio and television stations also serves as source of news. Almost all newspapers have a provision for monitoring to check whether they have all important news items. Radio and television news channels are regularly monitored by news agencies also and, sometimes, they prove of great help.

Then, there are press releases that directly reach newspaper offices. They are either passed on to the reporters concerned with the "beat" or handled by the desk (sub-editor's desk) depending on the discretion of the news editor.

Mobile telephones are in use by even the middle and lower middle class people these days. Therefore, telephone also at times serves as a news source as somebody from the site of an accident may ring up a newspaper office and give a tip, which would be later followed by reporters concerned or one specially deputed.

The above-mentioned sources that are normally reflected in the "by line" or "credit line"; there are other classifications of news sources, which find mention in the intro or body of the story. They indicate from where or how the news has come to the reporter. These include the following:

Press Release or Hand Out

These may be signed or unsigned statements issued by a government department, civic body, political party, institution or organization. These are released to the press for publication of the news contained therein. These are called press release, press note, or press hand out. These contain the version of the department or company; there may be omissions of significant points. These serve as one-way communication at best.

Press Conference or Press Briefing

Sometimes, a formal conference of pressmen is held. A dignitary invites the pressmen for press briefing or press conference. He makes not only the initial announcement on the subject but also delivers his statement covering all the important points in his bid to pre-empt as many questions as possible. As he gives his point of view or spells out the government policy decision, there is always scope for questions by the reporters. He remains ready to answer questions of newsmen. News briefing is also called news conference. Press conference is addressed by the dignitary himself.

Press briefing is similar to press conference. The newsmen are told something and they can ask questions. The difference is that briefing is done by a spokesman who is authorized to make a statement and answer questions on behalf of a dignitary, department, or party.

The distinction becomes clear by using an example. A Prime Minister holds a press conference, while a spokesman of the prime minister's secretariat or a spokesman of the external affairs ministry briefs the press. A party president addresses a press conference while a party general secretary briefs the press.

It can happen that the president of the political party may brief the press on the proceedings of national convention of the party. Similarly, the prime minister may brief newsmen (both domestic and international) on proceedings of a summit conference or he may brief only Indian newsmen travelling with him about what transpired between him and the head of the host state.

It is now clear as to the distinction between press briefing and press conference though there is a very thin dividing line between them: press conference sounds more formal while briefing is less formal.

Interview with Public Figure VIP, CEO, Celebrity or important person

Politician and press are made for each other. Therefore, interview method is also growing in importance these days. News items are based on interviews of dignitaries in good number. Chief Executive Officers of large corporations and Public Sector Enterprises are ever ready to give interviews, mainly to remain in the media. Not only the newspapers, but also sometimes, even news agencies' creed stories are based on interviews for publication by some paper or magazine. News stories based on interviews are considered more credible and statements therein more authentic.

Legislatures

Legislatures and local bodies (civic bodies), in session, become major sources of news. When parliament is in session, all government decisions are announced in parliament, as it is the privilege of the public representatives to get the first hand information on all policy matters. Similar position obtains in case of state legislatures and civic bodies including Panchayati Raj Institutions.

Courts

All the civil and criminal courts serve as sources of news.

The proceedings of various courts on important cases become news. Similarly, important decisions/judgments by High Courts and Supreme Court appear as news.

Conferences, Seminars and Symposia

These forums are also sources of news depending on the subject of discussion and the status of the organization involved.

Speeches

Speeches delivered in legislatures, seminars and conferences, public meetings, diplomatic dinners and in bodies like UN form a major source of news. Business and professional organizations and Industrial organizations organize discussions on various subjects of interest and pass resolutions urging the government to adopt or amend a certain policy, etc. Speeches made there give rise to large number of news stories.

Reports

Committees and Commissions are appointed by the government from time to time on important subjects, either on public demand or on its own. Therefore, the official reports published by government and sometimes by other institutions also serve as sources of news. In addition to the reports, eye-witnesses at the site of a crime or accident, police, hospital staff and district authorities also serve as sources of news. In international coverage, the United Nations (UN) and its affiliates or related bodies are also important news sources alongwith other countries, domestic and foreign governments, political and non-government sources. Similarly, large manufacturing and business houses try to remain in the news and, therefore, their Chief Executive Officers are willing to share findings of important business reports.

MORE ABOUT SOURCES OF NEWS

Whole Truth

Believe it or not it is hard fact that no newspaper can give the whole truth even if it wants to. A wealthy newspaper will have correspondents in most of the capitals, and many of these have done excellent work, but for the bulk of foreign news, it must depend upon the agencies. Some of these may have an interest in emphasizing or concealing certain items; they may be influenced by a particular government and will try to make the news fit that government policy. Or an agency may have connections with financial or advertising interests.

Most papers have their own correspondents on the spot in foreign cities and they often send in excellent reports. However, it happens frequently that the accounts have to be sent ready coloured to match the character of the paper which commissions them.

Due to demand for speed and yet greater speed and yet greater speed means that unverified reports are printed in large type, with no mention of the qualifications that the correspondent may have stressed. Often such reports are proved next day to be baseless or exaggerated, but the denial or correction, if any, will be put in small print in a neglected corner of the paper, if it is published at all. It is the impression made on the reader by the original rumour that nearly always remains. Tension between nations results out of this manipulation of the news at the source.

For example, it was reported some tears back that Germany had presented an ultimatum to Rumania, and that Englishwomen had been evacuated form Malta. Neither report was confirmed, but both contributed, though a little, to the nervousness which makes it easier for wars to start. The remedy for this is not suppression of the news in democracies. The correspondents on the spot are not necessarily to blame for misleading reports; they depend for their livelihood on supplying the demand for human interest, coloured news, and above all, speed.

Specific News Sources

Press Releases: Announcement stories that companies or individuals send out often plague the newspaper office. Most releases that come by mail are worthless, especially for the bigger paper, which cannot publish information on every activity of a company and its personnel. While most releases are self-serving, telling the general public what the person or company wants the public to know; nevertheless, sometimes releases can provide sources and ideas for news.

Reference Material

Releases are, however, valuable for setting up a directory of potential sources. The professional release has the name and address of the PR officer and the company which can be contacts, as can the names of new heads of divisions and other personnel mentioned in releases. Most newspapers rewrite any releases they decide to use, for several reasons.

Most standard releases have a release date, of "embargo" line, which tells the paper when to release or print. Editors should respect these restrictions, but they do pose a problem.

Investigative Source

It served as one of the best examples of the importance of reporters developing souring in the classical Watergate case back in the 1970s. How far would Carl Bernstein and Bob Woodward have got in the Watergate investigation without a basic source—"Deep throat", the insider—who whetted their appetite for information and supplied enough to keep them going? They also had a myriad of other sources as the following:

(1) Telephone Books
(2) Washington Post Police Reporter
(3) Library of Congress
(4) Personal Telephone Sources
(5) NP Researcher
(6) CBI and Justice Department Sources
(7) Call from an Unknown Lawyer
(8) Court Records
(9) All India Reporter
(10) Address on Envelope
(11) Plaint Sleuthing
(12) Many a Record like :

   (a) Birth Records; Death Records; Marriage; Divorce; Wills

Others like :

(13) Real Estate
(14) Property Tax Records
(15) Neighbourers on a City Block
(16) Building Permits
(17) Bankruptcies
(18) Judgements
(19) Corporations
(20) Voter Registration
(21) Auto Records
(22) Payroll Records
(23) Professional Records
(24) Permits and Inspections Records
(25) Traffic Accident Reports
(26) Military Records
(27) Income Tax Records
(28) Telephone Records

Experience shows that it is also possible to obtain these records by tricky methods. At least one reporter we know would stoop so low as to call the telephone company business office and, posing as the person being investigated to claim that he did not recall mailing certain long distance calls that had been charged to him. He would then ask the phone company to check the numbers and dates of the calls and report back. The same gambit is sometimes used by reporters who wish to check on the money a person has borrowed. They simply call the credit company to "reconfirm" the loan. Similar techniques can be used to check on someone's airplane reservations. Obtaining such information from the phone company, however, works both ways. So, if an experienced investigator is intent on protecting a sources identity, he or she may call from a remote pay phone or from the paper's subscription department rather than from a home or desk phone".

In the United States, there is a book for more detail on using records, John Ultman and Steve Honey Mari's Reporters' Handbook: an Investigator's Guide to Documents and Techniques, a project of the Investigative Reporters & Editors,

Inc. (New York: St. Martin's Press, 1983). The book, for instance, includes names and address of places to write in all 50 states for birth, marriage, divorce, and death records.

NEWS FROM PARLIAMENT

Parliament and state legislatures become major news centres when in session. The government is bound to make all announcements in the house. Political news also comes from in and around the house in session as political parties express their views on various issues and the relative strength of various parties is tested in the house. There are moves and counter moves by ruling and opposition parties which find place in news columns.

A reporter should know the rules and procedures of parliament. State legislatures follow similar rules and procedures with a slight difference here and there. During inter-session periods; there are conferences of presiding Officers of all the houses presided over by the Speaker of the Lok Sabha. This makes rules and procedures more or less uniform.

The Constitution provides for a bicameral Parliament consisting of the President and two Houses, known as the Council of States (Rajya Sabha) and the House of the People (Lok Sabha).

The Rajya Sabha

The Rajya Sabha consists of not more than 250 members. Of these, twelve are nominated by the President for their special knowledge or practical experience in such matters as literature, science, art and social service. The remaining seats are allocated to the various States and Union Territories, roughly in proportion to their population. Each State is, however, represented by at least one representative. The Rajya Sabha members are elected by the members of the Legislative Assembly of the States in accordance with the system of proportional representation by means of single transferable vote. The minimum age for membership of the Upper House (Rajya Sabha) is 30 years.

The Rajya Sabha was constituted for the first time on April 3, 1952. It is a permanent body not subject to dissolution;

but one-third of the members retires every second year by rotation and are replaced by newly elected members. The Rajya Sabha at present has 244 members (Total strength being 250 members).

The Lok Sabha

The Lok Sabha is composed of representatives of the people chosen by direct election on the basis of adult suffrage. The maximum strength of the House envisaged by the Constitution is now 547—up to 525 members to represent the States, up to 20 members to represent the Union Territories and not more than two members of the Anglo-Indian community to be nominated by the President if in his opinion that community is not adequately represented in the house. The total elective membership is distributed among the States in such a way that the ratio between the number of seats allotted to each State and the population of the State is, so far as practicable, the same for all the states. The qualifying age for memberships of the Lok Sabha is 25 years.

The Lok Sabha, unless dissolved sooner, continues for five years from the date appointed for its first meeting and expiry of the period of five years operates till dissolution of the House. However, while a proclamation of emergency is in operation this period may be extended by Parliament by law for a period not exceeding one year and not extending, in any case, beyond a period of six months after the proclamation of emergency has ceased to operate.

Following the first general election held in the country in 1952, the First Lok Sabha met in May 1952. Thereafter, general elections were held. Elections were last held in . . . to constitute the . . . the Lok Sabha. The strength of the Lok Sabha is 542 (525 elected representatives of States and 15 elected representatives of Union Territories) and two representatives of the Anglo-Indian community nominated by the President.

Functions

As in other parliamentary democracies, Parliament in India has the cardinal functions of legislation, over-seeing of administration, passing of budget and ventilation of public grievances.

The scheme of distribution of powers between the Centre and the States, followed in the Constitution of India, emphasizes in many ways the general predominance of parliament in the legislative field.

Apart from the wide range of subjects allotted to it in the Seventh Schedule of the Constitution, even in normal times Parliament can, under certain circumstances, assume legislative power over a subject falling within the sphere exclusively reserved for the States.

Further, in times of grave emergency when the security of India or any part thereof is threatened by war or external aggression or armed rebellion and a proclamation of emergency is made by the President, Parliament acquires the power to make laws for the whole or any part of the territory of India with respect to any of the matters enumerated in the States List. Similarly, in the event of the failure of the constitutional machinery in a State, the powers of the legislature of that State become exercisable by or under the authority of Parliament.

Besides the power to legislate on every wide field, the constitution vests in the Union Parliament the constituent power or the power to initiate amendment of the Constitution.

Under the Constitution, the Council of Ministers at the Centre is collectively responsible to the Lok Sabha. One of the effective methods by which parliament exercises check over the executive is through its control over finance. This financial power in the hands of Parliament helps in securing executive accountability. Besides, the procedures of parliament in India afford ample opportunities for the enforcement of ministerial responsibility, for assessing and influencing governmental policies as well as for ventilating public grievances.

The procedure of questions (with possibilities of supplementary and, in the case of inconclusive or unsatisfactory answer, half an hour discussions, calling attention, and short duration discussion), enable information to be elicited and attention focused on various aspects of governmental activities.

The more significant occasions for review of administration are provided by the discussions on the motion of thanks on the President's address, the budget, including demands for grants of various ministries, and departments and proposals to raise funds discussed through motions on matters of urgent public importance, private members' resolutions and other substantives motions. In extreme cases, government can be censured or a motion of non-confidence moved against it. Among with these, a close and continuous check on governmental activities is exercised through a comprehensive system of parliamentary committees.

Relative Role of the Two Houses

As between the two Houses, the Lok Sabha has supremacy in financial matters. It is also the House to which the council of ministers, drawn from both the Houses, is collectively responsible. On the other hand, the Rajya Sabha has a special role in enabling parliament to legislate on a State subject if it is necessary in the national interest. It has a similar power in regard to the creation of an All-India Service common to the Union and the States. In other respects, the Constitution proceeds on a theory of equality of status of the two houses.

Disagreement between the two Houses on amendments to a bill is resolved by both the Houses meeting in a joint sitting where questions are decided by majority vote. However, this provision of joint sitting does not apply to money bills and constitution amendment bills.

The Presiding Officers

In the Lok Sabha, both the presiding officers, the Speaker and the Deputy Speaker, are elected by the House. In the Rajya Sabha, the Vice President of India is the ex-officio Chairman of the House. He is elected by the members of an electoral college, constituting the members of both the Houses of parliament in accordance with the system of proportional representation by means of the single transferable vote. The Deputy Chairman of the Rajya Sabha is, however, elected by the members of the Rajya Sabha from amongst themselves.

The Constitution of India makes certain specific provisions in regard to the office of the Speaker; Lok Sabha laying particular emphasis on the importance and the independent character of the office in the context of the parliamentary polity. His salary and allowances are charged on the Consolidated Fund of India.

The Speaker of the Lok Sabha enjoys vast authority and powers, both under the Constitution and the rules as well as inherently. As the conventional head of the Lok Sabha and, as its principal spokesman, the speaker represents its collective voice. He is guardian of the rights and privileges of the House, its committees and members. It is through the Speaker that the decisions of the House are communicated to outside individuals and authorities; he issues warrants to execute the orders of the House wherever necessary, and delivers reprimands on behalf o the House.

Within the precincts of the House, his authority is Supreme. His conduct can not be discussed except on a substantive motion.

The Committees of the House function under his overall supervision and control. The Chairman of any parliamentary committee is nominated by him. Any procedural problem, in the functioning of committees is referred to him for directions. Committees like the business advisory committee, the general purposes committee and the rules committee, however, work directly under his chairmanship.

He enjoys a special position in so far as the relations between the two Houses of parliament in certain matters are concerned. He certifies money bills and decides finally what "money" matters by reason of the Lok Sabha's overriding powers in financial matters.

It is the Speaker of the Lok Sabha who presides over joint sittings called in the event of a disagreement between the two Houses on a legislative measure.

In his overriding concern to see that the Lok Sabha fulfils its rightful role as the prime centre for decision-making and policy formulation, and a major mediating force in the country's democratic policy, the Speaker has to strive to reach a position of dynamic balance in which the forum and the needs of orderly debate and efficient dispatch of the ever growing volume of public business are harmonized.

Sessions

Normally three sessions are held in a year:

(1) Budget Session (February-May)
(2) Autumn Session (July-August)
(3) Winter Session (November-December)

In the case of Rajya Sabha, however, the Budget Session is split up in two sessions and so the Rajya Sabha has four sessions.

President's Address

The Constitution enjoins that the President shall address both the Houses of parliament assembled together, at the commencement of the first session after each general election of the Lok Sabha and also at the commencement of the first session of each year and inform parliament of the causes of its summons. The address contains a review of the activities and achievements of the government during the previous year and their policy with regard to important internal and current international problems, besides a brief account of the programme of government business for the session.

The President's address is a solemn occasion. The President arrives at the Parliament House where he is received at the gate by the presiding officers and Secretaries General of both Houses and conducted in a formal procession to the high domed Central Hall of Parliament. As the procession enters the Hall, the Marshal announces the arrival of the President, and the members rise in their places. With the President reaching his seat on the dais, a band positioned in the lobby of the Central hall to the right of the President, plays the national anthem. During this time, everyone keeps standing. Thereafter, as the President takes his seat, the presiding officers occupy and members resume their seats. The President then addresses the members. After the conclusion of the address, the President rises from this seat followed by the members when the national anthem is played again, whereafter the President leaves the Hall in a procession in the same way as he arrived. The entire ceremony is marked by utmost decorum and dignity befitting the occasion.

Constitution Amendment

A bill seeking to amend the Constitution may be brought forward by a minister or a private member. Where the bill is from a private member, the bill, apart from being subject to the normal rules applicable to private members' bills, has also to be examined and recommended by the committee on private members' bills and resolutions, before a motion for leave to introduce it is included in the list of business.

Barring the requirement of a special majority (majority of the total membership of the House and a majority of not less than two-thirds of the members of the House present and voting) for its adoption, and in certain case of ratification by the legislatures of not less than one-half of the States. A bill for amendment of the constitution follows practically the same legislative process as any ordinary legislation.

The Budget

The annual financial statement laid before both the Houses of parliament embodies the estimated receipts and expenditure of the Government of India in respect to the ensuing financial year. In India, the "financial year" commences on the first of April.

The estimates of expenditure are split up into what are called "demands for grants". These demands are arranged ministry-wise and they generally cover the requirements of each administrative service. Under each demand, the estimates are sub-divided according to the categories of expenditure included in the demand.

In India, the budget is presented to Parliament in two parts: the general budget and the railway budget. The general budget is presented to the Lok Sabha by the finance minister usually at 5 PM on the last working day in February, that is, about a month before the commencement of the budget year. The budget speech of the finance minister is in two parts. One part deals with general economic and financial situation in the country and the other part relates to taxation proposals. A copy of the budget is laid on the table of the Rajya Sabha. The railway budget is presented by the railway minister about a week or ten days earlier.

The budget is discussed in two stages in the Lok Sabha. First, there is the general discussion when only the broad outlines of the budget and the principles and policies underlying it are discussed. Discussion and voting on the demands for grants of each ministry is taken up thereafter.

The Lok Sabha has the power to assent to, or refuse to give assent to any demand or even to reduce the amount of any grant sought by government. In the Rajya Sabha, there is only a general discussion on the budget. It does not vote on the demands for grants.

Vote on Account

Before the budget for the whole year is passed, a special provision is made, by which the government is enabled by Parliament to have finances, sufficient for running the administration for part of the year. This provision is called "vote on account".

The Finance Bill

The finance bill, which seeks to give effect to the government's taxation proposals, is introduced in the Lok Sabha immediately after the presentation of the budget. The provisions in the bill relating to duties of customs or excise, etc., come into effect immediately with the introduction of the bill by virtue of a declaration under the provisional collection of Taxes Act, usually included in the bill.

The Appropriation Bill

After the voting on the demands for grants has been completed, the appropriation bill is introduced. The appropriation bill seeks to authorize the government to draw monies from the "Consolidated Fund of India" to the extent shown in the budget passed by Parliament.

Supplementary/Excess Grants

No expenditure in excess of the sums authorized in the budget by Parliament can be incurred without the sanction of parliament. Whenever a need arises to incur extra expenditure, a supplementary estimate is presented to parliament. If any money has been spent on any service during a financial year in excess of the amounts granted for that service and for that year, the minister of finance/railways presents a demand for excess grant. The procedure followed in Parliament in regard to supplementary/excess grants is more or less the same as is adopted in the case of the expenditure estimates included in the general budget.

Parliamentary Committees

In India as elsewhere, the work done by Parliament is not only varied in nature, but considerable in volume. The time at its disposal is limited. It cannot, therefore, give close consideration to all the legislative and other matters that come up before it. A good deal of its business is, therefore, necessarily transacted in the committees.

Both Houses of parliament have a similar committee structure, with a few exceptions. Their appointment, terms of office, functions and procedure for conducting their business, are also more or less similar and are regulated under the provisions of the rules made by the two Houses under article 118(1) of the Constitution.

Broadly, parliamentary committees are of two kinds—Standing Committees and *ad hoc* Committees. The former are elected or appointed ever year or periodically and their work goes on, more or less, on a continuous basis. The latter are appointed on an *ad hoc* basis as need arises, and they cease to exist, as soon as they complete the task assigned to them and have submitted their reports.

Standing Committees

Among the standing committees, the three financial committees—committee on estimates, public accounts, and public undertakings—constitute a distinct group and they keep an unremitting watch over governmental spending and performance. (While members of the Rajya Sabha are associated with the committees on public accounts and public undertakings, the members of the committee on estimates are drawn entirely from the Lok Sabha). The control exercised by these committees is of a continuous nature. They gather information through questionnaires, Memoranda from representative non-official organization and knowledgeable individuals, on the spot studies of organization, oral examination of non-official and official witnesses. Between them; the financial committees examine reports on a fairly large area of the multifarious governmental activities at the centre.

These committees have adequate procedures to ensure that their recommendations are given due consideration by the government. The progress in the implementation of the recommendations as well as any unresolved differences between the committees and the government are set out in action taken reports. Other standing committees, in each House, divided in terms of their functions, are:

(1) Committee to Inquire

(a) The committee on petitions examines petitions on bills and on matters of general public interest, also entertains representations on matters concerning central subjects, and
(b) The committee of privileges examines any question of privilege referred to it by the House or the Speaker or the Chairman.

(2) The Committees to Scrutinize

(a) The committee on government assurances keeps track of all the assurances, promises, undertakings, etc. given by ministers in the House and pursues them till they are implemented.
(b) *The committee on subordinate legislation* scrutinizes and reports to the House whether the power to make regulations, rules, sub-rules, bye-laws, etc. conferred by the constitution or statues are being properly exercised by the authorities so authorized, and
(c) *The committee to examine:* The committee on

papers laid on the table examines all the papers laid on the table of the House by ministers, other than statutory notifications and orders which come within the purview of the committee on subordinate legislation, to see whether there has been compliance with the provisions of the Constitution, Act, Rules or Regulations under which the paper has been laid.

(3) Committee relating to the day-to-day Business of the House—

(a) *The business advisory committee* recommends the allocation of time for all items of government and other business to be brought before the House.

(b) *The committee on private members' bills and resolutions* of the Lok Sabha classifies and allocates time to bills introduced by private members, recommends allocation of time for discussion of private members, resolutions and examines constitution amendment bills before their introduction by private members in the Lok Sabha. The Rajya Sabha does not have such a committee. It is the business advisory committee of that House which recommends the allocation of time for the discussion of stage or stages of private members' bills and resolutions.

(c) *The rules committee* considers matters of procedure and conduct of business in the House and recommends amendments or additions to the rules, and

(d) *The committee on absence of members* from the sittings of the House of the Lok Sabha considers all applications from members for leave of absence from the sittings of the House. There is no such committee in the Rajya Sabha. Applications from members for leave of absence are considered by the House itself.

(4) *The Committee on the welfare of scheduled castes and scheduled tribes,* on which members from both Houses serve, considers all matters relating to the welfare of the Scheduled Castes and Scheduled Tribes which come within the purview of the Union Government and keeps a watch whether the constitutional safeguards in respect of these classes are properly implemented.

(5) Committees Concerned with the Provision of Facilities to Members—

   (a) The general purposes committee considers and advises the Speakers/Chairman on matters concerning the affairs of the House, which do not appropriately fall within the purview of any other parliamentary committee, and

   (b) *The house committee* deals with the residential accommodation and other amenities for members.

(6) *The joint committee on salaries and allowances of members of Parliament,* constituted under the Salary, Allowances and Pension of Members of Parliament Act, 1954, apart from framing rules for regulating payment of allowances and pension of members of parliament, also frames rules in respect of amenities like medical, housing, telephone, postal, constituency and secretarial facilities.

(7) *The joint committee on offices of profit* examines the composition and character of the committees and other bodies appointed by the Central and State governments and Union Territory administrations and recommends what offices ought to or ought not to disqualify a person from being a member of either House of Parliament.

(8) *The library committee*, consisting of members from both the Houses, considers matters concerning the library of parliament.

Ad hoc Committees: Such committees may be broadly classified under two heads:

(a) Committees which are constituted from time to time, either by the two houses on a motion adopted in that behalf, or by the Speaker/ Chairman to inquire into and report on specific subjects (for example, committee on the conduct of certain members during the president's address, committees on draft five-year plans, etc.), and

(b) The select or joint committees on bills which are appointed to consider and report on particular bills.

These committees are distinguishable from the other ad hoc committees inasmuch as they are concerned with bills and the procedure to be followed by them is laid down in the rules of procedure and the direction by the Speaker/Chairman.

The Secretariat

Each House of Parliament has a secretariat of its own headed by a secretary general who is a permanent official working under the over all control of the presiding officer of the House.

The main function of the secretary general is to advise the presiding officer, in the exercise by him of all the powers and functions that belong to his office. He also acts as the administrative head of the secretariat of the House.

Proceedings of both Houses begin at 1 p.m. When a correspondent enters the press gallery, he can get a list of business for the day. This is the order in which the House will take up its business for the day. Two other lists are also available, one listing the oral or starred questions and the other of unstarred questions, answers to which are laid on the table of the House.

If the member or members who have asked an oral question is/are not present in the House, the question becomes unstarred automatically and no other member is allowed to ask any supplementary question. A copy of the written answer which was to be read by the minister in the House is available to correspondents along with the answers to other unstarred questions.

MEDIA AND DEVELOPMENT

Communication for Development

The positive role of media in national development has been recognized in the third World countries because information dissemination plays a key role in bringing social change through opinion formation or re-orientation of attitudes among the receivers.

Nora Quebral (1975) defined development communication in the following words:

> "(It is) the art and science of human communication applied to the speedy transformation of a country from poverty to a dynamic state of economic growth and makes possible greater economic and social equality and the larger fulfilment of human potential".

The definition thus outlines the important role being played by information in expediting the process of development. More specifically and aptly, development communication can be described as the systemic use of communication channels in support of national development.

Fraser and Restrepo-Estrada (1998) defined development communication as:

> "Communication for development is the use of communication processes, techniques and media to help people towards a full awareness of their situation and their options for change, to resolve conflicts, to work towards consensus, to help people plan actions for change and sustainable development, to help people acquire the knowledge and skills they need to improve their

condition and that of society, to improve the effectiveness of institutions".

The new definition of development communication identifies the role being played by communication or mass communication in the beginning of the 21st century. The communication or mass communication will facilitate in making people understand their environment. For example, majority of the Third World population is illiterate and they may not be aware of the benefits of literary, and hence they need to be educated on the positive effects of literacy.

Development: An Overview

Development is the goal of every nation on the globe. Various strategies are planned to achieve development encompassing all spheres of life—political, economic, social, and spiritual. In the last six decades, scholars have proposed various theories and models while development agencies set various goals for the development of nations, and some of these theories have failed to yield results, and new theories that emerged have tried to offer solutions to speed up development; it is viewed as social change, Everet Rogers, an influential scholar, described development as:

> "A widely participatory process of directed social change in a society, intended to bring about both social and material advancement including greater equality, freedom, and other valued qualities of the majority of the people through their gaining greater control over their environment (Rogers, 1976)".

According to Chambers (1994), good change has the following attributes:

- Giving priority to the poor.
- Aiming to meet the basic needs.
- Striving to be endogenous to a society; it means that it should originate from the society's values and its perceptions of its own future.

- Making optimal use of natural resources, taking into account the potential of the local ecosystem, as well as the present and the future limitations imposed by global considerations for the biosphere.

Further, in the concept of good change, poor people are the focus of development who are in need of satisfying their basic needs of life. More than half of the world population is deprived of basic needs of life such as shelter, clean environment, and drinking water. Can these nations need to understand new theories of development?

Modernization Theory

Scholars have used three concepts—growth, modernization and development—to describe and explain the goals to newly independent countries. These countries while formulating their strategies of development after World War II followed the economic development model of Western industrialized nations. They believed that industrialization was the quickest way to development. Consequently, they invested in heavy industries like steel mills, hydroelectric dams etc., at the expense of the rural and agricultural sectors of economy. Meanwhile, Walt Rostow, David McClelland and other scholars in the 1950s and 60s put forth theories of development under the name of modernization for the benefit of the less developed nations.

Economic and Sociological Theories: *Rostov (1960), an American economist, suggested a five stage model for the development of a nation. Essentially he constructed a five-stage model of transition from a traditional economy to a modern industrial complex: the traditional society, pre-conditions for take-off, take-off, drive to maturity, and the age of high mass consumption. He believed that every society would pass through these five stages of economic growth leading finally to the last phase, the age of mass consumption.*

According to Rostov, a traditional society was one whose structure was developed within limited production functions based on pre-Newtonian science and technology and as pre-Newtonian attitudes towards the physical world. The social structure of such societies was hierarchical in which family and clean connections played a dominant role. Political power concentrated in the regions where aristocracy thieved with the help of soldiers and civil servants. More than 75% of the working force would get engaged in agriculture and, therefore, agriculture would be the basis of the economy.

Such societies would pass through the second stage, the pre-conditions for take-off. Rostow observed that radical changes would occur in this stage in three non-industrial sectors.

(1) Transport would develop to enlarge the extent of the market, and to exploit natural resources productively and allow the State to rule,
(2) A technological revolution in agriculture would take place to boost production and to meet the requirements of the population, and
(3) An expansion of imports would then take place. Because of these reasons, continuous development would be possible to expand the modern industry.

In the third stage, take-off was possible and this period would last about two decades. The conditions for take-off, according to Rostov, were: increase in net investment, development of manufacturing sectors, and the economy should mobilize large savings to create an effective demand for manufactured goods.

Because of these conditions, a nation would enter the fourth stage, the drive to maturity. In this stage, three changes would occur. First, the character of working force changes. Skilled people would emerge who prefer to stay in the urban areas. Second, the character of entrepreneurship changes as sophisticated and polite managers would emerge. Third, the society expects something new to happen. In the fifth stage, the age of high mass consumption, people migrate to urban areas by extensively using automobile while buying durable consumer goods and household gadgets.

While economic theory interpreted development as economic growth that would bring changes in the economic and social structure of a country, others argued that change at the individual level would pave the way for the modernization of a country. The works of two American scholars in the 1960s—David McClelland and Everet Hagen were highly influential in this direction.

McClelland (1961) propounded a theory that focused on achievement motivation or desire for excellence. He argued that the need for achievement (n ach) would propel an individual to meet challenges and take risks to succeed in the face of difficulties. The industrial nations, according to McClelland, comprise individuals with high levels of achievement motivation, which led to high rate of national economic growth. Entrepreneurship is one of the expressions of achievement motivation.

Further, McClelland explained the wide differences between the economic progress of cultures and nations; he identified a cluster of economic and cultural values that facilitate and account for development. Among the most important factors are:

- Universalism, as opposed to particularism, in which modern societies develop a universal set of codes, norms, and laws that apply to all people "regardless of who they are in particular".
- Anti-traditionalism, in which pressures for conformity are superseded by the individual's drive for economic success through impersonal entrepreneurial behaviour.
- Specificity of role relationship, a characteristic, that stresses individually motivated contractual economic arrangements rather than diffused, informal, traditional, and kinship-based arrangements.
- Achieved status, as contrasted with ascribed or inherited status.
- Collectivity, in which individuals must, to some extent, put the goals of the public interest above those purely individual aspirations.
- Rationality in planning, emphasizing the formal, scientific, and future orientations instead of magic of supernaturalism.

- Optimism and faith in the future, in particular, the idea that progress is not constrained by nature and fate, but is a function of human capacity.

The idea that achievement is a pre-condition of development carries with it an economic interpretation for McClelland, who argues that achievement is not solely the cultural propensity to seek social status, but more importantly for economic development, the "desire to do something better, faster, more efficiently, and with less efforts".

Hagen (1962) believed that developing societies comprised traditional personalities while industrial personalities had more innovative personalities.

Dominant Paradigm of Development

During 1960s, the modernization theories propounded by Lerner, and others were known as the dominant paradigm, which influenced and guided many national development programmes. According to Rogers (1976), the dominant paradigm grew out of the following:

- The industrial revolution in Europe and the United States.
- The colonial experience in Latin America, Africa and Asia.
- The success of the Marshall Plan in Europe's post-World War II development.
- The quantitative empiricism of North American social sciences.
- The capitalist philosophy of economics and politics.

The dominant paradigm aimed at raising the standard of living of the people by alleviating poverty while improving the economy. The essential features of the dominant paradigm, according to Hernandez Ramos and Schramm (1989: 10) were:

- Industry is the prime mover of the economy. Therefore, a major part of the investment must go to industry and what is required is raw material, transportation and training.

- Modern society requires more specialists than generalists in each field (e.g. Health and Industry)
- Public education is needed to raise the abilities of the entire workforce and encourage their participation in government. Healthcare and family planning are needed to increase the well-being of the population and curtail demand for jobs, housing and so on.
- The profit from centrally owned and managed industry, trade and sale of manufactured goods would be trickled down from the centre of the system to the periphery, from industries and central markets to agricultural sector and cities to villages.
- To increase rapid development, necessary information can be diffused and persuasion can occur through the mass media with the aid of an extension service.

The dominant paradigm saw mass communication as a powerful and direct force to diffuse information and innovations about development issues to the masses (Rogers, 1976).

Indian Press and Development Journalism

A movement for development journalism has started in India and newspapers are increasingly aware of development journalism.

Murthy (2002) summarizes the news contents in the mainstream Indian newspapers as follows:

(1) The Indian Press is influenced by the Western news values of sensationalism, sex, scandal, gossip and conflict. The news values of the third world like development, education, national integration, and social responsibility are relegated to the backseat.

(2) Scoop is the most sensational word in the journalistic profession. Journalists vie with each other to out-beat their professional rivals rather than to consider their relevance to society.

(3) Event reporting is given much importance than process reporting.

(4) Newspapers dedicate space to flimsy and non-relevant issues.

Though these news values are predominantly found in the newspapers, the Press can re-prioritize its values keeping in view the development of the country thus four key news values emerge such as culture and social capital, integrity, social development and social accountability to expedite national development.

Culture and Social Capital

Since the use of the word 'global village' by Marshal McLuhan in 1964, globalization is increasingly affecting social life. With the free movement of goods and ideas, globalization in its wake has impacted the world, particularly in the economic and cultural spheres. One perspective of globalization is that it has positive results for the developed world and the transitional corporation, as they are able to expand their business ventures. Scholars cite mass tourism, migration, McDonaldised consumerism and the spread of popular cultural form in music, film and television as an example of globalization's influence on culture (Casey *et. al.*, 2002; 112).

In sustainable development, local, social, and cultural values worked in support of the individual, community and society to sustain the planet. Since culture involves the passage of knowledge from one generation to another, newspapers can frequently report on cultural roots and norms of the society to preserve them for the future generations. Therefore, the newspapers in India can attempt to preserve the cultural values while giving less importance to modes of modern civilization.

Integrity

Indian society suffers from three problems—indolence, indifference and lack of integrity (Murthy, 2005). These three problems that impair development of the nation as a whole and also an individual; dishonesty coupled with corruption is the root cause of myriad problems and the politician and the bureaucrat equally share the responsibility. Kothari (1993) notes with concern that a significant portion of citizens do not get enough to eat, do not have a secure roof over their heads or enough clothes to cover bodies. Men, women, and children toil from morning to night. India's poverty is, therefore, not a poverty of resources. It is a poverty of justice. Stories in the Indian Press appear on dishonesty of politicians and bureaucrats. For instance, Sainath's stories (1996) on poverty adequately reflect the dishonesty of politicians and bureaucrats in siphoning-off the money meant for development.

When the newspapers argue that the space is a constraint in newspaper columns, how can newspapers publish splashy photographs on the front page? Newspapers, instead of publishing splashy photographs by allocating much space, can re-allocate that space to development related issues.

In a report to the Millennium Conference, the Secretary General of the UN, Kofi Annan (2000), identified some of the challenges facing the humanity at large at the start of the 21st century:

- Reducing the extreme poverty faced by 1.2 billion people who live on less than $ 1 per day.
- Improving the lives of 100 million slum-dwellers by 2020.
- Ensuring that all children complete primary education.
- Reducing HIV/AIDS infection in young people by 25 per cent by 2010.
- Preserving forests, fisheries, and biodiversity.
- Reducing the threat of global warming by reducing by 60 per cent the emissions of carbon and other greenhouse gases.
- Confronting the water crisis.
- Defending the social fabric.
- Preventing conflict.

ECONOMIC REPORTING

Economic reporting falls largely in the category of development reporting. It involves interpretation of facts and figures in a general and intelligent manner to the people.

Similarly, rural development encompasses not only agriculture but several related occupations, transport, electrification and other aspects of infrastructure.

The broad indicators of a country's economy consist of the growth rates in national incomes (GNP or GDP), the growth rates in agriculture and industry, exports and imports, whole-sale and retail prices, bank deposits and advances and the rate of money supply expansion, the level of foreign exchange reserves and the balance of payments position.

The growth in national income every year is computed by the central statistical or planning organization of a country and quick estimates are furnished. These are followed by provisional and later on by final estimates.

The wholesale price index has many sub-indices: for food-grains, edible oils, processed food, manufactured articles, power, fuel, other consumer goods, transport, and machinery. The price movement in each category has to be judged in relation to the movement of the particular group index.

In India, the Consumer Price Index (CPI) has 1960 (= 100) as the base year and it has been built with data obtained about the prevailing retail prices in about 50 centres. There is always a time lag for the Wholesale Price Index (WPI) to be reflected in the Consumer Price Index. While the WPI goes up in a given period, the CPI may be going down, and *vice-versa.*

Similarly, there are indices for measuring the progress of agricultural production or industrial production with sub-indices for various industrial products or manufactured items.

BALANCE OF PAYMENTS (BOP)

A country needs to earn foreign exchange in order to be able to import what it needs. When a country exports more and imports less, there is a trade surplus. When a country imports more and exports less, there is a trade deficit. Apart from trade surplus or deficit, there are other international transactions like receipts from airways and shipping, from remittances of nationals abroad and tourism as well as expenditure by a country on repayment of debts it owes to other countries.

The balance of payment account contains all these elements. A country may have a large amount of foreign exchange reserves but still it may be running a big payments deficit. This deficit is met partly by drawing down the level of the reserves or taking fresh loans or grants from abroad both from other countries which are ready to extend assistance and from inter-national institutions.

A country may draw each year, foreign assistance of a certain order and it would also be repaying old debts or paying interest on running debts. The net inflow of assistance is derived by deduction from gross receipts the amount of repayments.

Taxes

In the fiscal system there are both direct and indirect taxes which bring in revenue to the government. In India, the bulk of the tax revenue comes from indirect taxes.

Direct taxes include taxes on income and on profits of corporate enterprises, wealth tax, gift tax, and estate duty. Indirect taxes are made up of excise duty levied on all commodities at the factory before the goods move out for consumption and customs duty which is levied on imports. The duties are fixed at a certain percentage and often described as *ad valorem,* which means that as the value of the article goes up, correspondingly the tax also will go up.

These are other indirect taxes like VAT, GST, excise revenue, entertainment duty, motor vehicles tax; octroi is levied as a toll fee when vehicles laden with goods enter from one area to another.

DEVELOPMENT REPORTING

Everyone is familiar with the old saying that man does not live by bread alone. Nor do nations live by politics alone. But political news dominates the press in all countries, developing and developed. Newspapers are said to be history in a hurry. Conventional history books are full of the deeds of kings and statesmen, of wars, of treaties made and treaties broken. Social histories are far fewer than political histories.

THE ART OF INTERVIEWING

Some Tips

Keep Your Questions Short

Do not make along statements and ask your victim whether or not he agrees. Nor should you ask questions which call for long answers that go on and on. Long paragraphs are not attractive. The questions, especially the first few, should be so designed that the answers will be short, that there is progression and variety.

An interview is not a lecture punctuated with "And then"? from the interviewers. When the interviewee goes off into a by-way, get him back to the main road.

Equally important is not to but in when a person is about to say something interesting. On TV, the spectators resent the fussy and the super-clever interviewer.

The rule above all in an interview is that the correspondent should not be overbearing. He should never be rude.

"It is especially essential that the Radio or TV interviewer avoids being either savage or fawning. He should ask pointed questions that will draw revealing answers, especially in interviewing public figures. Antagonism is certain to produce a negative response from the audience as well as the interviewee".

(G. William L. Rivers: The Mass Media: Reporting, Writing, Editing).

While you have your list of questions, you should know what to skip. Inability to do so and going on to questions that have been already answered has ruined many a good interview.

Interviewing Statesmen

When interviewing heads of government and state:

Find out how much of time has been allotted. Some want the questions to be handed in earlier. They prepare answers. But you must know when to ask supplementary.

If you take a tape-recorder, be sure to ask for permission to use it. Keep your tape-recorder ready. Do not keep fiddling with wires when the interviewee is ready. Find out whether you are expected to show the text. Many make it a rule to see the text if verbatim questions and answers are being quoted. Do not waste too much time on formalities. Do not be too obsequious. Do not go on describing what you propose to ask. And keep confidence, if things have been told off the record.

Flexibility

The same technique will not work with all. George Bernard Shaw's advice to an interviewer was: attack everything that the other man stands for and he will come out fighting. This approach works if you are a Bernard Shaw but normally leads to a breakdown of the interview. There are some who just cannot be drawing out. In such cases, it may be necessary to have several meetings. When writing about a person, use language, which is appropriate to his background. Do not make a farmer speak like a professor of English.

An interview can often give you a useful peg to hang a good deal of background material on. A striking quote from an authority can make the background topical.

When the interview matter is brief, for want of time, as it happens in a chance encounter, the matter can be padded with background data on the personality.

Division of Labour in Newspaper Organisation

Industrial revolution introduced division of labour in industry, which facilitated mass production with better efficiency. The same concept has percolated to other organised activities, newspapers being no exception. That is why there is division of labour in the reporting staff. The units allotted to reporters and special correspondents are called beats. A reporter may be in charge of police, crime news or hospital news. Therefore, the police, crime or hospitals will be his beat. Reporters can have more than one beat. In fact, all the government departments, political parties and institutions where news is expected are listed and distributed as beats among the reporting staff.

The allotted beat becomes thus the responsibility of the concerned reporter. He should make all necessary arrangements to get all the news stories from his beat. If activity gets spurt due to situation and he cannot cope with it doing full justice to his function, he has to ask the news editor or chief reporter for additional hands. If he misses something, which is carried by the rival paper, he will come under fire from his superiors. Each newspaper has to be the first with the news to survive.

The reporter will have to look for his own sources in his beat, which could be relied on. He has to identify and nurture them. He cannot be present all the time but he has to be in touch with key persons who inform the press by duty or by habit. He has to be in regular contact with those who have information and also those who are enjoy decision-making power. Regular contract with these people ensures routine coverage of the beat. If he is vigilant and skilled enough, he may at times succeed with the help of those contacts in getting something exclusive, which may not appear in any other newspaper. Big news, broken by a reporter, is called scoop. A reporter cannot have scoops everyday, such developments take place seldom, but if he is regular at his beat, he will not miss a scoop when it is possible to get it.

Planning for Tapping Relevant Source

Many events are planned and sometimes they are informed to the pressmen, too. Therefore, news is not always unexpected and, therefore, news coverage of expected events can be planned. Of course, we cannot plan an accident or crime coverage before it happens or is committed. We can definitely plan follow-up coverage of the accident or crime.

For planning purposes, every newspaper or news agency maintains a diary and it is kept up to date. Assessing the nature or duration of an event and depending upon its importance, the necessary staff is organized and concerned members given time to do necessary homework, if possible. The newspaper organisation/management should ensure to make available necessary telegraphic, telephone or telex facilities to the correspondent if he or she is sent out of town or abroad to enable him/her to file news promptly.

There is a practice in all newspaper organisations to hold daily meeting of reporters presided over by the chief reporter and of special correspondents presided over by a bureau chief to finalize this kind of planning and tie up the loose ends. Both the chiefs confer with the news editor and the editor before holding and addressing such meetings.

There is practice in some newspapers that the editor himself presides over the meeting of the entire reporting staff. This may be done occasionally in some newspapers. This may happen in any newspaper if the situation warrants proper planning; the events may be international or national or otherwise highly significant for coverage.

The coverage of state legislatures and parliament is duly and definitely planned. Similarly, election coverage and coverage of budget proceedings need extensive planning. All available hands are used and everybody is given some job, some of the experienced and senior reporters given even extra work, depending on their special qualifications or capabilities or knowledge.

Follow-up of Events already Reported

Follow-up of news reports is a casualty in India. Very few news items are followed. Once reported, the matters are forgotten. It is the duty of the newspapers to ensure that the reports that have already appeared in the newspaper or other newspapers are properly planned. The follow-up should not only be confined to special investigative stories but also to the other ones.

It has to be clearly understood that newsgathering is basically a planed exercise but the plan has to be flexible so as to account for the uncertainty of events.

CHAPTER

5

Press Releases, Press Notes or Press Statements : As Sources of News

Press release, press note, press statement or press hand-outs mean the same thing. It is statement on behalf of government, political party, institution or even an individual given to the press. Normally, it is signed or on official stationery or cyclostyled or Xerox copy issued by an official which is competent to issue it.

It is an important source of news for journalists. Joint communiqués issued by the two governments, memoranda given to authorities and dignitaries, messages of dignitaries are also normally given to the press in this form. Sometimes, it carries the words "Press Release", "Press Note", etc., on the top but at times such words are not mentioned at all.

The first step to deal with a hand out or press release is to read it carefully and understand it. Then the reporter has to find out the important news points and evaluate them in the order of importance. Then comes his skill at news writing. He has to write the intro covering the most important point and then proceed to the body of the story in logical order.

There is large variety of such government handouts. These may be about a minister's speech, text of banquet speeches, announcement of government decision through a press note, summary of political reports, text of messages on behalf of ministers, or the content of agreement signed with different countries or firms. Programmes of dignitaries issued in the standard form can also be used as a source of information but the story is written giving just the highlights of the programme in the general inverted pyramid style of writing. Here is an example of a programme handout.

The above examples of government handouts mention the facts clearly though one can argue about the presentation. However, a reporter often has to deal with handouts which do not make much sense and has to write the story by doing some extra work so that it makes some sense for the readers.

Just hectic activity does not make news. The reporter should find out what happened in various meetings and get some important news peg on which he could tag the story. Further, there are two kinds of meetings—one with central ministers and the other with opposition leaders. There could be different stories on that. A reporter is supposed to do a lot of legwork on it, then only a good story would be possible. The handout only tells whom the Chief Minister met and where he is going. The reporter should use this information to get other facts from different sources.

While dealing with press releases, the reporter must give background information wherever necessary. Sometimes, major announcements are made by the government through press notes with only a few sentences. In such cases, the reporter has to add a lot of information and background while writing the story and give it the importance that it deserves.

FOLLOW-UP OF MATTERS OF IMPORTANCE

The reporter has to use his judgement and skills while dealing with such cases. He must read it carefully and then work on it to give it the shape of a news story it deserves. He should look for the gaps of information and try to fill them going beyond the handout. He should also add necessary background whenever required and should take care of other related activities before finalizing the story. All this depends on the judgement and the skill of the reporter. He can make or mar the story. He must try to make it.

CHAPTER

6

Reporting Speeches

Whatever the venue, politics or any other subject, delivered before legislature or out in the open, or else before select audience, speeches are expression of ideas, views, thoughts, policy, criticism, or to rouse popular or desirable sentiments. All will simply agree that speeches are a major source of news. Every day, many news items that appear in the newspapers can be traced back to some speech or the other. Sometimes, several speeches form part of one report. This happens in reports of seminars, symposia and legislatures. Public address by political leaders are also equally quoted and reported. In such situations, the most important speech, normally from the most important speaker, gets prominence.

It is observed that while covering political party conferences and international conferences on various subjects, one has to deal with several speeches in a row. Depending on the content and the speaker, a reporter has to decide who should come first. Effort should also be made to generalize observations if possible and then mention who said what. In such cases, the normal practice followed is to report the most important things said by different speakers. The different speakers should first be mentioned and then supporters of different schools of thoughts should be quoted and/or reported. One caution please, here again repetition of ideas should be avoided.

It is left to the reporter to judge the importance of speakers and speeches. However, the importance of speeches and speakers varies from occasion to occasion and relative importance of other speakers. A reporter must evaluate various factors and use judgement while writing the story. For example, if many ministers speak in a party meeting, their speeches are important and what they say will be important according to the content of their speeches. It needs hardly be emphasized if the prime minister speaks and he touches upon points which have been covered by other ministers already and adds something to it, he will get the maximum space and the rest of the ministers will be mentioned in the story with very little of what they said.

There could be an instance if in a special debate in the parliament; the speech of a minister of state gets prominence in case the cabinet minister of the same ministry/department does not speak. It can happen that the cabinet minister also speaks. In that case, the state minister is normally pushed out of intro. There could be a situation that the prime minister intervenes during the debate and says something on the subject. Then even the cabinet minister is pushed below in the body of the story. Therefore, while reporting multiple speeches, the reporter must evaluate all these factors before writing his report.

Many times, it so happens that copies of a speech may be supplied in advance. It also happens sometimes that the story is prepared based on the advance copy and a reporter goes to the site when the speech is made. He goes there just to check whether the speech was made and if so whether it followed the advance copy. The advance story is supplied subject to an embargo, which is lifted automatically at the time up to which it is embargoed (there is implied or express understanding that it should not be used before or should be used on or after. . .) A reporter or sub-editor who writes the story from such a speech has enough time at his disposal and should read the speech carefully and write the story on the top of which "not to be used before . . . (time) on . . . (Date) as mentioned in the embargo should be prominently typed for safety. Normally, this embargo time is the time of the event where the speech is to be made. Even the News agencies sometimes creed the embargoed story in advance. It is understood that the copy would be used only after the embargo is lifted.

There may be occasions when advance copy is not made available. In that case, the reporter must reach the place where the speech is to be delivered and check from the organizers if they are supplying a copy of the speech. If the copy is supplied before the speech, then the reporter should start working on it immediately. He should go through the contents carefully ad mark what he considers as important points.

He should also mark the order of their importance so that he loses no time when he has to type or dictate his story. He should carefully check the copy when the speech was made and see if there were any major deviations from the text supplied. Sometimes what is said by the speaker outside the supplied text is more newsworthy than all what is given in the text. Such departures from the prepared text should find place in the intro or body depending on their news value.

Many a time, a speaker does not read the prepared speech and says that the speech be taken as read while what he says is in addition to that. In that case, the reporter is supposed to listen to the speaker carefully and read the text also before writing the story.

If the organizers promised that the copy of the speech would be supplied but it was not distributed when the speech began, the reporter should start taking notes from the beginning of the speech imagining that the copy was not available. Many such promises of the organizers prove false and if the reporter does not take notes or record the speech when it is delivered, he will be in difficulty. Moreover, he will miss any departures from the text.

A reporter should make use of the copy if he gets it within a few minutes after the event otherwise he should rely on his notes and do the story. The copy can be used for quotations from the speech.

But there are occasions when the copy of the speech is not supplied. This happens in seminars and almost all the public meetings of political parties. A reporter can record them on a tape recorder. He must take care to take down important points in his notebook also. In this way, he can do the story quickly, for he will not have enough time to replay the full speech and then write. A tape recorder is useful for it helps the reporter in reproducing exactly what the speaker might have said on a controversial or important issue.

A speech can sometimes yield more than one story. In certain circumstances, a reporter can add colour to the story by describing the atmosphere or some sidelights. Such opportunities should not be missed.

It is interesting to see how the same speech is covered by different newspapers. The following is the address by the President of India to Parliament (February 20, 1986).

Presidents' Speech

Honourable Members,

(1) It gives me great pleasure to welcome you to this first session of parliament in 1986. I felicitate the new members.

(2) The year has seen Parliament transact its business in a purposeful manner and in an atmosphere of cooperation. I extend to you all my best wishes for the successful completion of the budgetary and legislative business that lies ahead.

(3) In July 1985, the government took a major initiative to resolve the complex and difficult problems in Punjab. Our prime concern was to strengthen the forces of unity and integrity. Policy was governed by the perspective of serving the highest national interest. The democratic process triumphed over terrorism. The peaceful elections in Punjab testified to the desire of the overwhelming majority of the people for peace and normalcy in the State.

(4) A great responsibility rests on those who have secured the mandate of the people. Their supreme task is to isolate those who are resorting to violence to disturb communal harmony and peace. In this task, they will have the support of all political forces

committed to the unity and integrity of India. There cannot be, and must not be, any compromise with the forces of disintegration. It is imperative that all secular and democratic forces join hands in a mass campaigning to safeguard the values enshrined in our constitution—nationalism, secularism, democracy and socialism—the bedrock of India's unity.

(5) The Assam settlement was followed by elections to the Legislative Assembly and the Lok Sabha. A new government has taken office.

(6) Governments are committed to the fullest implementation of the Punjab and Assam Accords.

(7) Governments express their deepest sympathy with the families of all those who lost their lives, or were injured, or suffered loss of property in violent incidents in different parts of the country. Violence in public life is the very antithesis of the ethos of our civilization. The frequent resort to violence to settle what are perceived as grievances of one group or another should deeply disturb those who uphold democratic values. While governments must firmly put down violence wherever it may occur, it is essential that political parties committed to democratic values should deal with the root causes of violence through purposive and sustained work among the people. The temptation to seek short-term advantages from communal and other types of violence must be eschewed.

(8) Communication continues to pose a serious threat to national unity. It is being reinforced by religious fundamentalism and fanaticism. These trends represent a reactionary social outlook, directed against the struggle of the poor and the under-privileged against the vested interests. The reconstituted National Integration Council will have to act decisively and systematically to strengthen secularism.

(9) In my address on January 17, 1985, I had outlined the major policies and programmes of the government. I recapitulate the main points:

(i) Commitment of a clean public life,
(ii) Administrative reforms,
(iii) Judicial reforms,
(iv) A new national Education Policy,
(v) A new national programme for women,
(vi) Participation of youth in programmes for promoting national integration and achieving excellence,
(vii) Establishment of a Wasteland Development Board,
(viii) Formation of a Central Ganga Authority,
(ix) A new textile policy, and
(x) Thorough examination of safety measures for industrial establishments.

(10) My Government has fulfilled in substantial measure the tasks it had set for itself for the past year.

(11) The Anti-detection Act is now on the statue book. Contributions to political parties by the companies have been permitted by law. Government has endeavored to set a new tone in public life. This has strengthened national confidence. A strong sense of involvement in public affairs among all sections of the people and a buoyant spirit have characterized the year that has gone by. We have to build on these assets to raise the standards of public life.

(12) Vigorous steps have been taken to combat corruption and to improve the performance of the public services. Strong emphasis has been laid on sound personnel management and training of personnel at all levels. Machinery for redressal of public grievances is in place. Its results are being continuously evaluated. A new Ministry has been set up to monitor the implementation of various programmes. All Departments of government have been directed to formulate detailed action plans for

the coming financial year, against which their progress will be judged. Administrative reforms are in process. Detailed exercises are under way to reorient the system to speedier decision-making and better implementation.

(13) Government is determined to eliminate delays in dispensation of justice. The experiment of Lok Adalats has proved that an innovative approach is required to cure this malady. The establishment of Administrative Tribunals will also lighten the burden of the courts, enabling them to devote more time to the liquidation of arrears. However, these are just the first steps in tackling the basic problem of making justice inexpensive and easily accessible to the poor. Drastic changes are needed. Government has entrusted to the Law Commission the task of recommending such changes.

(14) Government published in August 1985, a statute paper entitled "The Challenge of Education". This was intended to stimulate wide and intensive national debate on issues and alternatives. Government notes with satisfaction that the debate has involved all sections of the people and many useful ideas and approaches have emerged. A draft of the new Education Policy will be presented shortly to parliament.

(15) Government has set-up a new department to look after the development for women. A comprehensive national programme for women is being worked out. It will aim at enabling women to play their full part in developing a strong and modern nation.

(16) Programmes for youth development have made considerable headway but more has to be done in this area.

(17) The Wasteland Development Board has been set-up and has started work on an ambitious programme of afforestation. In a recent meeting, all the State Governments endorsed an integrated approach to a National Land Use Policy as well as the strategies and policies for wasteland development.

(18) The Central Ganga Authority has come into existence. With the cooperation of the concerned State Government, work has started in full swing on stopping the pollution of the Ganga.

(19) A new textile policy was announced in June 1985. It aims at production of cheaper cloth for the people. An equally important objective of the policy is to protect the interests of handloom weavers. It is envisaged that in the Seventh Plan, the entire production of 700 million sq. metres of controlled and janata cloth will be transferred to the handloom sector. The Handlooms (Reservation of Articles for Production) Act, 1985 has been passed to strengthen this vital sector which provides livelihood to millions. Steps are being taken to ensure full and efficient implementation of the policy.

(20) Government has completed examination of pocesses relating to industrial safety and management of hazardous substances and legislation will be introduced in this session of parliament.

(21) Government will establish seven Zonal Cultural Centres; three have already been set up to promote a sense of cultural cohesion. These centres, cutting across territorial and linguistic boundaries, would project the rich diversity of regional cultural traditions and their underlying unity. They would take the best of our culture to the masses, harmonizing it with their lives and struggles. Their essential thrust would be to break the artificial barriers created during the colonial era between the masses and the living tradition of India's age-old culture in all its forms. The centres will also aim at revitalizing folk art which has enriched the country's cultural life.

(22) I would now refer to the major trends in our economy.

(23) The Seventh Five-Year Plan was approved by the National Development Council (NDC). The basic strategy of the Plan is cast in a longer-term perspective of eradication of poverty and building a

strong, self-reliant and modern economy. The plan sharpens the focus on the anti-poverty programmes which will have an expanded coverage. It also envisages adequate investments in the core sectors to strengthen the growth potential of the national economy.

(24) The fulfilment of the Plan required total commitment and determination to mobilize adequate resources for investment. To translate the vision of a strong, prosperous self-reliant India into reality requires unremitting toil and capacity to sacrifice and to bear hardship. Adequate savings have to be mobilized to pursue a non-inflationary path of development. More importantly, these savings have to be used effectively. The challenge has to be met. There are no shortcuts to development, no alternatives to hard work.

(25) Vigorous implementations of anti-poverty programmes yielded significant results. The Sixth Five-Year Plan aimed at assisting 15 million families under the Integrated Rural Development Programme (IRDP): 16.6 million families were actually covered, of which 6.4 million belonged to the Scheduled Castes and Scheduled Tribes. These programmes are being strengthened and surplus foodgrain stocks will be used in 1986-87 to expand the National Rural Employment Programme (NREP) and the Rural Landless Employment Guarantee Programme (RLEGP) to cover one million additional families. An amount of Rs. 100 crores has been provided annually during the Seventh Five-Year Plan for the construction of housing for the Scheduled Castes/ Scheduled Tribes and freed bonded labour.

(26) By the end of March 1985, of a total of 2.31 lakh problem villages lacking safe drinking water supply, 1.92 lakh villages had been provided with at least one source of water supply. During 1985-86, the programme was further accelerated.

(27) In 1985-86, agriculture continued to make steady progress. In November 1985, foodgrain stocks with

Government were higher by nearly 15% over those of 1984. This has enabled the Government to offer subsidized rates in tribal areas and to other vulnerable sections, especially the Scheduled Castes, Expectant mothers and Children, etc. A comprehensive crop insurance scheme has been introduced in specified areas of the Kharif crop. The Government is considering further expansion of such schemes.

(28) During the first seven months of 1985-86, industrial production grew at the rate of 6.3%. The policy initiatives of the Government have created a buoyant investment climate. The infrastructure industries have performed well. Compared with the first nine months of the last year, power generation was up by 8.2%, saleable steel production by 12.9%, fertilizer production by more than 10%. Our ports handled 13.2% more cargo and the railways created an all time record in freight traffic movement.

(29) In 1985-86, the Central Plan outlays were stepped up by 15% over 1985-85, especially on anti-poverty programmes, human resource development and infrastructure. There was considerable increase in the outlays of State Plans. Government will have spent in 1985-86 Rs. 1650 crore on food subsidy and Rs. 2050 crore on fertilizer subsidies. Public Distribution System (PDS) was strengthened and prudent management of supplies prevented shortages. It is gratifying that a significant increase in public investment was achieved.

(30) Tax collections have been buoyant belying gloomy forebidding. The collection of direct taxes is up by about 23% compared to the corresponding period last year. Indirect tax collection has increased by 22%. Total tax collections have increased by 22% which is the highest in the last decade. An effective derive was launched against tax evaders, smugglers and black-marketers. Action has also been taken against personnel found guilty of colluding with economic offenders. Government is determined to

clean the economic life and to fight the evil of black money.

(31) For the first time, a long-term fiscal policy co-terminus with the Five-Year Plan has been announced. A long-term direction to economic policy has been provided. Government is confident that the policy will ensure economic growth and speedier expansion of productive investment and employment opportunities.

(32) It is necessary to focus attention on the structural problems of the economy to further our basic objective of growth with social justice. India's development depends upon steadily rising levels of public investment. How are these investments to be financed? Massive investments made in the previous plans must yield adequate returns. Costs of production have to be reduced. Every paisa of national savings has to be put to the most productive use. Otherwise, it will be difficult to find real resources of the larger and varied investments required for maintaining the tempo of self-reliant growth, for enlarging our anti-poverty programmes and for preserving our economic independence. Sooner or later, sooner rather than later, we have to face the realities of the situation. No one should be under the delusion that growth, social justice, price stability and self-reliance are achievable without efficiency, discipline and sharing of burdens. Contemporary history warns us of such pitfalls.

(33) We must reduce the costs of our inputs and prices of final products and services. We can not afford the luxury of pricing ourselves out of both the domestic and the export markets. A modern industrial society cannot rise on the basis of continuing low levels of productivity and high costs of production. New jobs cannot be created if existing enterprises incur losses year after year. Operational inefficiency increases the cost of production and is inevitably reflected in increased prices, which are a burden on the people. It raises cost all round, reducing real investment.

(34) The future of the planning process depends on our capacity to face difficult questions and to take hard decisions, that may involve sacrifices but without which forward movement will not be possible. Growth is absolutely vital to raise the standards of living of the poor. Can we evade decisions that protect and strengthen this development process? Nations are built by generations that sacrifice for a better tomorrow.

(35) The balance of payments position poses a similar challenge. Our exports have remained sluggish in 1985-86 but our imports have increased. The imports of petroleum products and edible oils are well above the limits the country can afford. The question basically is whether we want to stand on our own feet or not. If we do, there is no question that we have to curb the growth of consumption of petroleum products and we have to be self-sufficient in oilseeds. We also have to have a fresh look at our imports of capital goods. We do not want to shut out new technology because that will harm us, but we have to make sure that such technology meets the rigorous criteria of essentially. External financial flows are needed but government is determined that India must never be at the mercy of foreign banks and institutions. Economic independence and self-reliance are central to our philosophy of development. We shall pay whatever price is required to maintain our economic independence.

(36) The primary objectives of our foreign policy continue to be the promotion of non-alignment, advocacy of peace and nuclear disarmament, enlarging the area of friendship and cooperation and building of a just world order.

(37) We welcome the resumption of high level dialogue between the USSR and USA. It is imperative to take urgent steps to bring about a freeze in the nuclear arms race and a comprehensive nuclear weapon test ban treaty. The six nation initiative has called for these measures. The Delhi declaration of January,

1985 had a good impact on public opinion throughout the world. The leaders of the six countries are in touch with one another about further steps.

(38) During the last one year, the atmosphere in the sub-continent has distinctly improved. We have succeeded in making progress with our neighbourers in many fields. But we remain concerned about the ethnic situation in Sri Lanka, and Pakistan's continued pursuit of a nuclear weapon capability. We remain convinced that the situation in Sri Lanka can be settled only through political means. Attempts to seek a military solution will fail and will only result in the loss of a large number of innocent lives.

(39) The Government welcomes the establishment of South Asian Association for Regional Cooperation (SAARC) launched in Dhaka in December 1985. We expect that it will help strengthen forces of friendship and cooperation in our region.

(40) The Government has made untiring efforts towards the resolution of the major area of tension. At the Commonwealth meeting in the Bahamas in October, in which the Prime Minister participated, our delegation played a leading role in the adoption of the Commonwealth Accord on South Africa. We continue to demand comprehensive mandatory sanctions against the racist regime in South Africa. If the authorities there and other governments in a position to influence South Africa do not act in time, violence on a large scale will become unavoidable.

(41) The Prime Minister also attended the 40th anniversary of the United Nations. The necessary declaration on World Order, adopted by Commonwealth leaders, contained a strong plea for adherence to international norms and principles and the strengthening of the United Nations. Support for the United Nations system is one of the cornerstones of our foreign policy. We are concerned at the growing threat to the multilateral institutions and the increasing tendency to resort to unilateral action.

Government supports international efforts to combat international terrorism. While recognizing the rights of people under colonial occupation, to use all means to attain their just objectives.

(42) The Government deplores the fact that the Palestinian people continue to be denied their inalienable rights, including the right to an independent homeland of their own. Until this problem is tackled, West Asia will not see a basic lasting peace.

(43) The Prime Minister paid official visits to the USSR, Egypt, France, Algeria, the USA, Bhutan, the UK, Cuba, the Netherlands, Vietnam, Japan, Oman and Maldives. Our traditionally close and friendly relations with the USSR have been further strengthened following the Prime Minister's discussions with Soviet leaders in Moscow. The visit to USA has significantly enlarged the content of our bilateral relations with the USA. The Prime Minister visited Dhaka to express our solidarity with the people of Bangladesh during the cyclone disaster and participated in the meeting of Heads of State and Government for launching the South Asian Association for Regional Co-operation. The Prime Minister addressed the UNESCO during his visit to France. He addressed the annual conference of the I.L.O. in Geneva. We had the privilege to host visits by the Kings of Nepal and Bhutan, the Queen of the Netherlands, the Presidents of Mexico, Maldives, SWAPO, Sri Lanka, Tanzania, Indonesia and Pakistan, the Chairman of PLO, the Head of State of Ethiopia, and the Prime Ministers of Poland, Yugoslavia, Mauritius, Britain, New Zealand, People's Democratic Republic of Yemen, and Trinidad and Tobago. The Crown Prince and Princess of Norway and the people from there also visited India.

(44) Let me now outline some priority areas for 1986-87 and beyond.

(45) The need of the hour is to enable the poor to better

their lives. Science and Technology has to support this fundamental objective. To this end, the Government is mounting technology missions in the following areas:

Drinking water for all villages;

Eradication of illiteracy;

Vaccination and immunization of children;

Production of oilseeds and manufacture of edible oils; and

Improved communications.

(46) In the course of the year, more thrust areas will be identified with the object of using technology for improving productivity in industry and agriculture. In selected areas, science and technology missions will endeavour to place India in the front rank of scientific activity.

(47) A comprehensive agriculture policy will be formulated to promote an optimal cropping pattern, to improve water and soil management to increase productivity of all crops, to enhance the incomes of small and marginal farmers, and to enlarge our hard won self-sufficiency in foodgrains, and more production of oilseeds and pulses. A time bound action plan will be drawn up to take the green revolution to the eastern region.

(48) It is gratifying that a national consensus has emerged on treating water as a national resource. Government attaches high priority to the evolution of a national water policy which would optimize the use of water for agricultural, industrial and other social needs.

(49) Government has carried out an in-depth analysis of our family planning programmes. Profiting from the experience of the past, an effective strategy for family planning is being worked out and will be announced shortly.

(50) The focus on anti-poverty programmes will be sharpened. A new programme, which builds on the success achieved by the revised 20-point programme, is being formulated and will be announced soon. It will bring together all the elements, policies and

programmes for a major national effort to tackle the problem of mass poverty in all its manifestations, especially the problems of Scheduled Castes and Scheduled Tribes. Programme for the social, economic, educational and cultural development for the Scheduled Castes, Scheduled Tribes and other weaker sections will be vigorously implemented. The implementation of the 15-point programme for the development of minorities, with special emphasis on increasing economic opportunities, will be closely monitored.

(51) To rapidly increase employment to stimulate developments in backward areas and to enhance the efficiency of Indian industry to serve the masses better, a more comprehensive framework of industrial policy is required. Many changes have already been made in our industrial policy which now reflects the new thrust for modernization, absorption of new technologies and promotion of indigenous technologies. High cost and inefficient industry hurts the poor, because it absorbs resources that are needed to create new jobs for them. A vast increase in the production of goods and services for the masses in rural and urban areas is central to our strategy for the removal of poverty. This necessitates a fresh look at policies governing the scale of production, capacity utilisation, the role of indigenous technology, labour productivity, the detailed regulatory mechanism, the future perspectives for small and medium industry and the existing administrative and management apparatus. Industry must serve the large masses.

(52) To meet the challenge of maintaining a viable balance of payments position, a major thrust for promotion of exports and tourism is called for. Any slacking of progress on this front will jeopardize our overall development strategy. Government will take new initiatives in these critical areas.

(53) It is imperative to effect changes in our administrative system to bring it in tune with the

objective of growth with social justice. Management in Government has to be imbued with a new social outlook. It is not a question of imposing something from above. The impetus to reform must come from within. The national community as a whole must debate issues affecting the working of the administrative system. A concrete agenda of action will thus emerge for implementation. Our watchwords must be improvement of efficiency and enforcement of accountability.

(54) To safeguard the health and vitality of our basic political institutions, changes will be needed in our electoral and other laws. Government will hold wide ranging consultations with the leaders of political parties with a view to formulating concrete proposals to ensure cleaner public life.

(55) The vision of a mighty India will be realised soon in the actual lives of men and women who have strength of character, tenacity of purpose and commitment to excellence. Government's strategy for human resource development aims at developing these qualities in our national life. The new education policy will be an integral part of this strategy. It will aim at the physical, intellectual, cultural and moral development of society in a harmonious fashion.

(56) It is not enough to state objects. A national mobilization is essential to ensure that the resources required to implement the education policy are forthcoming. Even more important is the involvement of the youth, students, teachers, the intelligentsia, workers and farmers in giving a new direction to the national effort in this area. Education has to be transformed from an activity in the classroom to a social process for building the India of our dreams. It has to be integrated more closely both with production and our commitment to conserve and enhance our cultural heritage to make us proud to be Indian.

(57) The years ahead are years of challenge. Government

has taken a number of measures to accelerate growth, to modernize the economy and to give new content to our programmes for achieving social justice. It is imperative to impart a sense of urgency to the task of implementation.

(58) Much has been achieved in the past year, and the hopes and expectations of our people are high. As their representatives, you have the onerous duty to fulfil their aspirations. Above all, people's representatives and organizations of all political persuasions should work together to strengthen the secular and democratic foundations of our society. The forces of violence and agnosticism have to be fought. The economic capabilities we have built up since independence have brought us to a point where determined and concerted efforts to take us forward and to remove poverty are feasible. Now is the time to ensure greater political cohesion so that the battle against poverty and backwardness can be won. I wish you all success in the tasks ahead. Jai Hind.

CHAPTER

7

Reporting Press Conference

It will not be out of place to call the modern era as the age of press conferences as this is taken as the most appropriate medium to disseminate news and make public pronouncements. Almost everyday, newspapermen get invitations for press conferences. Some press conferences are over-crowded while some people keep on waiting for newsmen and sometimes, they begin only when the newsmen who have arrived on time threaten them with a walkout. The variety of subjects on which such press conferences are based is also unlimited. Any body who thinks he has something to say can invite newsmen for a press conference.

The in-house procedure goes like this: the invitation for press conference is marked to the reporter or correspondent who deals with the subject. If the press conference is important and the reporter thinks that he would need help, then somebody else is also asked to join and team with him. Sometimes, even editors attend press conferences. The tradition has been that editors are just present and they do not ask any questions. Now this tradition is fading out.

No press conference can be attended without preparations. Therefore, before going to the press conference, a reporter should do his 'home work'. He should prepare himself for the event and read as much as possible on the subject. He should look for the questions, which can yield news from the person who is to address the press conference.

Many reporters prepare a list of possible questions and actually write the language in which to ask. The more confident ones normally have the subjects in mind and phrase their questions when the opportunity comes. But if a reporter does his homework properly, there is no harm if he writes possible questions in advance. It is better that these questions be written in order of importance. A reporter can ask no question; in fact, many reporters who do very good copy do not sometimes ask any questions.

Since other reporters present also think along the same lines on the subject, some questions may be asked by the reporter. Then if the reporter gets an opportunity he should ask a related question to get more information before the subject is changed. He should open a new subject if he thinks that enough has been asked on the subject on which the previous reporters had been asking questions.

A reporter should not hesitate to ask relevant questions even if they are uncomfortable for the person addressing the press conference. However, care should be taken to be polite. Even if the person gets rude, the reporter should keep his cool. He must remember that he has come to get news and not to quarrel with the person on a point.

If the behaviour of the person addressing the press conference is unbecoming then the reporters can mention that in the story or make a small separate item. However, this behaviour should be reported only when it has news value.

After the fall of the Janata Government, the leader of the Janata Party, Jagjivan Ram used to get angry if somebody referred to Mrs. Indira Gandhi. Later, when H.N. Bahuguna joined Mrs. Gandhi even the name of the former irritated Jagjivan Ram. Many reporters described this behaviour of Jagjivan Ram in their stories.

The reporter should also try to use his sense of humour while asking questions if suitable opportunities arise. But he should not overdo it as it becomes funny and irritating if overdone.

A reporter should not ask long questions. He should be brief even while giving the background. He should remember that he is attending the press conference and not addressing it. A long question confuses the person who is addressing the press conference and also indicates that the reporter has not done his homework. Sometimes, the person addressing the press conference uses his sense of humour and asks the questioner to repeat his question, which he was unable to understand. He invariably generates laughter, which is humiliating for the reporter who asks such questions.

For important press conferences, it is good to have a tape recorder. However, the reporter should also take notes to ensure if some mechanical failure may mar the quality of recording, he should be able to do the story without it. Further, these notes will be time savers when the story has to be field.

Entire replay will not be required and the reporter will play only that portion which he wants to check to make sure he is accurate.

A similar problem arises with reporters who depend on shorthand. They concentrate on noting down each word and end up as confused persons. They read again and again what they have noted down in short hand and thus waste precious time and sometimes their copy is not in order because of the confusion in the mind.

One must remember that a tape recorder and shorthand are devices and skill, which should be used to help the mind in retaining and analysing. They are not to be substitutes for an alert and lively mind. Care should be taken that shorthand and tape recorder do not become a burden on the mind of the reporter. It is better not to use them if they burden the mind. The decision should be made by the reporter himself and he should make his own assessment about the use of these devices and skills. A reporter should not become dependent on these devices also because there would be occasion when despite his best efforts, he will not be able to get a tape recorder or his device may fail at the last moment.

During the press conference while talking notes and asking questions, the reporter should also keep an eye on news value of what is being said. This simultaneous analysis is easy if it is done at the end of the conference. However, looking at the notes, the reporter is free to revise his judgement.

Depending on the news value and the subject touched upon at the press conference, the reporter may file just one report or he may file several separate reports.

If a team of reporters from a newspaper covers a press conference, they should ensure they sit together so that they can communicate among themselves and decide which subject should be covered by whom.

Normally, the possible subject should be divided by reporters among themselves before the beginning of the press conference, but if a new subject comes up which they could not think of earlier, it should be allotted on the spot to someone.

In important press conferences, like the one addressed by the prime minister, all available hands who get invitations and accredited correspondents are used. Better planning yields better results on such occasions.

Sometimes, in important press conference reporters from news agencies divide the work in a way that one of them conveys a major announcement on the phone to the desk and it is creeded immediately to the subscribers. Other reporters take notes and do the final copy.

Sometimes, press conferences start with questions and answers but sometimes, the persons addressing the press conference makes preliminary remarks and then questions and answers follow.

Some people also supply a press note or a handout, say something to introduce the subject and then they take the questions from newsmen.

NEWS FROM PRESS CONFERENCE—AN EXAMPLE

PM'S Press Conference

Transcript of the Press conference of Prime Minister Rajiv Gandhi

Friends,

I had wanted to meet you much earlier. But the last six months were so packed that it was difficult to find time. In-between, we had the budget session and the two foreign tours; there was the Air India tragedy. This has caused us all great agony and I want to express our sympathies to the bereaved families. We have done a good many things in the last six months. I had outlined our programmes and priorities in my first broadcast and in parliament. We have placed before the country what we want to do.

The most urgent task of all is to lift the people out of poverty; we have to remove poverty and move forward. We have to see how to ensure fuller social justice; how to strengthen our society.

There are many other problems. Punjab is a major problem. It loomed large at the time of the elections. As a result, the path we have adopted in the last six months to the measure we have taken, the tension has considerably reduced. You find that the Akali Dal is coming forward again in Punjab. They are talking in terms of functioning within the framework of the Constitution. They are speaking out against extremists and against violence. Because of some of the recent incidents, the whole country stands against terrorists. It has been my effort all along to take the Opposition Parties with me in the work before the nation. Whichever major problem has been there, I have invited them and talked it over with them. We have met five or six times in these months and had serious discussions on all the major problems.

We are looking ahead now to the Seventh Plan. Our priorities are before you. The biggest task is in agriculture and we shall address ourselves to it. We shall place even greater emphasis on poverty alleviation programme and on strengthening the infrastructure. In the last few months, we have given a new thrust in several areas—in licensing policy, in capacity ultisation in our industries, in electronics, in textiles, and in many other fields—in order to speed up our work. We are looking into the 20-Point Programme with a view to speeding up its implementation. We must give more attention to the public sector; and we are doing so. We wanted the restructuring of the public sector to be done faster but some matters have arisen which require a little more time.

Our economic situation today is on the whole good. There is naturally discussion about prices. On this matter, I should only like to say that in the last three months, the inflation rate has been only of the order of 3.1 per cent which is lower than in many years. Prices are a matter in which we cannot afford to relax our vigilance. We are looking seriously into the matter, so that whenever there is any rise, we at once contain it and bring the situation under control.

We have promised to clean up our public life and take steps to remove corruption. We have made a beginning, but it is not enough. We are planning some more steps. We have brought in the Anti-Defection Bill and legalized donations to political parties and launched a two-pronged attack on black money by simplifying licensing and taxation on the one hand and by tightening administration on the other.

We have set-up the Wasteland Development Board. It is our hope that there will be vigorous plantation activity, as a result of which there will be more fuel for our people and fodder for our animals. We have also established the Ganga Authority to implement our programme of cleaning the Ganga. We shall make a beginning with Varanasi.

I undertook two foreign tours. Both have yielded considerable result and it is my earnest hope that as a result of these visits, our bilateral relations with the countries I visited will be greatly strengthened, that there will be more friendship and more cooperation. In-between the two tours, I also went to Bangladesh for a day, as a result of which our friendship with this neighbourer has improved.

I think I have spoken enough and now to your questions.

Q.1. It seems that the terrorist problem is being utilized by several countries to pressurize the Government. I refer in particular to the reports that the FBI arrested some terrorists, and some other terrorists were arrested who had received training, as it was said, in Eastern Europe. What comments do you have on this international pressure being applied on you through the terrorist menace?

PM: There is no way that the Indian government is going to succumb to any pressure, whether terrorist or otherwise.

Q.2. Mr. Prime Minister, this is about the reservation policy of the Government of India. You have just removed one Chief Minister in Gujarat yesterday. But the leaders of the agitation have said that they are not going to withdraw the agitation. Since the country became independent, because of the reservation system that we have created, it seems, a new caste system may crop up, and many people seem to have developed a vested interest in staying backward and we have different kinds of reservation system in different States. In the South, you have reservations from 65% to 75% whereas in the North, you have several States where it is only 20% or 25%. The Chief Minister of Gujarat was trying to increase it up to 50% and he lost his job. All this is because of his peculiar reservation system which goes by the caste a person belongs to and not genuine economic backwardness. Now, what are you plans? Are you planning to call a Chief Ministers' conference to discuss this and arrive at a national policy where you have a ceiling up to a maximum number of XY or whatever? What are your plans? This is what I would like to know.

PM: First, one point should be absolutely clear and that is that the reservations for the Scheduled Castes and Scheduled Tribes are in no way under question and there is no question of changing or our altering those at all. You have asked two questions, I think, one: What is going to happen in Gujarat? The new Chief Minister will tackle the problem. The agitation that has been going on in Gujarat, we have maintained, is a political agitation in which many Opposition parties are involved, and we would like that they do not exploit parochial feelings among the people for their political ends. They must rise above this and work for the political betterment of the country, not for their personal gains.

Q.3. I would like to know, Mr. Prime Minister, whether you have got any economic philosophy. If so, what is it? Is it Left or Right or is it Centre or Left or Right of Centre? If you have got any ideological background, would you kindly take us into confidence?

PM: Well, the questions you have asked will take most of our time allotted to this Press Conference to answer. But just to put it in a few sentences; there is no question of Left or right or Left of centre or right of Centre. It is a question of what is good for India today. The basis of our policy has been laid down by Panditji, by Indraji, and we are not shifting from that. But we have to modify their ideology and their thinking with today's conditions on the ground which means the economic conditions in India, the improvements that we have made, the progress that we have made, the financial constrains as we see them and the situation in the world monetary and financial systems. Today, we have to balance all that and produce a package which does not deviate from the basic Congress ideology and is dynamic and will take India ahead.

Q.4. Your Excellency, please evaluate the agreements signed recently between India and Pakistan. To what degree will they influence bringing of normalization to India's north-western borders?

PM: We have always been in favour of normalizing relations with all the countries, especially the countries in our neighbourhood. The progress that has been made in these talks has been good. We would, of course, have liked that we would have made some major advance in trade. Unfortunately, there were some differences. But we hope, in future meetings, that they will also be clarified. We have made progress in cultural exchange, in interchange of our people going to each other's country, simplification of various travel arrangements. In our talks, I think there has been a general understanding of each other's perspectives for the region.

Q.5. In your opening remarks, you referred to your desire to clean up our public life. The Opposition parties, or a few Opposition leaders, presented to you a memorandum of charges against the Haryana Chief Minister, Mr. Bhajan Lal. Do you propose to hold an enquiry into these charges and, if so, what is the nature of the enquiry you are going to order?

PM: The procedure that has been followed on all such complaints and which we also propose to follow for this complaint is that we will first ask the Chief Minister for his comments. Then, we will evaluate his comments with the charges that have been made. On the basis of that evaluation, we will decide whether to have an inquiry and what sort of inquiry to have. I have talked to the Opposition leaders who came, and I have promised them that if anything is substantiated in what they say, we will take action.

Q.6. If we can go back to Indo-Pakistan relations and the talks with Sahebzada Yaqub Ali Khan, for a minute, Prime Minister. During your visits to the United States, the question of Pakistan's pursuit of nuclear capability figured very prominently, and at the end of it, what we got were two contradictory statements. One that the United States has assured us that they will do all they can to dissuade Pakistan from going nuclear. Two, that the United States told us that they did not think that Pakistan was making or could make a bomb.

PM: I don't think they are contradictory at all.

Q.7. What is our own estimation of the state of Pakistan's nuclear pursuit and secondly, if this matter was discussed with Sahebzada Yaqub Khan and, if so, with what result?

PM: While our assessment is that they are fairly close to manufacturing of the weapon and that they do have a programme for manufacturing the weapon; their position is that they are not manufacturing the weapon. This has been brought to the notice of Sahebzada Yaqub Khan and he has taken the stand that they are not making the weapon. We pointed out that if they have the weapon, it will change the situation in this region and we would have to react in some manner.

Q.8. *(Hindi):* I have a short question. From coins to sugar, we are importing so many things. Is this a proof of our economic self-reliance?

PM: *(Hindi):* The meaning of self–reliance is not that we don't import anything from abroad. Japan is also a self-reliant nation but it imports a good number of things. This is not the only criterion. What matters is that we utilize our resources in order to achieve India's progress and development. If imports help us to conserve our resources, we should not hesitate to import. If we have to enlarge our domestic industrial capacity, we must do so. Sometimes, you will require something at once and importing it is the only way. But if you look at our economy and at our progress, you will then find that we have now achieved what we had not achieved earlier.

Q.9. It is months since you have assumed charge as the Prime Minister. You have not been able to organize your Cabinet fully. What is holding it up? There is a supplementary also which I would like to ask.

PM: What makes you think my cabinet is not organized? I think it is perfectly well organized.

Q.10. You have given additional charges to several of your senior Ministers.

PM: I see no fault in the functioning of the Ministers.

Q.11. You had talks with the Congress (S) President, Mr. Sharad Pawar. Is there any likelihood of the Congress (S) jointing your party?

PM: Not at the moment.

Q.12. *(In Urdu):* Sir, let me first congratulate you on your having used Urdu, which is forgotten language. We have been free for 38 years but the dependence on English continues. All your governmental media give preference to English papers over language papers, whether Hindi or Urdu. May I appeal to you to give encouragement to Hindi and Urdu papers instead of English papers?

PM: *(In Urdu):* Certainly. In whichever language the question is asked, I try to reply in the same language.

Q.13. *(In Urdu):* That is why I congratulated you. For the first time, the Prime Minister has spoken in Urdu.

PM: *(In Urdu):* Thanks.

Q.14. It has been seen that many non-Congress (I) States, particularly in the South, take to what is called populist programmes. In one State, they spent about Rs. 200 crores towards what is called a mid-day meal scheme. In another state, they spent about Rs. 180 crores towards what is called cheap rice scheme. A third State is also in the same way to supply rice and also cloth. Now my point is, all these constitute some kind of a non-developmental expenditure although they could be justified in terms of promoting human welfare? The real point to consider is that it causes erosion of funds for meaningful economic development. Now, this is putting pressure on the Congress (I) parties in those States, which are in opposition, and are likely to generate similar pressures for Congress Governments which are in power. Now, I want to ask you whether you have any intention to take up this matter either at the NDC or at any other appropriate forum so that there could be some kind of uniform norms and guidelines so that the poorer people in the Congress (I) States do not suffer in the process.

PM: You missed one out. One State is also distributing power free. I know this is very serious problem and it has to be looked at by all the States and the Central Government together. The fact is that such programmes are necessary and are required. But, as you said, they are not productive in the sense that they do not generate any returns which can be redeployed for development. So, they must be balanced with programmes which do generate such returns. And it is this balance which we must establish because if you spend everything on such programs, our development process will come to a grinding halt. These states must realize that there is no goose that lays golden eggs. They have to generate the wealth that they have to distribute for development amongst the poor.

Q.15. I have two questions Mr. Prime Minister. You were very prompt in passing the Anti-Defection Bill, but the first defection has taken place in your own party in Bihar. The second question is Ms. Gandhi used to describe her Government as "the government that works". How would you like to describe your Government?

PM: One that works faster.

Coming to your first question, we passed the Anti-Defection Bill and if there is any party which contravenes that, there are provisions in the Bill which will come into action. The matter that you are talking about has been taken up in the court. There it will be sorted out. It is a legal matter. We have categorically given instructions that no such people are to be inducted into our party. We are having some things like this in the North-East also. There, too, we have told them that nobody is to be taken in.

Q.16. Mr. Prime Minister, you said that you are going to do something for the upliftment of the poor people of this country. What exactly are the specific steps that you are going to take to help them?

PM: We have got our Anti-poverty programmes. Our main thrust in development is agriculture, which is targeted to help the poorest in the country. We have to develop our infrastructure. These are the three basic thrusts that we are giving.

Q.17. Coming back to Punjab, you referred to some hopeful signs with regard to the attitude of the Akali Dal. What do you think, how do you rate the chances of complete return to normalcy and the chances of having elections before the deadline expires on the 6th October?

PM: For normalcy, I give very high chances. As regards elections before October 6, it is very difficult to say at the moment because the situation is sensitive and we will have to watch it as we go along. We would, of course, like to have elections before October 6, so that we do not have to extend President's rule. But if it is necessary to extend president's rule, we will extend President's rule.

Q.18. In your talk with the leadership of USSR, France and USA, during your recent visits to those countries, did you find any accord in their approach towards the nuclear disarmament question and also what were the areas of discord?

The second part of my question is: are there any fresh initiatives in the offing from India to solve the Gulf crisis and the Palestinian questions?

PM: No, we are not taking any fresh initiatives at the moment. We are watching the situation. We are in touch with the various people.

The attitude of the countries on the nuclear question has been made very clear on a number of occasions. The non-aligned countries are for disarmament. The nuclear weapon States are rather more cautious when they talk about disarmament. The US has said that they are for complete disarmament. But they feel that the road to complete disarmament is like star wars. We feel that this is wrong and any escalation cannot lead to disarmament and we feel that this would be an escalation. France says that it has a very small deterrent, which is only relevant to France and the Soviet Union and does not affect the total nuclear picture. This deterrent is also totally on submarines; the weapons are totally on submarines and thus are not covered under the purview of the present disarmament talks. And their position is that if there is a substantial reduction in armaments by the major powers, they will start disarming themselves.

Q.19. I am Suman from Samachar Bharti. Mr. Prime Minister, the Kanishka tragedy has been a big disaster.

PM: *(In Hindi):* At least, Smachar Bharati should ask questions in Hindi.

Q.20. *(In Hindi):* You are right; I shall ask questions in Hindi. Prime Minister, I want to say that the recent

Kanishka mishap has been a big set back to the confidence in Air India. I want to draw your attention to the fact that all over the world, hijacking and terrorism are on the increase. What guarantee is there that such incidents won't recur? I want to ask whether government is considering any steps by itself and in consultation with the Governments of the United States and Canada to ensure that lives and journeys of passengers will be safe.

PM: *(In Hindi):* We have taken up these matters with both the governments. When I was in America, I had some talks with them. I am confident that the American government will take suitable action. I think that the Canadian government will also deal firmly with the extremists. Earlier, they were not as firm with them as they should have been.

As regards the larger question of international terrorism, as long as there is no worldwide agreement and everyone does not exert himself to put an end to it, until then it will not end. We find that there are many who condemn terrorists but the same people are also encouraging them. If this ends, then terrorism will also end. Meanwhile, we are taking all possible steps to ensure fullest safety on Air India, Indian Airlines and Vayudoot and also to have thorough search of luggage, goods and passengers.

Q.21. *(In Hindi):* Sir, a question arises out of your opening statement. When you took over the prime ministership, you emphasized two or three matters. Among them, the top priority was given to educational reforms. But you did not mention it at all in your opening statement. Would you please take the trouble of telling us what your comprehensive vision of education is in relation to the nation's progress and taking the nation to the 21st century?

If you permit me, I will also add one other question connected with this. In one of your speeches during your recent visit to America, you said that as regards scientists and technicians now working in America, it was your attempt to create conditions which would make them come back and work within the country and that a time would come when they should be ready to come to India. What opportunities are you creating to enable them to come back and serve the country?

PM: *(In Hindi)*: You will remember I had said that within five or six months, we would come out with our educational policy, so that there could be discussion and debate on it as a result of which we could get a picture which could then be put into a final shape and implement it from next year. There is no change in this. The policy will be ready in the coming month or two. A draft was indeed prepared two months ago on which there have been discussions and there will be more discussions and there are also some other reports. These will be before you in the next two months. There could then be a full fledged debate. We have to see that this policy will prepare workers for new industries in the next fifteen years and also our students for the technological innovations. We have to instill a work ethics in our countrymen, a sense of unity and a feeling that we belong not to a developing nation but to a developed country. This will be our objective in formulating a new education policy. At the same time, we have to see that we do not forget our history, our traditions, our ancient values.

Regarding your third question, we shall try to bring back all our technologists and scientists. We are providing opportunities to them and are assisting them. We have formulated policies to enable them to come back to this country and work here. Many of them have now thought of coming back to India and I hope that they will return. But it is not our intention that none of them goes abroad. We would like them to go there for education, experience, so that they could use these on their return to India.

Q. 22. Mr. Prime Minister, it is exactly ten years after the emergency. Do you think at this stage that the declaration of the emergency was the right step to have been taken and if similar conditions of unrest, as it was called, prevail, will you resort to the same measures?

PM: I think at that time it was the right step and there were various forces working. If these conditions are repeated, it might be necessary to have an Emergency. But that will have to be seen with the conditions that prevail. There can be no absolutely equivalent set of situations. Things will be different. I, personally, am not in favour of using such harsh measures if they can be avoided. But, if it is necessary, they must be used.

Q.23. In reply to an earlier question, you said that an inquiry will be conducted into the charges against Mr. Bhajan Lal on receiving his comments. But, two days ago, we were told that the government had decided to stop any further action on the Vaidyalingam Committee report on the two former Prime Ministers. Now, if follow-up action is not taken and inquiry reports are not taken to their logical end, what will be the sanctity attached to such inquiries? That is No. 1. No. 2: Do you have any alternative mechanism to ensure that people in high positions—the Prime Minister, and the Chief Ministers—are not allowed to get away with whatever wrongs they may commit during their tenures?

PM: One: We will take action if any of the points raised is substantiated. Second: On the Vaidyalingam report, although Justice Vaidyalingam has said that a *prima facie* case has been made out on three issues, on three points, and they should be followed-up, we thought that since in 1980 elections, the people had given their decision on those very issues, it is not necessary to follow that up further. We are trying to see how tc set-up fool-proof systems. We have seen the Lokayukta and Lokpal system working in various places. They are more successful in some places, less successful in some places and totally redundant in others. We would like to come out with a system which is effective and which works. And we are trying to see how this can come about.

Q.24: In the light of the forthcoming visit of the German Foreign Minister—after Mr. Gromyko's elevation to the Presidency, now the most senior one in the Western world, how do you rate the state of relations between India and Germany?

PM: I think our relations are good. We have a good trade relationship. We have fairly good understanding of our political positions. And I see relations between our countries improving with more technological and trade exchange.

Q. 25. (*In Hindi*): After the brutal assassination of Indiraji who was the beloved leader of not only this country but of the whole world, on what grounds is the government continuing to adopt a lenient attitude towards the Akali leaders and leaders of SSF who were responsible for converting the Golden Temple into a military base and headquarters of terrorists?

PM: (*In Hindi*): Partly on the grounds of their statements. We shall not allow them to repeat the same thing and if they try to do so, we shall deal with them firmly right from the beginning. We will not let it happen again.

Q. 26. Mr. Prime Minister, under your chairmanship, the Planning Commission had a dream that overnight the resources gap has disappeared. I would like to know how, without any specific steps being suggested, such a scheme has been visualized?

PM: No, I don't think that gap has just disappeared and I don't think the Planning Commission has had a dream of their resources. They do have a dream of what they want to make India, yes. The resources gap has been closed after discussing with the States and evaluating the additional resource mobilization that the States are willing to do and have accepted to do. On that basis, we have evaluated that we not only can but we will have a plan of Rs. 1,80,000 crores, and we are optimistic that we might even be able to do better.

Q. 27. Mr. Prime Minister, how do you react towards the efforts of Sant Harchand Singh Longowal towards Hindu-Sikh unity and amity in Punjab? Further, have you any plan to release all the Sikh detenues and for reinstatement of army deserters?

PM: Well, the army has its own rules. They have their own laws and they will deal with the deserters as per their rules. We are not going to interfere in that in any way. I think Sant Longowal has taken many steps, positive, to bring about normalcy in the situation and I congratulate him on that and we look forward to his moving even further ahead and bringing about complete normalcy in Punjab.

Q. 28. At your press conference in Washington the other day, you were asked whether you had any plans for removing Government controls on radio and television and you replied "none at the moment" and went on to explain that, as you put it, India is not yet ready for the change. Sir, except for a mercifully brief period, we have been a functioning democracy for almost forty years. We have a people's Parliament, we have an independent judiciary and we have an articulate press. All these have poorly enriched our democratic system. It is, therefore, rather too late in the day-to-try to convince the world that giving freedom to radio and television will be risky venture. Mr. Prime Minister, my respectful submission is this. Will it not be more correct, credible and convincing to say that in this particular matter at least, it is the Congress party which is not, and obviously will never be, ready?

PM: Well, that may be your submission. I don't think the Janata Party gave any autonomy to radio and television; neither did the BJP, nor did any body else.

Q.29. That is not a precedent?

PM: I am not talking of precedents. I am talking of what is right for the country at the time. It is when you are in government that you realize the responsibilities that you have to bear. It was very easy for the BJP to talk about autonomy for the radio and television but when they had the responsibility and they had to bear and shoulder that responsibility, they realized that the time was not ready for it and they did not do it.

Q.30. Sir ....

PM: Do you want my answer or do you want ....

Q.31. I am sorry, I just want to ask supplementary if you permit me?

PM: You permit me and then after that I will permit you. As you say, India has been a vibrant democracy for 38 years now and if this was really an issue with the people, they would have raised it. They have not raised it. We feel and I reiterate that we are not ready for total autonomy for these two institutions and we are not going to give it at the moment.

Q. 32. I know when the Janata party was in power, they were busy quarreling among themselves and they had no time for these basic reforms. But my point is the Indian people were never consulted in this matter and how do you say we are not ready for this particular democratic reform? In what respect are we not ready? Is it a risk?

PM: By seeing the way that you people print and publish, I don't think you behave responsibly at all.

Q. 33. But that has nothing to do with radio.

PM: Of course, but if it spreads to radio, there will be a tremendous danger to country.

Q. 34. But is radio a counter blast to the Press or creative?

PM: Do you want a debate or should we carry on with the press conference?

Q.35. I have two questions: Is the Congress (I) planning to withdraw its support to the G.M. Shah government in Jammu and Kashmir since the Congress-I has been openly criticizing that Ministry?

Second: Has the post of Principal Secretary to the Prime Minister been abolished?

PM: 'No' to both. We are not withdrawing the support, and the post has not been abolished.

Q.36. There is the recent case of a Muslim religious court sentencing a woman to 101 lashes. There is also a demand for deletion of Article 44 from the Constitution. This brings out the danger of religious laws and civil laws diverging from each other. Will the Government move in the direction of a uniform civil code and, if so, how soon?

PM: No, we have no plan at the moment to move away from the systems that we have at the moment and where discrepancies come up such as you have pointed out, we have High Courts and the Supreme Court which will handle that.

Q.37. In the field of telecommunication, Mr. Prime Minister, you would perhaps remember that you had called Mr. Thomas Kora to your residence and asked him to dial 100 and he could not get it. Now you promised in those days and of course your mummy also promised in those days that the telephone system would be improved in the country and perhaps an agreement was signed with a Fresh Company. A factory in Gonda has been installed to manufacture electronic exchange. My first question would be: what are you doing for the second factory and whether the country is going in for another technology in the field of telecommunication which has the worst infrastructure in the country?

PM: One, we are looking very seriously at communications. But as you are aware, we are under tremendous resource constraints during this period. The specific question of what has been happening about the second telephone factory, you better talk to the Communications Minister. He will be able to answer that better. But as a matter of policy, what we are developing is our own technology. We are hopeful that it will be ready in a couple of years and we are hopeful that it will be as good as or better than what is available anywhere in the world. We have got the best brains working on it and we are optimistic.

Q.38. Mr. Prime Minister, you have been generous enough to allow more than one question to your own journalists. May I be allowed to task three questions? Sir, I am from Pakistan. My first question is: What are the real difficulties in signing a No War Pact with Pakistan?

PM: There are many problems with this. We are in favour of a much more comprehensive treaty and we have put forward various proposals. We feel that a simple, pointed thing would not give the necessary results.

Q.39. My second question is, Mr. Prime Minister, Pakistan has proposed joint inspection of nuclear installations. What is India's attitude towards it?

PM: We feel it would not be adequate to give us the guarantee that we need and it would give an excuse for clandestine development.

Q. 40. My last question, sir, there has been a general feeling among masses, both in India and Pakistan, despite extensive clamoring and loud claims, nothing much could be achieved during the Indo-Pak Joint commission's deliberations, particularly in the field of travel and trade.

PM: Well, we have been very positive in our attitude and we are willing to do much more. It is for the Pakistan Government to come forward and help us to do that.

Q.41. Mr. Prime Minister, there is a new disarmament proposal initiated by two political German parties: one is the Socialist Unity party of GDR and the other one is the Socialist Democratic party of FRG. Both have elaborated a common framework for governmental agreement on a zone free of chemical weapons. How do you consider this proposal in the context of worldwide endeavours of peace loving forces for disarmament?

PM: We are very much for a ban on chemical and biological weapons, and we would like to see some agreement between all the nations to bring this about. It is something which must be seen on its own and we are disheartened that certain countries are now starting development of just such weapons.

Q.42. This is about cleanliness in politics. You did a very right thing at the time of the last Assembly elections by denying tickets to various party-men who were under some doubts and you had very good criteria and everybody appreciated that Indian people liked it and they gave you the verdict. But the point is the same persons who have been denied tickets are becoming Chief Ministers or they are inducted into State ministries. Is it consistent with your policy or do you feel that you have entered a chakravyooh and you cannot come out of it now? No. 2: There was a talk that you are sharing dual responsibility—one as the Prime Minster and one as President of the Congress Party—and there are a lot of things you have to do with many questions before the country as well as organizational problems. So, would you like to share your responsibility as President of the party with somebody else?

PM: I take the first question first. There were many reasons why we denied tickets to people. Corruption or bad image was not the only reason. One of the reasons was that if in their assembly constituencies, they had lost votes during the Parliamentary election, because we stuck rather rigidly to that, some people who were down only by a few hundred votes were denied tickets. And these are the sort of people that we have used after that. Where there have been serious charges of corruption, we have not rehabilitated those people.

About Party presidentship, this is for the party to decide. We are having party elections next year. We are building memberships now. It is for them to decide.

Q.43. You are holding both the positions. So, you must be having your personal thinking about it. Are you feeling comfortable in both the positions?

PM: Yes, I am very comfortable. They put me here and they must decide.

No Deviation in Economic Policy

New Delhi, July 7 (RTI). Mr. Rajiv Gandhi said today that the government's economic policies were governed by what is "good for the country" and not by ideological consideration of Right or Left.

Asked to define the "Economic philosophy" of his government, Mr. Rajiv said, "Our basic policy has been laid down by Nehru and Indira Gandhi and we are not shifting from that. But we have to modify our thinking in terms of today's approach, financial constraints and international monetary and financial systems. We have to balance them and produce a package which does not deviate from the basic Congress ideology. It will take India ahead", Mr. Gandhi said.

Earlier, in his opening remarks, the Prime Minister described the economic situation as good and noted the price rise. He said the rate of inflation at 3.1% had been the lowest in the last three months in relation to past several years. But he agreed that the prices of certain items were going up and that the government had to be vigilant to control the situation.

The Prime Minister set at rest doubts about the Seventh Plan outlay which, he said, would remain at Rs. 1,80,000 crore as envisaged in the approach paper. He said he was optimistic that "we may be able to do even better".

Asked about the reported resource gap for the Seventh Plan, Mr. Rajiv Gandhi said, "I do not think the gap has disappeared. But the gap has been closed after talks with the States and evaluating additional resources that they are willing to raise. On that basis, we have concluded that we can have a plan of Rs. 1,80,000 crores".

Asked if the Centre did not consider "populist" certain schemes of the non-Congress (I) governments such as mid-day meal and cheap rice involving hundreds of crores of rupees that cut into funds available for economic development, the Prime Minister said, "It is very serious problem and has to be looked into by all the States and the Centre together".

Such programmes, he said, were necessary but they were not productive in the sense they did not generate return which could be re-deployed for development.

"They must be balanced with programmes which generate returns. If we spend everything on such programmes our development programmes will grind to a halt. The States must realize that there is no goose that lays golden eggs", Mr. Gandhi remarked.

"Self-reliance does not mean that you do not import any thing", Mr. Gandhi told a questioner who said the government was talking of self-reliance and at the same time is importing such items as coins.

"There were many items that needed to be imported to meet the immediate needs and some that would enable the country to produce more and better things", he said. He pointed out that even developed countries like Japan could not do without imports.

In his opening remarks, the Prime Minister said, "the first priority of his government was to uplift the poor. It had chalked out many programmes. The anti-poverty programme would be implemented vigorously", he added.

Referring to the Seventh Plan, he said, "Priority would be given to agriculture where a lot of work needed to be done and would be done".

He said, "Many steps had already been taken to give a new thrust to improving infrastructure facilities. Greater attention would also be given to the public sector", he added.

CHAPTER

8

Reporting Parliament

Parliament and State legislatures become major news centres when in session. The Government is bound to make all announcements in the house. Political news also comes from inland around the house in session. Political parties express their views on various issues and the relative strength of various parties is tested in the house. There are moves and counter-moves by ruling and opposition parties, which find place in news columns.

A reporter should know the rules and procedures of Parliament. State legislatures follow similar rules and procedures with a slight difference here and there. During inter session periods, there are conferences of Presiding officers of all hc houses presided over by the Speaker of the Lok Sabha. This makes rules and procedures more or less uniform.

The constitution provides for a bicameral parliament, consisting of the President and two Houses, known as the Council of States (Rajya Sabha) and the House of the people (Lok Sabha).

The Rajya Sabha consists of not more than 250 members. Of these, twelve are nominated by the President for their special knowledge or practical experience in such matters as literature, science, art and social services. The remaining seats are allocated to the various States and Union Territories, roughly in proportion to their population. Each state is, however, represented by at least one member. The representatives of each State are elected by the elected members of the Legislative Assembly of the State in accordance with the system of proportional representation by means of a single transferable vote. The minimum age for membership of the House is 30 years.

The Rajya Sabha was constituted for the first time on April 3, 1952. It is a permanent body and so, not subject to dissolution, but one-third of the members retire every second year by rotation and they are replaced by newly elected members. The Rajya Sabha at present has 244 members.

The Lok Sabha is composed of representatives of the people chosen by direct election on the basis of adult suffrage. The maximum strength of the House envisaged by the Constitution is now 547—up to 525 members to represent the States, up to 20 members to represent the Union Territories and not more than two members of the Anglo-Indian community to be nominated by the President if in his opinion that community is not adequately represented in the House. The total elective membership is distributed among the States in such a way that the ratio between the number of seats allotted to each State and the population of the State is, as far as practicable, the same for all states. The qualifying age for membership of the Lok Sabha is 25 years.

The Lok Sabha, unless sooner dissolved, continues for five years from the date appointed for its first meeting and expiry of the period of five years operates till dissolution of the House. However, while a proclamation of emergency is in operation, this period may be extended by Parliament by law for a period not exceeding one year at a time and not extending in any case beyond a period of six months after the proclamation has ceased to operate.

Following the first general elections held in the country in 1952, the First Lok Sabha met in May 1952. Thereafter, eight general elections have been held. Elections were last held in December 1984 to constitute the Eighth Lok Sabha. The present strength of the Lok Sabha is 544 (525 elected representatives of

States and 17 elected representatives of Union Territories) and two representatives of the Anglo-Indian community nominated by the President.

FUNCTIONS OF PARLIAMENT

As in other parliamentary democracies, Parliament in India has the cardinal functions of legislation, overseeing of administration, passing of budget and ventilation of public grievances.

The scheme of distribution of powers between the Centre and the States, followed in the Constitution of India, emphasizes in many ways the general predominance of Parliament in the legislative field. Apart from the wide range of subjects allotted to it in the Seventh Schedule of the Constitution, even in normal times, Parliament can, under certain circumstances, assume legislative power over a subject falling within the sphere exclusively reserved for the State.

Further, in times of grave emergency, when the security of India or any part thereof is threatened by war or external aggression or armed rebellion and a proclamation of emergency is made by the President, Parliament acquires the power to make laws for the whole or any part of the territory of India with respect to any of the matters enumerated in the States List. Similarly, in the event of the failure of the constitutional machinery in a State, the powers of the legislature of that State become exercisable by or under the authority of Parliament.

Besides the power to legislate on a very wide field, the Constitution vests in the Union Parliament the constituent power or the power to initiate amendment of the Constitution.

Under the Constitution, the Council of Ministers at the Centre is collectively responsible to the Lok Sabha. One of the effective methods by which Parliament exercises check over the executive is through its control over finance. This financial power in the hands of Parliament helps in securing executive accountability. Besides, the procedures of Parliament in India afford ample opportunities for the enforcement of ministerial responsibility, for assessing and influencing governmental polices as well as for ventilating public grievances. The procedure of questions (with possibilities of supplementary and, in the case of inconclusive or unsatisfactory answer,half an hour discussions, calling attention, short duration discussion), enable information to be elicited and attention focussed on various aspects of governmental activities.

The more significant occasions for review of administration are provided by the discussions on the motion of thanks on the President's address, the budget, including demands for grants of various ministries, and departments and proposals to raise funds to meet the expenditures. These apart, specific matters maybe discussed through motions on matters of urgent public importance, private member's resolution and other substantive motions. In extreme cases, government can be censured or a motion of continuous check on government activities is exercised through a comprehensive system of parliamentary committees.

RELATIVE ROLE OF THE TWO HOUSES

As between the two Houses, The Lok Sabha has supremacy in financial mattes; it is also the house to which the council of ministers, drawn from both the Houses, is collectively responsible.

On the other hand, the Rajya Sabha has a special role in enabling Parliament to legislate on State subject if it is necessary in the national interest. It has a similar power in regard to the creation of an All-India Service common to the Union and the States. In other respects, the Constitution proceeds on a theory of equality of status of the two Houses.

Disagreement between the two Houses on amendment to a bill is resolved by both the Houses meeting in a joint sitting where questions are decided by majority vote. However, this provision of joint sitting does not apply to money bills and constitution amendment bills.

THE PRESIDING OFFICERS

In the Lok Sabha, both the presiding officers—the Speaker and the Deputy Speaker—are elected by the House. In the Rajya Sabha, the Vice-President of India is the ex-officio

Chairman of the House. He is elected by the members of an electoral college, consisting of the members of both the Houses of Parliament in accordance with the system of proportional representation by means of the single transferable vote. The Deputy Chairman of the Rajya Sabha is elected by the members of the Rajya Sabha from amongst themselves.

The Constitution of India makes certain specific provisions in regard to the office of the Speaker, Lok Sabha, laying particular emphasis on the importance and the independent character of the office in the context of a parliamentary polity. His salary and allowances are charged on the Consolidated Fund of India.

The Speaker of the Lok Sabha enjoys vast authority and powers both under the Constitution and the rules as well as inherently. As the conventional head of the Lok Sabha and, as its principal spokesman, the Speaker represents its collective voice. He is guardian of the rights and privileges of the House, its committees and members. It is through the Speaker that the decisions of the House are communicated to outside individuals and authorities. He issues warrants to execute the orders of the House, wherever necessary, and delivers reprimands on behalf of the House. Within the precincts of the House, his authority is supreme. His conduct cannot be discussed except on a substantive motion.

The committees of the House function under his overall supervision and control. The chairman of any parliamentary committee is nominated by him. Any procedural problem in the functioning of committees is referred to him for directions. Committees like the Business Advisory Committee, the General-purpose Committee and the Rules Committee, however, work directly under his chairmanship.

He enjoys a special position in so far as the relations between the two Houses of Parliament in certain matters are concerned. He certifies money bills and decides finally, what are "money" matters by reason of the Lok Sabha's overriding powers in financial matters. It is the Speaker of the Lok Sabha who presides over joint sittings called in the event of a disagreement between the two Houses on a legislative measure.

In his over riding concern to see that the Lok Sabha fulfils its rightful role as the prime centre for decision-making and policy formation, and a major mediating force in the country's democratic policy, the Speaker has to strive to reach a position of dynamic balance in which the forum and the needs of orderly debate and efficient dispatch of the ever growing volume of public business are harmonized.

Sessions: Normally three sessions are held in a year:

(i) Budget Sessions (February-May),
(ii) Autumn Session (July-August), and
(iii) Winter Session (November-December).

In the case of the Rajya Sabha, however, the Budget Session is split up in two sessions and so the Rajya Sabha has four sessions.

PRESIDENT'S ADDRESS

The Constitution enjoins that the President shall address both the Houses of Parliament assembled together, at the commencement of the first session after each general election of the Lok Sabha and also at the commencement o the first session of each year and inform Parliament of the causes of its summons. The address contains review of the activities and achievements of the government during the previous year and their policy with regard to important interval and current international problems, besides a brief account of the programme of government business for the session.

The President's address is a solemn occasion. The President arrives at the Parliament House where he is received at the gate by the presiding offices and secretaries general of both Houses and conducted in a formal procession to the high domed Central Half of Parliament. As the procession enters the Hall the marshal announces the arrival of the President, and the members rise in their places. With the President reaching his seat on the dais, a band positioned in the lobby of the Central Hall to the right of the President, plays the national anthem. During this time everyone keeps standing. Thereafter, as the President taken his seat, the presiding officers occupy and members rescue their seats. After the address, the President rises from his seat followed by the members when the national anthem is played again, whereafter the President leaves the Hall in a procession in the same way as he arrived. The entire ceremony is marked by utmost decorum and dignity befitting the occasion.

QUESTIONS

The first hour of every sitting is normally devoted to questions. Questions are of three types. A starred question is the one to which a member desires an oral answer in the House. Any member may ask a supplementary question germane to the main one, while it is being answered. In the case of an un-starred question, a written answer is laid on the table by the concerned minister. A short notice question is the one, which relates to a matter of urgent public importance and can be asked with shorter notice than the normal period prescribed for a question. For questions other than short notice questions, the period of notice prescribed is not less than ten and not more than twenty-one clear days.

Closely connected with question procedure is the provision for half an hour discussion. Under this procedure, a member may give notice for raising a discussion on a matter of sufficient public importance which has been the subject of a recent question, oral or written, and the answer to which needs elucidation on a matter of fact. Such discussions are held during the last half an hour of the sitting on specified days of the week.

Besides questions, there are various other means by which members may bring up matters of urgent and current public importance before Parliament.

Call Attention Notices

Calling attention notices, essentially an Indian procedural innovation, enable a member to draw the attention of the government to an important development of public interest and to elicit government's views or stand thereon. A calling attention notice may be admitted straight way by the Speaker at his discretion and the government have to come forward with a statement. The matter is normally raised after the question hour. Although there can be no debate at the time the statement is made, the members concerned may raise points for clarification and elucidation by the minister there. There is no bar also to a notice being given for a debate on a subsequent date on a matter contained in the statement. This procedural device, without the implied censure of the treasury benches, normally associated with an adjournment motion, is popular with members on all sides of the House.

Raising of Matter under Rule 377

A member who wishes to bring to the notice of the House any matter, which is not a point of order and cannot otherwise be raised through any other procedural device, can do so by giving a notice for the same with a full text thereof. On permission being granted by the Speaker for raising the matter under rule 377, the member concerned may make a brief and specific statement in the House relating to one matter only without any allegations of a defamatory or incriminatory nature. The Speaker in such cases does not direct the Minster to make a statement in response to the matter concerned. The minister may, if he so desires, make a statement on the subject with the permission of the Speaker.

Motions for discussion, No-day-yet-named and for Short Duration

Members may raise discussion on a specific matter of public importance by giving a notice of a motion popularly termed as No-day-yet-named motion. It is so worded as to record the decision of the House on the subject. A short duration discussion provides an opportunity for discussion of a situation or a statement, but there is no question of putting it to the vote of the House.

After admission of notices by the Speaker, any one of these motions may be selected by the Business Advisory Committee for discussion in the House and thereafter, it is included in the list of business. The mover of the motion in the case of a no-day-yet-named motion has the right to reply in addition to the privilege of initiating the discussion; no such right of reply is available to the member raising a discussion for short duration. The minister intervenes towards the end to clarify the government's stand. Experience has shown that the members make full use of these alternative procedures for raising discussion on matters of current public importance.

Adjournment Motion

The primary object of adjournment motion is to set aside the normal business of the House and take up for discussion an urgent matter of public importance. A motion for an adjournment of the business of the House for the purpose of discussing a definite matter of urgent public importance can be moved with the consent of the Speaker and of leave of the House. Normally, no business not included in the list of business, can be taken up in the House. The adjournment motion is an extraordinary procedure.

The Speaker may give his consent for moving an adjournment motion if he is satisfied that the matter sought to be raised is definite, urgent and of public importance and there is a failure on the part of the central government to perform the duties enjoined on it by the Constitution and the law.

The question of public importance is decided on merits in each individual case. The refusal to give consent is at the absolute discretion of the Speaker and he is not bound to give reasons.

After leave of the House to the moving of an adjournment motion has been granted and time fixed for its discussion, the Speaker allows the motion to be moved at the appointed hour, which is normally at 1600 hours. The time allotted for discussion is two and a half hours unless the debate concludes earlier.

Private member's Resolutions

Specific matter may be discussed also through private members' resolutions and other substantive motions. In an extreme case, the government can be censured on a motion of no-confidence moved against it.

The Legislative Process

A bill, that is draft of a legislative proposal, has to pass through the following stages before it becomes an Act of parliament.

First Reading

A bill can be introduced in either House by a minister or by private member, depending upon whether it is a government bill or a private member's bill. Money bills or financial bills attracting the provisions of article 117(1) of the Constitution can be introduced in the Lok Sabha only.

On the day appointed for introduction of a bill, the minister-in-charge of the bill (or member) moves for leave of the House to introduce the bill. On leave being granted by the House, the bill is introduced. If the motion is opposed by any member after brief statement by the member who proposed the motion and the member who moved the motion insists on its introduction, the question is put to the vote of the House.

Second Reading

The second reading consists of consideration of the bill, which is in two stages. First, a general discussion on the bill as a whole takes place, when the principles underlying the bill are discussed. At this stage, it is open to the House to decide to refer the bill to a select committee of the House or a joint committee of the two Houses or to circulate the bill for the purpose of eliciting opinion thereon or straight away take it into consideration.

In the event of a bill being referred to a select or joint committee, the committee gives it a close and detailed scrutiny clause-by-clause and makes such amendments therein as it deems necessary. Where necessary, the committee may also take evidence of associations and public bodies representing the affected interests or of experts who have special knowledge of matters having a bearing on the measure before it. Thereafter, the committee submits its report to the House, which considers the bill as reported by the committee.

The second stage of the second reading consists of clause by clause consideration of the bill as introduced, or as reported by select/joint committee, as the case may be.

Third Reading

When all the clauses and schedules, if any, of the bill have been considered and voted upon by the House, the member-in-charge moves that the bill be passed. At this stage, debate is confined to arguments either in support of the bill or its rejection, without referring to the details thereof further than is absolutely necessary. Only formal, verbal or consequential amendments are allowed at this stage.

Bill in the other House: After the bill is passed by one House, it is sent to the other House where again it passes through similar stages.

In the case of a money bill, the Rajya Sabha can only recommend amendments therein and return the bill to the Lok Sabha within fourteen days of its receiving the bill. The Lok Sabha may accept or reject any or all of the recommendations of the Rajya Sabha. If the Lok Sabha rejects the recommendations, the bill is deemed to have been passed by both the Houses in the form in which it was passed by the Lok Sabha. If the Rajya Sabha does not return the bill within fourteen days, it is deemed to have been passed by both Houses in the form in which it was passed by the Lok Sabha.

Joint Sitting

In the event of persisting disagreement between the two Houses on a bill other than a money bill or a constitution amendment bill, or if more than six months elapsed from the date of receipt of the bill by the other House without the bill being passed by it, the President may call a joint sitting of the two Houses to resolve the deadlock. At the joint sitting, the bill may be passed by a majority of the total number of members of both the Houses present and voting.

Assent of the President: When a bill is passed by both Houses is sought from the President by presentment of the bill to him for assent. The President may give his assent or withhold his assent to a bill, or he can return the bill (provided it is not a money bill) with his recommendations for reconsideration. If the Houses pass the bill again with or without amendments, the bill has to be assented to by the President. In the case of a constitution amendment bill, the President is, however, bound to give his assent.

Decision of the House

Any matter requiring the decision of the House is decided by means of a question put by the Chair on a motion made by a member. At the conclusion of a debate, the Chair puts the question to the House. Those in favour of the motion are invited to say "Aye" and those against it to say "Naye", and then the Chair says "I think the Ayes (or the Nayes, as the case may be) have it". If the opinion of the Chair as to the decision goes unchallenged, he repeats twice, "The Ayes (or the Nayes, as the case may be) have it", and the question before the House is determined accordingly. If the opinion of the Chair is challenged by any member or member exclaiming "The Nayes (Or Ayes) have it", the Chair directs that the lobbies be cleared.

On the Chair directing that the lobbies be cleared, the division bells are rung. When bells ring continuously, it indicates that a division is to take place in the Lok Sabha. (When bells ring intermittently, it indicates that a division is to take place in the Rajya Sabha. After three and a half minutes the Chair puts the question a second time and declares whether in his opinion, the "Ayes" or the "Nayes" have it. In case opinion so declared is again challenged, he shall direct that the votes be recorded by division.

Divisions

There are three methods of holding a division that is, by operating the automatic vote's recorder, by distributing "Ayes' and "Nayes" slips in the House or by members going into the lobbies.

In the case of recording of votes through the automatic votes recorder, members cast their votes from their seats, respectively allotted to them, by pressing according to their choice "Aye"/"Naye"/"Abstain" push buttons provided for the purpose. After the result of the voting appears on the indicator boards any member who may not have been able to cast his vote by pressing the button on account of any reason, considered sufficient by the Chair may, with the Chair's permission, have his vote recorded. Similarly, any member having by mistake pressed the wrong button may also be allowed by the Chair to correct his mistake. The result of automatic voting is thereafter declared by the Chair.

When the Chair directs that votes would be recorded on slips, each member is supplied by the division clerks, at his seat, an "Aye" or a "Naye" or "Abstain" slip according to the choice indicated by him on these slips, members are required to record their votes by writing their division numbers and signing them at the appropriate place. After the members have recorded their votes these are counted by the officers at the table and the totals of "Ayes", "Nayes" and "Abstentions" are presented to the Chair. The result of the division is then announced by the Chair.

Another alternative procedure for division is that members may be asked to record their votes by going into the lobbies. This procedure is not in much vogue now.

Amendment of the Constitution

A bill seeking to amend the Constitution may be brought forward by a minister or a private member. Where the bill is from a private member, the bill, apart from being subject to the normal rules applicable to private members bills, has also to be examined and recommended by the committee on private members'bills and resolutions, before a motion for leave to introduce it is included in the list of business.

Barring the requirement of a special majority (majority of the total membership of the House and a majority of not less than two-thirds of the members of the Hose present and voting) for its adoption, and in certain cases, for ratification by the legislatures of not less than one half of the states, a bill for amendment of the Constitution follows practically the same legislative process as any ordinary legislation.

NEWS OF BUDGET

The story of budgets, taxes and sector-wise, ministry-wise financial outlays of the government in tune with the priorities determined through the instrumentality of the Planning Commission and with overall approval of the National Development Council. This process and tool of budgeting is at the very root of the reporting of government—local government, state government as also the union government.

Outline of the Assignment: Truly speaking, there is nothing as more important to the cause of democratic self-government than a public presentation of the costs of government and the tax proposals through which officials seek to raise the funds to meet those costs. What the public wants to know, and what reporters must establish as their right of getting informed, is when a new budget proposal is presented, whether it will be necessary to increase taxes and if so, what kind of taxes, levies, surcharges, etc. and how much.

Reporter ensures that every budget story must be told with regard for detail. In outline, this is the way the story generally develops:

The total amount to be spent over the next fiscal .year (usually from April 1 to March 31 in India).

The amount of increase or decrease over the preceding year gives information about priority.

If there is an increase, the ways in which the local, state or union government will raise the money.

New taxes, and if so, what kind and how much; increased taxes now on the books, particularly for property and business levies, and how much of each.

Increases in fee and license charges and stamp fees or registration charges, etc.

Economics, such as staff reductions, and how many and how much is to be saved, elimination of service, exactly which ones and the costs involved, and revision of employee benefits and perquisites,

New bond issues (public Debt), and if so, how much and what will the interest charges to be charged to the Consolidated Fund.

Pay increases or decreases for employees, new hiring, if any.

The largest department expenditures in the budget, with each one listed, and the exact amount by which each is to be increased or decreased. Generally, this involves the defence, police and fire departments and the sanitation services, transportation and road/street repair and where the city makes a large contribution for its own schools and welfare services.

Statements made about the budget by the way of and/or city commissioner/Mayor and Finance Secretary and from the political opposition on the city Council/Corporation or other legislative body at the state or union level are important to get a peep into the objectives and reasons.

Explanation of the debt service item. This is always large sum in most corporation/municipal committee budgets. It consists of the interest charges that the city must pay to foreign financial institutions, bankers and private individuals who buy government securities, stacks and bonds, which are issued in order to raise money for specific projects or to meet various types of deficits. The debt service should be reported as an increase or decrease over the previous year and the story should give the latest charges of interest on the newest governmental obligations.

Making Tax Estimates

Sometimes, for understandable reasons, public officials are not willing to admit that their spending plans are going to cost the public more money in the form of higher taxes. It then becomes the responsibility of the reporter to determine how much of a tax increase is likely and what areas will it affect, usually property taxes and general business taxes.

Types of Budget

The budget outlined here is called an operating or expense budget, which is financed mainly by property and business taxes, fines, licencees' permits and service charges, revenue sharing from state and union governments and other miscellaneous sources.

Local Government and Budgets

The two principal types of local government consist of the following:

> *Mayor, City Council (also Municipal Council or Municipality or Municipal Corporation):* This is the most familiar type of local and other governmental authorities. The mayor is responsible for drafting the budget and submitting it to the council/corporation, which then has the authority to

make changes, but must finally adopt it before the beginning of the next fiscal year.

Whatever the system, some single person, either a mayor or a city commissioner or budget director Finance Secretary or the like, must take the responsibility for making up a budget and presenting it for adoption.

Making up an Operating Budget: An operating budget, the most common and necessary type of financial document, consists of two parts: (1) proposed revenues, and (2) proposed appropriations. Generally, income matches outgo, and that is called a balanced budget. Many local or state governments, or even central/union government amit, operate under laws requiring them to work only under deficit budgets.

Analyzing the Budget

The first thing any reporter should do on receiving a proposed budget is to look at the summary, up front, of income and outgo, the anticipated revenue and the proposed appropriations, and then read the mayor's or revenue/finance minister's accompanying message contained in his budget speech.

In case of Union government in India, Economic Survey is presented by the Finance Minister touching upon the previous year's economic conditions and a hint as to what needs to be done to boost up the economy and about the sectors/sub-sectors or areas to be accorded top priority, etc.

Next, both the covering message and the summary will point to the improvements in services that are being proposed such as the addition of more defence personnel, more police, for example, and the provision of more services for general interest or welfare.

Basic Facts

These are the principal things to remember about reporting on budgets, taxes and local government:

The first requirement is a basic knowledge of the functions of local government, the manner in which budgets are prepared and the manner in which the need for tax increases is determined.

If a budget is increased over the previous year, the reporter must determine as quickly as possible where the additional money is coming from. It must be derived either from economies through decreases in staff and services, increases in existing taxes or the levying of new ones, or the sale of bonds or tax anticipation notes.

If taxes are to be increased, the first test is to determine how much the property tax will rise and what this will mean to the average home owner. Pay increases or decreases for city employees should be noted, with exact amounts wherever possible.

Where there is an increase in debt service, the amount a local/state/central government pays in interest on the bonds it issues is given focus for comment. The reporter should know how much interest the government now pays on its bonds.

In writing budget stories, the lead should specify the total amount of the proposed or final operating budget and report on whether tax increases or new taxes are requested. A summary of the main points of the budget should follow, with the body of the story elaborating on the principal developments.

The tax levy is determined by dividing the sum needed for property taxes by the total assessed valuation of all property involved multiplied by 100. If the budget allows for a small percentage of property taxes that may not be collected, this should be subtracted from the property tax total before the final calculation is made.

Team reporting is often required at the local level if a detailed inquiry is being made into governmental affairs. Since governmental affairs at the state level are even more complicated, such devices as the in-depth report and the "take-out", a detailed account using a feature style approach, are sometimes used to describe such developments.

Budget Procedure

The annual financial statement laid before both the Houses of parliament embodies the estimated receipts and expenditures of the Government of India in respect of the ensuring financial year. In India, the "financial year" commences on the first of April.

The estimates of expenditure are split up into what are called "Demands for Grants". These demands are arranged ministry-wise and they generally cover the requirements of each administrative service. Under each demand, the estimates are sub-divided according to the categories of expenditure included in the demand.

In India, the budget is presented to Parliament in two parts—the general budget and the railway budget. The general budget is presented to the Lok Sabha by the finance minister usually at 5 p.m. on the last working day in February. That is, about a month before the commencement of the budget year. The budget speech of the finance minister is in two parts. One part deals with general economic and financial situation in the country and the other part relates to taxation proposals. A copy of the budget is laid on the table of the Rajya Sabha. The railway budget is presented by the railway minister about a week or ten days earlier to the presentation of the general budget by the finance minister.

The budget is discussed in two stages in the Lok Sabha. First, there is the general discussion when only the broad outlines of the budget and the principles and policies underlying it are discussed. Discussion and voting on the demand for grants of each ministry is taken up thereafter.

The Lok Sabha has the power to assent to, or refuse to give assent to, any demand or even to reduce the amount of any grant sought by government. In the Rajya Sabha, there is only a general discussion on the budget. It does not vote on the demands for grants.

Vote on Account

Before the budget for the whole year is passed, a special provision is made, by which the government is enabled by Parliament to have finances, sufficient for running the administration for part of the year. This provision is called 'vote on account'.

The Financial Bill

The finance bill, which seeks to give effect to the government's taxation proposals, is introduced in the Lok Sabha immediately after the presentation of the budget. The provisions in the bill relating to duties of customs or excise, etc. come into effect immediately with the introduction of the bill by virtue of as declaration under he provisional collection of the Taxes Act, usually included in the bill.

The Appropriation Bill

After the voting on the demands for grants has been completed, the appropriation bill is introduced. The appropriation bill seeks to authorize the government to draw moneys from the "Consolidated Fund of India" to the extent shown in the budget passed by Parliament.

Supplementary/Excess Grants

No expenditure in excess of the sums authorized in the budget by Parliament can be incurred without the sanction of Parliament. Whenever a need arises to incur extra expenditure, a supplementary estimate is presented to Parliament. If any money has been spent on any service during a financial year in excess of the amounts granted for that service for that year, the minister of finance/railways presents a demand for excess grant. The procedure followed in Parliament in regard to supplementary/excess grants is more or less the same as is adopted in the case of the expenditure estimates included in the general budget.

CHAPTER

9

Various Beats

All beats require background, understanding of the subject and constant touch with the subject and sources. This is the reason why newspapers allot beats to reporters and corespondents.

But in today's world of interdisciplinary approach, beats gather information on events or issues. The News Editor or Chief Reporter has to have information from many different beats. For example, crime, police, courts, hospitals and jails are different beats. But while dealing with a crime story, often the information has to be gathered from two or more of these beats.

Reporters should resort to this kind of multi-beat approach and should follow all the leads to make the story comprehensive.

Police : There is always a system for information flow to the press about crimes in every major city. However, at times, there are efforts to avoid disclosure of crime or delay it for various reasons. If the reporter is active on his beat, he may get information about an incident earlier than others. It is good to check with the concerned information man or the police chief's office about incidents regularly and more than once every day.

It is good to be known to the police chief but it is always useful to periodically meet station house officers of different police stations. In this process, good relations should also be developed with lower staff. It does not take much to build such relations. If a reporter talked to members of lower staff politely whenever he visited the senior officer, he would have done half the job. If he can remember names of some of them and can address them by their names, he has almost won them. Such people may give the reporter useful tips at times which may lead to big news breaks.

It is always good to meet various sources in the police set-up even when there is no work. Such contacts are helpful when the reporter is on the job and chasing a story. Building contact is building human relationship with people of different walks of life. Even in this very bad world, there are innumerable people who will be prepared to help a good and genuine reporter. This help will start coming almost without notice once he establishes his credentials as a good and well meaning reporter. This, however, does not mean toeing the police line. Even if you go against it but you do not have a vested interest in it, you will earn respect and this will lead to better contacts.

Many police officers try to use reporters to get some publicity and they may make false claims. Whenever there is any doubt, the reporter should try to cross check such claims with other sources in the set-up. By experience, the reporter will be able to judge who can be relied upon and to what extent.

If you get information from independent sources that relates to crime, it is always better to check it with the police. Sometimes, an additional angle may emerge from such cross checking. Story may carry independent information as well as police version.

What happens in police lockups and jails makes news occasionally. If you have good contacts at lower level, you may get tips, which may yield good news reports.

CRIME AND DEFAMATION

While writing crime reports, a reporter must be careful to avoid defamation. A case of defamation may arise over the publication of a statement by someone containing defamatory reference to another person or even a corporate body. One must remember that the fact that the person making the statement is named in the copy is answerable for it does not absolve the newspaper from the consequences of any action instituted by an aggrieved party. The use of adjective of a pejorative nature with respect to persons should be avoided in all circumstances.

The law, however, provides complete immunity against action for defamation in the publication of proceedings of Parliament and State legislatures. No reporter or sub-editor is liable for it in a court of law by way of either prosecution or proceedings for damages by persons complaining of defamation if the report is published in good faith and is substantially true. Similarly, publication of a substantially true report of the proceedings of a court of justice, or of the result of such proceedings, enjoy complete immunity and no action for defamation can be brought by an aggrieved person on the basis of publication of such proceedings.

Reporters unaware of the rights of citizens often mention a person or persons by name as having been arrested in connection with a crime. This is hazardous. Arrest for a criminal offence tends to lower the public image of a person. An arrest is confirmed only when a person is produced before a magistrate or released on bail by a commissioner of police (wherever so empowered). Until then, a person, even if taken to a police station, cannot strictly be described as arrested, for he may be allowed to go after interrogation, and if a report has described him as having been arrested, he can sue the paper for libel. A safe way to report the matter is to say that a person was detained for interrogation. The arrest, together with the name, can be mentioned after the person is produced before a magistrate.

This, however, does not apply to arrests of outlaws or persons declared absconding. Similarly, person taken into custody for political offences can also be named, since political offences do not involve any moral turpitude and thus there is no question of lowering of public image.

CONTEMPT OF COURT

Publication of any matter calculated to scandalize or lower the authority of any court of law, prejudice or interfere with the due course of judicial proceedings or interfere with or obstruct the administration of justice in any other manner constitutes contempt.

It is not open to a newspaper to publish an item charging a particular judge with corruption, whatever the circumstances, nor can his conduct in court be adversely commented. The courts have been armed with such absolute authority to ensure that the justice is administered without any fear or tension.

If in a case, the proceedings of a lower court including the judgement convicting and sentencing the accused are covered by a newspaper, it must follow the case in the higher courts also, if an accused secures acquittal in a higher court, it will be unfair to ignore it.

While covering these beats, a reporter should always keep an eye for human interest and basic principles. The Shah Bano case is an example of such a case which aroused much public interest.

Ordinary crime stories can be made readable if the reporter finds a human interest angle and treats it properly:

Example

A Battle Won at Last

After a long struggle, Mr. Narula will be richer only by about Rs. 10,000. He says he fought not for money but on point of principle, "The amount does not mean much to me. But the unjustness of the case pinched me".

The battle started when in October 1953, the Ministry promoted one Mr. Raj Kumar, Mr. Narula's junior, as senior clerk and fixed his salary at Rs. 155 while the former was drawing Rs. 150. Five other clerks senior to Mr. Kumar also drew less money.

Together, they made a representation to the Ministry. After nine years, the raise was granted to all except Mr. Naruala on the ground that others were given a benefit for additional work, which he did not do.

Mr. Narula continued to make representation till 1973, and then moved the High Court. Later, his case was transferred to the administrative tribunal, which finally granted justice on Monday.

Hospitals are also good source of human interest stories. Disease outbreaks, unnatural births, lack of facilities or addition of new facilities, problems of doctors or para-medial staff, corruption and mismanagement, success in sticky operation—all make news.

In hospitals and medical colleges, the reporter should develop contacts at all levels. Associations and unions of various categories of staff may be very useful in such contact development.

Contacts are useful if some VIP is admitted to hospital and one has to know about his condition. In such cases, all possible aspects of the disease, the report of checkup in layman's language, response to treatment, visits by outside specialists and other VIPs should be mentioned in the story. For example—

Arun Nehru Suffers Heart Attack

....

Jails: Here again, contacts at all possible levels are important. However, this is perhaps the most neglected but most talked about beat in India. There have been very crucial stories like Bhagalpur blinding, Ashwani Sarin's investigation of Tihar Jail but, mostly, the reporters neglect this beat.

All the important jails can be sources of many 'human-interest' stories. There are important or famous criminals who may yield interesting stories. Reporters should visit jails and meet employees at various levels to know what is happening inside their iron gates.

Civic Bodies

Civic bodies and institutions dealing with public amenities are also good sources of news. The news that comes from these bodies is important for general public. Interruptions in water and electricity supply may not look important as murder or bank robbery but such things affect more people directly. The news is of interest to a large number of local readers and, therefore, it is important. Similarly, news about upkeep of parks, maintenance of roads, condition in hospitals, water and electricity supply, chain snatching, traffic bottlenecks, illegal confinements, child abuse, ill-treatment of women, drug selling, gambling, cheating, frauds, cyber crimes, robberies, thefts, murders (particularly of aged people), dog menace, monkey menace, cattle on the roads as hazards to traffic, etc. are news stories of interest to the town dwellers or city residents.

Consumer Problem

In some newspapers, retail consumer prices and problems of consumers also find place. Whether enough milk is coming to the city or there is a shortage of vegetables or there is undue hike in the retail prices of some commodities, these matters make important news for readers. Similarly, there are cases of deficiency of service, which arise by invocation of the provisions of Consumer Protection Act, 1986; these make news, too.

Clubs

Various clubs run after newsmen for publicity. Here the reporter should make sure that he is not taken for a ride and should only give news, which is in public interest.

If a club is making some worthwhile contribution for the welfare of the people, due credit should be given. But one should avoid unnecessary praise of a president of a club or report minor activities of a club, which are of no significance.

Business and Commerce

In many newspapers, more than one page is given everyday to business and commerce. It is also an important section and should not be ignored.

Movement of shares, securities, performance of Mutual Funds and prices of various important commodities should be reported. Selection should be made according to requirement of the areas served by the newspaper. News agencies also give importance to such reporting for they have many business subscribers and they have the commerce page in newspaper also. Reuter's main profit comes from commercial service. With the growth of commercial activity in India, importance of this service will increase.

Education

Educational institutions also form an important beat because of direct interest of the readership. A reporter should keep himself in touch with the higher authorities as well as leaders of teaching and student community.

Student activities find echo everywhere. Various days are celebrated, sports and other fests are organized, seminars held, special lectures organized, contests held and many cultural activities are organized. In colleges and universities, elections are held to student organizations, academic councils and senates. These provide numerous news stories as many events take place and situations spring up as side issues.

Sometimes, educational institutions engaged in research can give good stories. The reporter should enquire about significant research projects going on and should keep an eye for any break-through or outcome of the research work.

Science and Technology

This field is becoming more and more important from the reporting point of view and many news papers have appointed reporters with a science background for this purpose.

However, this kind of qualification is not essential as a physics expect will be as ignorant about medicine as a layman. Science and technology, whenever reported in newspapers, it is for the laymen. If a non-professional reports, readers will understand it more easily for he will be on a par with the lay reader.

However, if an expert does the reporting, he may presume certain concepts as universal knowledge and do a story, which may not be easy to understand.

This does not, however, mean that a background of science will be of little use in reporting science and technology.

It will be definitely helpful if the scientist reporter always keeps in mind his lay reader.

It is always better to talk to the expert in the non-professional's language and find out an angle which will be interesting for a layman. A look at the following example will illustrate the point.

HAIR PRINTING FOR CRIME DETECTION

Chennai, March 30 (PTI): "Hair printing" may soon become a powerful crime detection device like finger printing.

According to geneticists at the Post-Gráduate Institute of Basic Medical Sciences (PGIBMS) at Tarmani near here, like fingerprints, hair prints were also distinct in every individual and the "Ultrastructure" of the human hair was different from person to person. Every human hair was different from person to person. Every human being's hair could be printed like fingerprints with the help of an electronic microscope and biological tools, Prof. K.M. Marimuthu, Head of the Genetics Department at the PGIMBS, said. (PTI).

He said, "a human hair with its root could also help geneticists identify as one belonging to a man or a woman by the chemical nature or protein chains in the follicles".

If this printing can be systematized and perfected, then it can become a valuable detection device in the hands of the police, who can help track down criminals by identifying them from the hair left behind at the scene of the crime. Human hair has a tendency to fall and at any scene of a crime "it is very likely the criminal leaves behind this valuable clue", he added.

A science and technology reporter should keep an eye on various laboratories and should keep monitoring the purposes and progress of various major projects. Information about delay or failure or success will come from the people working on the project.

A reporter dealing with science and technology should also cultivate the habit of reading scientific magazines and scientific journals with the help of contacts in the scientific community. This may help him in keeping track of various developments in this field.

Sports

There has been phenomenal growth in sports activity at all levels—local, national and international. It has become imperative to do advance planning for coverage of sports events which has become a specialized branch of journalism.

From the point of view of readership, the sports page is important, only next to the front page. Particularly, the younger generation and teenagers keenly follow various competitions more avidly than their elders do.

A special feature of sports readership is that different segments of population take interest in different games. Some have interest in cricket, others in hockey or tennis, or football or badminton, etc., each according to his or her taste. Boxing, wrestling, horse racing, polo, golf and chess too have their own large readership. Our indigenous games like kabaddi and kho-kho have emerged as major national games.

With such widespread year-round sports activity, the newspapers find it useful to employ journalists specializing in different sports. But many a time, a reporter has to deal with more than one game. It is always good to keep background information and records ready in a diary, which should be updated regularly.

It is also important that a reporter knows rules of the game and understands various tricks of the game.

Contacts are necessary in the sports field also. Key officials of various boards and federations must know you. It is good to meet them periodically so that the reporter is not left out on a crucial occasion.

Briefings are done by office bearers after the meetings of associations, boards or their committees. On a controversial issue, it is always good to cross check the facts with some other members, if possible. As in any other kind of reporting, the reporter should try to get more information than the rivals get.

Coverage of Olympics or Asiad is always a major exercise. Advance planning goes into it. The concerned reporters should divide the events, and prepare their own backgrounds. It is essential to know the system of getting information and adapt the strategy in such a way that the reporter gets official information together with or before other reporters. He should not be late.

In such major events, there is attendance of a number of sports personalities. Many of them can be interviewed. Interviews of sports stars are not only confined to sports magazines. They add colour to a sports page of newspaper also.

In every state, there is a sports department. At the national level, there is sports ministry. In parliament and state legislatures, sometimes issues related to sports are raised. After the Asian Games in Delhi, there has been increase in the interest of legislatures in sports. Questions in Parliament or Assembly are asked when sports department figures in questions or there is a special debate relating to some sports issue.

In short, all sorts of techniques, which are used in other fields, can also be used in sports. There is a similar word of caution here again. Sports reporters should not take for granted that everybody knows about sports as the reporters know. With the exception of very famous cups or trophies, they must mention clearly the name of the game along with trophy or cup. They must not presume that the readers know and understand their stories without such information.

Stories about sports events are interesting to the sports lovers. These concern who wins, who loses, who makes hat-trick, who scores century, who makes world record, who reaches zenith, who is disqualified, which team becomes world champion, which team is found steroid positive, etc. Most popular games are cricket, football, hockey, baseball, handball, basketball, lawn tennis and chess. Athletics have emerged as popular and interesting events throughout the world.

CHAPTER

10

Interview as Source of News

All engaged, connected or professionally attached to journalism world know that interview is one of the most dependable and credible sources of news. It has been established as a major technique of getting information in journalism. There is hardly any news magazine, which does not carry interviews. Many a time, the cover story and some other major stories involve more than one interview.

It has become a practice for the Sunday Magazine/ Sunday Newspaper or the magazine sections of daily newspapers often to carry interviews. Sometimes, several people are interviewed on a particular subject and different viewpoints are compiled in one feature, representing a spectrum of diverse views on an issue or subject or happening.

Magazines have special staff to take interviews. They often supply copies of their exclusive interview to daily newspapers and news agencies before they hit the newsstands so that news content of the interview may appear in newspapers. Transcripts of interviews are sometimes released by the press relations staff of the dignitary concerned (interviewee).

It is said that politician and newspaper are made for each other. Political persons and bureaucrats look for every possible opportunity to get their photos published in newspapers and magazines. It is this fact and also that truth is extracted/ ascertained from the horse's mouth on critical, controversial and policy matters through interviews that the importance of interview has been growing as a news gathering technique over the years. It is now seen more and more in news columns. At times, because of interview, a newspaper scores over its rivals in news coverage.

After police action in the Golden Temple (April 30, 1985), Amarinder Singh, the then Agriculture minister of Punjab, became the centre of controversy. Resident Editor of the *Indian Express* based at Chandigarh got an opportunity to interview him; it resulted in publication of that interview on the front page of the paper next morning.

A reporter has to do more home work for an interview than for a press conference. He is alone to ask all the questions. He is not invited to have interview as in a press conference. He has to fix the interview himself. Unlike the press conference, the success or failure of the interview depends completely on him.

PREPARATION

Advance preparation or homework of the reporter is not the same in all cases. The reporter can hold an interview in two parts—reading about the subject concerned and preparing questions to be asked.

Once the reporter has decided the general subject to be covered, he must decide what information he wants to get. The more specific his objectives, the better will be the preparation. It is obvious that he must know the person to be interviewed. If he has written any books, articles or made any speeches about the subject of interview, the reporter should read them. Such material will reduce the time and effort for preparation and help him in framing better and more precise questions. He should check whether any information has been published on the person. He should also find out the environment in which he works or lives.

This background reading will be of great help. He may get answers to superficial questions, which he might be thinking to pose initially. and new, more fruitful, areas of inquiry may become apparent.

It is always better to prepare all the possible questions and note them down in a logical order. The interviewee may want a list of questions in advance. Some more important questions could be given to him. The rest of the questions can be asked as supplimentaries during the interview.

Reporters who do not prepare questions usually run out of questions. On the one hand, it is embarrassing and on the other, the time available in not utilized properly.

It is neither correct nor necessary that the interview should proceed according to the order of questions listed with the reporter. If the list of questions is made available to the interviewee in advance on his/her request, the interviewee may reply to question number three first and then may start replying to question number seven. The reporter can and has to easily go back and forth on his list and keep on asking supplementary questions from the answers. However, a reporter should not hesitate in asking for clarification if he is in doubt about the reply or needs more clarity.

It needs to be kept in mind that questions should be framed with care. They should be specific and clear. One question should raise just one point so that the reply is complete and properly understood. The question and answer should not be long and confusing. If it packs too much information or raises many issues, it will create confusion and uncertainty about the validity of the answer.

Experience shows that some open ended questions should be included to draw out the interviewee. Such questions begin as: "what do you mean by. . . ?" Or "what do you think about . . . ?" Or still, "what factors do you think . . . ?" These kinds of questions may put the interviewee in a thoughtful mood. However, in doing so, one should not forget to ask the basic questions relating to the issue/problem/topic/subject. It has been noticed that sometimes, one may get new or interesting insight into old problems. A good reporter should not be afraid of appearing ignorant in an effort to get worthwhile story and that, too, from the horse's mouth.

As reporter asks questions in public interest; he should not hesitate to ask tough questions that cause a man to think, reflect and clear up any discrepancies in earlier statements on the same subject. If situations compel, there is no harm in asking uncomfortable questions if they are important. There is caution, too. One should not ask questions that are designed to embarrass the interviewee.

The homework or this preparation helps the reporter in many ways. He keeps himself updated on the subject-matter. He knows what to ask. He has time to think how best he can ask the question. Apart, he can convince the interviewee that he is interested in him and in the subject through intelligent questions. Many interviewees cooperate only if they know that the reporter is serious enough and can do justice with the interview. Thus, on the one hand, the preparation prepares the reporter for a better interview and, on the other hand, it helps in getting cooperation of the interviewee, which is so essential for success of the interview.

Considering the status of the person and time given by him, the reporter should introduce the subject skillfully and tell the purpose of interview in a few words in the beginning. If the reporter feels it appropriate, in view of the situation, he may devote a few minutes to pleasantries. This is particularly necessary for those interviewees who are not exposed to newsmen. Let such people be comfortable before you begin putting your questions.

There are dignitaries who keep meeting newsmen; for them, it is good to go straight to the point. This procedure will save time, which could be better utilized by asking more number of questions.

It is not uncommon that the interviewee goes off the track during the course of the interview. In such a situation, the reporter should bring him back to the subject by politely interrupting and asking another question. However, the reporter must make sure that he does not lose control over the interview; else he will fail in his objective.

It is always good and safe to take a tape recorder if the interview is planned but do take permission to use it. Still, it is important to take notes while asking questions for it will help if the machine fails or gets misplaced. Even otherwise, it is easy to deal with your notes than to wait for a transcript or replay if the story has to be done quickly. While taking notes, one should always note important sentences or phrases, which will be useful in assessing the interview and writing the story. A tape recorder helps if the interview is to be given in a question-answer form and if quotes are to be used from it.

CHAPTER

11

News Features : Human Interest and Depth Reporting

New areas of interest have emerged in all human activities. It is but natural that Journalism is affected by such changes and has to meet the expectations of the readership. It is in this background that interpretative reporting, investigative reporting, depth reporting and human interest stories are modern additions to journalistic terminology. They all have found place in reporting and feature writing.

Feature has also grown far beyond its pre-World War limits. It is difficult to draw a dividing line between feature and news story. Now, a news story can be "featurised" by playing up a human interest angle.

Article is not different from feature now. What appears on the edit page as main article is nothing but a category of feature—humorous or serious, or analytical feature. After all PTI feature Service, INFA, (India News and Feature Alliance), Publication syndicate, and Punjab Feature Service mainly supply articles that appear on the edit pages of newspapers as main articles.

Feature has even crept into the editorial column. What many newspapers publish as the interesting and light piece as third editorial is more a feature and less an editorial. It could be called "feature editorial".

Previously, interpretation and opinion were areas reserved for editorial columns. Now interpretation is part of reporter's duty. He not only gathers and reports the facts but also adds explanation or interpretation wherever necessary.

Though investigative journalism was regarded something new in pre-independence India, the nationalist press was full of such stories. This was the major reason why the series of repressive laws were forced on Indian press, particularly the Vernacular Press, by the British government. Several examples of such stories can be found in the history of *Amirt Bazar Patrika*.

If we compare today's concept of feature with the concept of news, we can say that news story deals with more important facts while the feature deals with more interesting facts. Further, timeliness is more crucial in news than in feature. These criteria are relative and not absolute. But together, they can be successfully applied to identify a feature or a news story.

According to the content, feature can be classified into following categories:

News Feature

It appears in news column but *its news value* content is lower as compared to hard news. Backgrounders, situationers and story describing 'how' of an event come in this category of features.

Wild Life Features

With the interest in environment and wild life on the increase, features dealing with these subjects are also increasing in newspapers and magazines. They are normally accompanied by suitable photographs.

Photo Features

Features that rest mainly on photographs are called photo features. This is the case where photographs are supported by words and not where photographs add variety and colour to the text. Loosely, any feature accompanied by photographs is described as a photo feature.

Like news stories, features can be exclusive (not given to any other newspaper) or syndicated (given to newspapers and magazines with an embargo). As news agencies supply news to several newspapers simultaneously, feature services or feature syndicates supply features to several newspapers simultaneously.

A good feature should hang on a news peg. It should contain interesting and important details of an event or person or situation. It should attract the attention of the reader and should be readable enough to take the reader from the beginning to the end. It should not have unnecessary details as they make the text very heavy. Necessary details that are difficult to understand should be interpreted. Sufficient background should be provided to put things in perspective. Language should be simple and the meaning clear.

DEPTH REPORTING

Definition

We find that just as there are as many definitions of news as there are editors, so is the case with definition of depth reporting. There are as many definitions of 'depth reporting' as there are reporters. Here are some definition-answers of depth reporting:

- Depth reporting is what makes readers aware of all aspects of a given subject by giving them all possible information, including background and atmosphere.
- Depth reporting treats a story with a kind of thoroughness of detail and background that a 300-word story cannot. It tells the reader not only what happened but also why it happened.
- Depth reporting means giving the reader the entire

story, in an exhaustive, balanced and well-organized way with full back-grounding.

- Depth report*ing is simply* good reporting with an eye for accuracy and details.
- Depth reporting is the explanatory story that accompanies or follows a breaking news story.
- Depth reporting means going into a news d*evelopment and explaining* its significance with the possible accompaniment of photos that help illustrate the story.
- Depth reporting is sound planning in anticipation of news and vigorous execution while the news is fresh.
- *Depth report*ing is not a one-man job but is the product of teamwork, allowing for maximum flexibility.
- Depth reporting deals in explanatory facts and not explanatory opinion.
- Depth reporting is that which leaves no occasion for more questions to be asked by the reader.
- Depth reporting is not just presentation of facts as they appear at first, but which delves into the origins, the logic, the pressures and the interests involved, making the reader understand not merely who and what, but how, and more importantly, why.
- Depth reporting is digging beneath the surface and coming up with facts that are not immediately visible, but which nevertheless contribute to an understanding of the story.

No matter how it is defined; depth reporting, in the final analysis, should tell us the whole, unvarnished story as it is.

It is a mistaken notion to think that an 'in-depth' story should necessarily be long, though New Yorker reports which are magnificent examples of in-depth reporting run into several thousand words. Length has nothing to do with depth. And, while obviously it is not always easy to cram many facts in a short piece, a perceptive reporter should be able to provide the maximum information in the fewest necessary words. Wordiness is not wisdom and padding is usually seen for what it is.

Often, the best in-depth reporting is done by a team, especially if one has to consider the time factor. While the total number of man hours put in pursuing the facts and writing the story may be about the same if the piece was written by just one reporter, team writing has the additional advantage of bringing the thinking of several men to the final story and should generally be preferable.

The line dividing an in-depth from a feature article or an investigative report is pretty thin indeed and one can often be confused for the other. The presumption usually is that in an investigative report, the object is to ferret out important secret information which somebody is determined to keep secret. But there is no hard and fast rule which says that a writer of a feature article should not reveal secret information or that in-depth reports should confine themselves strictly to presenting background information in detail. The *Indian Express*, in late April and early May 1979, ran a series on what it is like to be in a jail by one of its reporters, Ashwini Sarin. Sarin got himself arrested to get into the jail on purpose and provided some excellent inside information about life in Tihar Central Jail, Delhi. The four-part serial was part in-depth reportage, part feature and part investigative reporting at its best.

Depth Reporting versus Investigative Reporting

There is subtle difference between Depth Reporting and Investigative Reporting. When a story emerges out of police investigation and the accused is challaned in the court, certain aspects catch the imagination of curious reporters. They start finding out that there may be facts beneath not disclosed or purposely thrown under the carpet. The case looks to him as an iceberg, whose tip is visible but its full size is not visible being under water, that too muddy or unclear water or covered by sea-weeds. The Reporter undertakes this as a project and delves deep to find out more facts, sometimes very surprising and startling. This is depth reporting.

When a case is not solved and it is filed as 'untraced', the reporter takes it up and tries to find out facts, ferreting out truth. This is a case of Investigative Reporting. Even this type can be called depth reporting due to the fact of going deep into the simple matter.

Ever since Woodward and Bernstein of the Washington Post broke the Watergate story and followed it up to the point where President Nixon had finally to resign his august office, investigative reporting has received a fillip out of proportion to its real contribution to journalism. The fact is that much of what the two reporters put out was based on FBI reports that were passed on to them by sources that had their own axes to grind. And while this is not to minimize what Woodward and Bernstein had done, it is well to remember that investigative journalism is more than rephrasing leaks. At its best, investigative reporting is master detective work. It is a way of reporting that makes it a tool of the in-depth writer. Also, it is situation reporting rather than event reporting, although events may be involved.

An investigative reporter starts with the hunch that there is more than meets the eye in something of which he had heard. But he can only function best if he is assured of strong editorial direction and backing. Without that, the most perceptive reporter would be wasting his time and the paper's money.

This means that the investigative reporter will have to clear his assignment with the editor and function with the knowledge and consent of his seniors, because no investigation can be successful without the time to do a decent job. *A city Editor of the Detroit Free Press is qu*oted as giving the following suggestions to the prospective investigative reporter.

Don't overlook a tip from any source. Some of the best leads may come from the tips that don't look promising. Many projects won't be sound to plan out. But don't overlook any possibilities.

Stay within the law. Don't attempt to open safes or burglarize offices for 'evidence'. Don't be a policeman.

Make plans from the start. Don't leap into it. Check the evidence and keep checking as you go along. Keep up your lines of communication with those working in the field.

Keep going. The investigative way is hard, but don't stop if you think you have something. If your curiosity is burning you are sure to succeed.

Investigative stories may be written in a variety of ways. When the subject matter is familiar and little explanation is called for, the story can be written as straight news. But if the investigation deals with complicated issues, then a good deal of interpretative material will become necessary. The important thing to remember is that the writer must remain calm, restrained and detached if he is to make any meaningful impact on his reader.

THE CRUSADE

In a sense, all good editors are crusaders for a cause or causes. In the early thirties and forties, till indeed India became free, journalism in our country was largely crusading journalism where the national press was concerned. And the crusade, understandably, was for freedom. *The Free Press Journal* in its early days ran strong stories supporting the cause of Indian shipping.

A crusade implies not merely a cause to be fought for but steadiness and constancy, a strong heart and an unflagging interest. A crusade is not fought by writing one editorial or one news story. Perseverance, often against entrenched hostility from the powers that be, is hallmark of a crusade. Bal Gangadhar Tilak was a crusader, so was Mahatma Gandhi. At the turn of the century, Lovat Fraser, then editor of the *Times of India* ran a crusade exposing the inhuman working conditions in Mumbai's textile mills where men worked 12 hours a day. Fraser ran a tearing campaign starting with an article entitled "Bombay's Slaves' which was to result in a succession of Factory Acts that brought the Indian industrial system in line with world practice.

A crusade can be for any good cause, against child marriage, in favour of prohibition, for ushering in linguistic stages. Several are the causes that the Indian press has fought for over the years. The obvious characteristic of a crusade is that it is concerned with the public good as seen by the editor. In conducting a crusade, the editor may bring to the battle all the ammunition he has, through his editorials, depth reporting, investigative reporting, even cartoons.

It was Joseph Pulitzer who first established the crusade as a way of life for American newspapers by setting up a prize for such kind of journalism. He himself ran crusades against predatory financial interests, bad housing, and the white slave traffic, to mention only a few causes that he strenuously espoused. Today, in the United States, the Pultizer Prize remains a major incentive for journalist to carry on with the Pultizer tradition.

It may be mentioned in passing, however, that neither in the United States nor in any other country, India included, is a crusade necessarily inducted in the public interest. A crusade is just one more gimmick to raise the paper's circulation, not that this is necessarily wrong. If the public interest coincides with the paper's interest; there is no reason why eyebrows should be raised. What shines for public weal may turn out to be another way to augment private profit.

In itself, a crusading newspaper is neither good nor bad. That depends, as one of the distinguished American publicists, Robert J. Blackely, pointed out in his R. Mellett Memorial lecture:

> ". . . in large part upon its motivations. There are newspapers that 'crusade' for ulterior reasons to build up circulation or to grind an axe rather than to sharpen the sword of justice. These are contemptible. They injure the innocent. They rarely accomplish beneficial results that endure, always stopping short when the cream of sensationalism has been skimmed and never pressing to where they touch the really powerful and dangerous elements of the community, but to me the free press reaches its zenith in a good newspaper looking for a fight in a good cause in its own avenues and alleys. Few personal satisfactions can match the knowledge that one is making one's community a better place in which to live . . ."

CHAPTER

12

Interpretative Reporting

INTRODUCTION

It is an established fact that we look back into the past to find out how things have occurred or made to appear as they seem at the present moment. Therefore, looking into the history of Journalism, its concept, as it has evolved, and is currently also held, is news dissemination and sharing. Its extension concludes in the statement—Journalism is news-gathering, fact-finding, reporting without value judgement and thus accurately and substantially true. It is important anywhere at any time.

Sharing and dissemination of information is indispensable in a democracy. People cannot live a truly social life without information. No matter what changes—social, economic, political or others—occur in the future, it is inconceivable that there ever will come a time when there will not be those persons, by whatever nomenclature called, whose full-time function will be to find out what is going on. It would be their mission to transmit that information to others, together with a proper explanation of its significance, impact or consequence, making it clear and understandable to the common man.

The world's population has been zooming further. It has become possible on vehicles of latest technology to visit all parts of the globe in a few hours, and even in minutes. Therefore, the problems and areas of interest with which the editor of to-day is concerned have multiplied many times. The complexity and interdependence of all aspects of human living, furthermore, continue to enlarge both the opportunities and responsibilities of the news-gatherers and disseminators. Although chip technology has introduced miniaturization and opened up infinite possibilities of contact with the media audiences yet there are undeveloped or underdeveloped or developing areas/countries/regions where the traditional go-betweens are slave runners, town criers, newsletters, carrier pigeons, telegraphs, telephones, printing presses, and motion pictures.

There are developed countries or fast developing countries, which have in place the modern modes of communication like radio, television, cable television, satellite communication networks, or even thought waves.

With constantly growing knowledge and its sharing, as envisaged under the World Trade Organisation (WTO), this seems certain that it is going to take better men and women to report and edit the news of the world in the future than it has done in the past. The basic and desirable educational and professional qualifications required of those who enter the specialized and missionary journalism will continue to broaden as they have been doing steadily during the past four decades. More and better education, both general (in relation to the subjects) and related to different types of jobs to execute with the required finesse, will be needed. There will be an augmented need and tremendous scope for those capable, after adequate preparation as general practitioners, to become specialists in a multitude of fields. This is discernible in almost all the developed and developing countries.

E-commerce and E-banking are in place in most of the countries. In this backdrop, the improvement in the quality of the personnel engaged in journalism will continue to be both a business necessity and an essential feature to future existence of democratic society. Only a competent and responsible journalism can provide the knowledge and understanding of information needs of the masses and classes of mankind in order to maintain government of the people, by the people and for the people. From the standpoint of the young person choosing a career, this means that there is no other field of endeavour more likely to provide challenges and opportunities for personal development and service to mankind.

THE NATURE OF REPORTERS' WORK

Newspaper reporters do not often emulate detectives in exposing murderers, kidnappers and subversives, nor do they shout "stop the presses" and compose headlines over the telephone after profanely "telling off" unreasonable superiors. Rather, they put in a regular full day's work in and out of remarkably quiet and orderly newsrooms, where they remove their hats.

It is seen that in large cities, some reporters spend their entire working days on "beats". On smaller newspapers, beat men visit their news sources once or twice daily, returning to their offices to compose their own accounts of occurrences. At times, they may also double their role as "general assignment" reporters, covering news, which occurs at places other than the familiar spots. In whatever way they may operate, they are in all instances under the careful direction and scrutiny of the city editor; the latter, in turn, is responsible to the managing editor that has general charge of the entire news-editorial operation.

We can witness a growing complexity of the news in the modern era. This complexity is augmenting the trend toward a multiplicity of semi-autonomous departments. News today relates to business and finance, real estate, travel and tourism, environment, science and technology, literature, art and culture, sports, etc. Apart from the foregoing types of news, there is one area of criticism and comments as well as interpretation for the common reader. Specialized reporters often constitute one-man departments and have considerable leeway in assignments. Likewise, team reporting by specialists is a new but welcome development. The classic system of deploying reporters geographically is no longer in vogue. Specialists are fast replacing them and, obviously, their borders of news coverage often cross.

The reporter is himself haunted constantly by deadlines: the deadlines are the last minutes at which copy can be submitted for editing. With changes in the working system, there is generally less monotony and consequently less danger of "getting into a rut" in newspaper work. Such situation obtains in almost anything else he could do today. There is a greater pride of workmanship and sense of accomplishment in journalism than is possible for workers in most industries and offices in the present.

It would be wrong to say that the world of reporter is a dream world or fool's paradise. The reporter, in reality, is a responsible person. However, there are several other persons having a part in determining how whatever news he handles appears in the paper. Nevertheless, he has "first crack" at it. The occupational disease that newspapermen must guard against is cynicism (disinclined to recognize goodness, contempt for human nature, heartlessness). Whereas skepticism is a journalistic asset, a hard-boiled or flippant attitude towards the so-called "realities" of life can lead not only to a flagrant disregard of the public interest but also to personal deterioration.

Celebrities in journalism who are persons of worth have tried to settle the controversy, which continues unabated, whether journalism is a profession or not. In fact, much superfluous effort has gone into the attempt to determine whether journalism is a profession, business or trade. What really counts is the attitude of the individual towards his work. Professionalism can be present or absent among carpenters, hotel clerks, nurses, doctors, lawyers, taxi drivers, newspapermen and anybody or everybody else. As for journalism, there is no field, which offers greater opportunities for the development of a professional point of view, idealism, public service and the like. It is the place for the starry-eyed youngster who wants to help "save the world". There is no better way for one who wants to help make democracy work more effectively to devote his talent. As in every other worthwhile endeavour, the road to the top in journalism is long and strewn with obstacles. At the summit, however, are the prestige and power, the Zenith, which make the struggle worthwhile.

THE NEED FOR INTERPRETATION OF NEWS

It needs to be borne in mind that the successful journalist of the future has to be more than a thoroughly trained journey man, if he is to climb up the ladder of success. He must be capable of more than routine coverage and to interpret as well as report what is going on.

For a Reporter to be able to interpret the news, it is necessary to understand it, and understanding means more than just the ability to define the jargon used by persons in different walks of life. It involves recognizing the particular event as one of a series with both a cause and an effect. With their perspective, the historians of the future may be better able to depict the trends and currents of the present. But if the gatherer of information is well informed, through his reading of history, his study of economics, sociology, political science and other academic subjects, and has acquaintance with the attempts of other observers to interpret the modern scene in books and magazine articles, he will at least be aware of the fact that an item of news is not an isolated incident but one inevitably linked to a chain of important events.

It is based on experience to say that the interpretative reporter of the future should be as shock proof as a psychoanalyst and a practical philosopher in his general outlook on life. He cannot succeed if he is hampered by prejudices and stereotyped attitudes, which would bias his perception of human affairs. Modern psychiatry has proved that the first step in ridding a person of complexes is to make him aware of their bases. Hence, the news-gatherer should have a firm understanding of how men think and why, both to avoid pitfalls in his own search for so-called truth and to understand the behaviour of those whose actions are his responsibility to report.

The Reporter, the so-called (but expected) interpreter of the news must see reason where ordinary individuals observe only overt happenings. And he must study them as the scientist scrutinizes the specimen in his microscope, scientifically. Ordinarily, he cannot be a participant in the events of which he writes. Otherwise, his viewpoint will be decidedly warped. To convey meaning, or feeling, to readers, however, it may become necessary to "role-play" to learn what makes others "tick". That means joining the action as stunt reporters do when they get themselves committed to jails or take employment of one sort or another. Features, stories or exposes which result from such reporting still are valuable, but the complexity of contemporary problems demands more than skeptical journalistic detective work, rather it demands sympathetic participation if feeling is to be conveyed to others. Unless reporter can make readers understand what an event means to its principals, he may have failed in his effort to interpret it. Sill, doing his best, he may err constantly; scientific method is nothing but being as approximately correct as possible. His mistakes, however, will be honest ones of an expert and not the blunders of an ignorant one.

THE GROWTH OF INTERPRETATION IN JOURNALISM

It was the World War-1 that actually provided the first important impetus to lend interpretative aspect to handling of the news. When it broke out, most Americans were surprised and dumbfounded in fact and utterly unable to explain its causes. In his doctoral dissertation at the University of Wisconsin in the Mid-30's, the late Maynard Brown suggested the extent to which the news-gathering agencies were responsible for this phenomenon. Brown wrote in part as under:

> "Where the Associated Press failed most was in preventing its reporters from sending background and informative articles based on politics and trends. It smugly adopted the attitude of permitting correspondents to report only what had definitely transpired. It wanted no interpretation of events but the mere factual reporting of the obvious. Some of its correspondents were trained in foreign affairs, but too few were able to interpret or discern significant events and tendencies".

The demand of the Readers for more than mere drab objective reporting of domestic news grew tremendously after the stock-market crash of 1929 and during the depression years of the 30s and the period of New Deal experimentation. The newspapers were slow to modify their basic news formula. Nevertheless, the newspapers expanded their contents to include signed columns by political analysts, most of which were syndicated at reasonable cost so as to be available for moderate and small sized newspapers. They also tried out various forms of daily reviews, expanded Sunday magazine or feature sections and increased the number of supplemental articles to provide historical, geographical, biographical and other background information to help make current news more understandable and meaningful. A whole new vocabulary developed to categorize these writings. Instead of lumping them all under the general heading of "think pieces" as in the past, newsmen talked of sidebars, explainers, wrap-ups, button-ups, blockbuster and other types of explanatory enterprise, off-beat background, sub-surface, creative, speculative or interpretative reporting and writing.

A considerable amount of attention was at first devoted to definitions to determine what difference, if any, there was between interpretation and explanatory material, background facts, editorializing and opinion. The question of policy was, however, fundamental: whether or not to permit writers any leeway to go beyond the mere objective reporting of the news.

As Readers' expectations have become known, the future reporter must prepare himself to help meet the increasing need and demand for "sub-surface" or "depth" reporting, to "take the reader behind the scenes of the day's action", "relate the news to the readers' own framework and experience", "make sense out of the facts", "put factual news in perspective", "put meaning into the news", "point up the significance of current events", and so on, to use the expression of various authorities.

Foremost defender of interpretative reporting against its critics has been Lester Markel, long time associate editor of the *New York Times*, who wrote as under:

> "Those who object to interpretation say that a story should be confined to the "facts". I ask, "What facts?" and I discover that there is in reality no such thing as an

"objective" article in the sense these objectors use it or in any sense, for that matter".

Take the most "objective" of reporters. He collects fifty facts, out of these fifty, he selects twelve which he considers important enough to include in his piece, leaving out thirty-eight. This is the first exercise of judgement.

Then the reporter decides which of these twelve facts shall constitute the lead of the story. The particular fact he chooses gets the emphasis, which is important because often the reader does not go beyond the first paragraph. This is the second exercise of judgement.

Then the editor reads the so-called objective story and makes a decision as to whether it is to be displayed on page I or on page 29. If it is displayed on page 1, it may have considerable impact on opinion. If it is put on page 29, it has no such emphasis. The most important editorial decision in any paper, I believe, is what goes on page 1. This is the third exercise of judgement.

In brief, this "objective" news is, in its exponents' own terms, very un-objective, and the kind of judgement required for interpretation is no different from the kind of judgement involved in the selection of the facts for a so-called factual story and in the display of that story.

In other words, just as the Constitution is said to mean what the Supreme Court says it means, so is news what newspapers and other media of communication decide it to be.

REPORTER'S PREPARATION FOR INTERPRETATIVE JOURNALISM

The basic rule to follow in preparing for a career in journalism is "learn as much about as many things as possible and stay intellectually alert". The ignorant reporter is at a tremendous disadvantage. He annoys news sources because he does not obtain all of the essential facts, and may make gross errors of fact as well as emphasis when he writes his story.

To be able to cover intelligently a police station, criminal court, local body's office/municipal hall, country, state or centre, or political headquarters of all, more particularly of major political parties, one must understand the set-up of government, the nature and functions of various offices. The reporter must be able to read and quickly digest the contents of legal documents. He must know the meanings of such terms as "corpus delicti", "habeas corpus", "injunction" and "certiorari". He cannot say "divorce" when he means "separate maintenance", or "parole" when he means "probation". He must be able to read a bank balance sheet, know when a financial market is bullish and when bearish and what it means to sell short or long, hedge and stockpile. He must understand what it means to refinance a bond issue or liquidate the assets of a corporation. He may not confuse craft unions with industrial unions.

Unless the Reporter knows the procedure by which slum-clearance projects are developed, it is impossible for an interpretative reporter to write that the last obstacle to beginning a slum-clearance programme has been removed. He can not explain the status of a pending city ordinance unless he understands what the rules provide for future consideration of it. It is impossible for him to interview a prosecuting attorney regarding the course of action he may take in a particular case unless he knows what the alternatives are.

The Reporter must know which reference books and clipping files to consult to obtain historical and other explanatory information to "round out" a story although most editorial offices today are equipped with good libraries, or morgues as they often still are called. As he gathers experience, he becomes a veritable storehouse of knowledge himself. Aware of the nature of different organizations, public and private, he knows which ones to consult on which occasion and what each group's slant or interest is likely to be.

In the absence of background knowledge in a field, a reporter cannot fill out an account by declaring that the home run was the longest ever hit in the park. That the shit was the first time a certain ward gave a voting majority to the candidates of a particular party, that a fatal accident occurred at an intersection where the municipal committee/corporation once refused to permit the erection of stop signs, that what seems to be a new proposal for civic reform really was based on (or resurrected from) a decade old report by an elder statesman.

It is left to the interpretative reporter to "read the fine print" of a news story in order to answer the readers' queries, "What does it mean"? To keep a particular news event "in focus", the interpretative reporter shows its comparative importance. "Statistical methods and statistical terms". Huff wrote in his introduction, in his book "How to lie with Statistics", "are necessary in reporting the mass data of social and economic trends, business conditions, opinion polls, and the census. But without writers who use the words with honesty and understanding and readers who know what they mean, the result can only be semantic nonsense".

To be able to present anywhere near a true picture of the housing situation in any community, a reporter must consider the age of the community and of the dwelling units, the adequacy of zoning and building codes and their enforcement, the influx of newcomers and the effect, including that caused by prejudice against certain types of persons because of race, national origin, religion or other reasons, the extent of overpopulation, transportation and parking facilities, educational, cultural and recreational advantages, the income and cost of living indices, nearby urban and suburban growth and similar factors. With such data, he can provide readers with an understanding of the situation and enable them properly to evaluate proposals for change. It would then be situation reporting due to interpretation and judgement applied.

When mere announcement is given that consumer credit outstanding at any given time is such and such means little or nothing unless the reader knows how the figures given compare with similar ones for comparable periods in other months or years (comparison helps to understand implication or gravity).

It is for the Reporter to know and then tell the motives of persons in the news to make their actions understandable. The interpretative reporter knows that cornerstone laying, dedications of buildings, opening of parks and other public facilities and similar acts are times so as to have the maximum beneficial effect for the office-holders in charge. To write with the perspective of the cultural anthropologist or historian of a century means to be aware of "schools of thought", climates of opinion and social, economic and political trends, a journalist scholar should know when the views of an educator are consistent with those of an outstanding scholar or organization or with what has been attempted elsewhere which has improved the matters.

The studious interpretative reporter is certain of this; he knows that nothing just happens. A wave of intolerance has a cause. So has a revival movement an excessive hero worship. A bullish stock market, an increase in superstition, or any fad, fashion, craze or mass movement create followers and opponents, too. For instance, when violence erupts and persists simultaneously in many parts of the world, it is shortsighted to treat a local incident as an isolated phenomenon.

CHAPTER 13

Investigative Reporting

It is an established fact that almost all stories need some investigation. A reporter should, therefore, not hesitate to do this for it will improve the story and he cannot be taken for a ride by some smart public relation exercise.

There are situations where an investigation is on a large scale involving some major government development or big business or multinational company or corporation or some prominent political party or politician or some mafia king or other gangs involved in illegal activities and influencing government. In such a case, a lot of preparation and planning is required.

The Reporter needs to understand that he/she is an investigative reporter and he/she is more like a judge and not like a public prosecutor. He should assess the evidence he gets with an open mind. He is not to tilt the evidence in favour of the hypothesis on the basis of which the investigation has been started. Investigative reporter must be fair. Therefore, he should not shut his eyes or ears to anything, which does not suit the line of investigation. He must keep his mind open from the stage of the conception of the investigative story till it is published. At any stage, he should welcome any information or evidence for a fair evaluation. A biased investigative reporter will after all become what is called a "yellow journalist".

History tells us that Yellow Journalism sprang up in America by conscious design to increase circulation. The circulation war started by William Hearst, Editor of *New York Journal* to overdo Joseph Pulitzer's "The World". The latter raised topical subjects through representation of surrogate of a Colony boy, The Kid. Hearst imitated the style and made the Kid a "Yellow Kid" to give better attention and created sensational news. Pulitzer followed suit to remain in race. Thus the New York readership got two yellow kids and found the punch lines and comments interesting.

IMPORTANCE OF POSSESSING OCCUPATIONAL AIDS

The one in the journalistic profession should have the ability to use a typewriter as well as use shorthand; it is essential. As observed, when it often is necessary to interview news sources in the company of other reporters or to attend news conferences at which only a few get opportunity to ask questions, a verbatim record of what transpires is often valuable. He can also take down the testimony in court or proceeding at the committee hearings in shorthand; both at in-house or before Press Council sub-committee. In view of this utility, more and more news-gatherers who specialize in such kind of work are learning it to their advantage.

Still, there are cases of those who have not cared to do so. They usually develop their own system of short of longhand. They may know some of the commercialized systems which are based primarily upon abbreviations for common syllables and combinations of letters. The reporter who develops his own system uses abbreviations for frequently used words and phrases. For instance, "2" is used for "to", "too", and "two", and "c" for "see", "u" for "you", "r" for "are", etc. The reporter can use simplified spelling in note taking if not in actual copy and can make use of such common abbreviations as "rr" for "railroad", "inc" for "incomplete", etc. He may even use foreign words which are shorter than English, as the French "selon" instead of "according to". Instead of "capital punishment" he may write down "cp" and instead of "labour union" he may write "lu". Still used by some old timers is the Phillips Telegraphic Code patented in the late 19th century by the Associated Press Official. Typical code abbreviations are lgr for "legislature," bd for "board", sap for "soon as possible", cn for "constitution" itxd for "intoxicated", etc. There are several similar systems all using abbreviations, including Zinman Rapid Writing and Streamline.

Tape recorders today are in widespread use by magazine and freelance in which they are circulated.

It is becoming a realization that interpretation is required here and there in almost every story. There are certain stories that are basically the result of interpretation of events, circumstances or various kinds of data available from different sources. Such stories are called interpretative stories.

For reporting of this kind, the reporter should have a strong background of the subject. He should not forget checking all sources of information before writing such a story. If there is any doubt regarding facts, it is better not to do a story than to give a wrong interpretation based on half truths. It is truly said that a wrong interpretation is worse than no interpretation.

This kind of reporting offers a reporter the opportunity to give his opinion in news columns. But one should avoid editorialing news stories. Attempts in the interpretative story should be to use logic and background knowledge; conscious effort should be made to keep personal bias away from the report.

There is no bar to one's expression of opinion based on analysis of facts but distortion of facts to suit one's bias should be avoided. An interpretative reporter should always have an open mind. He may have a hypothesis to begin with, but if the facts do not support it, he should never try to mould facts to do his story.

INVESTIGATIVE JOURNALISM

The surge of interest that developed in the 1970s, largely

as a result of Watergate, generated much argument about investigative reporting. Some authors/writers opined that an exotic new media form had been created, and that its application represented a daring and dangerous extension of the journalist's constitutional franchise, which was to report only facts as they appeared with no comment or value judgement as these involved bias.

You may call it *muckraking,* expose, whatever you wish. Investigative reporting has been part of American journalistic tradition since the early eighteenth-century days of John Peter Zenger. If helped break up the Tweed Ring in New York City more than a century ago.

We come to answer a question as to what is the difference between investigative reporting and just good reporting. The answer can not be either yes or no. The fact is that there is no difference and a lot of difference. No difference because good reporting assumes an investigative attitude and investigative methods, a lot of difference because investigative reporting in its more recent manifestations has begun to change the definition of news values. Essentially, the big difference is a gradual shift from the old style of reporting on spectacular single incidents and personal crimes to more original and conscientious reporting on the systematic operations of society.

The style of today's investigative reporter has undergone sea change: he does not always wait for things to happen. He or she is not geared to events. Since inception of Journalistic concept, and for too long, too much of journalism has been organized into locational beats, like the police station, the city clerk's office (municipal town hall), the courthouse. The beat system encourages the reporter to accept the official version of events. It restricts his movements. It does not motivate him to find out, for example, what happened in the years before an industrial safety problem grew into a lawsuit on his court beat. Pressures of time, space, tradition, training, even commercial constraints, keep him from asking the essential questions. "Why did it assume these proportions?"

There is changed pattern of working in investigative journalism. The modern investigative reporter inverts tradition. He resists daily deadlines. He cuts across beat lines to pursue trouble wherever it originates. Conscious aversion to the accepted way is perhaps the most important attribute of today's investigative reporter. His choice of story subjects forces him into new thinking about standard definitions of news and of the role of the newspaper. He is not content to score a scoop saying that a public figure is under official investigation. He is rather bothered to search for the problems that officialdom ignores. For instance, he wants to know why one class of citizens virtually escapes prosecution for income tax evasion while another class faces swift retribution. In short, he is concerned about the equitable operation of the entire social system. It follows obviously, therefore, that the job of every newspaper is to examine critically and report on all the institutions of society.

It boils down to the fact that the best reporters try to go beyond catching criminals or unmasking single incidents of corporate cynicism. They try to define not only what is operationally unsuccessful but also what is conceptually false. The risks, the pains, and the pleasures are exemplified in the storm of Watergate. It created the tidal waves that would cause to sweep back and forth through our society for decades to come. There were strong, traditional arguments against reporters probing into banking transactions and the tax records of public persons. It is satisfying that, in retrospect, the painful and dangerous individual and collective decisions of reporters, editors, and publishers were, for the most part, justified.

The storm created by the Watergate Scandal also induced a sudden jump in attempts at investigative reporting, though much of it was ill-conceived and poorly executed. Watergate was to make hometown editors and reporters realize that investigative reporting carries heavier burdens when it deals with real people than when it deals with remote, symbolic figures.

Investigative journalism requires a certain amount of missionary zeal, or what Bill Lambert calls "a low threshold of indignation. Investigative reporting is unavoidably complex. That does not mean, however, that it cannot be accomplished successfully by the determined team. But a word of precaution: investigative reporting is high risk journalism on any level.

There are some instances where the dare devil Reporters did wonderful job in investigative journalism. One unforgettable personality is Paul Williams.

PAUL WILLIAMS

Paul Williams was indefatigable investigator. He was a gentle and modest man of intelligence, the kind of person you would like and respect even if you knew nothing of his work. He represented a conventional and unimportant tradition in journalism, which is not so unusual. But he also personified a new and significant reality. He met the old convention of the proper reporter and editor. He had once been a paperboy, a "little merchant". One summer, he even worked in a paper mill. He had been a copyboy doing odd jobs inside a newspaper office, all before became a professional reporter and editor. This is the old fashioned idea of a "real newspaperman", the mythical creature who somehow had ink in his veins from birth.

He represented something new and different in modern American journalism. He knew that the mechanical and technical skills were important, that you must get details accurately in hand, and that you must be capable of fast work. But he also knew something far more important: you need a sense of morality about your society and you need to accept personal responsibility for your role in that society. In his first years, he demonstrated that all the proven power of the press and of individual reporters when given support and freedom is not terrible, and world society do not arise from overtime parkers or welfare mothers but from negligence and crimes of large, prestigious organizations.

It is not only duty but also the quality of a good reporter always to discover enough about his or her subject to test the validity of information that is printed. But the big difference that gives new meaning to "investigative reporting" is, as he has written, "a gradual shift from the old style of reporting on spectacular single incidents and personal crimes to more original and conscientious reporting on the systemic operations of American society.

Paul assumed leadership of teams of reporters who used careful and intelligent analysis of the masses of data by which modern organizations do business. He demonstrated that the individual reporter working on complex stories is still important but there are some stories like complex corporate and governmental crime that are best done by coordinated research by a team of disciplined journalists. Records reveal that Paul led a bright journalistic career; he won Pulitzer Prize for weekly paper and earned the credit to personify what was best in American Journalism.

INVESTIGATIVE NEWS

There is a school of journalistic thought that curls its lip and sneers at the very mention of the words 'investigative reporting'. It argues that, since all reporting is investigative, the phrase is meaningless. If only that were true! But some reporting is investigative only in the most basic sense. It is the journalistic equivalent of the single cell creature and bears about as much resemblance to the subject of this chapter as amoebae do to humans.

INVESTIGATIVE REPORTING

Investigative reporting is substantially different from other kinds and there are four features that distinguish it.

(i) *Original Research:* Investigative reporting is not a summary or piecing together of others' findings and data, but original research carried out by journalists often seeing the rawest of material. It can be extensive interviewing, or matching and comparing facts and figures and discovering previously unknown patterns and connections.
Often, you have suspicions of wrong doing or negligence but have no proof and neither does anyone else. You need to accumulate evidence and this requires far more time and prolonged effort than ordinary reporting. It may also involve more than one reporter.

(ii) *Information Secret:* Investigative reporting starts at the point where the day-to-day work stops; it does not accept the secrecy and the refusal of officials to give the information. It finds out for itself.

(iii) *The States:* the kudos and pride you get when the story works out can be considerable, but so can the amount of dirt hitting the fan when it all goes wrong. Consider the Cincinnati Enquirer's experiences in 1998. In May of that year, they published a front page story and an 18 page section devoted to a year long investigation into the international banana firm, Chiquita Brands. Headlined "Chiquita Secrets Revealed", the paper alleged that Chiquita secretly controlled dozens of supposedly independent banana firms, that it and its subsidiaries used pesticides that threatened the health of workers and nearby residents, that employees engaged in bribery in Columbia and that its ships had smuggled cocaine into Europe.

(iv) *Sniff of a Story:* Investigative reporting starts with a sniff of a story, or the hunch that in some subject lie the seeds of one. The main thing at this stage is to think carefully about the 'best case' outcome and consider whether the story will be worth the effort and time required. If it is not going to be page one, forget it. Specialized investigative units in particular can easily get obsessed with a story that is far too narrow to be of importance to general readers. Submit your planned inquiry to the headline test; if the anticipated outcome does not make a startling headline, then you are probably going to water your time.

Potentially, good investigations can be found in almost any area of public life. Two broad categories, however, are particularly fruitful activities and organizations that do their work in remote places or otherwise away from the public gaze, and people and institutions that suddenly get thrust into the spotlight, appear to have come from nowhere and around which a mythology has speedily grown. They are the people and institutions which seem to have no background. But they will, and in that background, there is almost sure to be a good story.

Reporters from the Boston Post newspaper were discovering this past. The 'Greta Ponzi', it turned out, was better known to the authorities in Canada as prisoner no. 247, the number he bore while jailed for forgery, he had also done time in Atlanta for smuggling aliens. The Post ran the story, Ponzi's company duly collapsed, and he went to jail for four years.

Reporting Skills

Investigative reporting can be undertaken by anyone with the determination both to see the job through and to handle all the inevitable frustrations. It requires no grater skills than those demanded by general reporting. But there are a few things that make the job easier and which will make you more efficient at it.

Public Access

What is the law on this in your country? Do you know that public records and documents you are entitled to see is not 100%. This is vital. Some investigations have resulted from secret documents being passed to journalists, but many more have resulted from reporters discovering that certain records or registers are kept and that they have a right to consult them. Most bureaucracies do not exactly advertise the existence of such information and they erect all kinds of barriers to prevent people consulting them, by making them available only at certain times, or by storing them in out of the way places.

In the United States, the 1966 Freedom of Information Act, strengthened in 1971, has opened up all kinds of documents to journalists. As a result of their use in investigations, all manner of scandals have been uncovered by the press:

Unreported Accidents at Nuclear Sites

X-ray machines at cancer detection centres which were emitting 25-30 times the correct level of radiation (within months of disclosure, all such centres in the United States had reduced amounts of radiation).

Unaesthetic drugs routinely given during child birth even though they could and did cause brain damage to babies.

There was also the paper in Louisville, Kentucky which obtained federal inspection reports on nursing homes showing the abuse of residents. As a result, new state legislation was introduced, many homes were closed and the owners of several others were charged with fraud.

Standard Reference Sources

Lists of official publications, reports from legislatures, lists of public bodies, company ownership, reference books or registers of bodies receiving government funding are reference resources.

The Contacts

The reporters obviously need contacts, but investigative reporters more so.

Computer Literacy

This means not just the ability to search effectively online, but also the ability to use database software. Examples of the value of this in investigations now abound. One of the most instructive was that by the Atlanta Journal constitution in Georgia, which won a Pulitzer Prize in 1989 for a series analyzing racial discrimination in bank lending.

The investigation started with an off-hand remark by a white house developer. He said he was having trouble building houses in the black areas of south Atlanta because banks would not lend money there (something that would be illegal, if done for discriminatory reasons).

Dedman discovered that banks and other institutions were making five times as many loans in white areas as in black areas. By examining bank policies and practices, he also found that they were not looking for business in black areas and were otherwise discouraging black borrowers. Blacks, in turn, could only resort to unregulated mortgage companies and loan sharks. As he says, only then did I turn to anecdote'.

He collected personal experiences, which gave his series real lives, and showed how the policies of banks affected people.

Investigation Operations

The subjects for investigations come to papers in all kinds of ways—tips from contacts, by accident, a seemingly routine story that subsequent information indicates is far bigger; a reporter's own observations, a run of the mill story which escalates bit by bit, or one where every question you ask throws up other, increasingly important questions.

This was the case with perhaps the most famous journalistic investigation of all—Watergate. It began in June 1972, with a break-in at the Democratic Party's headquarters in the Watergate Building in Washington. It ended just over two years later with the resignation of the most powerful man on earth, President Richard Nixon. The role of the President and his staff in the original burglary and much else besides (phone-taps), lush funds and, most important of all, the cover up of these illegal activities) would never have been known had it not been for investigative reporters. The two main ones were Carl Bernstein and Bob Woodward of the Washington Post.

When they started working on the story, in a mood of mutual distrust, it was a routine crime story. Five men had been caught breaking into the Democrat's Head Office to plant a listening device. Woodward went to the courtroom the following day and noticed a prominent lawyer taking great interest in the case. What was he doing there? Woodward also learnt at the court that several of the men had worked for the Central Intelligence Agency. They were also carrying large amounts of cash on them when arrested and two of them had note books, inside one of which was a telephone number for a man who worked at the white House.

The moral of every investigation ever mounted is to lay your hands on every document that you can and throw nothing away. Bernstein and Woodward, the Watergate reporters, filled four filing cabinets after just a few months.

(a) *Be Persistent* : Read the story of any investigation and the persistence of the reports the thing that strikes you. During the Watergate investigation Woodward and Bernstein often spent days going through records, sat at their desks making phone calls all weekend, or waited outside lawyers' offices all day for the chance to see a perhaps vital source. On one occasion, they obtained a list of the hundred or so people who worked at the Committee to Reelect the President, the seta of much of the wrong doing. Since they obviously could not visit thee people at their offices, they spent many weeks calling on them at their homes after their normal day's work at the paper.

Old Sources : As long as an investigation is in progress, there is no such thing as an old source. Woodward and Bernstein each kept a separate master list of phone numbers of contacts.

Cultivate Sources: During the Watergate investigation, Woodward contacted a man who worked at a senior level in the government to ask him if any word of the wrong doing had reached him. It had. He knew an enormous amount and clearly regarded it as his duty to assist the exposure of the conspiracy.

Executive Support: The news editor or editor must commit staff and other resources to the project.

Going Undercover: Most of the time, there is a better way of collecting information than going under cover. But occasionally, very occasionally, it might be the only way to write the story.

The other hands will take a lot more lying down. First, undercover work always becomes some deception, so the wrong doing you are reporting needs to be serious enough to justify that dishonesty. Second, the physical dangers in such a situation can be immense and last long after you have surfaced to write your story. Third, if you are investigating criminal activities undercover, you may well be drawn into participating, which makes your actions even harder, if not impossible, to defend.

Social Services

Andy Knott, a hard driving six footer with the energy of a threshing machine, became an investigative reporter of the *Chicago Tribune* soon after his graduation from the University of Tennessee. For three months, he worked undercover as an emergency Medial Technician for five private ambulance companies in Chicago. Then he wrote a six part series for the *Tribune* entitled 'Ambulances Unsafe at Every Turn', which disclosed scandalously poor maintenance of many private ambulances and widespread abuse of patients. The result was—major reforms, made mandatory by new state and city laws and regulations.

Comparing Objectives

It used to be said that the primary objective of most campaigns was to put wrong doers in jail and get innocent persons out of jail. These, naturally, are the most spectacular results of campaigning.

Future Prospects of Investigative Journalism

The nation will have need of a more efficient and broadened system for the dissemination of news, ideas and opinion. What we are seeing today is the adaptation of newspapers and wire services to the computer age and the development of the electronic media is only the beginning of the changes that are ahead for journalism.

The genius of science, investing with the laws of supply and demand, will determine how much instant journalism we can live, what form it will take and how much we can actually absorb.

There are several things that are more important to the journalist than research and development, much as they are needed in a profession that has been backward for too long in such matters. The first and greatest of these is the continued protection of the freedom guaranteed in the First Amendment, which are under increasing challenge in times of social change and worldwide political upheaval. For without a free press, the journalist becomes a mouthpiece for government, a lackey of the powerful, and a robot that performs mindless duties in a graceless style.

While it is a temporary relief to have the United States Supreme Court strike down judicial gate order and other prior restraints on publication, no journalist can feel secure if reporters sit in jail in violation of judicial orders to disclose their source to the authorities and act, in fact, as servants of the government. It is a disturbing, even a threatening trend.

Second only to the perpetuation of the rights of a free press is a reconsideration of the substance of journalism. The current definition of what the journalist treats as news is simply not good enough. Television and radio will have to be something more than glorified bulletin boards. Newspapers, wire services and news magazines will be obliged to shape their reports to a greater extent towards areas that are more deeply after the public interest.

Finally, journalism must stand for something if it is to continue to be respected enough to be the harbinger of bad tidings, in primitive societies; such messengers were killed and journalists, in modern times, have frequently felt the sting of public animus merely because they did their duty. No less than the holding of public office, the difficult task of informing the public is a trust. It is therefore, inevitable that the concept of journalism as a public service is bound to increase in strength. Today, it is a trend. Tomorrow, it will be a necessity.

Salient Features of Campaigning and Investigative Reporting

Campaigns must have the wholehearted support of the news organization newspaper or magazine or broadcasting station or reporters will find them helpless to continue.

Campaigns based on the premise that the press is the watchdog over the public's business show results.

It is manifestly true that not every campaign or investigation that is undertaken will pay-off in a dramatic way. The ratios of success to failure are about one in five in the United States.

Reporters undertaking investigations of crime or suspicious organizations are always in personal danger and they and their editors must realize it. Don Boles of the Arizona republic was murdered during his crime inquiry. Terry Thompson of the Nashville Tennessean remained under police guard for a long time after he became a Clan member for a year and then wrote an expose.

TV investigation, because of the visual nature of the medium, usually takes a lot longer to complete than newspaper requires. On network TV, with the exception of special programmes like 60 minutes, the time allowed for national coverage is relatively modest. TV reporters usually have to do a much tighter job of writing than their colleagues in print.

The substance of many an investigation is based on examinations of public documents such as land sales, tax records and court actions. The objective, in examining such data, is to determine first of all if there is a pattern of suspicious circumstances that might indicate wrong doing. If the matter exists, it should be followed up with a detailed inquiry.

A campaign or an investigative report should be written in a calm, restrained manner. This is not the place for typifying. The lead ought to indicate broadly the nature of the inquiry and the principal results, the reason the investigation was undertaken, the length of the inquiry and the participants.

Whether campaigns are undertaken in the public or private sector; they ought to be so fashioned and so directed as to serve the public interest.

REPORTERS AT WORK

Situations could be:

At the laboratory testing eatables, at questioning and tape recording replies of alleged murderer (suspect), at contemplative state of mind getting inspiration that a high official must have evaded tax payments, at study or morgue reading reports or memorandum or data to arrive at patterns, at interview confirming a fact, interviewing key person, critically testing records to cue how stores got siphoned-off, reading numbers to attempt zeroing on possible culprit, talking to a friend while eating lunch with him about police corruption thus conceptualizing, waiting in a telephone call for teaming, scrutiny of high court judgement to assess possible error in libel case, visiting a telephone company or railway office or where public distribution of essential commodities is managed to find out any irregularity and not serving public interest, viewing with surprise or remorse the feeling of trees without authorization or without regard for environment, spotting duties not performed or neglected or awfully and badly performed incurring wastage or public annoyance or insulting responsibilities to society, all persons engaged in these activities or more of such activities, thoughts, on hunch or intuition or suspicion or on small insignificant trails or leads—are all investigating men and women.

These are the persons really as brave as soldiers, as curious as the cat, as full of vitality as a child is—defenseless especially in India where physical protection is not provided and being like a parallel agency to official police and allied investigating agencies pruned upon and harassed and endeavoured to doom in failures—not considered as challenge to be more efficient and coordinate for a common objective bringing wrong doing to light from the depth. The causes, the maladies, the contradictions and apathy to place before the society and authorities for debate and rectitude to stem the rot and improve situations and also to provide better safeguards for regulated social functioning are the matters reported in public interest.

Some of the reporters are doing it in the old fashioned way, using private sources to get leads to concealed information. Others are using more modern methods, discovering patterns that once were beyond the ken of the pencil and paper reporters. They vary widely in age, experience, and approach, yet each of them is changing the nature of news work. They are breaking away from the conventional beats; they are viewing events as parts of processes. They are challenging and questioning the official version of the significant issues.

Day after day, year after year, investigative reporters are plagued with the question of whether what they do will change things. For most of them, change is the inner motivation, spoken or not. That comes slowly, if it comes at all, but no change is the case of inner frustration.

A general feeling among the mass media reporters is that one of the things that make so many people feel frustrated these days is that they feel everything is out of control. There's nothing they can do about their lives. There are forces here, there and everywhere that have just taken over.

The trend has changed in recent years. This different approach many reporters are taking to their work. They still expose specific instances of individual wrong doing. But more and more of them are pressing beyond, searching for conceptual and structural problems in the social system. They are doing investigative reporting.

WHAT EXACTLY IS INVESTIGATIVE REPORTING

The word "reporting" comes from the Latin word, 'reportaire', which implies carrying something back from another place. The word investigative, of course, also has a Latin root: vestigium, which refers to a footprint or track. The analogy seemed simple enough a few years ago. The reporter went on the trail to find a predator, to quarry its footprints, watched the trees and rocks for claw marks or tufts of fur. He stayed on the hunt day and night, trying to anticipate that quarry's next move. Eventually, he bagged it and hung up its hide in public. Much of the thrill was in the chase, and the hunter was honoured as a hero for outwitting and capturing a cruel individual beast. But the game has grown somewhat stale. We have learned that it does not keep away all beasts. They want more from their hunters, the reporters, than vicarious sensation. They want to learn about real life and how to live it successfully.

To build a workable definition of investigative reporting for tomorrow, then, start with this injunction: You are here to tell how things really work, not how the civics book says they work. If you think about and work at reporting with this principle in mind, you begin to find stories where nobody else thought to look.

If you start looking at how things work in a business, you try to find out about the relationships between the managers of that business and the agencies of government that are supposed to regulate it. You think about the decision-making process, about the relative priorities given, for example, to profit, to pollution control, to other community or national goals.

When you start looking at how a police department operates, you try to determine what internal controls it has, what criteria it uses in deciding which laws to enforce. The resulting stories describe system wide corruption and failure of the top bureaucracy to do anything.

David Burnham advises that the concept can be summarized in the following words:

> "Corruption is much more than a moral issue. It really is a failure of the bureaucracy to function. Corruption means the bureaucracy can not recruit the right people. You attract the wrong people and repel the right people. It means the discipline is all shot to hell . . . it means, of course, that the laws are not enforced".

Telling Reporter how things work inevitably leads him on trails far outside the conventional paths of the beat reporter. It leads to another way of defining the challenge: it is a job of pulling things together for the reader.

Pulling things together

In view of the preceding views, the investigative reporter is the antithesis of the beat reporter. The beat reporter is expected to produce several hundred meaty words each day about activities of immediate consequence to thousands of persons; the investigative reporter may work for months without writing a paragraph for print. The beat man must know and cultivate all of the key people in his building, which sometimes means scratching their backs in exchange for the first break on an official announcement. The investigative reporter, on the other hand, is skeptical if not scornful of such an announcement. He devotes little effort to winning friends in the official hierarchy. The beat reporter's world is bounded by the walls of his courthouse or police station, the investigator views these buildings as way stations along a torturous trail of observation, documentation, and interview.

While the beat reporter's job is to report that something happened, the investigator's challenge is to find out why, and to tell why it may happen again. His job is to pull things together. Not surprisingly, this challenge leads the reporter, after his training on the beat, to abandon the beat itself.

Penetrating Secrecy

In addition to telling how things work and pulling things together, there are two other aspects of investigative journalism: penetrating secrecy and preserving the system. "Investigative reporting", says Robert W. Greene, "usually involves the gathering of important information which some person or agency is trying to keep secret". This definition.... presupposes that the information gathered is the original work of the reporter, not the investigative product of another person or agency. Greene's definition emphasizes "the original work for the reporter" and stresses the penetration of secrecy. Unless these elements are present, Greene believes, reporting may be called good, but it cannot be called investigative.

The reporter goes beyond the official version of an event or circumstance. He looks at things not from the self-interested viewpoint of the prosecuting agency but from the viewpoint of the reader. By far, the toughest aspect of investigative reporting is the penetration of secrecy. It requires ingenuity, resourcefulness, planning, guts, guile, salesmanship, and obstinacy in the face of hostility.

PRESERVING THE SYSTEM

The persons in charge of various functions and services are aware of problems, but time and again, it has been seen that they make serious errors of policy and tactics because they misread the public's perceptions of important problems and their causes. Investigative journalism does not and should not preclude the reporting of good news. A free press, Walter Lippmann said, "is not a privilege but an organic necessity in a great society".

It needs to be clearly understood that the press is not free solely for its commercial good, nor because publishers and editors should have special license to vent their own ideas or opinions. Its freedom is based on the common right to know not only what is going on, but what ideas to do things differently are followed abroad. The latter right is every bit as important as the former. It makes change possible and change is unavoidable for development.

We know that the political scientists and lawyers will continue to argue about precisely how our journalistic right to free inquiry and debate fits into the system. Free enquiry's main purpose is to help citizens participate in the decisions that affect their lives. The system has never worked precisely that way. Perhaps it never will but the ideal is there and is worth striving for.

THE DEMANDS ON THE JOURNALIST

Given the complexities of life today, finding out how things work is a full-time job and needs skilled help. Such work makes special demands on the journalist. It calls for personal integrity and a strong sense of right and wrong. Stories based on a single source are, by definition, not descriptive of how investigative reporting is conducted. They do not pull things together. They perpetuate and give stature to the biases and special interests of the single source. They contribute to misunderstanding. The reporter who lives on them is denying the very basis of investigation, which is to compare and contrast, to strip away irrelevancy and obfuscation, to provide solid information.

The everyday challenges and problems of investigative reporting are obviously not for everybody. It is a much more demanding form of journalism than reporting the visible, daily activities of life, the wins and losses that a professional football game symbolizes or the personal struggles of men and women trying to cope with a system they find unable to control.

It is expected of the investigative reporter to shed light on the future. The reporter who decides to follow the investigative route will be exploring the frontiers of journalism. But before he embarks on it, he will need to re-examine his standards, his thought processes, and his reporting techniques.

The Intellectual Process

Investigative reporting is not stereotype reporting or simple/routine type of reporting. It is an intellectual process. It is a business of gathering and sorting ideas and facts, building patterns, analyzing options, and making decisions based on logic rather than emption including the decision to say no at any of several stages involved.

Seymour Hersh says, "The hardest thing to do in any reporting is when you don't have a story". His statement crystallizes the greatest daily pressure on the investigative journalist. His colleagues, his boss, and his sources, even he himself—all expect to see some results from all that sitting around and reading, that clipping and indexing, and that travelling and telephoning. Too often, under such pressure, the reporter hypnotizes himself. He begins to believe that the story is there. He ignores or fails to look for evidence that it isn't a story.

The Investigative Reporter has to satisfy himself that the content of what (his source) said is true. The veteran journalist has ingrained within himself a special style of reasoning. He knows how things normally work. If he observes a phenomenon, an effect, he wonders what caused it. He develops a hypothesis and begins checking it against observable facts. He works to back up the chain of facts, searching for information that will either support or negate his hypothesis. He tries different combinations of conflicting versions of a story until he finds the one in which salient points overlap.

Conception

As an established reporter, you get lots of tips. Some are single sentences spoken in a half whisper. Many are telephoned, some come in letters, signed or unsigned. Look for proof of two or three essential facts that might support the tipster's claim. Equally important is evaluation of the tipster, if she or he is known. Is it proper and reasonable to assume that this person knows the facts? Is there any information available about the tipster in the morgue? Is the tipster already known by other members of the news staff? What axe does this person have to grind? If a story develops as a result of this tip, will the informant personally benefit through job promotion, financial gain, or by advancement of political interest? Is he or she trying to "get" somebody hooked such as an ex-boss or an ex-lover?

There is the operating principle that hardly anybody, ever, provides a tip without an ulterior motive. The motive will likely bias the tipster's version of whatever is going on. The Reporter does not want to rush into print with a story that can damage a person's reputation. Still, if the tips are handled carefully, the Reporter can get the conception for a story.

Sometimes, the tipster has no motive but good citizenship. Your final evaluation of a tip should be based on the probability of the allegations it involves, not on the character or motives of the tipster. Even if your tip doesn't pass your first screening, it is a god idea to file and cross index it. Some day, another bit of information may pour in that fills a gap in your fragmentary knowledge and then surprisingly a story begins suddenly to take shape.

Sources

Sources are identified and nurtured; they are not tipsters. Sources are the people who are in a position to tell you what is going on. Every time you make a new contact on a story, you have found a potential source. As you go along, you acquire sources in law enforcement agencies, in banks, in key government agencies, in the criminal community, in the professional fields—(law, medicine, engineering), in public relations, in labour, in politics, in the courts, in education, in science—ideally in every field of human endeavour.

An Intelligent, discreet, and well-placed source is a help in story conception, an adviser in appraising tips, a guide to valuable research records, and a knowledgeable interpreter of your research. The search for story ideas is unending. Story ideas can come from anywhere—legal advertisements, estate sales, bankruptcy notices, and transfers of business executives, company and professional newsletters.

Legwork

The smart reporter, however, makes a point, even while carrying on a major investigation, of moving around, of seeing people outside the news business.

Tangential Angle

Many times, in the middle of one investigation, another

story is possibility conceived. It is a new angle, but one you cannot chase down right away. So, you write a memo on it to review at the end of your project.

Observations and Files

Investigative reporting needs patience and lot of reflective ideas or conjectures. He has to sit and stare at the wall and ask: "What things happen in this town that affect a lot of people but about which nothing ever has been written? What are the institutions—public, educational, non-profit, and corporate—that manage to stay out of the news?"

It so happens that sometimes a subject emerges clearly. However, more often, you will decide to start building a file on the basis of conversation with people around the institution. You may find that the initial results confirm your suspicions. Then, you go into the next phase of story development.

Case Story

In 1972, for instance, Ed. Pound was investigating a minor political kickback scheme in Chicago's 43rd Ward. A friend told him about a young man who was being intimated by John J. (Jack) Clarke, a probation officer. Pound made a note in his diary went back several months later with colleague, Tom Dolan, to find out who Jack Clarke was. They found that Clarke was more than a probation officer. For special missions, he reported directly to Mayor Richard Daley and to Judge Joseph Power, former law partner of Daley's. The reporters found Clarke also drew $ 1,500 a month as a consultant to the police department, and that he further drew questionable fees as a security consultant to the Port of Chicago. In a series of stories in April of 1973, the Sun-Times exposed Clarke's multiple and mysterious roles. Within eight months, Clarke was indicated for income tax evasion and obstruction of justice, pleaded guilty, and was sent to jail. It was a dramatic payoff to systematic pursuit of a tangential angle.

Feasibility Study

There are a few pertinent questions about feasibility of

undertaking Investigation. These are: Is it possible to do the story? Is it feasible? Are people, time, money, and technical skill available to pull it together? Will the story literally take time long enough for our examination? What blocks stand in its way from being fully and accurately told? Further, unavoidably, the most basic question of all: Does the story mean anything to my reader?

Before deciding to initiate the feasibility study, it may consist of twenty-minute talk with your editor, or it may involve a couple of weeks of intermittent conversations. It should cover the following points—news value, protection, green· signal from editor, and goal-setting.

News Value

What if there are obstacles, resistance, resources and protection. How many readers does it affect? Is the effect clear and direct, or is it abstract and theoretical? Is it something a significant segment of the audience needs to know but can not find out?

Protection

There are two aspects to protecting your story. The first is to preserve security within your own organization in order to prevent knowledge of the investigation from leaking back to the target. Keep your files or memoranda and documents locked up and discuss the project with others only on a "need to know", basis. The second aspect of protection is to prepare for the backlash or counterattack from the target.

Green Signal from the Editor

The upshot of the feasibility study is a decision on whether to proceed with the investigative story. The Editor examines the memorandum or note submitted and authorizes to proceed.

Goals

Limiting the dimensions within boundaries fixed by that decision, of course, is the matter of goals: what the paper hopes to accomplish by publishing the story. This approach towards determining goals makes life easier at both the start and the finish of an investigative project. If the goals are clear, the go/no-go decision is far easier to make. If, on the other hand, there are too many unanswered questions about the feasibility of the story, or it is one that the editor feels the reader won't give a damn about, or is too expensive to get and too uncertain in the getting, the editor is likely to say, "No go", Even if the answer comes out no, you should be able to satisfy yourself that you have given your best. You can close the file or put it in the "observation" category and move on to your next idea. But if the decision is go, you can start planning how to do the job.

PLANNING AND BASE-BUILDING

As in other areas where scientific management is called for, any investigative story involves planning. It also involves learning and understanding the norms of the subject area under study; it might be termed base-building. Planning pertains to methods, tasks, roles, and schedules.

Methods

Information obtained along the way in pulling together an investigative story must be compiled and organized. Maintaining files is also an important method. Files should be organized so that related information falls naturally into patterns.

Tasks

Tasks are specific activities you will have to perform in connection with any investigative story: records to be checked, persons to be interviewed, data to be put on file in the computer and processed, files to be maintained, references to be read. As best you can, try to estimate the time your tasks will take and pencil them in on a calendar in the order in which they are to be done.

Roles

You may organise roles in any of several ways; simply be sure that every task you have identified is covered by someone who knows that is his job.

In view of what has been discussed above, it follows that the goal of base-building may be defined simply as understanding the norms of the area under journalistic investigation. If you don't understand these norms, you won't have a story. You may write one and somehow get it published, but it may transpire that you will not have asked the right questions and your reader will not understand what you are trying to say. Moreover, your target will be able to shoot holes in your story. It may so happen that he may be able to get other reputable experts to do the shooting while he stands aside, look righteously aggrieved.

Research Records: *Written evidence of what the reporter sees, to whom he talks and what the person said, observations, and speculations are the seeds of investigative stories. The records suggest a pattern the investigator can follow, which no other method can suggest.*

Observations

The most significant of all methods is direct observation. It places the reporter right at the action scene. He may watch from a distance, he may be an anonymous participant, he may play roles. All of these activities force the reporter to weigh and examine his ethical values.

Comparing and Contrasting

The Reporter develops nerves closer to the surface than most people can. Comparing and contrasting as the reporter sifts through the accumulation of records, an instinct for the telltale clue. He collects the facts unlike other Reporters do.

Gap-closing

There is a suggestion. Just sit down at least once a week with the material and review it. Bring your chronology book up to date and decide whether the new information points in new direction or requires further checking. It is the business of resolving conflicts among your different records, observations, and interview notes.

Whatever the case, no matter how many record searches are made, interviews taken, and observations made, one thing is certain and that is to make effort to close the gap. No matter how often you and your co-workers compare and contrast the information gathered, the gap must be closed.

Key Interviews

The interviews of key persons are to be postponed for the last. Three important points to remember about it are: you should prepare for it carefully; you should keep control of it, and you should use it to gain new information.

Preparation

Reread all the files carefully. Bring the chronology up to date. Check and recheck crucial documents. Study the whole of this material until you can talk about any aspect of it without fumbling.

Frame and rewrite the questions. Study them for their clarity and import and arrange them in a logical order, going from the most general and least difficult ones at the start to the tougher and most specific ones at the end.

Control of Interview

It has been the experience with most of the people that the interview becomes an intense contest of wills and wits. Proper planning and execution enables you to keep control of it.

New Information

The objective of conducting the interview is to get new information. The target person (subject) may not want to see you, but don't use this as an excuse to avoid the interview; not until you have tried and exhausted all approaches can you conscientiously write, "Mr. Ashok refused to comment".

FINAL EVALUATION AND FINAL DECISION

You must discuss the negative decision with your editor, but do not talk yourself into a go decision just "because of all the work we have put into it". "I spent weeks reading transcripts of court material and several thousand pages of transcripts and depositions," says Al Delugach of *The Los Angles Times*. He says that the original tip was to have led to some hanky panky in a national political campaign. "After talking to a number of people", he says "I decided it was not the story that it was cracked up to be. . . . It did not have the potential". You have to develop such a tremendous self-discipline to deal with this frustration of finding blind alleys.

WRITING AND PUBLICATION

Mature suggestion rather command is to write only what you know. Again, write with conservative accuracy. You can write from the facts and still have a readable piece. It is often best to write the central part of the main story before you decide on the lead and the ending. If you can put together a clear narrative, organized chronologically or in some other easily understandable manner, the lead may suggest itself.

Follow-up Plan

Follow-up is essential, otherwise the authorities concerned may gloss over and ignore the story and take no action to find out cause and effect rectification, besides ensuring no recurrence. Therefore, people go about following up on their published story in different ways, but all agree that the follow-up is necessary. Follow-ups themselves develop into stories.

None can authoritatively suggest a recipe for doing an investigative story. There is no single way in which to do the investigative story because circumstances alter cases. The essence of investigative work is imagination, determination, perseverance and motivation.

Better way in which to begin developing ideas is to start on significant but not sensational "depth" stories about local issues. Bob Greene says, "At least do the motherhood issues; crime on the streets; drug addiction among the young: this is the sort of stuff that you want to work on first. These are motherhood issues. You know that your advertisers will applaud . . . but at least you are starting to accomplish some good. If you can get people used to that profile, then put your foot in. Put another step into the water and keep going. Go as far as you can".

The Matter of Records

Authorities in Journalism say that the first and great commandment of investigative reporting is this: get the record.

There is no doubt that all reporters and editors know there are public records in the local body, the court, secretariat (Revenue records), Tehsils, Districts, Government Agencies including autonomous bodies. They publish some of these records—real estate advertising. They get a lot of stories out of records of police activity, fire calls, zoning applications. Unfortunately, that's about as far as most reporters ever go.

Being skeptical and conservative, the investigative reporter looks at records in different ways. First he recognizes that there is an institutional record of almost everything. Second, he does not limit his search to standard public sources. He reasons that all sorts of records, including many that are customarily thought of as private, are worth digging for. He knows that records are often the best evidence, far better than prejudiced recollections or oral accounts of what happened.

Investigative Reporter does know by experience that before he begins interviewing, he must build a firm documentary base. During his cub and journeyman days, initiation into journalism, he learned to get acquainted with clerks, librarians, book-keepers, auditors, purchasing agents—all sorts of people who maintain records. He also learned that many of them know more than what may be found on the pieces of paper in their files and that many of them will let their friends from the newspaper know when special records pass over their desk

FILES AND PROFILES

The ferreting reporter does not restrict himself to records of transactions and events. At the very start of his project, he begins to build profiles of people. He thinks of all the human activities, i.e. birth, death, marriage, divorce, travel, major purchases, licences, education, military service, credit applications, voting, organizational membership that is preserved in records, and he then proceeds to draw documentary pictures of the people he is dealing with.

THE LAW

There is system and procedure for accessing or getting copies of public records. Therefore, to get public records, you must know the laws governing them

BEATING THE BUREAUCRATS

A difficult situation may arise. What happens when information is withheld? Suppose, for example, a state or local government record you want is being restrained, and suppose your publisher and his lawyer tell you it will be a long and expensive job to get it by going to court. What are then the alternatives available?

The first principle to remember is to go only as high as necessary to get access to public records, no higher. Only when denied at the lower level do you go higher, first through the civil-service hierarchy, and finally to the political appointee level. At each level, be prepared to quote the law by section and paragraph number. It is good also to quote case law, if it happens to be recent and on your side, and to demand the legal citation under which access to the records is being denied to you.

The aim is that you want to get the records with a minimum of fuss. In such instances, look for a way around the obstruction. Try going to a friendlier person in another section of the same department. Or go to a source in a different department who has access to the records in the course of his official duties. He can ask for the files and then make photocopies for you.

Another tack is to look for similar or partial records in other offices. Get all such documents, interpret the gaps with common sense, then go back to the mine-safety department and ask for information to fill the gaps.

Fortunately, now Right to Information Act has eased the situation. On application in the prescribed form, copies of records from public office/government agency are made available. The hassle of yesteryears has gone. The only rider is that the information/record is required for general good.

However, there are exempted categories of classified documents in the interest of security of state.

Get it All

Once on the job of getting the record, get all of it. Taking photocopies is the best way. But if you have to copy the information by hand, copy all of it, including the initials of persons who approved it, the noting, the dates of various actions, the serial or file number, marginal notes scribbled by file clerks or previous recipients.

For having general records search, follow the following broad and major guidelines:

- Get the whole record, not just notes or excerpts.
- Evaluate each document's validity and possible weaknesses.
- Compare and contrast similar or overlapping records, in other words, "triangulate".
- Build and maintain a workable system of record-keeping for your self.
- Get to know the people who keep records, and learn their systems.
- Know the laws covering public access to records, help protect and extend the public right of access.
- Don't break laws to get non-governmental records.
- Persist.

You should not at all begin to undertake significant interviews until you have done these things at the start of a major project.

TALKING AND LISTENING : INTERVIEW AS A SOURCE FOR INVESTIGATIVE REPORTING

Conversational ability is the greatest asset of a reporter, more so of the one who takes interviews frequently. The professional reporter spends his whole career developing and polishing his interview skills. In college, he studies psychology, sociology, and survey methods to learn about motivation, bias, and interviewers-interviewee interaction. Early in his career, he uses trial and error. He questions other reporters. He reads other writers' stories to deduce their interviews worked. If a colleague taped an interview, he borrows the tape and plays it back, analyzing the success or failure of particular lines of questioning. Before any significant interview, he sits down with a colleague and tests different lines of questioning—working to get his questions in the right order, to anticipate what turns the interview may take and how he will respond to them. Gradually, he develops mental reflexes so that he can interview anyone, anywhere, any time, and obtain usable information. He develops the self-control to ask challenging questions under pressure without losing his cool and without letting the interviewee dodge the questions.

The big question is—what is the best approach to investigative interviewing? To paraphrase a popular saying: any way that turns them on in any interview situation. Remember:

- Preparation,
- Control, and
- Information.

Plus listening patiently. The reporter listens to what the respondent is saying. After all, the purpose of the interview is to obtain information. A good interview involves knowledge of the background of your topic obtained through base building. A Well prepared reporter has detailed knowledge of the elements of his story, accumulated through documents and notes of previous interviews. He has knowledge of being interviewed, obtained by him through building a personal profile. Finally, preparation includes making lists of questions, then screening and rearranging them in an order intended to extract neutral, factual information before more controversial questions of opinion and motivation arise. Such planning also entails careful phrasing of critical questions so that answers to them are truly responsive.

It is the solid preparation for an interview that results in its being controlled by the reporter. Control includes being courteous and restrained while asking the most pointed questions and refusing to be disconcerted by angry counter questions or challenges from the interviewee. Establishing control begins with the kind of grooming, dress, and demeanor that can cause the interviewee to regard you as slightly enviable.

It may sometimes appear that the subject is taking control of the interview and is deviating from the subject in focus; you may regain it by asking an unpleasant or unexpected question that causes him to stop in surprise or fear. Careful listening is the best way in which to secure information. As the interviewer, you analyze each answer against your framework of independent knowledge and of the answers the subject has already given. If the answer does not fit the framework, ask your question again in slightly different words, preceded by a phrase such as "Do you mean that . . . ?" or "In other words . . ." or simply ask, "What does that mean?" Answers to such questions will confirm and solidify your understanding of what the subject has said.

THE SOURCE

"There is one cardinal rule you have to live with", Jack Tobin cautions the investigative reporter. "If you deal with people (sources) in public places or in public positions, you have to keep their identity absolutely consecrated. Because once you burn (that source) you will burn every other guy in his line of communications, and pretty soon you cannot get to first base.

Remember that a source is different from a tipster. A tipster is a more or less casual contact who gives you a piece of information about something he is not involved in and asks to be kept out of the story. On the other hand, a source gives you information and assistance under an explicit agreement that he or she is never to be identified in connection with that information. A tipster is essentially a gossip monger whereas a source is an expert with whom you have established mutual trust.

Case

Sources are rarely all good or all bad. David Burnham recalls that one of his best leads came from "a little lawyer who represented a lot of corrupt cops, a kind of a nice guy, even though he was an evil person essentially. His heart was, may be, one-third in the right place". The lawyer, for his own reasons, told Burnham of a secret police report which showed that a district attorney had dropped corruption charges against a policeman even though he had the ironclad supporting evidence he needed. The story became an important part of Burnham's systematic report on official apathy towards police corruption.

Case: It is not uncommon that at the other end of a spectrum is the source which is literally self-sacrificing. For example, a secretary working in a Maryland direct mail firm began talking to reporters about suspicious things she was ordered to do on behalf of the firm and its part owner and major client, the Pallotine Fathers. She provided information to the Washington Post and the Baltimore Sun, both of which carried several stories over a period of several weeks. After less than two months, her boss traced the leak, fired her, and threatened to sue her for a million dollars in damages. In a story in the Post later, she explained: "I felt that if I kept quiet I would be compromising my values . . . I felt I had seen an abuse (of donated money) . . . I do not consider myself a crusader at all. . . . My conscience would not let me sit back and not do something about what I saw".

Such experiences should constrain the reporter who works with a relatively "innocent" source to consider what will happen if the source is uncovered.

Bob Greene says : In the first place, an investigative reporter has a cop mentality; anybody who says he does not have it is full of crap. You are an investigator; the cop is similarly an investigator. You think in investigative hypotheses. When you start working on somebody, you say he may be innocent, he may be guilty; you can not come to definite conclusion. But as more proof comes in, you become more convinced he is guilty. No matter how hard you try, you start seeing more things as evidence of guilty than of innocence. . . . There is no question that you get into a police mentality. Therefore, investigators are investigators, whether the newspaper investigators, CIA investigators or any other class of investigators.

Avoid the Single Sources

Be extra careful to plan and work to get information from all kinds of people and from all kinds of records. Use your judgement about what is true and fair; avoid being overly influenced by single person. It is a fact that the truth is elusive; don't be hobbled or steered in your search to get it.

The Exploratory Visit

An investigative story begins with interviews that may occur as early as the base-building phase. These are preliminary exchanges, which are, by their nature, exploratory. You have thereby developed a general assumption; you are now beginning to test it. You know you are dealing with a person you don't know. It is likely that you may have to go back to him several times. Therefore, there is need rather a primary consideration to establish sincerity and competence. The thing you do not want to do in this process is frighten or threaten the subject.

Two Objectives Formulated

The moment you decide to get in, you have already written on your note pad or engraved in your brain a number of questions. As prudent person in this sensitive professional relationship, you must not normally plunge into them right away. You have to keep in mind that you are beginning a relationship that may become quite complex. So, spend some time getting acquainted and letting your subject become comfortable with you. In this process, you are trying to do two things—

- Gathering all relevant information/data about the subject (person-interviewee to be), i.e., to learn his strengths and weaknesses, his relationship with others involved in the issue under investigation, his attitude towards the matter at hand. Knowledge of these matters will help you phrase questions that appeal to self-interest.
- To establish yourself convincingly as a person of professional competence.

Be alert and tactful at this early stage; follow-up hard on only one or two questions (not key questions just yet). What you principally want to do is demonstrate an ability to control interview situations and show that you are not going to let him snow you.

Body language and particularly facial expressions tell subtly what goes inside. So, look your subject straight in the eyes as he answers a question but don't rush to ask your next question. Do not try to feign doubt or cynicism. Just wait he will probably say more and it may provide lead to more information.

It is likely that you are still in doubt; so, avoid playing psychological games in this first interview. It is far better to gather information, to get clues about where the bodies are buried, to see where the road is leading. Always be sure, before you leave, to ask for other sources of information. Ask for copies of letters, policy statements, working reports, memoranda. Ask for the names of others who may have more detailed knowledge.

Normal and major question: Why People Lie:

> It is a matter of experience and generally true. In any interview, you have to realize that the respondent will not be telling the whole truth. He will be protecting himself. He will try to steer away from ideas or information that may reflect unfavourably on his colleagues, his institution, or the people he respects. You should accept this as part of human nature. But in investigative work, things are different and unwelcome: you must also face the prospect of being told bald faced lies.

Before you finish the exploratory interview, you should have:

- Fair knowledge of how the person fits into the overall situation and how he feels about the people involved in it.
- Possession of some documentation, even if fairly superficial.

- Knowledge about specific places to look for more information.
- Manifestation of the person's respect, which may be based on fear, professional admiration, or even altruistic interest in what you are doing.
- A fair idea as to the person's truthfulness.

Be sure to note to specify what is on or off the record, attributable, or background.

THE ESTABLISHED CONTACTS

Contact person is important and necessary. An established contact is a person either within the target institution or with close connections to it. You may know him well and who may be able to provide attributable information and records. You may feel that you are, in effect, going to play on your friendship with this person, who is more than a tipster or a confidential source.

DEALS AND DECISIONS

For you to move into your assignment smoothly or properly, the temptation always is to make a deal with the person at the lower-echelon. You may in effect give him "immunity" in exchange for his assistance. In that case, you have chosen to make him a "source". The choice should be considered carefully. Even if the idea comes up early in a conversation, do not do it on the spur of the moment. Give it a day or two for thought. Think of other ways of getting information without this person.

Alternatives must be explored. The more deals you make, the less freedom you have. By agreeing to block one line of investigation, you are depriving your readers of your best skills in investigation.

It is a sane advice to weigh the pros against the cons in any given case and make your choice with care. The limits are fairly obvious: if your story is based entirely on non-attributable sources, it will be sharply challenged or ignored: if it must rely solely on quotable persons, you may not get the facts you need. It is a dilemma with which you have to live.

ENEMIES AND FRIENDS

Tim Leland says, "The good thing about talking to someone's enemies first is that they give you all the dirt they have on him and more, and they don't tip him off".

In such a situation, your first job is to sift out the "more"—to find out what fact is and what opinion is. Keep in mind, particularly when you have not told the "enemy" you are doing a story, that probably less than half of what you get is true. Check neutral records and other people's recollections of dates and events.

You must especially guard against rumour and opinion that build up around a person who is strong and active, as your target will likely be. Apocryphal anecdotes imbued themselves in mythology about such a person; they must be checked.

As it happens in such cases, the other major problem is screening out what is relevant to your story. It is easy to learn surprising, titillating, or shocking things about a person. You must use discipline and discretion to decide how much of this information, if any, belongs to your story.

It is helpful to give credence to the general feeling that everybody has friends with whom he shares his secrets, his feelings, his ambitions, his fears. Most people enjoy talking about friends who are powerful, famous, or fearsome. They will know things that help you understand your subject well.

EXPERTS AND INNOCENTS

Outside experts are engaged for some job during investigation. For example, in translating almost any major investigative subject into the languages of your audience, you have to look for outside experts who can help define the norms and standards of a given profession, business, institution, or lifestyle.

THE VALUE OF ASSOCIATIONS

Society functions: The good news about this category of interview is that there is a national association of almost everything, and it has several to hundreds of staff members who are experts in their fields.

Always look for associations and institutions that are not funded by the local target. These groups include consumer organizations and agencies; purely technical agencies that live on foundation money.

The Value of Proximity

It generally happens that the people involved in a questionable activity without being accomplices are innocents. They are the clerks and secretaries, the draftsmen, the mechanics, the orderlies, the book-keepers. Their value is in their proximity to the target and their relatively neutral view of things. By having friends among innocents, you can pick up accounts of conversations, minutes of meetings, detailed knowledge of the way things work inside the target area.

At times, the innocent may be generally responsive but afraid to "get involved". A different problem is the innocent who wants to be too involved, too, cooperative. He or she wants to play cloak and dagger when approached. He or she may try to answer questions too completely, going even beyond what he or she knows. He or she may make wrong assumptions, based on incomplete information and misunderstood measures. Your job is to be visibly receptive but inwardly resolved to check, to compare, and to contrast.

The tact of the trade demands the realization that it is important to build a relaxed relationship so that you can go back again and again to check other clues. If an innocent supplies what he claims is solid eyewitness knowledge of an illegal act, and if you may have to depend on him as your sole proof of that point, it is a good idea to ask him to make an affidavit and sign it in front of a notary. Signing an affidavit is serious business for most people. If your innocent refuses, you may lose him and perhaps the story, but that is better than losing a libel suit or printing wrong or exaggerated information. And even though the affidavit may be attacked in court, the fact that you obtained it tends to show you used caution in preparing your story.

To be successful with innocents, you have to deal with them as individuals of varying morals, motivations, and methods. Some may nurse secret grudges against people above, below, or around them. They want you to "get the bastards" to book. Some do not want to get involved. Some do not care. So, you may have to talk to 25 to 30 to find four or five who can provide usable information and stick to their information.

TELEPHONE INTERVIEWS

Mr. Bell, Uncle ITT, and their collateral relatives have provided you a device that is at once a boon and a bane (hero and villain at the same time).

Advantages

The telephone spans continents and ocean with its magic beeps. It demands answering. It lets the interviewer build his own image, often larger than life, in the mind of the interviewee. It is cheap compared to the air fare, taxis, hotel bills, and time involved in getting a few hours of interview time in New York, Washington, or Los Angeles or in any big city if Indian sub-continent. Used lavishly, the long-distance call may even impress an interview subject with your determination to get the facts. When a person does not want to talk to you, the telephone can pursue him

Disadvantage

The phone can cause the interviewee to develop a negative image of the caller, particularly if the latter has a thin voice or halting or unclear speech. Because the aural message is not reinforced by gestures or facial expressions (that is non-verbal communication, particularly body language and physical gestures, etc.), it can easily be misunderstood. Calls are often screened through operators, receptionists, assistants, and secretaries (or, at home, wives and children). When you are in a hurry, the line is always busy; many home telephone numbers are unlisted. Worst of all, the phone can be hung up and then left off the hook.

A general rule: Do not use the telephone to interview significant people whom you have not met. "Significant here means not just "big" or "important" people, it means people you expect to quote, the people who do not like you, people you hope to develop into sources and, of course, key interview subjects.

There are, to be sure, many exceptions to the rule. One exception occurs when you want to reach someone who is ill, recently bereaved, or facing sudden or unwanted publicity. In these instances, the apologetic phone call often works best. Abrupt or persistent questioning will not only get you nowhere, it may cut you off from contact with friends or relatives as well.

When the call goes through, keep the approach friendly and relaxed. Take a few moments to let him get to know you. If someone else referred you to him, by all means use the other person's name. If possible, flatter the interviewee a bit and then background him on what you are dong. This is sound practice because of the lack of reinforcing non-verbal communication. Unless you know a person well and unless both are talking from the same level of understanding, it is easy to misinterpret short statements over the telephone.

CIRCLING AND SHUFFLING

The tactic of "Circling" explains the application of "compare and contrast" to the interview phase. It is a matter of taking a bit of information from one source and running it back around your circle of contacts for refutation or confirmation. "Shuffling" is a term used by Les Whitten, and implies building from a single bit of information. It involves "shuffling" around to other persons who may have been involved in the transaction, levering an additional tidbit from each until a complete picture emerges.

The activities that represent circling and shuffling are important aspects of investigative reporting. Their importance is evidenced by the fact that any time you have a tip that more than two or three persons are part of a significant transaction, you have a pretty good chance of reconstructing the event in detail and of getting more information.

The shuffling procedure is followed for getting more information; it requires patience, judgement, and guts. Wait till the pieces begin to weave into a solid pattern. Avoid naming others you have talked to during the process. But once the pattern is clear, change tactics and start presenting as much rich, attributed detail as you can.

THE KEY INTERVIEW

The key or main interview (some call it the target interview) is an essential part of any planned investigative piece. It is the interview with the person or persons directly in control of whatever you are writing about the person, you are bringing to account before the public. If you work according to plan, it turns out usually to be the final interview. It has two purposes:

- To let the target feel free to comment on or refute the information you have and the assumptions you believe this information proves.
- To obtain additional information believing that there could be more to the situation, still placed under the carpet.

It invariably turns out to be a hostile interview. As a rule, you are dealing with a person who is almost always a tough, worldly, and experienced one in dealing with media. Except in rare instances, he knows approximately what you have found out and whom you have talked to. He has briefed himself fully, has gone over the problem with aides and advisers, and has chosen strategy and tactics designed to knock you out of the box.

MAKING THE APPOINTMENT

Your first consideration is to do everything reasonably possible to obtain the interview. A simple refusal, transmitted over the phone or through an intermediary, is not sufficient excuse to say the person "could not be reached for comment". Try personal confrontation. Try going to his home. Try talking to his lawyer, his closest friends, and his fellow members of the board of directors about getting to see him. Bear in mind Denny Walsh's general advice about going to see people rather than calling them on the phone for interviews: "I want to make it uncomfortable if not impossible for the person to avoid seeing me".

If we assume that one of these ploys works most likely on the courteous person, your next major decision is one concerning the structure of the interview. Think first about how well you know the person, what he thinks of you. Is your factual case complete, or do you need significant new chunks of information from him? Where will the interview be held? How much time will you have? Whether to take a hard, soft, or intermediate approach to the interview depends upon your thinking about such things, as discussed before, particularly the questions, just mentioned, which will help you decide.

Preparing for the Meeting

You must remember the early stress on preparation, control, and information. Preparation is vital, both for facilitating your control of the interview and the information to be gleaned to depend; both depend on your preparation. Begin by working with the person who will accompany you on the key interview. A second person is essential for corroboration of whatever exchanges take place in the interview, and for tactical purposes that will become clear later. If he is a member of the team, he will be up to date on your files and plans. If not, you will need to brief him and rehearse the interview.

In following the steps towards preparing for the interview, first reread the entire file, making notes of information yet to be obtained and of "why" questions to be asked. Classify the questions. Place the neutral, information gathering questions early in the phrasing of critical questions so that they are clear and that answers to them cannot be evasive.

Hi, How Are You

Plan opening the interview with a courteous approach to open up to the human warmth. Then, give a brief, general statement of what the story is about. Avoid any accusatory remarks that might make the interviewee more tense than he already is. Your first goal is to get him talking. The more freely he talks, the better your chances of getting him to answer the difficult questions later.

Control Techniques

The subject knows he has been under investigation. It is almost always the case. If the target does prove talkative, it is fairly easy to lead him into questions about factual points. If a particular fact is essential to a later, harder question or to a point of your assumption, ask for it when the target is relaxed and talkative and before you move into the tough questions. Note that it may be impossible to get the information later if the subject becomes angry and decides to throw you out. If you have done your homework, the factual questions should be relatively few. If they can be phrased as simply refining or confirming knowledge you already have, they should also help build in the interviewee's mind an impression of the depth of your research.

Confrontation

Once the fact finding stage is over, it leads naturally to the confrontation stage. When your questions become more specific, it is the time to start showing documentation. If you have a document, the interviewee can not refuse his statements. If he does so, show the document to him. Similarly, if you have an "on the record quote from another person", use it at the time when it will be most likely to confound him. The point is to catch the target in contradictions and lies. Even if the contradictions are so minor that you do not intend to write about them, it is usually to your advantage to point them out.

However, there is danger in carrying this tactic too far. Going into a third degree grilling may literally confuse the target into giving mistaken answers or may cause him to invite all wits at his command to make up answers. All the experienced reporters tend to agree that in nine out of ten cases, neutral, persistent questioning will obtain more information than an impassioned, sledge-hammer inquisition.

Shifting Gears

There may be occasions, and they do crop up surprisingly suddenly, when the conversation becomes too heated. If such be the case, and the target begins to refuse answering questions, the better course would be to shift gears. Let your partner take over the questioning for a while. Let him be easy and friendly. Some people call this maneuver the "Mutt and Jeff technique". One questioner pursues a hard line and presents a skeptical ear. The other breaks in, perhaps even remonstrating with his partner, and asks questions in a friendlier tone. The interviewee welcomes the change, and may tell the second questioner things he would not like to tell the first one.

There is apparent advantage of double teaming. While one reporter is carrying the questions, the other can sit back and analyze the answers. If he spots a fuzzy or inconsistent answer, he may break in with a series of questions that bursts the bubble.

Registering Indignation

There are times when the interviewer keeps his temper under internal control despite believing that the target is telling a lie. Still, there may be need or urge to let the target believe he has become indignant about being lied to. Such indications of displeasure are best used when dealing with an experienced public figure, an elected official or a top level bureaucrat who is clearly accountable and who is trying to avoid his responsibility. The Investigator would say, "This is a serious problem and I want to know the answer. I asked you this question and I want to know your response. I want to take it down very carefully, because you are going to be held accountable to it. You have got a responsibility under the law, now what is your explanation? I am going to take it down and I am going to read it back to you so we do not have any quibbles about whether I am quoting you properly".

Under such questioning, the evasive bureaucrat "sometimes backtracks". If he is in a tight enough bind, he probably says just about what he has to say. But you don't have to trick him to get answers.

Learning from Others

There is one more point about questions: wherever you can, observe and talk to experienced questioners. They have learned a lot of common sense applied psychology. Trial lawyers are experts at developing lines of questioning, though their purposes are generally different from yours. Their tactics are basically designed to "crack" a witness, to break him down. These are, however, questionable practices for the reporter who is only trying to get information. What is interesting and useful to observe, however, is the skill with which such questioners absorb and analyze answers, then ask specific challenging questions designed to find weakness in the story of the witness. This ability to think clearly in the midst of a series of questions and answers is worth your study.

Results

Various combinations of all questioning techniques are used by the reporter. He must still expect to come away from most key interviews with little more than formal denials or at best "no comment" responses to his crucial questions. It happens most often to the inexperienced reporter who has not prepared himself properly. He simply reports "no go" to his editor, and goes on to the next job, a little wiser but no less confident.

Whether Taking Notes is Conducive to Interview

Except in the full-dress key interview, don't take too many notes. Most people get nervous when they see you scribbling their words down. Keep good eye contact with the subject. Fairly common tricks of veteran reporters are not to start writing when the subject makes a startling or unexpected revelation. Instead, they keep the subject talking for a few moments. At some less tense time, they make a few key word notes. Later, after the revelation has been agreed upon a bit, they may go back and review it, taking more notes as necessary.

It is necessary to learn to memorize the key points of conversation without taking notes. Work at this, and test yourself in non-story situations. There are times when the appearance of your pencil and pad will stop an interview cold. So be prepared to work without them.

When you find absolute necessity to take notes, do this task as quickly as possible. It is better to learn to use shorthand. It is not hard. Such notes are used to break down a politician who cries "misquote". The main advantage of shorthand is that you don't have to spend as much time writing, you can keep the conversation flowing. I humbly reiterate that it is imperative always to transcribe all of your interview notes invariably on the type-writer the day you take them; no let up permitted.

Tape Recordings

It is not advisable to use tape recorder in all cases. The tape recorder is not a good instrument to use on a nervous interviewing, but it can be useful in key interviews. There is a great deal of anti-tape mythology among pencil and paper reporters. They believe that machine scares interviewees even more than a note pad.

If permitted, the use of tape recorders might help build credibility for reporters and newspapers. Many of the people you will deal with in key interviews and expert interviews will not be intimidated by the machine. The tape recorder can also serve as a reference and for the target, too. We do not rely on the tape recorder as the principal instrument. We take notes as any reporters do in terms of answers to the key questions. We use the recorder only to clarify notes or for the exact quote. So learn to use a good, unobtrusive hand size cassette recorder. Yes, there can be problems in using a tape recorder. The batteries can run down if you don't put fresh ones in before an interview. The microphone may pick-up unwanted noises such as the tap of a pencil or the rap of knuckles on a desk. A single microphone may not pick up the voices of two persons on opposite sides of a desk. Therefore, if you do use a tape recorder, make pencil notes also. Experience shows that defective fluorescent lamps' buzz can ruin a recording.

Summary

As investigative reporting is more than routine daily reporting, the responsibility for accuracy is more severe. Above all, investigative reporting is an intellectual process. Logic not emotion must rule when decisions are made, ideas gathered, facts sorted, patterns built, and options analyzed. Since a source can be mistaken or biased, the reporter must check everything carefully. Experience tells that the truth is elusive, and the reporter is responsible for the truth of every word. It is in appreciation of the fact that reliance on one source is risky.

The investigative reporter should develop the patience to run information from one source to another and on to another and another if need be. Moreover, interviewing is an art, and good interviewing involves talking and listening. Interviewer may ask questions, even what might be regarded as dumb questions. In fact, the reporter's objective is to get information, not to impress the interviewee with his own brilliance. Depend upon the time tested advice that careful listening is the best way to gain information.

By combining listening with strategic periods of silence, the source will be encouraged to go on talking, often telling the reporter more than could be gained by firing off questions in rapid succession. One strategy is to put the subject at ease early in the interview. While this is important in any interview, it becomes doubly so when the session plunges into serious questions or allegations.

It pays to make full use of eye contact during the interview, rather than hastily scribbling notes. Practise to learn to memorize the key points to conversations. Maintain control of the interview by being flexible in your pattern of questioning, shifting gears to maintain the element of surprise. Allow your team partner to help over when needed. At a less tense time in the session, commit the key points to paper and go over them again with the source if necessary to achieve accuracy. It is helpful to support the taped interviews with penciled notes. Later, at the personal computer and as soon as possible after the conclusion of the interview, record the major facts and important comments. In the interest of lending more credibility, transcribe direct quotes from your notes.

Be watchful while all this confrontation and drama are going on; be aware that you have some additional responsibilities. Be alert before, during, and after the interview. Pay attention to the colour and circumstances that occur accompanying the occasion. Be observant of detail and record these with your notes for future reference. Direct observation is an effective and useful technique for the investigative reporter and interview serves that objective best.

DIRECT OBSERVATION OF REPORTER

It is sheer common sense that tells the investigative reporter that direct observation is the best way to get the facts. It is the best way to get information unfiltered by others' biases, faulty memory, or incomplete records.

While planning the project, rather than making snapshots, the investigative reporter is drafting the script for a full length documentary movie. He must not consider just the given moment but more extensive actions covering all possible angles of the subject. He must describe the strategy, tactics, ambitions, misdeeds, reasoning, and motives of antagonists in one sub-plot of the continuing drama of human existence. He may have to become part of the action.

SITUATIONAL ETHICS

It has become a practice to use two words, "morals" and "ethics; these are most often invoked in discussing undercover work. The word "moral" is derived from the Latin word, "moralis", which means customs and folkways in short, the ways in which people or communities act towards one another. The other word, "ethical" may also suggest "conformity to a code or to the conclusions or considerations of right, fair, equitable conduct". Situational ethics has been around for a long time. In short, it relates to the idea what may be "wrong" in one situation may be "right" in another.

Whether the reporter likes the idea or not, he is unrealistic if he pretends it does not exist. He decides whether to carry story about the sexual behaviour of an errant school teacher or to pursue a tip about corruption in the police department. The investigative reporter applies situational ethics when he decides to go "inside" or "underground" to get his story. If the reporter is going to find out something that people less moral than himself are trying to conceal, he must use imagination, guts, guile, and yes, sometimes deception, to do it. If he has a low threshold of indignation, he is going to be as aggressive as his conscience will permit him to be. He may not have much fun going underground, but he may finally decide he must do so to do his job.

Once the reporter identifies what society expects of its institutions, he can better diagram its malfunctions. He will have a model against which to measure reality. Before going into the gutter to face a real or metaphorical beast, the reporter wants to know that the stakes, including the mental and moral strain, are worth the effort. He does not want to dissemble, to play a false role or to ask others to do these things unless he can see clear rewards for his readers as a result.

Temptations and Perils

After weighing the stakes and risks, if the investigative reporter decides that some kind of covert or inside activity is needed, the reporter should then impose controls on his own discretion and judgement. Constraints also include seeking as much corroborative evidence as possible. He keeps "discretion" at the top of his checklist. He does not expect to publish everything he finds out. For both ethical and pragmatic reasons, he avoids such temptations as:

- Deception for its own sake—that is, playing secret agent for kicks.
- Entrapment or provocation—that is, inducing or encouraging others. To commit illegal or immoral acts in order to fatten the reporter's story.
- Self-hypnosis—that is, imputing evil motives in everything he sees to persons he is covertly investigating.

While his prime concern is to uncover the hidden facts, the investigative reporter must also guard against committing either a crime or a violation of someone else's civil rights. In such a situation, he should hold consultation with a lawyer who specializes in publications law. There are five major kinds of legal perils about which the investigative reporter should be aware. These are :

- Burglary is a felony almost everywhere. In most places, you are guilty of it, if you overcome the slightest obstacle (such as turning an unlocked doorknob) to enter a place with intent to take something that does not belong to you.
- Trespass can occur if you enter a private place without permission of the owner or inhabitant. Some lower courts have held that reporters trespass when they accompany policemen or firemen inside a house where a crime or fire has taken place.
- Larceny, in varying degrees, occurs if you take something. Not only is it a crime, it can also open a reporter and his publication to civil suit from the victim of impersonation.
- Invasion of privacy is usually a civil matter, though some federal and state laws in USA also carry criminal penalties.

In view of the complexities involved, you have to weigh pros and cons and discuss these perils with your editor and attorney. Then only the reporter should consider the precise mechanism through which he will undertake covert observation.

VOLUNTEERS AS SOURCES— HOW MUCH DEPENDABLE?

The foregoing perils are not all. There are still other perils. Anyone who voluntarily becomes your source is usually trying to use your journalistic clout, your ability to get a story published to achieve a personal end. The end in his focus is the one that he cannot accomplish on his own. Rarely are his motives pure or altruistic. Indeed, he may even be a double agent or a provocateur trying to set-up a situation that will reveal the reporter in the most unfavorable light.

A volunteer may be less threatening, but no less false and frustrating; he bamboozles the reporter for selfish reasons. Conversely, the volunteer source can be solid gold, altruistically motivated, and the only person who can get the information the reporter needs.

Case

In 1974, an executive of Combustion Engineering, Inc., walked in on Jonathan Kwitny of the *Wall Street Journal* and delivered copies of documents describing a series of contracts the firm had made the previous year. While public investors had bought Combustion Engineering stock at rising prices in 1973 on news of $ 565 million worth of new orders announced by the company, thirty-six Combustion Engineering officers, directors, and other insiders were selling their stock at good prices. The documents handed to Kwitny showed that the publicized new contracts (actually only letters of intent) carried unusual warranties, penalties, and cancellation clauses that could hurt the company's profitability. The stuff made a good story. Before the Journal published the story, of course, it checked many other sources-spokesmen, other combustion engineering executives to be sure what the volunteer had handed over was authentic and significant.

THE RECRUITED INFORMANT

Based on experience, there is a caution about paid informants; they are trouble. The risk in using them almost invariably outweighs the possible payoff.

The paid and the unpaid: Sometimes, a tipster, anxious to sell you information, will give it away if properly motivated. There is in the minds of most newsmen, of course, considerable difference between paying for inside information and buying dinner or drinks for an informant who has delivered usable information. For the reporter, the old political definition of purity may be the most reasonable one: don't give an informant anything he can't eat, drink, or smoke in a single sitting. The most dangerous kind of informant is the one who has a vested interest in providing reports in dribs and drabs. He makes certain that a steady supply of payments is forthcoming and that information that might contradict the reporter's investigative assumption, and hence kill his golden goose, is not divulged. This kind of recruited informer is of no value to the reporter in backing up his story. And if the cash-for-information deal is ever exposed, the reporter's credibility is badly damaged. The recruited, unpaid, informant on the other hand, can be invaluable.

Case

Al Delugach and Denny Walsh used this kind of informant in reporting on corruption in the steamfitter's union in St. Louis in 1966-69. In this instance, the unpaid recruit proved to be the best way in which to find out how union officials were using member's dues to make illegal political contributions, to take over an insurance company and pay themselves agents' commissions, and, in general, to subvert trade-union ideals. To get both specific information and leads about records to search, Delugach says, "we found and cultivated some dissident members who really could not afford to have it known they were talking to us. This was a pretty rough outfit. They were able to tell us what happened at union meetings, what kind of assessments were put on and that these political assessments were not legal". The reporters, of course, could have tried burglarizing union offices, bugging telephones, or seducing secretaries, but working with informants was by far the soundest course.

It is, incidentally, not always a crime to possess pieces of paper. From a criminal standpoint, some monetary value must be established in order to prove larceny. Still, issues of trespass and privacy are to be considered in holding secret papers. As Bob Greene says, on this question the investigative reporter walks a tightrope.

Obviously, a reporter should not recruit an informant who does not want to be recruited. The reporter must be especially careful not to threaten the informant with exposure if he refuses to cooperate, to do so would be to flirt with extortion. The informant must be convinced that the public good and his own interest will be served by working with the newsman. The thoughtful reporter does not want the kind of plea-bargaining or "protection" leverage that police and prosecutors have when they turn a suspect into an informer. What he does want is an informant who will help because he believes that to help serves the community's best interests. And he wants the informant to know all the risks involved, and to protect himself against either taking unwarranted chances or fabricating information in the hope of obtaining rewards.

Protection

It is imperative that the reporter must also have a firm policy about what to do. He may be called before a grand jury or investigative agency seeking to learn the identity of his informant. If there is no shield law, he must have the backings of his editor and publisher. The reporter must find the legal technicalities that will provide maximum protection for himself and his informant. The best method to adopt for the protection of an informant is to think about whether his information, if published can be traced back to him. There are ways in which to obscure the trail. Alexander describes "take the document and put it on so-and-so's desk tomorrow morning when nobody's there. So-and-so will pick it up and say, 'What the hell is this?' And he will tell somebody else, perhaps he will duplicate it. And then two or three people know about it".

There may be more open contacts. In dealing with them, the reporter can also ask guarded, tangential questions about the same topic on which his informant has provided data. If the open contact seems willing to talk, the reporter can then lead the discussion until it has covered enough ground to encompass what the informant reported. Using this variation of the shuffling technique in a series of interviews shortly before publication, the reporter can effectively cover a trail leading back to his informant. Depending on how highly placed the informant is, he may have to use diversionary tactics to maintain his credibility.

The Legman

This kind of person is usually very important and also dependable. Well, a legman is a reporter on a loose leash. He gathers information by settling in where his antennae tell him tantalizing information lurks. Some, but not all, legmen do not write well but have a genius for searching out stories. Many investigative reporters believe one of the best methods for gathering authoritative information is to get right inside a target organization where they know what to look for and how to record and relate it accurately. The Boston Globe Spotlight Team and others have used legmen particularly for investigations of consumer swindles.

Case

Reporter Bill Jones got a job as an ambulance driver and wrote a Pulitzer Prize series about it for the Chicago Tribune in 1970. Five years later, he became assistant managing editor. As a result of Jone's inside technique, the paper's task force was formed in 1970 and operated under a succession of directors. The legmen exposed systematic vote fraud in Cool Country (another Pulitzer effort, directed by George Bliss). And they have uncovered the operations of fast-buck dealers in franchise sales, bill collection agencies, career schools, money grubbing nursing homes and private hospitals. The task force also unmasked abuses of city patronage jobs, police brutality, and a full range of other misdeeds of the kind for which Chicago is famous.

Drawbacks

There are, understandably enough, drawbacks to inside work. It cannot always be carried through. For instance, there are times when some of its results are best left unspecified. Sometimes, you have to curb your enthusiasm. It can also be dangerous if the person being written about is almost certainly a private person and chooses to use the legal protection available. This factor must be weighed carefully in writing a story based on inside observation. Other drawbacks to inside work include the heavy expenditure of time. The target may ensure that the reporter's cover is stripped away. In general, it is best to get into and out of an undercover situation as quickly as possible.

Impersonation

It is a tactic to uncover wrongs buried deep. The readers also tend to admire and support the reporter who spends time—days or months—playing the fictitious prisoner or mental patient or cheating salesman or corrupt precinct worker in order to report authoritatively. Yet readers also tend to scorn a reporter who poses as, say, a credit or insurance investigator in order to get information that would not knowingly be given to a reporter being purely private.

It is worth pondering over the question; ponder also the reliability of information obtained through such a ruse. If presented to people who believe their information will be held confidential, it will produce at best a mishmash of knowledge, opinion, gossip, and impressions. It would be not only unfair but professionally foolhardy to use information gained by a ploy and to attribute it either to the person who had been duped or to vague sources like "neighbourers" or "close associates". The absolute maximum evaluation that a reporter should give to such information gathered under misleading circumstances is "interesting, to be confirmed elsewhere".

Certainly any questioning by ruse should, for both moral and pragmatic reasons, be conducted with one goal, to verify or refute the leads suggested by the unwitting informant.

Surveillance

It is important and full of danger and hazards. Any reporter on the police beat learns some of the secrets of surveillance. He learns that only rarely does a law exist against watching a person or an activity—as long as he does not eavesdrop on private conversations or break into a home, office, or other private place. He learns about the use of an innocent looking panel truck to conceal a photographer armed with telephoto lenses. He also learns that police use exotic equipment like sensitive directional microphones to pick up conversations hundreds of yards away. And if he has not learned all the secrets of surveillance first hand, there is the nightly television show to fill him in.

Personal observation and skill to listen conversations are essential assets with the Reporter engaged in investigative projects. Therefore, from observations and from conversations with detectives who have sat for hours on fruitless stakeouts, the reporter learns a good deal about covert surveillance. He learns, for instance, that it is time consuming and frustrating unless the stakes are high and the information about impending action is solid and precise. He also learns, particularly from the public reaction to post Watergate disclosures of FBI and CIA activities, that covert surveillance is unpopular, often morally reprehensible, and susceptible to abuse.

It does not suit all temperaments. The conscientious investigative reporter, therefore, generally avoids surveillance. He never even considers it without also analyzing and weighing the possible consequences. He may decide that there are occasions when surveillance is the only way to get information of crucial importance to his readers. If the occasion does arise, it does probably only once or twice in most reporters' career, he elects to do his own surveillance (usually with a partner, a photographer, or both) in order to be sure it is reasonably and discreetly carried out. As always, he discusses it with his editor. And he does everything he can to be sure the surveillance produces solid evidence (like publishable photographs) with minimum risk.

The best kind of surveillance is passive; simply making unobtrusive observations of what many may see but fail to recognize. Reporters observing activities from a distance get only a myopic view that still must be clarified by direct questioning. Surveillance, then, with its ethical problems is a radical and certainly not a scientific tool, to be used rarely and with caution.

The advice is if your plans for getting a story can pass test and if it is the last alternative in a search for illegally withheld facts of overwhelming public importance, then you can undertake your investigative reporting with a clear purpose. Very few cases, however, can pass these tests. Virtually all of them require you to think in legal technicalities and to rationalize your action according to your perception of the public interest. Beyond that, conscience and a strong belief in individual human dignity are the best controls on irresponsible covert activity.

Computer Power

Human ingenuity played great role in introducing computers to solve problems promptly and accurately. The most advanced mathematical work in newsrooms used to be done with comptometers on election night. Somehow, the results turned out to be reasonably accurate unofficial returns for each precinct in the newspaper's circulation area.

The tables turned out by the newsrooms were studied next afternoon when political writers would study these tables, talk to ward chairmen and state party leaders, then produce impressionistic stories about why the vote went the way it did. Today, the computer is in the newsroom, and its presence has been prompted by a change in the attitude of the journalistic hierarchy about the interpretation of numbers. Television networks and wire services began to use them for national and regional political analyses in the early 1960s, but only a handful of newspaper men were visionary enough and resourceful enough to obtain the technical training and facilities for local use of computer power. By the mid-1970s, however, publishers in droves began to find it profitable to install integrated computer systems for book-keeping, billing, classified advertising, purchasing, circulation control, type setting, page layout, and numerous other non-editorial functions.

The investigative reporter, however, must provide himself with a good grounding in the general use of numbers before he begins to use computers. He must know how to analyze public budgets and corporate balance sheets and how to check quantitative measurements made by social scientists, by the legitimate ones as well as by fakers.

The Challenge

Knowledge of Mathematics helps. So, the understanding and routine use of mathematics, at least to the level of college algebra, is assumed as part of the investigative reporter's background. Jay Harris, professor in the Medill School of Journalism, North-western University, has phrased the challenge this way: "In many important areas, there has been quiet shift in the foundation of language from verbal to numeric. The language and vocabulary of most institutions, and thus the foundation of their decision-making processes, are more numeric/scientific than verbal/intuitive". This statement explains how important it is now to learn to analyse and interpret numbers.

It has been observed that the reporter who thinks of right and relevant questions has built his own base of knowledge of accounting principles. He is able to sit down with his pocket calculator and develop his own pro-forma statement from the readers' viewpoint. He now has the basis not only for checking records but for conducting key interviews with those who use numbers to persuade them.

Budgets and Reports

Hayes advises rather emphasizes the importance of thinking creatively about measurement and comparison of unit costs. The person who presents and advocates a budget (or any other set of figures) is naturally going to do so in the way most favourable to his own cause. The reporter must look for ways in which to test the budget presenter's premises. "The 'divide and compare' strategy takes time, effort and information", Hayes points out. "But it need not be done comprehensively, a reviewer can pick his spots, concentrating on areas of greatest importance ... it need not be done all at once, since the executive budget is usually before the city council or state legislature for one to three months".

"Governmental budgets", Harris adds, "reflect priorities, trends or responses to extra governmental pressures". The investigative reporter who is trying to measure the influence of a given lobby can sometimes use the statistical approach to advantage. He may find clues for its influence by tracing the amounts spent by government over several years to serve the lobby's interests.

There are threads leading to the forces behind both corporate and governmental budget decisions. They may hide in several places: the officers and advisers through which the document travelled on its way to the chief executive, the style (frantic or reasoned) of the public presentation, and the reactions to portions of the budget. Reporters themselves can find help in understanding budgets from their newspapers' accountants and tax attorneys and, by translating the budget into human terms, can present important insights to their readers.

HYPOTHESES AND PROCESSES

Granted that there will be application of creativity, imagination, and everyday arithmetic to visible questions, still there will arise need to formulate appropriate hypotheses. It has been observed that more elegant problem definitions and more exotic deductions are available with proper hypotheses processed through more sophisticated machinery. These definitions and deductions involve the following skills:

(i) Merging data collected from diverse sources, (ii) Undertaking analyses of larger masses of data than have heretofore been available, (iii) sorting of the mass of data by verbal factors rather than numerical in order to build patterns, and (iv) proper defining of "social reality".

It has been seen that many investigative problems require sorting, grouping, and patterning bits of information. If there are more than a few possible combinations to study, the analytical work quickly becomes mind boggling.

Finding Patterns

Every reporter is continuously exposed to tips and rumours that a judge has taken a fix in a given case. Any reporter who has tried to substantiate these tips has found that he needs doubly corroborated, crisply photographed, and tape-recorded evidence in order to even begin to get his readers' attention. The legal system allows great latitude for judges to make the critical choices regarding sentences *versus* probation, the degree of intent, and the likelihood of recidivism in deciding the fate of a defendant. There are umpteen instances of recorded experiences where the majority of citizens tended to side with a judge who invokes his legal rights in defense against a reporter's claim that he did wrongly in a single case.

However, if analysis of 100 cases handled by the judge shows wide divergence from the norms or the spirit of the law, the reporter is on much stronger ground. His readers will be in a better position to understand the issues and make their feelings known.

COUNTING, SORTING AND CROSS TABULATION

Computer is best known for tremendous computing power. So, the ability of the computer to cross-tabulate several variables represents a major expansion of the reporter's intellectual power. Many large law firms and law schools now use computer systems for studying legal problems.

The following three advantages of the computer have been convincingly demonstrated:

- By unraveling, sorting, and then rearranging data accordant to several variables, it performed a task that would have been literally impossible to do by hand.
- By relieving him of much tedium, it gave him time to conduct extensive interviews with scores of senators, committee staff members, and outsiders.
- By building on a broad base of factual data, it obviated much of the criticism a reporter can expect if he relies solely on hunch, tip, and judgement to select "typical" examples.

LEARNING TO USE COMPUTER

The student of journalism can take courses in college that make him familiar with sampling, statistics, and the principles of the computer programming. He should learn the techniques of simple card sort and complex cross tab methods. He should learn how to design, test, administer, and analyze simple questionnaires. If he is serious about applying this knowledge to investigative reporting, he will try analyzing existing programs and then write some of his own programs in order to analyze something new and interesting.

Hugh, F. Cline says in his introduction to Data-Text Primer: "I would strongly recommend that students have at least one course in statistics, including descriptive statistics, inferential statistics, non-parametric and multi-variety techniques, covering regression, analysis of variance, and factor analysis. They will be able to understand all of the material (necessary to use Data-Text).

The student reporter should also read standard texts and current periodicals while beginning to learn these new disciplines. He must read Precision Journalism, Philip Meyer's landmark book, and more recent works such as Handbook of Reporting Methods by Maxwell McCombs, Donald's Lewis Shaw, and David Grey.

The nearest large university probably has several types of computers and dozens, if not scores, of Ph.D.'s or doctoral candidates who can earn professional or academic credits by working with a reporter to analyze a new social problem.

Case

Once, Paul N. William had a mildly investigative piece handed to him by Prof. Ralph Todd at the University of Nebraska at Omaha. While some reporter-friends were chatting about another subject, Paul William learned Todd was studying variations in real estate tax assessments in Omaha. After Todd told him he saw story possibilities in his project, he had to do little but wait about a month for his computer printouts. He broke down the printouts by sectors that roughly matched the circulation areas of the four core Sun Newspapers. His tables, which his associates translated into maps, showed that homes in the old (eastern) half of the city were being assessed at much higher percentages of market value than were homes in the newer and more affluent (western) half. In short, the rich were getting richer and the poor were getting poorer. The reporters spent no more than twenty hours to complementary research on the story, interviewing country officials, real-estate brokers and community club spokesmen for comments and explanations.

Official Mistakes

Experience shows mistakes in official records due to negligence of the data handling people. Irritants have been known to develop, however, in connection with "official" computerized information. Sometimes an agency of government puts records on computer tapes or discs and then wants to charge the user for printouts. All kinds of errors and discrepancies may almost always be noticed. Your own computer serves you better for analysis of data.

New Paths

The paths opened up by computers are open for further exploration by any investigative reporter. To enter them requires, primarily, planning and thoughtful study of the records and procedures surrounding the target.

Currently, more pragmatic perils in connection with the computer confront the investigative reporter. One is the danger of computer hypnosis or loss of perspective. Jay Harris has written: "The Journalist is in danger of holding the computer in awe and adopting the proposition that whatever the computer says is incontrovertible fact. As the journalist works more regularly and closely with computers, he is in danger of losing touch with the people and the reality that the people constitute". He may also overrate the importance of "each statistical gyration, each individual finding, each percentage" fed to him by his beloved machine", Harris warns.

There are chains of computer computations. If the error begins early in a chain of computations, the final result may be a picture that is far from reality. As Meyer points out:

Some statistical programs have been discovered to contain flaws or limitations which produce computational errors .... (Found only) after the programmes were in use for several years and learned journals had published paper with substantive findings based on the inaccurate statistical manipulations. Roy W. Wampler of the National Bureau of Standards tried a mathematical problem on twenty different computer programs and got nineteen different answers, some of them not even close to the right answer.

The chief flaw was rounding error. Some of the calculations required very long numbers, longer than the storage capacity of the computer could accommodate and dropping of the excess digits threw the results badly out of line. The problem had a historical basis: programmers worked from textbook formulas designed for desk calculators.

But a man with a desk calculator could see when a rounding error was likely to be a problem and allow for it. The computer did its rounding out of sight and plodded mindlessly ahead, spewing out wrong numbers to unsuspecting users.

Social Reality

By far, the best tested application of computer technique to news work is the statistical analysis of sample surveys. Pre-election predictions and post-election analyses have become almost standard fare for larger newspapers. Each year, social scientists and reporters go a little further in thinking of ideas to count and measure, and of the ways in which to interpret the results.

The Politicians

Local politicians are as capable of ignoring social reality as their national conveners. Editors and reporters of the night Newspapers in America began defining social reality in 1967. Meyer, fresh from Harvard, directed a special study of the Detroit Urban League, which was published in the Detroit Free Press a few weeks after the July riot. With carefully trained black interviewers, a fifty six-item questionnaire, and a random sampling method, the Free Press reported findings that contradicted much of conventional wisdom about why people rioted and how black people felt about "the system".

The Social Scientists

Harris has suggested a danger that reporters will identify too closely with the social scientists. He urges that the journalist must not be content to look only at the "summary and recommendations" of survey, but also to check the methodology. "The social science community should not be afforded the luxury of telling the journalist what is important or what fact is," he writes, "nor should the journalist rely on him to do so.

The Dangers in Surveys and Interviews

Designing a survey is important. Any self-designed survey effort is dangerous. Careless design and an unwittingly biased interview technique can lead to disastrous results. The act of surveying can itself change people and their ideas, resulting in what social scientists know as the Hawthorne Effect (the testees' unconscious effort to please the testers) and what the physicists call the Heisenberg Principle (when you measure something, your actions or the effects of the testing device change it).

Experienced journalists are aware of these principles when they conduct one on one interview. When they propose, therefore, to conduct scores to hundreds of interviews through intermediaries, they should seek expert advice and then be conservative about interpreting what they find. If they take the proper precautions, however, they will likely have better evidence for their generalizations than they would have had through the old-fashioned "highlight" interviews with opinion leaders or with "typical" persons on the street.

There is more pernicious danger for investigative reporters. In that regard, Meyer says that it is "you become so entranced with the tools that you spend all your time enhancing and fine-tuning them and never get around to doing any reporting.

The problem most likely stems from the fact that computer problems, quite unlike problems in the real world, can always be solved if you work at them long enough. It can make you develop a taste for computer problems to the exclusion of your real purpose."

Getting the Message Across

Writing investigative stories is skill. There is no formula for writing such stories. Good writing is not done by formula. There are, unfortunately, a number of formulas for traditional news writing, and many reporters and editors are unduly influenced by them. Clarity is one principle. It requires that your theme, your language, your construction of the overall story as well as your individual sentences and paragraphs be easily understood. Clarity implies getting to the point quickly in language that is clear to the reader and carrying the story through to a clear conclusion.

There is no substitute for creativity. So, creativity is another principle. It requires giving careful thought to the tone of the writing. Creativity suggests judicious use of comparisons and metaphors which are strong and effective while remaining factually accurate and intellectually honest. If these principles seem to pay little homage to the traditional inverted pyramid formula for writing news stories, it is good enough. Little homage is intended.

Most investigative stories are not traditional "news". They are stories of discovery. They involve piecing together unknown or little known facts in new ways, they are contradictions of official and traditional views. By their nature, they are also often overloaded with facts.

Sometimes, they expose unfamiliar schemes and machinations whose vocabulary and processes are alien to the reader. When they deal with the shuffling of money from one party to another through subordinated notes, dummy corporations, blind trusts, debentures, stock swaps or other arcane machinery, the writer should not assume that the readers understand. When the story involves recognizing tax abatements or deeds of trust, it needs to be translated not only into words but into images that are relevant to the readers.

Getting Ready to Write

The reporter should write out answers on a piece of copy paper to several questions before beginning to outline a major investigative story:

- What is this story about? What am I trying to prove?
- Who gives a damn? Where, among the many interests and personae (taxpayer, union member, church deacon, business executive, and parent) of my reading public is the primary audience for my story?
- Why will my primary audience care? To which of their interests does the story appeal?

The exercise of writing down clear answers to these or similar questions will help the reporter find the voice, vocabulary, and pace that are most familiar and effective to the potential reader.

What is this Story About?

It should not be very difficult to determine what the story is about. It still requires a clear appraisal of its point and its features. Only then can it be told with clarity. For example, a story about a provable crime is possibly the one that is defined by law and that threatens the traditional inverted pyramid form because its images and implications are readily perceptible. But a story about a possible crime, one in which the elements of proof are missing or strongly contended, is a different matter. If the suspected crime is against property or is "victimless", it will require careful explanation and interpretation for it to be related to the readers' interests.

The writing problem becomes even more complex if the story is not about a legally defined crime but about the manipulation of a system or institution to the advantage of an individual or group. The writer must define terms, establish norms, and explain the effects of the abuse or manipulation. He must adopt the viewpoint of his perceived audience, and he must be confident he knows his audience even if the story is a relatively neutral "how things work" piece.

Illustration

For example, there are instances or cases involving writing about the payment of gratuities, finder's fees, consulting fees, or commissions to purchasing agents of foreign governments; such writings present a choice of viewpoints. A common business rationale is that such fees are a necessary means to the end of obtaining contracts, as long as the word "bribe" is not spoken, no bribe occurs. But a more common viewpoint among the mass of citizens is that payment of money to a person who does no work except make a decision in favour of the payer is a bribe, regardless of what noun is used to describe it on the company's books. The writer then is writing about a bribe, and in order to prove bribery, he has to prove intent and agreement. He must provide strong evidence and contemporary documents and testimony from neutral sources proving intent and agreement.

There may be situation where these elements are not clear. Then, the reporter should ask himself, "What am I trying to prove"? He should try to prove "how things work". What devices and deceptions (including mental self-deception) are used in making such deals? His story is about the real life operations of an institution, and he is wise not to assert that the evidence proves anything more.

Why Will the Audience Care?

Be sure that the individual reader in your audience will most likely care if the story spells out to him a threat to his (or his family's) person, property, pocket book or pride. The threat may be as direct as the danger of being mugged on the street or as remote as a rise in next year's taxes or fuel bill.

Designing the Story

After going through these mental exercises (which for an experienced writer takes less time) to think about than read about, the reporter should pencil out the central line or theme of his story. He should then write only that line in his main story. Within the first few paragraphs, he should make clear what the theme is. Then he should develop the theme, and finally, he should summarize it. This method for getting the message across is simply the exercise of an old rule of lecturing or public speaking: tell them what you are going to tell them, tell them what you have told them.

Choosing the Lead

Do not hasten to write the Lead or Intro. Often, the least painful approach is to avoid writing the lead until after you have blocked out the main narrative. But most writers can not do this. They know too many things are decided in the lead: the limits of the subject, the direction of the writing, the tone, the control. Once the lead is clear, the points sketched out, and the rest of the story follows naturally and quickly. There are several options. The hard lead that summarizes the main points, the anecdote lead that relates personally to the reader, the soft lead that intrigues, the bullets and dashes lead that relives a story overloaded with faces, and the easiest of all "this is the story" lead.

The Hard Lead

The hard lead is similar to the traditional spot news lead. It rises to summarize in a succinct paragraph or two all of the important information, then proceeds to a series of paragraphs of progressively lesser importance. It is the standard inverted pyramid construction.

The hard lead has drawbacks for most original investigative stories. Often, there is too much important information to pack into a single paragraph. Some of the impact of this information is lost when it is strung out in clauses or phrases. Sometimes, the information means little to the reader who lacks technical or legal background.

Similarly, the meaning of an investigative story cannot be reduced into a reasonable number of words without danger of distortion. If three or four major statements are packed into the lead, and if there are countering or opposing views about the importance of each statement, the explanatory (or "denial") paragraphs become a confusingly long, disjointed series. The reader is getting arguments about facts he has not yet been given. And if he is going to become confused and frustrated before he gets to the corroborating details, he will very likely quit reading and the investigator's work will have gone for naught.

It is better to think of a hard lead only if all of these conditions prevail:

- There is a single major revelation to be made.
- Its nature and context are familiar to the average reader's perceptions.
- The evidence to be detailed later will firmly support the specific charge or revelation.
- The remainder of the story can be developed in inverted pyramid style without major concern for chronology or for the developments and tying up of sub-plots.

Only a few investigative stories meet all of these criteria. But at their editors' insistence to fit them into the traditional mould, an unfortunate number of writers try usually to pack summarized view in the lead.

The Soft Lead

The soft lead purposely avoids conveying startling information. It may seem to be almost a throwaway paragraph; it is not so. The good soft lead is a carefully designed series of sentences intended to:

- Intrigues the potential reader, hinting at revelations to come.
- Guides him into an orderly sequential understanding of the story's elements.
- Provides him (usually) with one or two details of pertinent background.

The skilled writer's challenge is to beguile the reader without confusing him, and to inform him without boring him. The best soft lead normally runs no more than two or three paragraphs. It gives the reader a few dozen words summarizing what is to come and then moves briskly ahead from background to hard fact. The major revelation may be several paragraphs down in the story but when the reader reaches it, he understands it and probably appreciates, too.

Finishing-up

The "Far View" series contains some strong final paragraphs but investigative stories should close with a punch—a pithy quotation, a summary of the thesis, a surmise about the future, a promise by someone in power that things will change, or that they won't change. Some writers finish by lifting their fingers that things will change, or that they won't. Some writers finish by lifting their hands from the typewriter, others leave their readers something to remember.

Presentation

The most common problems in displaying investigative stories are:

- Extremely long text,
- Complexity of story structure, making late trims in the composing room difficult and risky, and
- Inadequate art: too few photos, and these often static and unimaginative.

All of these problems can be anticipated and dealt with if both the reporter and editor plan for good presentation from the moment base building begins. Consider these options.

Photographs

- Head shots of principals including series of close ups taken during interviews, posed medium shots with office, home or outdoor background, informal shots in other settings.
- Shots of the action being investigated (for example, a trade school salesman making his pitch).
- General background pictures, including historical and file photos of the principals and their activities in earlier years.
- Reproductions of key documents.
- Aerial views (for instance, of land to be re-zoned) to which an artist can later add boundary lines, directional arrows, and other identification.

Drawings

- Maps showing land holdings, traffic routes, location or flow of activities, spheres of influence.
- Block diagrams or charts showing relationship of the target with other groups or persons.
- Simple bar graphs illustrating single points in the text (for example, comparisons of activity or treatment of different subjects against the norms of the target's profession or industry).
- Line graphs demonstrating historic trends.
- Mood-setting illustrations or artist's conceptions based on facts reported in the text.

TYPOGRAPHIC ELEMENTS

- Headlines.
- Sub-heads within the text.
- Side heads, surrounded by ample white space, running near major points of the text.
- Boxes, used in moderation to emphasize short sidebars.
- Drop-in or read-out heads spaced through the text to relieve masses of body type.

- Reverse or overprinted headlines running into or out of halftone art.

Planning for Art

In base building and basic research, the reporter should begin to acquire file and background photos setting the scene and illustrating the history of activities being investigated.

The Layout

The story should be presented in easily readable form. Ease of reading should be the rule in laying out the story on the page. Just because sixteen kinds of display elements have been listed above, don't try to use all sixteen in one story. Instead, decide on an appropriate amount of display space, then place the elements so that the main text runs in the most compact, uninterrupted form that is reasonably possible. As a guideline, figure that fifty-five to sixty per cent of the available space should be devoted to heads, art and display elements. If the mix drops to the forty or forty-five per cent range, you are flirting with monotonous grayness.

I have my own preference and that is to frame the main story with display elements, leaving the text in squared-off units. If I use art or boxes, I will try to place them at the top or bottom of a column in order to leave the text modular. I don't want the reader to have to make a decision or a mistake in mid-page, trying to find out whether the story reads around a photo or jumps back up into the next columns. As in writing, so in the layout should the reader's convenience be the yardstick.

MEMOS TO THE EDITOR

The Plan: The newspaper editor should consider adopting the following plan consisting of nine steps for developing an investigative program:

(1) Take decision to the effect that you want an investigative tone in the local news report and that you are willing to accept the pressures this decision implies.

(2) Ensure to marshal carefully the reasons for your decision and discuss them with the publisher, telling him you won't raise the budget or hire new people just yet.

(3) Share your investigative attitude to sub-editors and reporters conveying in decisive tone. Reinforce it by asking challenging questions and assigning reporters to make aggressive follow-ups on stories that have been treated superficially. Make it concrete by asking reporters and editors for lists of investigative ideas. Study, screen, and merge these ideas into a few attractive, feasible story ideas, then settle on one.

(4) For building compact team, pick the staff members who show the best combination of investigative attributes. Give them at least a week to study the feasibility of the story before reporting back directly to you.

(5) The reporter's study should be given hard look and if it confirms the feasibility of the project, clear him of other duties so he can begin basic research. Set-up a schedule of meetings, at least once a week, to review progress and discuss problems.

(6) At the moment the reporter believes he is ready for the key interview, evaluate his research and discuss the key interview plan with him.

(7) After the interview has been taken, block out the time to do a "feet up" editing job, the kind Neale Copple describes in Depth Reporting. "This editing entails a single, clear-cut sentence of your purpose and thesis, a background to help the reader understand the circumstances surrounding the story, and interpretation". Interpretation is used here as a super definition of the why of the investigation, and the details of the investigation, the facts beneath the surface, and fitting the story into the readers' world. Make your hypothesis work or knock it down.

(8) Being convinced that the story is solid, let the publisher know it is coming. Be prepared to argue for it but don't try to slip by him if he is not used to high-risk, hard nosed reporting. If he is not prepared

for strong public reaction, it could cost you and the reporter your jobs.

(9) Take a review or a look back a week after the story has run; get the staff together and discuss the story's impact. The way in which individuals respond will help identify other investigative reporting prospects on the staff. The meeting will also help reinforce in staff members' minds your own commitment to quality journalism. Such commitment is a *sine qua non* for further development.

In other words, your direct expression of interest, motivation, support and counsel for good and feasible projects will stimulate at first a nervous trickle, then a steady stream of ideas, which may be too many, as a matter of fact. It is very likely that the readers will be phoning in tips or walking in with inconclusive documents and fascinating but unprovable theories and ideas. Reporters will be baying for scalps. That's when your editing judgement will be put to its severest test. You have to keep on top.

Qualities of Investigative Reporters

The first rule is to pick good people. Because: (i) Established, responsible investigative reporters are very expensive. (ii) Some self-styled investigative reporters float from city to city, looking for chances to collect scalps and prizes without accepting responsibility. (iii) Even if you find a diamond in the rough, he will take several months to get the feel of your town, its local power structure and political scene. Unless you and the publishers are prepared to wait, you may be disappointed. My second piece of advice, therefore, is equally simple: pick people on your own staff. Choose between own staff and new recruits, the latter to be sized up, who seem to have investigative potential. Here are the qualities to look for in a reporter who has investigative possibilities.

(a) *Self-Discipline:* He may work on a team or alone; the best reporter keeps himself under control. He does not act hastily. He thinks constantly and analytically.

(b) *Mental Toughness:* He possesses the ability to stand up under fire, to outstare, outtalk, and outthink people who try to foil him. It is the quality of being decisive and determined and that is necessary in this kind of reporting.

(c) *Persistence:* Given mental toughness, persistence implies a sort of oriental patience. Situations may present when direct tactics cannot be applied; persistence will then payoff. When the front door is closed, the investigator walks around the block and finds the landlord, the deliveryman, or a telephone repairman to help him get to the people inside.

(d) *Deferred Gratification:* He takes to journalism as mission. So, the investigative reporter does not live for tomorrow's by line. He enjoys the business of dogged pursuit, of careful deduction, of patient construction of a framework of facts.

(e) *Single Mindedness:* He consciously keeps his work in focus.

(f) *Personal Integrity:* This sterling quality connotes a devotion to truth. It enables the reporter to withstand personal abuse, uncertainty, jealousy, backbiting, loneliness.

(g) *A broad and open mind:* Out of many desirable traits present in the reporter, two traits are paramount in the investigative reporter: he avoids rigidity of ideology or investigative theory, and he looks far and wide for patterns. The true professional also talks openly about his work. He is willing to defend it against criticism.

(h) *Independence of thought:* The strings or blind alleys in thought process mar investigative acumen. Therefore, this quality comes as standard equipment with any model of investigative reporter, new or old/experienced.

(i) *A sense of outrage:* This term is Les Whitten's and it means about the same thing as Bill Lambert's "low threshold of indignation". It is an essentially humanist orientation, most often manifested as a desire to defend the little guy against the big guy.

(j) *Competency in writing:* As the subject-matter for investigation is strictly defined and report on it is equally straight, no comment or imagination permitted, the nature of investigative writing sometimes makes it less exciting than a dramatic rescue story. But you must look for a clear writer, one who puts together a well-structure story.

COACHING THE INDIVIDUAL REPORTER

Providing training to your own investigative people entails headaches, false starts, and frustrations. A new reporter needs lots of testing before he can be turned loose. He needs to develop judgement and poise. If he can spell and write declarative sentences and shows a lot of ambition, hire him and send him to the police station.

Stay at the Police Station creates sensibility. But the truth is that the police station and the editor can not carry the burden of training alone. Fledgling or tyro-investigators can greatly benefit as well from seminars and academic training; though these should not substitute for practical experience. Most major schools of journalism offer courses that immerse advanced students in investigative concepts and techniques, putting them under study or sending them on minor independent assignments for practical experience.

COACHING THE TEAM

While the outstanding journalist seems to get himself trained and to get stories by flashes of genius, it is not the case with all newcomers to the profession. Many have to struggle before learning the art and craft of it. The investigative reporter often substitutes intuition about a source's reliability for some of the drudgery of building a massive documentary case. But for most mortals—reporters and editors alike—tackling a large institutional or system story in pairs or teams is more practical and efficient. Teaming helps encourage the flow of ideas; teammates check each other and increase the effectiveness of key interview. A team following a good plan can be far more productive than two journeymen working separately on day-to-day assignments from a city editor.

THE PERMANENT TEAM

Experience tells that permanent teams have been highly successful. The advantages of the permanent team are worth analyzing:

(i) *Volume:* The team members become familiar soon with a wide variety of reference works, basic and special sources of documents, and bureaucracies. They have the advantage of moving on several lines of inquiry simultaneously rather than sequentially; it is a fact that can be crucial in probing a changing, developing situation. If there is lone reporter, he may be simply outpaced by events. Changes in policy, elections, personnel turnover, death or transfer of key persons, loss of sources—these may cloud or negate the meaning of facts gathered nine or ten months (or two years) earlier. It has been seen that most teams plan their projects to last no more than two or three months from conception to publication.

(ii) *Success Rates:* Largely because they are more thorough, team projects generally produce greater public impact changes in laws or policies, rises or falls of businesses or government agencies.

(iii) *Breadth of contacts:* The members of permanent teams usually have had experience on two to half a dozen beats. They are assiduous about keeping up those contacts. On a given project, a team may split tasks on the basis of members' backgrounds. Or, as Bill Lambert points out, a team can merge information from individual members' sources and effectively conceal the origin of key leads. Thus a team has rarely to generate and develop as many new sources on a project as does an individual reporter.

(iv) *Synergism:* The effect of three or four minds analyzing a problem is more than the sum of the parts. At times, the effect seems most exponential. It can produce unconventional ways of viewing a set of facts, of putting together observations.

(v) *Interviewing:* In case, a key interview comes up, the solo reporter must choose between going it alone or briefing another reporter to accompany him. But the team member already has one or more fully briefed veterans working with him. They can concentrate on scripting the interview, on planning roles and tactics, rather than each worrying about whether the other team can produce a complete series or story and sidebars promptly. The story has to be produced without undue delay. Thus speed of production minimizes the risk of a leak to the opposition or a counterattack by the target.

(vi) *Continuity and momentum:* It facilitates and permits one project to follow another quickly without cumbersome phases of slowdown and start-up. Sometimes, it happens that the base-building for a long-term project may begin while a current project is being wrapped up.

(vii) *Self-Checking:* The risk of error is sharply reduced if team members check each other's daily notes and story drafts.

(viii) *Self-regulation:* As human infirmity to fall victim to, at the end of a long, hard job, even good reporters can fall into devil theories or impute evil motives to characters that may only be incompetent or stupid. The presence of one to three colleagues, when each is presumably a strong and independent thinker, reduces this risk of lost perspective.

(ix) *Simpler management:* Management finds that an experienced team can be easier to supervise than a number of individuals. Wisdom of editor lies in the skill to hold the team leader accountable. In case of conflicts or divergence of opinion cropping up during investigation, he spends a good deal of time with the leader and finds this much easier than having to resolve the individual problems and conflicting needs of three or four persons.

(x) *Training:* It is generally a practice that about once a year, a new member is taken abroad while one veteran returns to general assignments or a beat. This rotation reduces professional jealousy among other staff members. Job rotation is also helpful to test and train.

(xi) *Team Problems*: We are aware that team operation, like any other, is not without costs and problems. Because the team works with more direction and fewer burdens than most of staffers, its salaries may be more efficiently spent. The biggest problem is to maintain secrecy. Security is harder to achieve when five people (including the lone editor) know something than when a single reporter knows it.

It is to the advantage of organization to be able to carry on several lines of inquiry at once. However, gaps should not be left and the same trial should not be crossed several times. The ego and the navel are also matters to reckon with in team efforts. The stereotypical investigative reporter has a strong ego. He may refuse to let others share his prized sources. If a person with an excessive ego turns up on a team, he will upset his colleagues and will himself operate at less than maximum capacity. Such cases are sometimes cured by incanting the classic definition of a courageous managing editor. He is the one who fired a Pulitzer winner. And reporters not on the team can, of course, become jealous. They can refuse to pass along tips and ignore tips given to them by team members. They complain about their own workloads and resent the time investigators spend reading books, encyclopedias, and magazines. The good editor, the coach, has to manage things to minimize the problems and maintain the advantages of the team.

THE *AD HOC* TEAM

It has been seen that the temporary team put together for a specific story is even more work for the editor than a permanent team. It can, nonetheless, produce spectacular results. After the project is finished, team members return to their beats. The *ad hoc* team might include one expert and a few specialists selected to supplement his skills and knowledge. But the strengths of the permanent team offer simpler management because of a strong team leader. Standard writing procedures for keeping daily reports and producing final drafts, and especially continuity and momentum are lost with an *ad hoc* team. The members of the permanent team practically rush on their own. The editor has to intervene more with the *ad hoc* team. With little operating continuity, he must take special pains to see that the team is protected from other assignments, that the schedule is followed, that the daily reports are written, that the project files are maintained.

Usually, there is also the greater danger of leaks. It is so when the effort drags on for months and several people pop into and out of it; word of the project will get on the grapevine and circulate.

EDITING THE REPORT

The investigative editing calls for the same kind of sleuthing as investigative reporting does. The editor should take the draft into his office, shut-off his phone calls and read it through several times. He examines the story from a different point of view, more particularly as under:

(i) Is the thesis proved? If not, make notes about what is missing and go on to the next reading.
(ii) Is the thesis important? Will a significant number of readers see it as important?
(iii) Does the story flow? Does it move in a continuous, logical line?
(iv) How can it be trimmed? A story in which the reporter has invested weeks or months will probably be laden with detail, excessive restatement, tedious qualification, and unnecessary attribution. Try to arrive at a balance between enlightenment and boredom. You want to get the story told quickly with strong, clear words. This is the time, for example, to strip out quotes that simply make an interviewee look silly without contributing information about his motives.

(v) After the cuts and adjustments, will the story read?

(vi) Now it is time to test the reporter. If he is a pro, he can stand it. If he cannot, you would rather know now than after the story is printed. Write down in blunt words every question you can think of that challenges the accuracy of the reporter's arithmetic, the credibility of his quoted sources, the logic of his assertions. By now, you have spent at least a couple of hours with the story, and have made marks all over the copy, plus a list of pertinent and impertinent questions. It is time to call the reporter in and go through the list.

Discussions, Revisions

Sometimes, the ensuing discussion can become a morass. Your job is to keep things moving briskly towards reasonable solution of the problem, and that is how to get the piece in print. A good reporter appreciates it. You can establish that the story has a sound thesis, proved by evidence; the next step is to deal with the hard questions that came up in the last reading. These are questions that you, the editor, may have to answer in a phone call or visit from the aggrieved person or his attorney. The reporter should have answers to every one of them.

There is no serious confrontation on 99 stories out of 100 if and only if you have a competent reporter at work. If you avoid the challenging questions, you are making a terrible mistake. Once the critical questions are answered, the irritants disappear and the rest of the conference should be a breeze.

The Final Hurdle

There are some important steps for crossing the final huddle. The first step is to seek out a trusted colleague city editor, editorial writer and veteran reporter who have not been involved in the story and show them the rewrite. Take care not to ask for a detailed editing at this stage but a fresh viewpoint and a candid evaluation of the thesis, approach, and structure. At the next stage, visit the lawyer. Lawyers think in terms of evidence and proof. That is not a bad viewpoint to have just before you publish. After the page is made up, read it again in the interest of accuracy. If you have time, have yet one more new person look at the page. Sports editor, the life-style editor, the wire editor, or some other trusted but uninvolved staffer; hé may spot an error that everyone else has missed. At this point, the final huddle is complete; now stop and congratulate the reporter for persistence and professional performance. And make sure that he or the city editor is geared for follow-up not just the next day but two weeks from now or a month hence.

THE BOYS TOWN STORY

Conception

In mid-summer of 1971, Sun group of newspapers decided to try the Boys Town story. The idea was simply to report how Boys Town, an organisation, raised its money and how it spent the money.

Case

Boys Town had been founded by Father Edward J. Flanagan in an old mansion near the centre of Omaha in 1918. About 1921, it moved to a farm ten miles west of the city. It had many financial problems until M-G-M made its famous movie in 1938 with Spencer Tracy and Mickey Ronney. After that, Boys Town's national image grew rapidly. Immediately after World War II, Father Flanagan started a major building project that included some $ 10 million worth of new dormitories, a stadium, industrial training shops, and administrative buildings. He died in 1947, less than a year before the project was completed. For all practical purposes, that was the last big capital expenditure made by Boys Town.

Every spring and every Christmas season, Boys Town sent out a lot of letters, asking people all over the nation for money. In the 1960s, Sun paper had made a couple of tentative passes at the Boys Town story. They went to the public relations people, the assistant director, and the director (Monsignor Nicholas Wegner) asking, among other things, how much money they took in and how they used it. We were turned down cold every time. "We just don't discuss our fund raising programme" was the general nature of the replies. "It takes a lot of money to care for a thousand boys".

But it was obvious that Boys Town was not going broke. Its physical appearance (a huge green campus dotted with brick and stone buildings, a large farming operation using boys as low priced hired hands) and the size of the payroll (some 600 employees) were enough to set aside that possibility. But Sun felt that the public, both local and national, had a right to know a little more specifically how its donated dollars were being spent. And Sun papers were in the best position to find out.

After proper planning of steps how to go about finding out facts, the Sun story of 1972 merely pointed out that Boys Town management was lethargic. Money flowing in was huge; the Boys Town could do better. The fall out was that Monsignor Wegner was retired in October 1973, and replaced by Rev. Roberts Hupp, pastor of city's richest parish. He was charged with implementing changes recommended by Booz Allen and Hamilton, a Management consulting firm. Hupp did many changes and introduced innovative ideas like proper budgeting. Unlike his predecessor who was reluctant to give information, Hupp declared that the Sun stories "really activated the whole operation into the idea of doing something more".

THE INSTITUTIONS OF OUR SOCIETY

It is observed that much of latter day investigative journalism has concentrated on individuals, their peccadilloes and their piracy. Such stuff is often highly readable. The play it gets usually reflects conventional editorial wisdom about what people will read, watch, listen to, and talk about. But it also reflects, undue concern by editors with traditional definitions of news, single spectacular incidents, events, conferences, court actions and political fire and counter fire. A reporter and his audience become bored and frustrated chewing over and over the standard fare of political chicanery, misfeasance and malfeasance, influence peddling, business embezzlement and stock swindles, sloppy or corrupt professional practices. If they remain preoccupied with these single case stories, they may miss the main point—the nature of the system itself.

The powers of government are limited. We have, therefore, created a host of institutions to serve the specific interests of different publics. They have also created institutions to serve the interests of the public at large "the people", as it were. These institutions may be governmental, quasi-governmental, public in purpose but non-governmental in origin, or strictly limited to technical functions. These institutions may be governmental (bureau of employment services, public utilities commissions, economic and community developmental, district council on ageing, programme for the mentally retarded, state rural electric cooperative), public in purpose but non-governmental in origin (state pharmaceutical association, state restaurant association, cancer association), or strictly limited to technical functions (state geological survey, state building authority, state construction trades council, canners and food processors association). All these institutions should interest the investigative journalist. A basic duty of the newspaper is to examine all of the institutions of its society and to report not only how they work, but how they really work.

Definitions

We may define an institution here for our purposes. An institution is defined as a body of persons working through mechanisms they have designed, and control its affairs in order to serve common interests which they have defined. What is important is that institutions are created by people who make their own rules. Most of them are created and supported by such large numbers of persons that they have a power and inertia (both at rest and in motion) of their own. Their formal decisions are usually collective ones. The decisions may be formulated and promoted by relatively few persons, but they are ratified by much larger populations. These populations agree on their goals and define the rules (subject only to principles of law) for achieving them.

A simple analogy: Let us build an image of an institution. An institution is like a dinosaur in some respects. It has a large body and a small, slow brain. Innately, it is neither imaginative nor aggressive, but once its power has been activated and directed, results are inexorable. It leaves big tracks wherever it goes. It is designed for the long haul rather than the short sprint. Once it has grown to adulthood, it usually protects itself and its territory fiercely.

For obvious reasons, the society tends to create its institutions along dinosaurian lines. It wants institutional actions to be deliberate. It wants institutions to have sufficient power for limited purposes, but not enough to destroy the delicate natural order. It wants institutions to be durable, to carry on long-term purposes and causes. Well thought and good creation. But our metaphorical dinosaur also has inherent weaknesses. It can be fooled by cunning people. It can be hypnotized by a skilled sorcerer, making its gestures meaningless. It can be knocked down by kicking by a well-directed blow to a vital point. When this happens, the wild thrashing of its extremities can harm others nearby. And when it dies, the stink and the mess can be awful.

Analytical Questions

Considering the above analogy, what should a reporter think about when he looks at an institution? Is there a public interest in its activities? If the institutional interest diverges from the general public interest, what are its impacts on my public? How significant are they? Does the public know what the institution's goals are? Are these goals being met?

As it usually happens, the wise investigative reporter is sensitive to the pervasive influences of institutions both private and government owned or sponsored. He reads the papers every day, including the business and women's news sections. He keeps constant check on his community's power structure, on those who run its institutions. He tries to find out how these work and inform the readers. Unhealthy trends or apathy for general interest or misuse of power or funds are brought out clearly and fearlessly by the investigative reporter.

Freedom of Information

Reporters have by now known in India how to use the Right to Information Act like most experienced reporters covering the government do. The Freedom of Information Act in the USA establishes the right of citizens in the USA, similar to that in India, to have access to and receive copies of any document, file, or other record in possession of any federal agency except:

(1) Information properly classified under criteria set by order as secret for reasons of national defense or foreign policy.
(2) Information related solely to the internal personnel roles and practices of an agency.
(3) Information specifically exempted by statute (such as income tax returns, patent applications, and completed census forms).
(4) Trade secrets and commercial or financial information obtained from a person and privileged or confidential.
(5) Inter-agency letters or memoranda that would not be available by law to party other than an agency in litigation with the agency.
(6) Personal and medical files whose disclosure would constitute a clearly unwarranted invasion of personal privacy.
(7) Investigatory records and even here, the agency must prove that disclosure of the records would produce one or more of six specific harmful effects.

The fact remains that the union government is also made up of mortals, most of them very sensitive to public pressures. Any reporter who has been schooled in municipal and statehouse bureaucracy, and who has learned how to gain the confidence of honest functionaries, can open at least 95 per cent of the inner doors if he plans wisely and works doggedly and persistently. The US governmental system is still one of the most open in the world, and the journalist who reports on it will help prevent the self-dealers from closing those doors.

CHAPTER

14

Crime Reporting

Crime stories, judging from the practice followed by the newspapers in the country, are more the staple of evening papers than of morning newspapers. In our country, morning papers also publish them. Since evening papers are published mostly from the major cities, it is hard not to draw the inference that crime is largely urban in nature and is only of interest to urbanites: this view is held in the West.

This, of course, is not true in India's context. There is probably as much, if not more, crime committed in rural India as in urban India. A murder in a distant village does not interest the urban dweller. Small town papers are sufficient in number to draw journalism students to them.

In the cities also, till about 15 years back, it was the political story that largely made the front page and very rarely the crime story. An occasional murder such as that of Prem Bhagwandas Ahuja (in what came to be known as the Nanavati Case) in Mumbai, which hit the headlines.

Writing a crime story can be as complicated as writing a political story. It is mostly the novice reporter who is assigned to the police beat. Fortunately, the police beat is the best training ground for future diplomatic correspondents. As Richard Critichfield writes in the Indian Reporter's Guide, "while speech reporting trains the ear and sports reporting the eye, crime coverage gives the new reporter a broad range of events on which to exercise his talents, usually providing action stories with a narrative as well as human drama".

WHAT CONSTITUTES CRIME?

The dictionary meaning says crime is "a wrong act that is against the law" or "a violation of law". It is also defined as an act of omission or negligence punishable by law.

An offence means any act or omission made punishable by any law for the time being in force. Offences can be bailable or non-bailable; bail is security offered by the accused for his appearance before the officer or court granting him bail. Any person is eligible for bail if he is accused of a bailable offence and arrested or detained without warrant by an officer in charge of a police station.

Some of the more common crimes may be classified as follows:

(1) Abatement that is, aiding and assisting, instigating or facilitating, a crime (usually the punishment is the same as for the offence).

(2) Criminal conspiracy is an agreement between two or more persons to commit an offence, where some perform act, done in pursuance thereof by one or more parties to the agreement.

(3) Offences against the state. These include sedition, assaulting officers of the state and others.

(4) Offences relating to the army and navy, such as mutiny, desertion, harbouring a deserter, impersonating a member of the military and insubordination.

(5) Offences against the public tranquility, such as rioting, being a member of an unlawful assembly, hiring persons to take part in an unlawful assembly, assaulting public persons, and promoting enmity between classes or committing affray.

(6) Offences by or relating to public servants. These include illegal financial gratification, corruption, impersonating a public servant or offences by a public servant such as disobeying a law with intent to cause injury, framing an incorrect document, unlawfully buying property or unlawfully engaging in trade.

(7) Offences related to elections such as bribery, false statements, and failure to keep election accounts.

(8) Contempt of the lawful authority of public servants such as absconding to prevent service of a summons, giving false information, threatening or obstructing public servants.

(9) False evidence and offences against public justice as giving false evidence, destroying documents, harbouring capital offenders, escape or resistance to lawful apprehension, insult to public servant during judicial proceeding.

(10) Offences relating to coin and government stamps. These include counterfeiting, possession of counterfeit money if it is known to be so, fictitious stamps.

(11) Offences relating to weights and measures such as fraudulent use of false instruments for weighting or measuring or constructing such instruments for false use.

(12) Offences affecting the public health, safety, convenience, decency and morals. These include deliberately spreading disease, adulterating food and drink, adulterating medicine, defiling pubic water supplies, driving or riding on a public way so negligently as to endanger human life, dealing with possession of fire, explosives or machinery as to endanger human life, imitating to guard against probable danger by a fall of any building over which a person has right to tear down or repair. Committing a public nuisance, sale of obscene books, obscene songs or keeping a lottery office.

(13) Offences relating to religion such as defiling or damaging a place of worship, maliciously insulting

the religious beliefs of any class, causing a disturbance to an assembly engaged in relics worship, trespassing in place of worship or disturbing a funeral with intention to insult, or uttering any word or making any gesture with intention to wound religious feeling.

(14) Offences relating to the human body:

(a) Offences affecting life:

(i) Murder.
(ii) Culpable homicide, act done with knowledge that is likely to cause death, with or without intention to do so.
(iii) Causing death by rash or negligent act.
(iv) Abetment of suicide committed by child, insane, idiot, delirious or intoxicated person.
(v) Abetting suicide.
(vi) Attempt to murder.
(vii) Attempt to commit suicide.
(viii) Being a thug.

(b) Causing miscarriages, injuring unborn children, exposure of infant with intent of abandoning it and concealment of birth by secret disposal of dead body.
(c) Voluntary causing hurt by dangerous weapons or drugs; to extort property and/or information, to deter a public servant from his duty or to give grave and sudden provocation.
(d) Wrongful restraint or confinement.
(e) Criminal force and assault such as to deter a public servant from performing his duties, to commit theft, assault or threat to a woman to outrage her modesty, to dishonour a person or to wrongfully confine someone.
(f) Kidnapping, abduction, slaving and forced labour:

(1) Kidnapping.
(2) Abduction in order to murder.
(3) Kidnapping a woman to compel her for marriage or cause her defilement.
(4) Procuring of a minor girl or importation of girl from foreign country or buying and taking possession of a minor for purposes of prostitution.
(5) Kidnapping to subject a person to slavery, causing grievous hurt or abducting of child with intent to take its property.
(6) Unlawful compulsory labour (begar).

(g) Rape by a man with his own wife less than 12 years of age and in any other case, and unnatural offences.

(15) Offences against property:

(a) Theft.
(b) Extortion, blackmail, obtaining illegal compensation.
(c) Robbery and dacoity such as simple robbery, or robbery on the highway between sunset and sunrise, or belonging to a gang of persons for the purpose of habitually committing theft (decoity).
(d) Criminal misappropriation of property.
(e) Criminal breach of trust, as by a clerk or servant, banker, merchant or agent.
(f) Receiving stolen property, or assisting in its concealment or disposal.
(g) Cheating, by impersonation or by dishonestly taking delivery of property or by altering or destroying a valuable security
(h) Fraudulent removal or concealment of property or false deed execution.
(i) Mischief; causing damage to the amount of fifty rupees or value, or by obstructing of public drainage, causing diminution of agricultural

water supply, damaging public road or bridge, removing landmarks, mischief by fire or explosives.

(j) Criminal trespass such as lurking, house trespass by night or dishonestly breaking open any closed receptacle containing property.

(16) Offences related to documents and to trade or property marks such as forgery, counterfeiting seals or plates with intent to commit a forgery, defacing or destroying a will, falsification of accounts using false trademarks, counterfeiting of banknote.

(17) Criminal breach of contract of service.

(18) Marriage offences such as a man by deceit causing a woman not legally married to him to think she is married and cohabit with him on that belief, or enticing with criminal intent a married woman, or adultery.

(19) Defamation or printing matter known to be defamatory or selling defamatory matter.

(20) Criminal intimidation, insult and annoyance such as starting a false rumour, circulated with intent of offending the public peace, or intimidation by anonymous communications, or by inducing a person to believe that he will be rendered an object of divine displeasure, or uttering any word and making any gesture to insult the modesty of a woman, or appearing in a public place in a state of intoxication and causing annoyance to any person.

This is pretty exhaustive list of criminal acts and a reporter covering crime must familiarize himself with it. It is equally important that he is familiar with the process of dispensation of justice.

In India, there are following classes of criminal courts. To begin from the lowest:

Magistrate Third Class: He may pass a sentence of imprisonment not exceeding one month and a fine not exceeding Rs. 50.

Magistrates Second Class: He may pass a sentence of imprisonment not exceeding 6 months, including solitary confinement and a fine not exceeding Rs. 200.

Presidency Magistrate and Magistrate First Class: He may pass a sentence of imprisonment not exceeding two years, including solitary confinement and a fine not exceeding Rs. 1,000.

Courts of Session (Sessions Judge or Additional Sessions Judge): He may pass any sentence, but a sentence of death is subject to confirmation by the High Court.

High Courts: they may pass any sentence, authorized by law.

Above them all, of course, is the Supreme Court of India. Mercy Petition is sent to the President of India, if necessary, in case of death sentence.

When a person is arrested and charged with crime, he is first taken to the police station where he is held until he is produced before a magistrate. Arrests may be made with or without a warrant, depending on the crime. (As an example, if someone is accused of buying or selling of any person as a slave, IPC 370 lays down that he may not be arrested without a warrant but if the criminal is habitually dealing in slavery; IPC 371 permits arrest without a warrant).

A warrant is a written out authorization from a magistrate to the police giving them the right to carry out an arrest.

An offence can be either cognizable or non-cognizable. In the case of the former, no warrant is necessary. In the latter case, a warrant will be necessary.

There is a further classification of cases into warrant cases (for offences punishable with death or imprisonment for a term exceeding a year) and summons cases (for offences punishable with imprisonment for a term not exceeding one year and fine).

Arrest: If a person complains against another demanding the latter's arrest, he must affirm under oath that he has reasonable grounds for belief in the guilt of the accused. A search warrant is issued to seize evidence of a crime, to be found. But in certain specific circumstances, the police have the power to search without a warrant.

A person has constitutional right to be brought into court promptly to be confronted with the charges against him. He can not be held in custody for longer than 24 hours without a special order from a Magistrate (who can authorize the detention of the accused for not more than 15 days at a time).

Information relating to commission of a cognizable offence if made by a witness or informant is reduced in writing, read over to the informant, signed by him and entered into a book. This is called first information. Anyone acquainted with the circumstances of a case and whose statements are recorded by the police are called witnesses for the prosecution (Remember the famous Agatha Christie's play by that name).

An investigation is carried out by the police starting with their first knowledge of an offence committed; this can go on until the police officer is satisfied that he has all the information necessary to form an opinion as to whether the offence has been committed or not.

An inquiry is begun after the police officer has sent up the case to a Magistrate. If no *prima facie* (on the face of it) case is made against the accused, he is acquitted. If, on the contrary, the Magistrate is satisfied that a *prima facie* case has been made out, he frames a charge. He may then try the case himself or commit it for trial to the Court of Session.

In his charge sheet or completion report that a police officer submits to the Magistrate, he must state (a) the names of the parties (b) the nature of the crime (c) the names of persons who are acquainted with the criminal case and (d) whether the accused has been forwarded in custody or released on his bond with or without sureties. This is the final report of the police officer after completion of his investigation.

A police officer making an investigation has the following duties to perform on a day-to-day basis:

(1) He must set forth the time when the information reached him.
(2) He must put down the time when he began and closed his investigation.
(3) He must name the places he has visited.
(4) He must record the circumstances ascertained.

How does one report crime cases? Hereunder is a partial list of questions to be asked by a reporter; partial because questions depend on the situation or circumstances.

Casualties: Was anyone killed? If so, how? Similarly, was anyone injured? How? What were the weapons used? What happened to the dead? Was any of the killed well-known?

Property Loss: What was the value of the property lost or damaged? What exactly was stolen, defaced or destroyed?

Method of Crime: How was the crime committed? What weapons, if any, were used?

How were the victims treated by the criminals? Was this a repetition of any similar crime? (Remember the similarity of crimes committed by the murderer Raman Raghavan in Mumbai and its suburbs).

Motive: What moved the criminal to commit the crime? What did the victims report? What did the police or other witnesses have to say?

Arrest: State the names of the arrested people, along with their age and occupation. What formal charge was preferred? How did the police apprehend the criminals? Where were they taken to?

Clues: Did the criminal leave behind him any clues? What clues did the witnesses provide? What clues are the police investigating?

Description: Is there a description of the criminals available?

Contempt of Court: it is extremely difficult to define the term "contempt of court". It is an aspect of reporting that the crime and crime report has to be constantly aware of and guard against. By and large, contempt of court can be defined as "any conduct or action that tends to bring the authority and administration of the law into disrespect or disregard or will interfere with or prejudice the parties litigating or their witnesses during litigation".

Contempt is of two kinds: (a) Contempt committed in the face of the court, and (b) indirect contempt or contempt out of court.

Some instances of contempt are obvious: A reporter surreptitiously returning to the courtroom after having once been excluded from it violates the order of the court. A reporter who photographs an accused person in spite of the order of the court not to do so is again in violation of the court and can be cited for contempt. Similarly, publication of proceedings of a case being heard in camera is a disobedience of the court's orders.

The out of court contempt may be divided generally into (a) False and grossly inaccurate report of court proceedings, (b) such publications that may have reasonable tendency to interfere with the orderly administration of justice, and (c) publication that scandalizes the court, judges, counsel, parties or witnesses.

Under Section 3 of the Act, it is an offence if any person for any purpose prejudicial to the safety or interest of the State:

> (a) approaches, inspects, passes over or is in the vicinity of, or enters any prohibited place, or (b) makes any sketch, plan, model, or note which is calculated to be or might be or is intended to be directly or indirectly, useful to an enemy, or (c) obtains, collects, records or publish or communicates to any other person any sketch, plan, model, article or note or other document or information which is calculated to be or might be or is intended to be directly or indirectly useful to an enemy.

Under this act, it would be hard for any Indian reporter to publish the Indian equivalent of the Pentagon Papers.

CHAPTER

15

Government, Media and Social Responsibility

Walter Lippmann made a distinction over fifty years ago between "news" and "truth": "The function of news is to signalize an event; the function of truth is to bring to light the hidden facts, to set them into relation with each other and make a picture of reality on which men can act".

Because news reporting and truth seeking have different ultimate purposes, Lippmann postulated that "news" could be expected to coincide with truth in only a few limited areas such as the scores of baseball games or elections where the results are definite and measurable. Lippmann concluded pessimistically if the public required a more truthful presentation and interpretation of the world they live in, they would have to depend on institutions other than the press.

That is not the first, nor will it be the last, time that the press has been lambasted, and not just for falling short in the pursuit of truth. Though an occasional editor, in the manner of Pilate, might with justification ask "What is truth"? The fact remains that the press, in general, has been somewhat remiss in other fields as well as, for example, in the matter of social responsibility.

"Social responsibility" is an omnibus term that covers a wide range of activities. One of the most trenchant critics of the press, Prof. N.S. Ramaswamy, Director of the Indian Institute of Management, Bangalore has asserted that "a survey of the various professions, including the mass media, would reveal that their social relevance is not high".

Responsibility and relevance are two different concepts, but are deeply intertwined. According to Prof. Ramaswamy, "social relevance" of society can be deemed to be high, as indeed that of any profession, "when its economic, social and political ideologies and instruments are oriented to meet the essential needs of the masses". One would presume that when the profession becomes socially relevant in a conscious and organized manner, it fulfils its responsibility.

Everybody would agree that the communications media are important instruments to involve the masses towards achieving national aspirations. Next, perhaps, to politics, the mass media is the most potent instrument of a society for economic and social transformation. And yet, claims Prof. Ramaswamy, "the way professions and institutions are now structured, organized and compensated, has resulted in low social relevance".

A few observations and conclusions are immediately possible from the findings noted above. One is that Indian papers are predominantly urban centred and what is worse, urban-oriented. Another is that they are obsessed with politics, whether Indian or foreign. A third is that developmental journalism still remains unattractive to large number of editor-journalists. Yet one other possible conclusion is that editors are indifferent to the welfare of masses because of the vast wall separating them.

But why are newspapers obsessed with politics? One reason is that their editors and owners, until 30 years ago, took a leading part in the struggle for independence and cannot tear themselves away from the peculiar fascination that the struggle for power has cast on them in the intervening decades. No matter how indifferent they claim to be to the goings on in state capitals and in Delhi, these men have a natural affinity to the politicians that they cannot easily shed.

Another reason, one may presume, lies in the fact that a second generation of newsmen, trained in the humanities, social sciences and other sciences have yet to get hold of the levers of editorial power. The older generation, still to a large extent, holds the key to the gate. It is this generation that still dictates what should go into each edition and what should not. This brings us to that new vogue word in communication vocabulary the "gatekeeper problem".

The media Gatekeepers, as we all know, are the ones who regulate the traffic in and out of any sanctora. And one thing certain about gatekeepers is that they are certain about themselves. And while certitude is no test of certainty, as that wise American judge Oliver Wendell Holmes rightly remarked, the certitude of our newspaper-gatekeeper and the news editors is such that there is apparently no appeal beyond them. What they say is news or becomes news.

For a brief—all too brief period—in early 1979, the Indian Express bravely tried to get off the beaten path but quickly reverted to journalistic beaten track. The "gatekeepers" were to have the last laugh and the last word. Were the "gatekeepers" moved by knowledge, reason or public opinion in opting for the known rather than experimenting with the unknown? Importantly, is public opinion necessarily a safe guide? It is a well-known axiom that there is always a conflict between the popular and the salutary, between priya and hita and obviously, at least in the case of the *Indian Express*, the priya won over the hita, the popular over the salutary.

It is noticed that not everybody has the courage of an Abraham Lincoln who, finding that on a difficult decision he was outvoted in his cabinet seven to one, firmly declared, "One for and seven against, the ayes have it, the ayes have it". Most editors in India prefer to play safe. Non-conformism becomes a habit when editors have nothing to lose. A Sadanand would have dared the government of his day as indeed he did and faced closure of his paper, in the pursuit of principles. Today's editor evidently is made of less stern stuff.

We know that in today's India, there is no Tilak to be found; a Tilak who knows about the aspirations and the agonies of the ruled and who remains relevant even today; only, we do not have Tilak.

It would be unrealistic to expect that in any conflict between the popular and the salutary, the latter should necessarily win. There is always a hiatus between the ideal and the possible and while one should aim at the ideal, it is unrealistic to believe that it can ever be attained, except in an authoritarian society where the needs of the regime more than the profit motive rein supreme. The experiment was carried out in India during the emergency; results we know now.

Take it to your heart and hand that the sole aim of journalism is service. Mahatma Gandhi said, "The press is a great power, but just as an unchained torrent of water submerges whole countryside and devastates crops, even so an uncontrolled pen serves but to destroy. If the control is from without, it proves more poisonous than want of control. It can be profitable only when exercised from within". If this line of reasoning is correct, how many of journals in the world withstand the test? But who would stop those that are useless? And who should be the judge? The useful and useless must, like good and evil, generally go together and man must make his choice. Similarly, the readers make the choice of media.

Majority of the critics of the press would give much the same kind of policy guidance to the news editors: "Transform yourself into something quite different from what you are, stop giving the customers just anything they want—any amusement, any violence—anything that sells. And give them, instead, information they need to know to be good citizens in a democracy.

We observe two flaws in this way of thinking. One, as Reston amiably put it, "it is not much use advising grasshoppers to be cockroaches, or newspapers to be monographs on foreign affairs, (since) the problem is to see whether, human nature being what it is, the people who sell newspapers can change to meet all these new responsibilities without losing the patronage of the people who buy and advertise in newspaper". Obviously, newspaper publishers cannot serve the national interest by going broke.

The other flaw observed is in thinking and that is to underestimate the absorption capacity of the ordinary even illiterate citizen. Newspapers did not have to tell the Hindi belt citizen that the Emergency was bad for him: he knew it without having it explained to him in lengthy features, informed news stories or profound editorials.

Conduct a survey of press and you would find that many newspapers are not solely devoted to pornography, violence or human aberrations but are trying to do as good a job as circumstances would permit them. Their editors are not always machines turned on by their paymasters but often they are men of conscience, if sometime ill directed.

There is a further point that can be argued. And this is that power lies not in the media but in the idea. The idea gains validity by its own truth, not by the number of people subscribing to it. There were no printing presses in the time of the apostle Paul or even in Sankara's time and yet too powerful were their ideas that they spread far and wide. Too often, those critics who castigate the press for all its sins of omission and commission forget that the Buddha's ideas travelled over land and seas without the coordinated assistance of All India Radio and the Indian press.

In appreciation of the circumstances, it is not what the mass Indian newspapers say or do not say that really matters as what even one newspaper prints and wins respect by its proven creditability. A newspaper's sense of purpose and integrity, rather than its circulation, would determine its influence although the two need not be and are not mutually exclusive. A newspaper that does not take itself seriously is not taken seriously by others as well, no matter how small circulation-wise it is. Or else why would the government of India have pounced on A.D. Gorwala's opinion during the Emergency?

When there is thesis, there is anti-thesis too. So, there will always be two opinions as to what exactly a newspaper should do, or a government should do by way of compelling newspapers to be socially responsive. Critics are treading dangerous, mine strewn grounds here. As knowledgeable an individual as H.Y. Sharada Prasad—he has been news editor of the *Indian Express*, editor of *Yojana*, Press adviser to Mrs. Indira Gandhi before and during the Emergency, has cautioned against too much governmental interference with mass media:

"I am afraid" he said in his extension lecture at Bangalore University, "we have been a little thoughtless in seeking to bend the traditional media to development purposes. It is true that the traditional media have always carried a message, most often a religious message, but whether all such are forms that could carry an official message without losing their distinct characters is open to question. A person with extensive knowledge of Indonesia was telling us recently that the highly publicized success story of Indonesia using the shadow play form and puppets in aid of the literacy drive was not really an unalloyed success. Indonesian puppeteers who tried to tell villages that Kauravas were defeated by Pandavas because Kauravas were illiterate whereas Pandavas were literate and the chagrin of finding whole village audience waling out on them. In our own country, there is a true story of a popular folk singer who knew five to six hundred songs by heart and when he was induced to learn twenty "development" songs, he forgot all the others he had known".

The clashes between government and the Press, it would seem, are mostly in the realm of domestic politics because it is here that power not only is exercised but is seen to be exercised.

By and large governments and the newspapers of their countries are in harmony over foreign policy because perception of what is good for the country *vis-à-vis* other countries is notably common between them, though Jawaharlal Nehru in his time and his detractors in the press differed over how to handle the cold war. This has been true not only in India but also perhaps even more so in foreign countries as well.

James Reston once called, *The Times of London* as "a king of house organ for the British government Establishment"—a charge, incidentally, that *The Times* might with some justification, have levelled against Mr. Reston's own paper, the *New York Times*. The Media is used to convey views which the administration in that country does not want to put in formal diplomatic communications. One reason for this, as Reston noted, is that the old diplomacy, with its polite but geometric language, has broken down, and the new diplomacy part secret, part public, part propaganda has devised new techniques of communication between governments and peoples.

It is historical fact when the French government indicated in 1966 that it intended to withdraw its military forces from the integrated command of the North Atlantic Treaty Organization (NATO) and force all NATO troops to accept French control or get out of France, the American government, hoping to forestall the move without threatening the French, "inspired" certain news stories through American reporters on the unpleasant consequences of such action by France. The meaning of those news dispatches was quite clear to the French government, though they did not bring about a change in the French policy.

Believe it what holds good in the international field does not necessarily hold good in the field of domestic affairs and correspondents who cooperate with politicians ostensibly with the laudable object of news gathering cannot be doing any good to anyone but their politician friends. The close liaison that has been noticed between Charan Singh and some members of the press may have helped the Deputy Prime Minister in conveying to Morarji Desai what he otherwise would not have dared to say in a face to face meeting that some correspondents lend their good offices to such politicking is a fact of life that could be deplored but cannot any longer be ignored.

We know that there is no way in which reportorial behaviour can be neatly categorized into right and wrong. In the end, it will have to be left to the good sense of the reporter himself. As long as politicians and papers exist and democracy functions in its ineluctable ways, correspondents can be expected to work in cahoots with favoured friends in power. That is the name of the game.

CHAPTER

16

Academic and Miscellaneous News

SCIENCE NEWS

The specialists are absolutely necessary in science, medicine, law and economics. In such fields as consumerism, the environment and atomic energy, a certain amount of special training, background knowledge and experience also are necessary particularly for investigative reporters.

Covering a Quake

The way a specialist covers an earthquake is somewhat different from and a lot more detailed than the way a general assignment reporter would go about the same job. He reports:

Quake results
Timing and damage
Danger discounted
Magnitude of quake
Extent of quake

Trains still run
Road damage
General damage

Progress in Science Writing

Humankind's giant vault into space has done as much as anything to stimulate the trend towards specialization in journalism. When Neil Armstrong in 1969 stepped on the moon's surface and said, "This is one small step for a man, one giant leap for mankind". He also marked a major development in the reporting of science news.

Energy Crunch

Nowhere is there greater need for informed and dispassionate reporting than in the field of energy.

The Consumerism

Consumer reporting is one of the big new fields that change has forced upon us. Consumer protection is a fact of life. It is not going to go away; even if it does, it would set your advertising manager to trembling.

The Challenge

A group of knowledgeable consumer specialists are reinforced from time to time with staff people.

Growth of Coverage

A few pioneering consumer organizations, with pitifully small resources and skimpy publications, struggled for years to awaken the interest of the public in a crusade against shoddy products, overpricing, misleading advertising and the other signs of an overly commercial age. But for much of this century, few consciences were stirred except among the more progressive editors and managers of the news media. Along Madison Avenue, it was even hinted darkly that people who suspected the good faith of big advertisers were dupes of Communism at best and plotters against the security of the republic at worst.

The first to break through the barrier of indifference and neglect was a public spirited lawyer. Ralph Nader, who managed to marshal the support of a group of talented young adherents in a whole series of campaigns to protect the interests of the consumer. Then, in a period of soaring inflation that sent the cost of living rocketing, the public itself began to face up to a distressing situation. The nations' campuses, ever sensitive to such movements, became staging areas for consumer groups that sought new recruits. And consumerism, at last, became a fact of life for the American Press. Even the broadcast media had to take notice when the crusade against cigarettes reached such a pitch that cigarette commercials were eliminated from the air by law. Health news, on a day-to-day basis, became important to a larger and demanding public.

Range and Methods

Editors approach consumer reporting in various ways. The larger news organizations use specialists who do nothing else. Business writers can do specialized pieces on how consumers can get satisfaction for their complaints. Sports writers can give much more advice than they do on such consumer details as where to park cars outside stadiums, the best methods of travel to various contests, costs, availability of meals and other details. All receipts in the family pages should carry approximate costs, and in travel and entertainment stories, costs should be included as a matter of course.

In a report by Jack Foster, editor of the Palm Beach (Florida) Times, he said, "Consumer reporting is all around us. It is no longer something out of the ordinary, if indeed it ever was".

Consumer Campaigns

Consumerism has been effective in journalism in several different ways. Leading newspapers are originating their own inquiries in response to complaints.

Campaigns that once were considered taboo are now being undertaken with the helpful resources of a news organization. The Des Moines Register, for example, gave full support to Nick Kats's examination of unsanitary practices in meat packing plants; the result was the passage of the Federal Wholesale Meat Act and a Pulitzer Prize for the reporter. Campaigns against unsanitary restaurants now are considered almost routine in some cities of the nation. And major papers like the *Wall Street Journal* do not hesitate to expose unscrupulous business practices wherever they are found. The 1982 Tylenol scare was a national sensation.

The automobile industry, despite its heavy advertising budgets, has been forced on the defensive in numerous instances to justify its safety standards and merchandising practices. The food sections of family pages, so long immune from critical inspection, have undergone an even more searching examination.

Just how far consumer reporting will develop depends entirely on the skill and devotion of the journalists who undertake this specialty and the amount of support they receive from their news organizations.

No less than consumerism, the relationship of people to their environment and the increasing public concern over pollution have generated broadening interest in the news. The great industries that recklessly contaminated the atmosphere, despoiled the earth of its beauty and polluted the water supply are being called to account. Cities that casually dumped their sewage in rivers, lakes and inland seas are finding themselves threatened by their own filth. New York City, a special case, has learned to its cost that it must cease dumping sludge in the ocean because it contaminates beaches for miles around. And even well-meaning citizens have learned that, through their own foolish disposal measures, they are among the worst polluters of all.

A Measure of Progress

There has always been a certain amount of interest in the conservation of natural resources in the United States and the development of the resources of the earth for the benefit of all peoples.

Environmental developments were covered, of course, but there appeared to be no special concern over the state of the earth and the atmosphere even after World War II. Once again, it was a book, Silent Spring by Rachel Carson, which called public attention to a development of consequences, the effect of the pesticide DDT on wildlife. Out of the national debate that ensued, a new consciousness was crated of the precarious nature of humankind on earth.

But when the Love Canal scandal broke in New York in the late 1970s and editors realized thousands of families were living over or near abandoned chemical dumps that threatened their health, local reporters did not have to do a great deal of investigating to find that similar situations exited in their own areas. The upshot was the issuance of a national list of dangerous abandoned chemical sites that had to be cleaned up. It was a major step forward in the development of environmental reporting as a daily newspaper assignment in many parts in the country.

ENVIRONMENTAL NEWS

When Henry Ford succeeded in manufacturing his first automobile, it was a revolution in the means of transportation on the personal and commercial level; an achievement which changed the world. Decades later, scientists have begun to realize that cars also emit harmful gases through their exhaust systems which affect our health and environment.

The issue of protection of the environment becomes a matter of awareness. Most of the projects and problems in the developing countries have their basis in their relationship to the scientific and environmental facts. These facts should be recognized by decision-makers as well as by the public.

The environment reporter's role is to keep up a continuous effort to inform the public and to make a constant effort to increase this awareness about the environment.

Among the environmental problems which need special attention in the Third World are the problems of air pollution, especially in the big cities, the manufacture and use of pesticides, and the misuse of agricultural land and forests.

In India, the Bellhop disaster exposed the problem brought about by some big industrial multinational pesticide companies. They shipped the hazardous and banned pesticides as separate chemical compounds to a developing country; then re-assembled them into a pesticide under another commercial name.

In most of the capitals and large cities of the Third World, there is serious air pollution, and this does not get the proper attention of research in an effort to put it under control or at least to lower the level of pollution.

In Egypt, an ancient practice was using mud bricks for building since the time of the Pharaohs. The Nile River annual flood brought a fresh supply of millions of tons of mud and silt, but after the Aswan High Dam construction, mud sediments were deposited in front of the dam, not making their way down the river as previously. Then farmers began to sell layers of their topsoil to persons deprived of their usual supply of mud for bricks. This practice led to the loss of fertile top soil in large areas. To solve their housing needs, they began to build on agricultural land. But recent laws have banned both practices of building on farm land or excavating topsoil for production of mud bricks; now there were severe penalties for doing this.

In Colombia, in the vast Amazon forest, illegal cocoa plantations have had a large scale development with big profits for labourers and farm owners who produce cocaine in laboratories in the forests. The government has used airplanes and army troops to fight this practice. But the problem has a negative effect where there has been damage to the tropical forests and of course, in the exporting of the drug to other countries.

A Veteran Journalist Observes

Investigative reporting sometimes could be a suitable way to deal with environmental issues. One can depend on relatives or friends to get information which may not be available through official channels all the time.

In Sudan, the medical team found that noise had had a bad effect on health causing loss of hearing; high blood pressure and tension which can lead to heart disease.

Another field of environmental reporting is that of wildlife protection. Third World countries are the home of many wild life species which are becoming endangered because of development and expansion of agricultural land uses, taking away their natural habitat. Efforts should be made to preserve the wildlife species and native plants.

For environmental reporters, scientific background is an advantage. But an interested reporter can obtain a good knowledge in the field by reading environmental materials published by international organizations, such as the United Nations Environmental Programme. Contact with the U.N. Programme can put a reporter in touch with the organizations working in the field and with their publications. For example, the international journal for environment and development ((magazine) is available.

The environment is a multi-disciplinary subject, which includes science, medicine, public health, meteorology, engineering, city planning, economics, and many more facets of man's life. So, a stream of continuous awareness is needed until we reach the point of the optimum development of our resources with a minimum disturbance to the environment. Having that awareness is the job of the environmental reporter.

ECONOMIC NEWS

The seriousness of the American economic situation, however, promoted a turn about in general economic reporting. Efforts were made to find reporters who knew the difference between a bond and a stock, an expense budget and a capital budget.

The long deferred recognition of economic news was accompanied by equally important changes in the way it was written and told. There is no longer an excuse for making economics dull. In professional hands, such a story can be told in informal, popular and often uninhibited style.

LABOUR NEWS

In the columns of a good newspaper, news of labour affairs is by no means confined to unemployment, strikes and lockouts or violence on the picket lines. A more sophisticated approach to the reporting of conflicts between industry and labour has developed, so that a good newspaper takes care not to label itself a pro-industry partisan in every dispute but tries to give both sides of the story.

EDUCATIONAL NEWS

The old journalists' weakness for emphasizing trouble rather than achievement is only a part of the difficulty in achieving a balanced presentation of the news of education.

There is little possibility for constructive dialogue; school and press drift into postures of mutual hostility.

When the schools are in the forefront of the news, however cool, careful and impartial, reporting must become the order of the day.

RELIGIOUS NEWS

The news of religion for many years suffered an extremely low priority in the daily press except on weekends and religious holidays.

Editors specializing in news of religion for the wire services and the larger newspapers dealt with many issues beyond the regular religious observances. The struggle waged by the forces for and against abortion, for example, was probably the single most emotional issue in American life during the 1980s and it deeply involved communities in every part of the land. It was a symbol of changing times.

CULTURAL NEWS

The audience for cultural affairs in the United States now is larger than the sports audience in most major metropolitan centres, but the news media have been slow to take advantage of it. Most of the reviewing and critical writing about the lively arts appears in the larger newspapers, the weekly magazines and the wire services.

While television itself does very little reviewing and criticism of a serious nature, it is the one universal medium with the capacity to bring great theatre and great music to nearly all American homes.

Editorials

The editorial page is undergoing a much needed revival in importance and editorial voice of radio and television is a little stronger. Even some news magazines are coming around to the end for a separate section for editorial comment. The new stress on editorial opinion is due in large part of the expansion of public service journals, for without the strongest kind of editorial support and the total mobilization of the resources of the entire news organization, many a crusade would wither and die in a few days.

There are many definitions of what editorial opinion should be and how a properly conducted editorial page or editorial programme should operate. Properly conducted, an editorial section should represent a community or region of the country; many, of course, contend that they speak for the nation but not very many could prove it if challenged. Moreover, such a section should be a market place of ideas, and not a drab bag of columns and reprints intended to please all segments of the audiences.

What Editors Believe

Editorial pages rank comparatively low in any survey of readerships of newspapers. The programmes devoted to editorial opinion are close to the bottom in radio and television audience measurement. Despite low total diffusion, the editorial section can have an impact on the decision-making process; community leaders are well aware of it.

TIPS FOR SPECIALIST IN JOURNALISM

- Every young reporter should begin, as early as possible, to cultivate a specialty. In today's complicated world, journalists with specialized knowledge are very much in demand.
- Science writing is of importance in everything from the coverage of earthquakes to claims about instant cures for the common cold. It is of special interest in anything having to do with atomic power and other aspects of the energy crunch.
- Consumer reporting cuts across all departmental lines in a news organization. A consumer reporter has to have specialized and dependable sources and

the strength and courage to stand by the reporting of unpleasant and controversial facts.

- Environmental reporting was given a big boost through the discovery that hidden sites for the dumping of chemical waste, much of it toxic, existed in most parts of the United States. The reporting of water shortages, the opening of national lands for private exploitation and other aspects of environmental concern are regularly in the news.
- Any recession brings renewed interest in the reporting of economic news. It is no longer something that can be safely relegated to the financial page and it can not be done solely by the Wall Street Journal or Stock Exchange Reports.
- Every news organization now is trying to find better ways to tell the economic story and it is going to take specialists to do it. The same is true of labour news, particularly in times of high unemployment.
- News stories about education, religion and cultural affairs; all have their specialized aspects and are important on larger news organizations. In smaller organizations, the reporter with all interest in any one of these often does work on such stories without being specially assigned. Many give their own time to the job, even though it is not demanded of them.
- It is a rare beginner who makes the jump from school or a first job directly to the editorial page or a spot as a columnist. It has been done, but each case is extraordinary. It pays how an editorial page operates and what makes columnist run but the one thing young reporters cannot do is to let the paper's editorial policy guide their reporting. No reporter can go out on a story with a fixed idea of what he or she is looking for and expects to do a fair and honest job.

SPORTS NEWS

Typical Combination: In the mythology of the sports world, sports reporters are supposed to confine themselves to the stories of who won and who lost, or game called-off on account of the weather, when they don't, it's news.

There is generally a feeling of unease when we think about sports, both college and professional, in terms of the fact that we are not really doing a job of reporting on the true conditions. I am talking about not only college cricket, baseball, basket ball, volleyball or football in particular, but also most college sports, the money involved and the practices involved. One has a hard time getting sport writers, interests in digging into that story.

Interviewing Sports Personalities/Figures: Bob Mathews, sports columnist for the Rochester (New York) Times Union, has these suggestions for interviewing sports personalities:

- Make sure your first question is a good one so the subject will know you have something on the game/ ball.
- Always be on a first name basis with every player in a team. Sooner or later, one of them will stand up with 'V' sign and it's sports writer's job to ask him about it. Nothing turns-off an athlete faster than a reporter who hasn't said hello to him all season but is quick to arrive after a costly error or lovely score.
- Try the specifics. Don't settle for generalities. Ask why the centre fielder dropped the ball in the last half of the minute, enabling the opposition to score the wining run.
- I have one pet question I often ask athletes: "what do you think of sports writers?" They usually have definite opinions and branch off into how they have been misquoted, misrepresented, etc. It's a good way to build rapport and can lead to some good exchanges.
- Before I interview a national sports figure, I often phone a sports writer in his particular town for background and tips on how to approach the subject.
- Invariably, there is a question I forget to ask or a point that needs clarification. So I always ask where the subject can be reached later in the day, just in case he is needed.

Basic Facts

Here are some of the basics that should be remembered about sports reporting:

- Sports reporters are measured by the same standard as all other reporters are measured. They have to do more than just report the score; it is their business to be aggressive to dig for the hidden story, to make sports pages mean something more than a repository for columns of agate results.
- One of the foremost problems today is access to athletes and locker rooms, at both the professional and the amateur levels. Reporters have to make it their business to ask the tough questions which mean that they can't let themselves be turned aside by a stern locker room janitor.
- Most beginners in sports get their first job stringing for a neighborhood paper and reporting high school scores. The high school sports best is a testing ground for the next generation of sports writers. Usually, the best of the stringers gets first crack at an opening for a high school sports reporter and the progression starts there.
- The three necessities for a sports writer are accuracy, restraint and a decent knowledge of and respect for the English language. Phone expertise and cliché ridden writing are the principal faults of new comers.
- In a contest featured on TV, the newspaper sports writer has to emphasize something other than the score, even though the score does have to be repeated high up. This can be anecdote, a sharp quote, an interview or an explanation of some occurrence that was fuzzed up by the TV reporters.
- In the thousands of contests that sports writers cover with little or no broadcast competition, the emphasis is still on writing the story straight and featuring the manner in which the game was won or lost. But

even there, the feature approach always helps and except for the brief summary story, good quotes are mandatory.

- Keeping statistics is an important part of the sports reporter's job and he or she should devise a system that can be quickly scanned and summarized at the end of the game. Too many states will spoil a story; too few will make it unusable. The point is to find the happy medium.
- Everybody in the business emphasizes sports writing styles. But mostly, this refers to the elite, the columnists and commentators who speak and write pretty much as they please. The young sports staffer is bound to the same rules that cover all reports, however, and should not deviate from them without permission.
- In India, the Sports Authority of India puts up grand plan for development of facilities and to identify and support talented and budding players. Mostly, it is individual effort in India and politics plays havoc and the real talent is relegated to the background.
- There are competitions at Regional, State and National levels to report. There are State level Associations, sometimes parallel organizations too, which organize competitions and Olympiads. There are elections and malpractices galore. Budgets are misappropriated and there is sporadic mud slinging, too.
- There are Asian Olympics. There are also Commonwealth Games and the most important involving all the nations—the once in four year event—the World Olympics. Sports reporting is mostly relating to who wins, who is defeated; who makes record, which breaks previous record. The most interesting news is the new player making impressive presence; he may make a century or half century in cricket.

India Women's Team and its Achievements

- There are various kinds of sports organisation. These are sport or game specific. These may be at different levels—local, regional, state and national. These may be government aided or voluntary. Their activities are also reported like their sources of funds, constitutions, membership, elections, groupism, disputes etc.
- Disputes may reach courts and there may be reported.
- Government may have plan to expand sports facilities, particularly in the rural areas. India may be constructed and coaches may be appointed.
- There may be maladies afflicting the organisations. These may be reported. Selections to constitute teams to take part in competitions may not be on merit causing resentment and disappointment. These are to be reported.
- Match fixing is the new strategy followed by the private companies whereby the best players do not play according to their skill, stamina and as per past performance. These cases make news in the whole sports world.

PART 2

EDITING

CHAPTER

17

The Editing Jobs

THE FUNCTION OF THE NEWSPAPER

The authorities have acknowledged certain functions of the newspaper as the foremost ones: these are to inform—about news, views, opinion—on events, happenings, occurrences—emanated from society, governments, legislature, international relations and happenings anywhere on the globe nay even inter-planetary developments like space. Not only this much but also woven through this function run the threads of its other duties—to instruct, to interpret and to mould public option, apart from entertainment.

There is broad pattern of the news presentation: story for story, varying across a broad range; it is like news stories, in varying degrees, being momentous, inconsequential, interesting, dull, sad, and funny, edifying, and revolting with again a variety of colour, texture, dimensions and particularly depth. The editor's raw material is the entire flux of human events; there are human beings individually and in groups creating news all the time. It is the skill and art of the Editor to blends his ingredients with lights and shadows, balances and contrast to present what he considers to be a fair, accurate, and interesting report of the day's news thus serving as gate-keeper of what should enter the canvas and what should be left out.

The first aim of the newspaper, which is the responsibility of both the Editor and the Manager are to attract and keep readers to stay live by remaining financially sound through circulation and advertising. Newspapers develop a formula for their news presentation. They have to be innovative and creative continuously. Joseph Pulitzer and William Randolph Hearst became crusaders of felt necessity; they made crusading one of their ingredients. Horace Greeley emphasized editorial opinion. Charles A. Danna developed the human-interest treatment of news. Edwin Lawrence Godwin published a journal of political science. William Rockhill Nelson fought for civic betterment.

It is noticed that since the beginning of the twentieth century, the American newspaper has developed a common denominator. This consists of culling from the amorphous flow of world events those stories which will both inform and interest the reader and putting them into a package that by typographical arrangement emphasizes and grades the news and attracts readers. This common denomination is like a balanced meal. A diet of meat and potatoes alone will not sustain the newspaper; or will one of salad alone or dessert alone. Put together in proper proportions, the menu is balanced; the newspaper informs, instructs and entertains. Therefore, each day's news differs, and each day's flavour varies.

However, the editor is always in a dilemma: he constantly faces the admonition to print not what the reader wants to read but what evangelists think the reader ought to read—sheer gate-keeping. Other critics, and particularly the inexperienced, insist to undertake some aspect in editing and believe that the editor's responsibility is to ram his ideas of justice and human improvement down the reader's throat. The seasoned editor has little patience with either view. He has developed the tempered state of realism that is the necessary alloy for the practical world of gathering and printing the news. He does not believe that the newspaper's sole duty is to reform the world and save readers from themselves. I may put it in another perspective: any concept that places upon the newspaper entire responsibility for the virtue of public underestimates the intelligence of the American reader. More than that, it is blind to the fact that news must have a flesh and blood component; that it must come as nearly alive as the persons and the events it describes. The responsible editor does not publish a scandal wheel, but neither does he publish a Sunday school paper or a journal of sociology or economics. The editor serves a constituency that wants and deserves to know about the human interplay that manifests itself in all facets of the news. Thus he is somewhat akin to an umpire who calls the strikes and the balls as they are pitched to the plate. His job is to tell what is happening and his concern is the objective presentation of events and persons.

The experienced editor does not leave scope to be guided by others: he lays down but one general rule by himself. It is to make the world come alone every day in the stories, in the headlines, and in the make up at the newspaper. Fulfilling this requirement calls for imagination, understanding, sympathy, a knowledge of human affairs, and an insight into people. Those qualities apart, it requires also knowledge of the technical devices used by the copy reader, the news editor, and the make up editor. These three are the architects who each day build the final product that comes off the presses. With this backdrop, I make an attempt towards an exposition of their techniques, like :

(1) *Copy reading*: The editing of news stories and the writing of headlines for them.
(2) *News editing*: The handling and display of all the news in the paper.
(3) *Make-up*: The fitting together of the news stories and the illustrations to form an attractive, inviting paper.

THE THREE PROCESSES IN CO-ORDINATION

In almost any medium size or metropolitan newspaper office, we will see a horseshoe desk and a number of men sitting around it. At the elbows of each are number of pencils, erasers, paste pots, scissors or rulers, and copies of the paper in various stages of being clipped and torn up. This is the copy desk and thousands of newspaper men spend their lives working on it; they edit the stories that appear in the newspaper and they write the headlines for the stories.

The News Editor sits at a nearby smaller desk, through whose hands the news is funneled. The general handling and the emphasis of the news is his responsibility. He determines the content of the paper subject to the ultimate approval of the managing editor. He decides which stories merit page one display, fixes location where on the page they are to appear, and how, in terms of typography, they shall be presented. He decides which stories shall be relegated to the inside pages. He also determines how the news is to be illustrated.

The make-up editor sits across the desk from the news editor. His job is to fit the news and the illustrations into the paper. He works with a set of dummies that constitute the blueprint of today's edition. The dummies are page size in miniature. The dummy for each page shows the amount and the position of the advertisements in it and the amount and shape of the space in which news can be displayed. In the space available for news, the make-up editor dummies the slugs of the stories and the illustrations that are to be displayed there.

There is no gainsaying that the function of copy reading, news editing, and make-up is the same in all newspapers—large and small. On all these newspapers, stories are edited and headlines for them are written: someone determines how the news shall be displayed and emphasized. On all, some system determines how stories and illustrations are placed in the pages. Although the function is always the same, the processes by which these three responsibilities are discharged and the care and time devoted to them vary widely in relation to the size of the newspaper.

THE COPY DESK

There is no copy desk in many small dailies. The city editor usually does what editing is done on local stories and writes the heads for them, while the telegraph editor (or the managing editor, for the two jobs often are combined) edits the wire copy and writes the heads for it. On the smaller paper, little attention usually is paid to refining and improving the copy. The local news appears approximately as the reporter has written it, and the wire copy goes into the paper with little editing beyond the marking of paragraphs and the trimming of stories for space. This explains lack of editorial man power, not indifference, as the reason for this.

However, the process on the medium size newspaper is more detailed. The staff of the medium size paper is larger, and the duties of the members are less general and more clearly defined. Several staff members devote their time to editing the copy and writing the headlines, and each story subsequently receives greater scrutiny.

The copyreaders work on what is known as a universal desk; it is so called because all main news is edited on it. The copyreaders sit on the outer of the horseshoe and are called rim men on the medium size daily and on the average metropolitan newspaper. The Slot man is the head copyreader, or head of the desk. He sits in the slot formed by the inner rim of the desk. He calls the stories to the rim men, overseas the editing of the stories, and improves the headlines after they have been written. The universal desk similarly handles all news except sports, financial, and society news; these are edited by staff members in those departments.

Some metropolitan newspapers have practice to subdivide the copy reading process into a separate desk system. The main news copy is read on three or four separate desks. A few large metropolitan newspapers that use the separate desk system divide the work among local, telegraph, and cable copy desks. The local copy desk handles local stories, which include the news of the city, its suburbs, and the metropolitan area. The telegraph copy desk handles all news that originates outside the city editor's territory but within the boundaries of the country: this is the general practice followed in the United States. The cable copy desk handles all news that originates outside the country. News of sports, finance, and society usually is handled separately by those departments, each with its own copy desk. Other metropolitan papers split the news three ways across a local desk, a telegraph desk, and a state desk. Here the state copy desk handles news that originates outside the city editor's territory but within the state, and the telegraph desk handles national and foreign news. Thus some metropolitan papers channel the news through six copy desks—local, telegraph, state, sports, finance and society. Others divide it among other fixed desks.

In the newspapers in which the separate desk system is used, a city editor or an assistant city editor usually is slot man of the local desk, the telegraph editor is slot man of the telegraph desk and the cable editor is slot man of the cable desk. When the arrangement includes a state desk, the slot man there is the state editor.

There are other variations that occur. Some medium size papers handle their copy on two desks—a local desk and a wire desk; the latter reading copy on state, national, and foreign news. An assistant city editor might be the slot man of the local desk and the telegraph editor the slot man of the telegraph desk. In such a situation, the state editor might devote his time to editing and rewriting copy from correspondents and bureaus throughout the state, while copy readers on the telegraph desk put final touches on his copy and write the headlines for it. There is still another variation; the job of telegraph editor includes the supervision of cable news, with the telegraph editor working at one end of the horseshoe that is at the slot man's elbow. In such an arrangement, the telegraph editor puts together the telegraph news and does a rough job of copy reading it, and the final copy reading and the headline writing are done on the copy desk. Also, sometimes, the state editor, working similarly to state news, sits at the other end of the horseshoe and at the slot man's other elbow.

There are four or five copy readers in a small city daily using a universal desk. A larger paper with a universal desk might employ a dozen or more copy readers. A large metropolitan paper, publishing many editions daily and operating round the clock, might have as many as fifty.

There is one manifest advantage in having separate desk system. Each copy reader tends to become an expert in the field in which he works. Copy readers on the local desk can be expected to have a wide and accurate knowledge of the city—

its geography, its personalities, and its politics. Those on the telegraph desk are experts in national news, and those on the cable desk should be specialists in foreign affairs. The separate desk system, by dividing the work among many copy readers, makes possible the exercise of greater attention to each story, which should result in better copy reading, better headlines, and, overall, a generally improved paper.

THE NEWS EDITOR

It is universally accepted that half of the job of news editing is judging and evaluating the news minute by minute, hour by hour as it flows into the news room. The other half is displaying the news so that the completed product is an attractive, interesting, readable, informative, and coherent newspaper.

Nineteenth century has witnessed a revolution in news editing. Early newspapers were small and circumscribed by mechanical limitations. News was dumped helter skelter into their slimy pages. Little attempt was made to evaluate their content. The use of typographical devices to emphasize and to grade stories in terms of their relative importance was unknown. The burden of piecing together the pattern and the relationship of the news was placed upon the reader, who had greater patience and more leisure than the reader of today.

Take the page from newspaper of a century ago; it shows that it consists entirely of advertising. What at first elegance appears to be a news story in column four proves, upon inspection, to be an adverting prospectus for another newspaper. The page is seven columns wide and is typical of the journalism of a century ago.

Here the news is evaluated and graded. It is accented typographically in relation to what the editors consider its relative importance and interest. The page is alert and inviting. News editing is what has been done to it.

The routine activity and the magnitude of the news editor's job vary. On small papers, the chief news executive is the managing editor. He is often managing editor, city editor, copy reader, news editor, make-up editor, and editorial writer—all in one.

However, on the medium size daily, the managing editor is a supervising executive who delegates principal authority to a news editor and a city editor. The news editor's duties there resemble more closely the classic definition of his job—the editing of the news. He is the overall supervisor of the editorial production of the paper. He determines the space allotted to each main story. He determines which story is the day's best and as such merits principal play, in terms of headlines and space. He determines the appearance of page one. He decides which stories shall run on the inside pages and on which pages they shall appear. He decides, in consultation with the picture editor, the details of illustrating the paper front page, inside pages and picture page. Customarily, he draws a dummy of the front page for each edition. The dummy shows the headlines and the position of each story in the page. Depending upon the size of the newspaper, perhaps the news editor draws dummies of inside pages, showing the headline and position of each main story and each picture. Editorial make up men in the composing room supervise the placing of the type in the page in accordance with the dummies.

Do not go by the news room titles; these are, however, but approximate descriptions of the duties performed by the title holders. It happens that in one metropolitan office, the managing editor may discharge his duties from a private office and be seen or heard rarely in the news room. In another, he may work in the news room flanked by an assistant managing editor, a news editor, and a make-up editor.

Quite often, in his office, the managing editor may read in dupes or original copy of proofs each main story for each edition. Instead of the news editor, he may draw the page one dummy of each edition, specifying the place of the main stories; he may also designate the filler items he selects for the page. He, along with the news editor and the picture editor, may examine each photograph and select pictures for page one, for the inside pages, and for the picture page. His principal assistant, the assistant managing editor, may perform the duties of city editor, aided by day and night assistant city editors.

In this manner, the news editor may be a liaison man among managing editor, city editor, telegraph editor, cable editor and picture editor. Instead of bearing detailed and original responsibility for the contents of the paper, the news editor here is a back-stopper for the managing editor. He confers with the managing editor and with subordinate editors in executing the managing editor's instructions. He confers with the managing editor on details of illustrating the paper. He arbitrates jurisdictional disputes. He does not, however, dummy the paper. That job is done by the make-up editor, who works at the news editor's elbow.

THE MAKE-UP EDITOR

The title, make-up editor, is unimportant. The executive whose responsibility is the detailed assembling of the paper may or may not determine the page one play, but he does dummy the inside of the paper. He may be the news editor of the medium-size paper or the make-up editor of the metropolitan paper.

Front-page play having been determined, the make-up editor dummies the inside pages. He works from a schedule that lists all the news on hand for the edition. The schedule shows the slug and the length of each main story. Working with dummies showing the space available for news, and with the schedule, the make-up editor dummies the news and pictures into the paper. He classifies the news, dummy-related stories together throughout the paper. He dresses the pages with picture and other illustrations. He groups together stories and related pictures.

Dummies leave his desk to go to the composing room. Here, the type is placed in the pages. The process is repeated for each edition throughout the day. Changes are made on page one and on inside pages as the news changes and as stories grow or diminish in importance. Content and appearance sometimes changes considerably between first edition and final edition.

CHAPTER

18

Newspaper and Magazine Page Make-up

THE FUNCTIONS OF MAKE-UP

Make-up is the typographical arrangement by which a newspaper displays its contents. Appearance and readability are determined by it. Make-up, moreover, is a manifestation of a newspaper's personality.

First Impressions

A prospective reader's first and often lasting impression of a newspaper is derived from make-up. Between some papers, there exists the difference that is apparent between a cultivated gentleman and a raucous fishwife. Some papers are quiet and dignified. Some are stately. Some are dull. Some are strident. Some are alert, lively, and human, yet poised and mature. Make-up to a large extent is what does it.

Appearance, and thus make-up evokes an immediate visual reaction from the reader. A crisp page invites the conclusion that the paper recognizes the news, discerns which of it is important, which is interesting, and which is inconsequential. Its orderliness inspires confidence in its contents. A cluttered, disorderly page discourages reading. Slipshod, unattractive appearance arouses suspicion that the contents have been prepared with similar unconcern.

An unfavourable first impression may well be erroneous but the impression, once made, is likely to persist. Judgments of content and policy are secondary, in the first impression judgment of the interior personality of a newspaper is an intellectual process derived from closer acquaintance, although some clue to the character usually is apparent from the paper's typography. Some papers, because of their staid and subdued make-up, are looked upon as conservative.

Two factors determine the first impression. They are : (1) the size and the arrangement of the headlines, and (2) the manner in which headlines, body type, and picture and other devices of illustrations are integrated in the page.

Grading the News

Within the framework of a dignified yet vigorous and readable appearance, the most important function of make-up is the grading of the news. A newspaper stands or fails, ultimately, through its judgment and treatment of news.

On the average day, one story stands out in the news editor's judgment as the No. 1 story, the day's biggest. Throughout the day, several stories might compete with one another for the No. 1 position. Examination and weighting of stories against one another result in the rapid elimination of many as contenders for No. 1 play. Moreover, a last minute development sometimes moves a hitherto weak contender into the No. 1 position; another development may reduce a potential No. 1 story to its subordinate position.

Although the news editor never reduces it to an arithmetical problem, the day's better stories rise to the top and the weaker ones sink to the bottom. Some day's when the news contains but one story of commanding interest, the choice is simple. Other days bring several stories which, had they occurred on separate days, would each have commanded no. 1 position. This day these stories might be played equally.

Or, with three or four stories of approximately equal value, the editor's preference or the newspaper's policy determines which is played in the No. 1 position.

Typographical emphasis enables the editor to establish a variety of story grades within a page.

Make-up v. Design: Newspaper personnel use the "design" in three different ways:

> In one sense, this term means the basic format of the entire newspaper. It is its lay-out. The format of a newspaper is fixed and is rarely changed. In another sense, this term, design, means the structure or arrangement of news on an individual page or the page design. A page design is the way the elements on a page—headlines, datelines, by lines and other credit lines, body text, column rules, boxes, etc. are arranged. Newspaper design or make-up personnel try to maintain consistency of individual page design within the overall design (format) of the newspapers. A third meaning of the term design is to plan or conceive the total structure or arrangement of a page.

The term 'page make-up' simply means arranging the various elements one a page. Thus make-up or arranging the elements is a part of the designing process. But both the terms, make-up and design, are used inter-changeably by most newspaper people. However, designing means planning the page, giving proper importance to the stories and other elements, and arranging them in a particular format or pattern. Page make-up, on the other hand, means merely filling the space on a page by putting the stories on it.

Most newspapers opt for page make-up as they are always under the pressure of a deadline. Thus there is no control over how the page would look finally. However, when newspaper pages are designed, the designer has mental picture of the entire page and has a number of alternative make-up patterns. The designer chooses the alternative that best suits the contents of the news.

Objectives of Newspaper Page Make-up

A Newspaper is a collection of many news stories, features, articles, editorials, pictures etc. When these are haphazardly arranged, it becomes confusing and difficult for the readers. So, the primary objective of newspaper make-up is arranging news in an orderly manner and making it convenient to reader. Secondly, make-up should also try and create a distinct personality for the newspaper. Thirdly, newspaper make-up should be more exciting to the reader. This is because the newspaper is competing with other media that are highly visual, dramatic and attractive.

So, the newspaper make-up people should create an attractive and interesting design that brings out the inherent drama of the stories and the newspaper can compete with other mass media.

Principles of Design Applied to Newspapers

Designing a newspaper page is a graphic art form. It involves certain principles of graphic designing. These principles are: *Balance, Contrasts, Proportion and Unity.*

Balance means equilibrium or a state of rest. It deals with the visual weight of the various elements of a newspaper page like the news stories, visuals, etc. Balance in newspaper means that the pages should not be top heavy, bottom heavy or side heavy, etc. it means that the pages should not be extremely heavy in any one section and extremely light in another.

The things that make a page heavy are headlines, visuals, and the size of the stories, the use of boxes and screens, use of bold text, etc. Balance in newspaper design is achieved by visually weighting the elements on both sides of a page. It does not require precise mathematical weighting. A properly balanced page has all the elements (headlines, pictures, etc.) so distributed as to give a pleasant look to the entire page.

Formal or symmetrical balance involves placing equal sized objects on either side of a page to form a mirror image. This kind of a design may be unbalanced from top to bottom. So, most newspapers use the informal balance. Here, the two sides and the top and bottom halves are not mirror images of each other, but there is a feeling of equilibrium.

Contrast in designing means the use of two or more elements that are dramatically different from each other. This difference could be in size, shape, shade, colour, etc. So, a headline set in lighter types is in contrast with a bold headline. A bigger picture contrasts smaller pictures. And black and white is in contrast with colour.

Contrast helps is highlighting certain elements. For example, a picture surrounded by body text would stand out on the page. The ultimate objective of contrast is to achieve a pleasant look for the newspaper page. However, too much of contrast makes a page unattractive and harsh.

Proportion is the principle of comparative relationships in terms of length, size, shape, etc. For example, a square shape is rarely used in designing as it is dull and uninteresting. It is also monotonous as all the sides are equal. Unequal proportions are usually more attractive than equal proportions.

Accordingly, the most widely used shape in designing is the *rectangle*. And this is the reason why the outer shape of the newspapers, the shape of most news stories and the shape of all photographs are always rectangular. The most common proportions used in newspapers are the 2:3 and the 3:5 proportions.

The *principle of unity* concerns the effect that a page design has over the readers. A newspaper page should create a single impression rather than multiple impressions.

A single impression makes a page pleasant and interesting. Unity on a newspaper page can be achieved by visually weighting all the stories and pictures and then shifting the placement when a satisfactory arrangement has been found out.

Other design principles that need to be considered while designing a newspaper page are *harmony, rhythm, and direction.*

Newspaper page make-up has always been a tough task as the make-up people do not have much time for planning and they always work under the pressure of a deadline. Also, manual makeup, either through arrangement of composed material (hand composition) or the cut and paste method (photo composition) are time taking.

However, these days, page make-up has become much faster and easier because of computers. Many a software package (like the Quark Express) has been specifically created for this purpose. So, the make-up people can change the placement and arrangement by pressing a few keys.

VISUALIZING THE TOTAL PAGE STRUCTURE

Although we have discussed about the basics of newspaper page make-up yet we know that it may be difficult to visualize the structure of page. To overcome this difficulty, there are two things beginners can do. The *first* one is to take a newspaper page and draw thick block lines around each story on the page. You can see the design now. To be able to critically analyse different types of page make-up, repeat this practice for different newspapers.

The second method is to copy the design of a newspaper page on to a plain sheet of paper. First, draw very thin and light lines with the help of a pencil marking the columns. Then mark the space covered by the stories and pictures on the newspaper page on to the plain paper. Fill the complete sheet and you will have a newspaper page design. Now, collect different design styles from different newspapers for your reference. You can create new page design from these design ideas.

Guidelines for Newspaper Page Make-up

(1) Front page make-up starts by indicating the amount of space that the name of place will take. A name plate usually appears at the top centre. Some newspapers (like the *Punjab Keṣari*) have the name-plate at the top left corner of the front page. Some people call it the mast-head and some others call it the flag.

(2) Often, stories are assigned numbers. So the headline, the allotted number of the story should be put on the page in the space marked for the story.

(3) The number of columns should also be indicated (S/C for single column, 2/C or D/C for two columns, 3/C for three columns, etc.)

(4) In case of single column stories, a straight, downward pointing arrow is drawn to mark the depth or height of the story.
(5) In case of multiple column stories, a continuous arrow covering all the columns should be drawn to show where the story is continued.
(6) Carry over or jumps should be marked properly along with the page number to which the story is to be continued.
(7) Pictures, cartoons, and other visuals should be properly labelled. The most common practice is to put a large cross (X) covering the entire space to be taken by the visual.
(8) Boxed items are also properly marked by drawing rectangles and labelling them with the word 'box'.
(9) Column rules, special marks, etc. are to be used judiciously, only to distinguish columns from each other or to highlight some part of the story.

Traditional Make-up Concepts

Many newspapers have been using certain traditional page make-up practices for decades or more. The main characteristics of such traditional make-up are:

(1) Name plates are always placed at the very top of the front page.
(2) No news story is placed on top of the name plate.
(3) All stories are placed after the name plate.
(4) Bigger headlines are placed at the top with smaller ones placed below.
(5) The most important story is placed at the left hand top corner of the front page. In the western newspapers, the most important story is paced at the right hand top corner.
(6) Date-lines are placed at the beginning of the story. Date-lines are often composed in the same type face and type size as in case of the news stories in traditional make-up.
(7) Mostly, a large picture or illustration is used singly at the top of the page. When more visuals are used,

they are also placed in the top half of the page. Newspaper designs using the traditional make-up practices usually are gray in the bottom half with no picture.

(8) Inside pages also have pictures placed in the top half.

(9) In the traditional makeup practices, column rules are used to distinguish columns. Also, cut-off rules are used to mark the end of stories and thus separate them.

(10) Traditional make-up practitioners use formal balance where the left and right sides are balanced. Thus the pages often are top heavy.

Contemporary Make-up Concepts

For many years, newspapers used traditional make-up practices. However, with changing times and changes in tastes of people and changing designing practices, modern design concepts are being adopted by many newspapers. Another major reason was the new technologies of newspaper production, particularly better printing technologies and the use of computers.

Three basic modern make-up concepts are being used by newspapers these days. These are: *Modular, Grid and Total Page Design.*

Modular Make-up: This concept is the oldest among contemporary approaches. Here, the stories are arranged in modules. Stories of similar type are grouped together into separate units or modules. A module could have a single story also.

Often, the module is enclosed in a box or a lot of white space is used around each module to separate one module from others.

A module clearly separates the story or group of stories inside it from others. This way, the entire page in divided into a number of modules. Each module can hold one, two, or more number of stories. Another benefit of the module system is that it is relatively easy to change the stories inside a module, as required in case of late breaking stories.

The modular concept is easy to implement as it can fit into any style of make-up. The modules are usually marked on the outside with one, two-or three point thick lines. Use of white space around modules makes them more attractive.

The grid concept is an extension of the modular concept. A grid is a pattern of intersecting lines forming rectangles of various sizes and shapes. In a newspaper, the column space (space separating columns) and the spaces separating stories (at the top and the bottom) are used to form the grids.

Grid lines are used to divide a newspaper page into very clear-cut portions. Stories are usually composed into either vertical or horizontal shapes. The division of space on a page is always unequal both sideways and vertically. This gives a contemporary look to the page as opposed to the traditional and formally balanced page. Here, the placement of stories is on the basis of their importance. Thus each story gets a chance of being seen.

The total page concept, like the previous two also divides the pages into the different rectangular portions. But it is much more exciting as it involves dramatization of content presentation. This overcomes the basic problem of the grid concept which the mostly dull.

Although dramatization is one of the most important features of the total page concept (TPC), these days the news stories decide the format. Spectacular or dramatic news stories demand dramatic presentation, while sober news stories demand sober treatment. In total page concept, the page is divided into broad portions that are pleasingly proportional.

Only rectangles are used here. Rectangles of various sizes, shapes, weights (shadowed or screened) provide the required differentiation for an attractive total design. TPC does not use odd shapes. It also does not use critical devices like stories shaped round, oval, triangular, etc.

However, TPC uses a lot of white space to enable the different stories to breathe without competing with each other for attention as happens in case of a cluttered design. Another attention getting device is the use of large stories and photographs for dramatic impact.

The Mixed Concept : Many newspapers today are adopting a mixed approach. They combine the best elements of the grid concept, the modular concept and the total page concept. This gives them complete flexibility in terms of arrangement of stories and visuals on the paper.

Traditional make-up practices and their evaluation: Most newspapers are now slowly changing their old and the so called established principles of make-up. One of the rules is that which has changed the use of capital letters to set headlines. Research has proved that lines set in lower case are much easier to read than uppercase letters.

Another such old rule was that the most important sorties on a page should be placed at the top. Newspaper make-up in the early days was over-simplified to help readers find the most important stories by putting them at the top. This kind of placement of stories, however, leads to the belief that stories placed at the bottom are unimportant.

Now newspaper people want the readers to read the entire page. The importance of the stories is not to be judged by the placement or position, but from the size of the story, the size of the head lines, and the treatment given to the story (*boxes, screens,* etc.)

Another point of contention is the placement of the name plate of the newspapers. Some newspaper people went to place other important matter at the top and move the name plate else where. However, the nameplate has got strong connotations and associations. And the best place for the nameplate is at the top. Also, placing of the nameplate at any other place could complicate the entire make-up process.

However, on very rare occasions, when there is *an all important story* and it demands complete prominence, then it may be *placed above the name plate.*

Some newspapers eliminate the *ear panels* and put the name plate on the top left corner. As far as headlines are concerned, the traditional make-up practitioners thought of headlines as large display type faces placed at the top of the story. However, in the modern practice, particularly with horizontal rectangular stories, the headlines may be placed at the left or right of the story. This gives a modern and contemporary look to the page.

Other contemporary make-up practices also include *elimination of column rules* and the use of white space to separate or distinguish columns. Also eliminated are cut-off rules that were used to separate stories at the top and bottom. The use of such rules (lines) makes the already gray pages even darker. *Use of white space,* instead of these lines, brings "light" to the pages and makes the pages much more inviting with less of black.

Another modern practice is the *reducing of the number of columns* on a page. In India, newspapers like 'The Hindu' and the 'Jansatta (Hindi)' use six columns on a page instead of the traditional eight columns. Some western newspapers use only four columns.

Also, *headlines are no more centred; they are "flush left"*. This gives a free form appearance to the page. Similar is the case of body text, which again is set flush left and dragged right just like in case of manual type writing.

Another feature of modern make-up is the *extensive use of sub-headlines*. Sub-headlines break the monotony of the gray mass of body text.

Modern make-up practices have also eliminated ear panels. Set inside boxes, the ear panels always attract attention to themselves and distract readers from the news stories. An important development in modern make-up is the dramatic treatment of pictures, and the use of larger pictures. This adds to the look of the paper. Also, the *shape of the pictures* used these days is *usually vertical or horizontal* and rarely square shaped.

Front Page Make-up

In the past, front page make-up was old-fashioned, artificial, unattractive and inflexible. The reasons behind this were unplanned and hap-hazard placement of stories and photos, and non-adherence to any design principle. *Modern front page make-up is highly functional, attractive and very flexible.*

The front page is the showcase of a newspaper. Thus it should be easy to read, attractive and inviting. It should be orderly. And it should have a distinctive personality of its own.

One way of getting a well-designed front page is to use the principle of *artistic dominance*. Front pages, being showcases, carry a lot of important stories, which compete with each other for attention. This kind of situation is often confusing for the reader. So, the front page has to have a posing of dominance. It could be a story with accompanying picture, or a group of similar stories clubbed together.

Dominance can be achieved by way of *size, shape, and placement,* etc. In India, the traditional method of front page make-up is to place the most important story in the top-left corner followed by the second important story in the top right corner. The most important place was the bottom left or hanger story followed by the bottom right corner, which often was taken up by an advertisement. This is referred to as the *Z-pattern.* In the West, the traditional pattern C-shaped and the places in order of importance are top right, top left, bottom left and bottom right. *Both the Z and C-patterns produce top heavy front pages.*

Now, the ordering of stories on the front page is not on the basis of position on the page, but on the basis of size and other treatments (boxed, encircled by white space or dominant shape). And stories can be placed anywhere and the readers can find them easily and there is no need to follow the Z or C-pattern.

Other guidelines for an exiting and more readable front page include:

- Creation of an open page with lot of white space between columns, between stories, pictures, etc.
- Using a news summary rather than having many small stories on the front pages.
- Making the bottom half as interesting as the top half by using larger pictures, boxed stories, etc.
- Avoiding too many boxes, lines and other attention getting devices (like asterix marks, screens, etc.) that put the readers away from the stories.
- Using cleaner, easy to red type faces.
- Incorporating a sense of freshness and vitality to the page by making small changes to the basic format on different days.

- Creating an elegant but different look by having columns of different widths, use of simpler and uncongested nameplate.

Inside Page Make-up

Inside pages almost always have advertisements. As ads bring revenue, they are given priority above news. In fact, it is the ads that are first placed on the pages. The remaining space or the 'news hold' is left for the editorial matter. As the number of and total space taken by advertisements each day are different, make-up personnel have to deal with different amounts of space everyday. This makes the job of page make-up personnel very difficult.

The designer of inside pages thus has to deal with two things:

(a) The editorial content, and
(b) The structural position of advertisements. Inside pages cover a variety of content. And the editorial content decides the design pattern within the available space. One of the techniques adopted for inside page make-up is creating of a Center of Visual Impact (CVI) which is usually the most important item on a page. The other stories are arranged around this centre of visual impacting in accordance with their editorial significance.

The structural position of advertisements also needs to be considered for bringing about a harmonious blend between the adverting and editorial content.

Advertising Placement

Often, the make-up personnel have no or little control over the placement of advertisements. But it is wise to consult with the advertising department and suggest about advertising placement on the pages in such a way that allows proper designing of editorial content on these pages. The usual ad placement formats include the pyramid and the double pyramid.

Pyramid Style (Step Style)

When ads are placed in the pyramid style or the double pyramid style, lay-out of editorial content becomes a little easier. Otherwise, when half the page is filled with ads or they have been placed in a haphazard way, page make-up becomes much more difficult.

Some techniques that brighten the inside page include boxing of stories, use of photographs and other illustrations, etc.

Make-up of Editorial Page

The editorial page is often shabbily made-up. But 'life' can be injected into editorial page which is otherwise sober and serious content-wise. The techniques of brightening editorial page include:

- Setting the editorials in large types than ordinary body type used for news.
- Setting editorials in wider columns.
- Boxing editorials and other stories or articles on this page.
- Use of more white space.
- Placing the mast-head at a lower position (removing it from the top left corner where it does not compete for attention with the editorials).
- Using photographs on the additional page. This may be not a traditional practice but it would enhance the 'look' of page.
- Use of flush left and right ragged style of setting to make it distinct from other pages.

But the problem with an editorial page is that it remains the same always. Being rigid in structure, it never varies on a day-to-day basis. So, it looks boring. However, make-up personnel can plan three or four slightly different alternatives for the editorial page to be used on different days which will remove the monotony.

Make-up of the Sports Page

With the variety of photographs, we expect the make-up

of sports pages to be exciting. But this is not the case. This is because the large number of sports stories often create problem for the make-up people.

The best solution here is the grid concept. Use of photographs in large sizes and with careful cropping can enhance the look of the sports pages. But smaller photos cluttered together make a page look unattractive and repulsive. Also, sports photos can be cropped to exciting shapes and enlarged to emphatic sizes.

Life style and feature pages: These pages strike a balance between serious and exciting topics, hard news and soft news, and always try to involve the readers. Such pages also serve the 'scanners' well by having a lot of quotes, sub-heads, boxes and also by breaking stories into small segments.

The key to successful *feature page designing* include the following steps:

- Stop the readers,
- Sustain their interest, and
- Surprise them.

Doing all the three things every day of the week is difficult. But still the designers try to achieve this by using certain techniques. The first such technique is the *Centre of Visual Impact (CVI)*. This could be text matter in dominant position with a large or prominent photograph or an illustration.

This CVI holds the attention and sustains it. Other techniques include use of modules, use of wider column, use of informational graphics, use of colour, etc.

Make-up of Tabloid Newspapers

A tabloid is half the size of regular newspapers (broadsheet). Many small newspapers (mostly avengers) are brought out in this size. Many publishers, particularly in the western counties, are bringing out tabloids because of the maintainability (ease of handling), design possibilities (can be experimented with many patterns and designs), advertising potential (people buy more full page ads in tabloid, and departmentalizing (separating news and features into separate segments).

Tabloids use more design strategies than regular broadsheet newspapers. One of these is the use of lesser number of columns (three, four or five) while four column-pages are most readable and most attractive, still people use three (for special pages where full page treatment is required) or five columns.

Style-wise, the tabloids fall in between newspapers or magazines. Most tabloids adopt a mixed style by having formats of both newspapers and magazine for news and features pages, respectively. Often, the tabloids use the centre pages (called the center-spread) to create what is called the double truck. Some use it for showing the most important feature while others use it for advertisements.

Recent Changes

Newspapers started to experiment more with typography and design only in the 1960s. This trend, however, caught up in India only in the 1980s. Slowly, the newspapers started experimenting with new styles: smaller headlines, larger photographs, etc. As a result of the better designing practices, today one rarely sees a newspaper in which the pages are unbalanced, types are mixed up and stories and articles are lost in a mass of grey types. Most news papers today have clean, orderly and organized pages.

Let us see what makes a newspaper attractive visually. It should excel in packaging the contents in an easy to find, and easy to follow style. It should offer surprises to the readers in spite of the highly formatted structure of its pages. It should combine a magazine look with the traditional newspaper-orientation.

It should mix type styles and faces in a usual manner like 'serif and sans serif' headline styles (Sans-serif type faces have no projection at the extremities like in E, T, S, etc.)

It should have informational graphics like sketches, diagrammatic representations, graphs, charts and computer generated graphs. This can sometimes make lengthy descriptions unnecessary. This also helps the scanners to make the stories short and easy to read. It should have a lot of colour. It should experiment a lot.

This is what 'USA Today' did when it was first published on September 15, 1982. This newspaper changed the whole concept of newspaper page make-up the world over. It was loved by its readers, and hated or ignored by its competitors. But 'USA Today' created a strong graphic awareness among the readers and newspaper people alike.

In India, 'The Times of India' is trying to do something like this and it has introduced colour; The personnel experiment a lot with their pages make-up. They also give more photos. And its competitors are following it.

A few years ago, newspaper paid little attention to the way they looked. Designing was not practiced. Page make-up meant putting text and visuals together on pages. Now, things have changed. Television and magazines have changed all this. Readers have become more demanding being aware of graphic sophistication. And today, the newspapers have started doing a lot to improve their look. These include the following factors:

Importance to Journalism over Artistic Decoration

Readers look for information in newspapers. So information needs to be presented in such a way that the readers' job becomes easier. A well designed newspaper presents information through a series of visual signals like headlines, text, photos, chart and graphs, maps, blurbs or summarizes at a glance.

Good design is not mere decoration. Newspaper design should emphasize on the information content as its primary goal is to communicate or express rather than impress.

Boxes, columns, headline size, colour backgrounds (screen) and other visual elements are not mere ornamentations. These help guide the reader through the maze, etc., make stories stand out by attaching significance to them. Good newspapers' design presents information in the most organized and visually appealing form.

Page Architecture

This is the internal space management of the pages. This helps in giving the pages a clearer look.

Choosing the right Illustration

Most newspapers use only photographs. However, other visuals like sketches, charts, maps, graphs, computer graphics, etc. can be more useful than just photographs.

Legibility

The information content of newspaper pages should be easy to read; designers need to choose type faces, type sizes, lines, spacing, etc. with legibility in mind.

Surprise

A well designed newspaper page stops the reader and surprises him. And this surprise could come in the form of larger photographs, dramatic use of colour, etc. Surprise on newspaper pages delight the readers and makes the routine job of reading newspapers interesting.

Newspaper page make-up has evolved from simply putting the stories and pictures together within the available space to a *highly intricate graphic art*. And the factors that have contributed to this evolution are:

(a) The changing tastes of readers.
(b) Graphic designing and the technical advancement like the advent of computers and better printing presses and processes.

Designing for the Market

"Design the newspaper for the market it serves, understand the readers: their reading habits, preference, life styles and design accordingly", was the advice of Richard A. Curtis, design editor of the 'Miami News' in 1978. Now, after more than twenty years, the advice still holds good. In fact, in today's market-driven situation, there is an urgent need to study the reading habits and design tastes of readers before choosing a make-up or design patterns.

The 'Times of India' calls itself a product and it is designed to suit the readers of today.

Simplicity in Page Make-up

Simplicity is perhaps the most important feature of

designing and make-up of newspapers today. In this regard, the KISS rule (keep it simple and short) of writing applies to make-up. A newspaper page contains a few elements like the text, the headlines, visuals, lines, boxes, colour and white space. These elements need to be integrated in such a way that it makes finding and reading the stories easier. And things like fancy type faces, tricky type setting, crowding of stories, etc. make newspaper pages more complex and slow-down reading.

Design to Communicate

The sole objective of newspapers is to communicate. Thus designing or page make-up should also have the same objective. To be able to communicate effectively, the page make-up should be developed from the content.

Magazine Make-up

Magazines are different from newspapers and other mass media in a unique way. They are considered to be much more than the sum total of their ink and paper. That is magazines are considered more than a store-house of a variety of articles, stories and features. This 'extra' factor comes from the personal relationship built between the magazine and its readers.

Both magazine editing and make-up is done towards encouraging and maintaining this relationship which is hard earned and asks a long time to be established.

Personality of a Magazine

Modern magazines exist in a visual age. They compete with the highly visual and entertaining Television. Now, the emergence of the Internet has added to this competition. And readers of today have been converted into more "viewers" who rely on images for their information and entertainment.

With everything becoming much image-oriented, we can safety modify Marshal McLuhan's statement: 'Medium is the message' into 'Image is the message'.

With readership and understanding dependent on the visual aspect of presentation, magazine editors and designers must be experts in the art of communication by means of pictures, layouts and other such means.

Illustrations in Magazines

While photographs are the most important illustrations for a magazine, there are many other factors, too. We use black and white colour for tone-photographs with different types of treatments or special effects. We also use pencil sketches, line drawings, water colours, oil painting, etc. Other illustrative devices include charts, bars, maps, graphs, etc.

Functions of Illustration

Using the illustration can have five functions. These are:

- Attracting attention.
- Illustrating a point.
- Telling a story by itself.
- Telling a story along with other illustrations.
- Giving visual relief to a design.

Any illustration usually accomplishes one or more of these purposes.

Use of Colour in Magazines

Almost everything on a magazine page—text, visuals, borders, etc. can be in colour. But colour for colours' sake is not a good practice. For example, body text in colour does not have as much of contrast as black and white body text. Certain practices in the use of colour adopted by designers include:

- Use of colour for display types (headlines, sub-heads, etc.)
- Use of colour for lines and borders separate and dramatise the stories.
- Use of colour for typographical dingbats like initial letters, stars, etc.
- Use of double-tone photos instead of black and white photos.
- Colour enhancement of graphs and charts, etc.
- Use of coloured screens.

Visual Personality for Magazine

A magazine to be successful needs to find out its target

audience and provide the content needed by the audience in the way they want it. As magazines are directed at different audiences, they should have different personalities. According to the audience it is directed at, a magazine could be conservative or traditional, modern, action-oriented, classical, fashionable, etc.

Here, the designers look for what is called the 'intensity of interest' on the part of the audience members. For technical magazines or other serious magazines, the readers want more information and less entertainment. So, the 'flashy' designs are avoided in such magazines.

In case of film magazines or fashion magazines where the readers want more of entertainment and less of information, then the magazine should be 'dynamic' in physical presentation. By blending type elements, visuals and white or coloured space, the page should be inviting.

Designing Continuing Pages

These pages are relatively constant like the cover page. These include the cover page(s), the editorial page, letters page and the pages with continuing feature columns. While these pages have fixed formats, efforts should be made to break monotony with simple changes in the make-up in different issues.

Establishing the Page Structure

A magazine may have fixed or flexible page structures; the page structure refers to the 'type page' (space inside the margins), the number of columns, the column widths, etc. Magazines usually have two, three or four columns. Many magazines today do not use a fixed number of columns for all pages or different pages. They use different number of columns. A lot of bleeding (illustrations intruding into space of text matter and *vice-versa*) is done.

Establishing Typographical Policy

The most important consideration for selecting type faces for magazines is easy reading (legibility and readability). Traditional magazines used fixed type faces and this policy provided continuity. But contemporary magazines use a wide variety of type-faces, sizes, and variations to give different looks for different stories or article.

Other practices include use of dingbats (decorative type devices like stars, bullets, and raised or drop letters).

- Determining the exact amount of space available for a story or article.
- Deciding how many columns to be used.
- Determining the space to be used for the text and the visuals, respectively.
- Designing and positioning display types for headlines, etc.
- Positioning body text and illustrations.
- Deciding what typographical devices to be used.

Earlier, make-up personnel designed through the various stages of lay-out. They drew thumb nail sketches, made roughs, created comprehensive layouts, and finally made the art-work which was ready for printing. But now computers have made the lay-out job much easier. Any kind of effect in lay-out can be created just by pressing a few keys or at the click of the mouse.

CHAPTER

19

Photo Journalism

PHOTO EDITING

Photo Journalism has become an integral part of print media. For more than one hundred years, print media have been publishing photographs. What was once revolutionary novelty has become one of the most common and indispensable elements of modern journalism. With a few exceptions, editors inquisitively look for the best photographs to illustrate dozens of stories. Their aim is to turn out newspaper or magazine pages with an attractive and effective mix of bold headlines, masses of type and eye-catching images.

While the glamorous TV is having an edge over all other media, the print media are concentrating on juicy scandals and scoops, reporting with elegant photographs for their survival.

A picture enhances the meaning of news story, feature or article. It gives the visual dimension to an event. And what is more important is that seldom or never does a picture err. Raghu Rai's photo depicting typical female anxiety on the face of the former Prime Minister, Mrs. Indira Gandhi, while she was waiting for a Russian dignitary, won applause from the readers. Raghu Rai, a well-known Indian photographer, won president's Gold Medal for outstanding photography.

Well, now the question arises as to what is actually meant by photo editing. Photo editing is an art and craft for effective communication with the help of journalistic photographs by selection, cropping, enlarging (or blowing up), reducing, sizing, retouching, reproducing, insetting, grouping, clubbing, etc. for appealing presentation.

(I) Selection

Selection of photo is an extremely vital and tough job. This is because valuable space is wasted if the picture does nothing more than depicting a scene that could be described more efficiently with words. The old slogan that one photograph speaks more than thousand words is not necessarily true always. If the picture adds nothing to the readers' understanding of a story, it should be rejected.

On the other hand, some pictures capture the emotion or flavour of a situation more vividly than words can do. In other situations, words and pictures provide perfect complements.

A creative and capable picture editor, experienced in visual communication, can provide the guidance necessary for successful use of pictures. Similarly, papers without the luxury of full-time picture editors can turn to their photographers for advice, but often the news editor or copy editor must make such a decision. When that is necessary, an appreciation for the importance of visual communication is essential for the results.

The selection procedure of a journalist photograph differs from newspaper to newspaper, some allow the photographer to make the decision, the pictures he or she submits to the desk are the only ones considered for publication. This procedure assures selection for the picture best in technical quality, but that picture may not be best to complement the story. A photo editor working closely with both the photographers and copy editors should have a better understanding of the story and be able to make the best selection.

(II) Cropping

It is the process of cutting the unwanted part of a

photograph. Earlier photographs were either totally selected or totally rejected but in the present era, some photographs are selected, but only their relevant and related parts are used and the rest is cropped.

(III) Enlarging

It is also called blowing up. Sometimes, some photographs are originally very small. But since they are very relevant and valuable, they need to be enlarged or blown up. So, it depends on the importance of the photograph and its degree of news value.

(IV) Reducing

It is the reverse of enlarging. These days, both the newspaper and magazines are running through space crisis. Thus, depending on the relevance, importance and degree of news value, some photographs are reduced. These days, even a group photograph is used in single column by reducing it.

(V) Sizing

The sizing of a picture should be preferably determined by the value of the photograph. It should not be determined by the space available. Too often, newspaper editors try to reduce a photograph to fit a space and destroy the impact of a photo in the process. Common sense should dictate that a picture of fifteen individuals will be effective if it appears as a two-column photo. More likely, such a photo will require three or even four columns of space.

Many skilful photo editors are acquainted with the fact that, when sizing photos, the biggest danger is making them too small. If the choice is between a two column photo and a three column photo, the rational photo editor opts for the larger size. Pictures can be too large, but more often they are damaged by making them too small. Another alternative may be available. Modern production techniques make it easy for an editor to publish a two and one-half column photo. Text to the side of it is simply in a wiser measure to fill the space.

Sizing of any picture is very significant job, but sizing of pictures in multi-photograph packages is especially significant.

In such packages, one photograph should dominate. These multiple pictures allow the photo editor a lot of flexibility that may not be available in a single photo situation. If a photo editor selects a photo of a harried liquor store clerk who has just been robbed and a photo of the outside of the store where the robbery occurred, he or she has only three opinions.

(1) Give equal space to the two photos. This is the least desirable option since neither picture would be dominant and consequently, neither would have eye-arresting effect.
(2) The outside shot should be made dominant and the close-up of the clerk may be given secondary position. This would work, but the dominant picture, which merely serves as a locater, would have little impact. The impact of human emotion, evident in the clerk's face, would be diminished.
(3) The facial expression should be made dominant with good sizing and the outside shot should be made as small as possible. The outside shot, standing alone, would look ridiculous if used in that size. But used in conjunction with another larger photo, it would work well.

Dramatic size contrast is an effective device to use in multi-picture packages. A photo editor trained in visual communication understands the usefulness of reversing normal sizing patterns for added impact.

(VI) Retouching

Retouching is a process of toning down or eliminating extraneous distraction within the frame. Retouching can improve some pictures. It can be accomplished with an airbrush, an instrument that applies a liquid pigment to a surface by means of compressed air. Retouching can also be done by brushing on a retouch liquid or paste or by way of retouching pencils of varying colours.

Retouching should be done so minutely and meticulously that the meaning contents of the picture are not changed. Retouching a picture to change its meanings is unethical in the same manner as changing a direct quotation to alter the meaning of a speech.

(VII) Reproduction

There are mainly four mechanical processes of reproduction. These are:

(a) Metal engraining
(b) Plastic Plates
(c) Veloxes or screened positive
(d) Windows and photo negatives.

The method to be used is directly related to the page make-up and printing technique used by the newspaper or magazine.

(VIII) Inserting

Inserting is an innovative and creative way of photo journalism. For example, there was a massacre in a village of Jehanabad, district of Bihar. The people who were killed were shown in the picture indicating where that particular village of Jehanabad district in Bihar is located. Another example of inserting is that when a debate in Parliament is going on and along with that report a picture of the Parliament is also inserted, then it is called insetting. Yet another example is that if a person is brutally murdered whose face in the picture is not identifiable, and then a clear and distinct picture of that person is inserted. This is also insetting.

(IX) Grouping

When two or three or more photographs are joined without overlapping one another, then it is called grouping.

(X) Clubbing

When two or three or more photographs are joined in such a manner that they overlap one another partially, then it is called clubbing. It is done in a very creative, imaginative and innovative way with a sense of graphics.

The photo journalist moves through four steps in handling a story.

(1) Idea generation
(2) Planning
(3) Observation
(4) Writing Captions

The photo journalist develops an idea or concept, decides on the appropriate lenses, spread and aperture and selects locations from where to shoot, decides when to shoot, and then does the darkroom work that will enhance the story.

For a feature, the photo journalist moves carefully and deliberately through these stages on a breaking news event, the thinking and the decisions come quickly, seemingly and instinctively.

More significantly, pictures can also tell a lie. Does the picture tell the whole story or only part of it? Does it distort, editorialize, mislead? Does it omit important details or include details that create an erroneous impression?

The point was raised by James Russell Wiggins, former editor of the "Washington Post" during a lecture at the University of North Dakota (reported in "Editor and Publisher", February, 22, 1969). "The camera", he said, "can be a notorious, compulsive, unashamed and mischievous liar".

To illustrate, he said, he once declined to print a photograph of President Harry Truman walking across the platform of Union Station before a backdrop formed by row of casket just shipped in from the Korean War. What that camera said was that the Korean War was "Truman's War, just what thousands of president's critics were saying".

He has also commented on the distorted portrait of policemen during civil disorders. The picture may have been representative of the action but they failed to tell what really happened in perspective and why.

If the camera does not tell the truth, skepticism about the media arises in the minds of readers. A picture may be striking and it may be narrative. But if it conveys a false or distorted impression, it would be better left unpublished.

Picture editors often can show subjective judgment in the selection of pictures. Suppose an editor has four or five pictures of a public figure. Some editors will select the picture showing the figure more favourably, others will pick one depicting him less favourably. Many of the pictures used for former President Nixon, even before his resignation, were editorialized. Pictures of two Labour leaders, John L. Lewis and George Many, invariably showed them glowering.

The cocktail glass is another picture syndrome. If the president is toasting a visiting dignitary at a state dinner, the picture doubtless will show the president holding a cocktail glass.

PHOTO CAPTION

It is the short description of photographs published in a newspaper or magazine or any other journal. If a photograph is accompanied with a story, then the job of caption writing becomes much easier. But if there is no story with the photograph, then caption needs to be written in a comprehensive way.

More importantly, a picture editor can help control the photographic image with a photo caption. The primary purpose of the caption is to get the reader to respond to the photo in the manner intended by the photographer and the picture editor.

First of all, the readers concentrate on the focal point of the picture, then glance at the other parts. Lastly, they turn to the caption to confirm what they have seen in the picture. The caption provides the answer to question of who, what, where, when, why and how, unless some of these are crystal clear in the picture.

The photo caption interprets and expands upon what the picture says to the readers. It may point out the inconspicuous but significant. It may comment on the revealing or amusing parts of the picture if these are not self-evident. The photo caption helps explain ambiguities, comments on what is not made clear in the picture and mentions what the picture fails to show if that is necessary.

The ideally suited caption is direct, brief and bright. It is a concise statement, not a news story. If the picture is accompanied by a story, the caption does not duplicate. It should, however, contain enough information to satisfy the readers who will not read the story. Ideally, the photo and its caption will induce the readers to go through the story. Normally, the photo caption with a story is limited to two or three lines. Even when the photo relates to the story, the caption should not go beyond what the photo reveals. Nor should the facts in the caption differ from those in the story.

Moreover, the caption writer must examine the cropped picture, not the original one. The caption has to confine itself to the portion of the picture the reader will see. If the caption says a woman is waving a handkerchief, the handkerchief must be in the picture.

The following are some precautionary measures for writing a caption:

(1) Use present tense to show immediacy or recency. This is especially applicable to the English language.
(2) Identify the photograph correctly. Wrong identification of a person in a picture is considered an insult to that person. Hence, double-check the photo with the caption. The wrong person pictured as "the most wanted fugitive" is sure way to invite libel.
(3) Don't comment. Don't write that the girl is beautiful or ugly. But if she is smiling then you must say as to why she is smiling.
(4) When something is crystal clear and transparent in the photograph, then it needs no caption. But if something is complicated, then it needs to be repeated even in the caption.
(5) Be specific rather than general. Don't say an old lady, just write a lady, 65, don't say a voluminous book. Just say a 1000-page book.
(6) While explaining the picture of a person, it should be written in bracket (from left) rather than (from left to right).
(7) Typography used in the photo caption should be different from body i.e., it may be bigger or smaller in point size (than the body type), bolder or differently coloured.

(8) Because the readers know you are referring to the photograph, so avoid writings like "as shown in the picture" or the picture above shows".

(9) There is a time lag between photo taking and photo publishing. So, the caption should be updated. For example, three persons were found killed after an earthquake according to photo, but later, it was found that five persons were found killed, then the caption should tell about five persons

(10) If the picture is exceptional or exclusive, then credit must be given to the photo journalist in the caption as credit line.

(11) The mood of the photo caption should match the mood of the picture. For example, if a carnage or massacre has taken place, the caption should also be written in a serious tone. Moreover, the caption for a feature photo may stress light writing.

(12) Don't editorialize. The caption should not judge whether somebody is happy or troubled.

(13) Check, cross-check and recheck the photo and the caption.

(14) The caption should describe the event as shown in the picture, not the event itself; otherwise the readers will be confused if you describe action which is not there.

(15) Caption writing differs from newspaper to newspaper. Some newspapers use one style for captions with a story and another style for captions on pictures without a story (called stand alone or no story). A picture with a story might call for one, two or three words in boldface caps to start the caption. In stand alones, a small head or catch line might be placed over the caption.

(16) News agencies and syndicates send the same photographs to different newspapers. Some papers only reset the caption supplied with the pictures. Most, if not all, such captions should be rewritten to add to the story told in the picture and to indicate some originality on thepart of the paper.

TYPES OF PHOTO CAPTIONS

Photo captions may be broadly classified under two types, i.e. functional and structural.

The functional photo caption may be classified as: (i) Null caption, (ii) Identification captio,n (iii) Mechanical caption, (iv) Commentary caption, (v) Creative caption, (vii) Cumulative caption, (vii) Explanatory caption, and (viii) Satirical caption.

The structural photo caption may be classified as: (i) Horizontal caption, and (ii) Vertical caption.

Types of Photo Caption

Functional
(1) Null caption
(2) Identification caption
(3) Mechanical caption
(4) Commentary caption
(5) Creative caption
(6) Cumulative caption
(7) Exploratory caption
(8) Satirical caption

Structural
(1) Horizontal caption
(2) Vertical caption

(i) Null Caption

When the photograph is self-explanatory and it does not require any caption, then it is called null caption. For example, many a time, a well known cricketer, Sachin Tendulkar, is shown in action, but there is no need to write who he is.

(ii) Identification Caption

When in a photo caption, the personalities or places are only identified, then it is called identification caption.

(iii) Mechanical Caption

When the photo explains hard news, then it is called mechanical caption. For example, RJD Chief Laloo Prasad meets SJD Chief Mulayam Singh Yadav.

(iv) Commentary Caption

This kind of caption is mixed with comment, opinions

and views. Such captions are generally found with news features or features or articles, etc.

(v) Creative Caption

This type of caption is written in a creative and innovative manner. This type of caption is generally found with feature or any other type of creative write-up.

(vi) Cumulative Caption

This relates to photo feature. When there is a series of pictures (and the captions of the pictures are written in the list indicating the numerical position of each picture, then that collection of caption is called cumulative caption.

(vii) Explanatory Caption

When the picture is without the story, then the picture needs details or explanation. It includes the entire background of the story very briefly so that the readers can comprehend the picture.

(viii) Satirical Caption

When the caption is full of satire and sarcasm, it is called satirical caption. This type of caption is used for features, columns, or cartoon type of pictures.

Now, as far as structural caption is concerned, it is either horizontal or vertical. Earlier, there was no concept of vertical caption. But with the advancement of information technologies and printing technologies, there has been graphical and typographical revolution. This has resulted in new experiment like vertical captions.

(1) Horizontal Caption

Horizontal caption is written in the bottom of picture. This type of caption is written in as many columns as the space taken by the photograph. This is additional style of placing the caption.

(2) Vertical Caption

This type of caption writing is a new experiment in the world of photo journalism. Here, the caption is written on the right hand side of the photograph and it runs vertical rather than running horizontally. It is generally half-column matter vertically running with either one and half column picture or two and half column picture or so on.

PHOTO FEATURES

Photo is an integral part of a feature. Seldom does a feature go without a picture. Pictures enhance the liveliness of a feature. But photo feature is altogether a different aspect.

When a feature is dominated by photographs, both qualitatively and quantitatively, then it is called photo feature. In photo features, more space is occupied by pictures than by written words. It is more a visual communication. It is such a skilled art and craft that picture speaks more effectively and dominantly. Here, the presentation of visual readily establishes an immediate bond of believability and familiarity with the readers of the printed page.

Photo feature sometimes can tell a story without words. It is just one of the allied arts that newspapers employ to heighten the force of the written words. Several Indian newspapers published photo features when Mrs. Indira Gandhi died covering her life from childhood till her death. Similarly, many newspapers published photo features when princess, Diana died, covering her life from the beginning to the end with the help of photographs.

Thus photo features, though interesting presentations are few and far between. 'India Today' and 'Front Line' have a reputation of using excellent photo features. Life magazine from the US is one such international publication which is known for its photo features.

SUMMARY

- Photography gives visual dimension to story.
- A good photograph has intense thematic appeal; it arouses desirable sentiments, feelings and emotions.
- A photograph is equivalent to a thousand words.
- A picture adds flavour to story.
- Photography is both skill and art, more an art.

- Photo should be activity related.
- Photo containing bizarre incident or subject should not be published.
- While doing clipping and cropping and touching, misrepresentation should not be encouraged.
- Camera is both a hero and a villain.
- No value judgement should be given for a photo.
- Do not impinge upon privacy. Photographers followed Diana wherever she went, those photographers were charged with Papparazzi.

CHAPTER

20

The Copy Reader

The Copy Reader stands midway between the reporter and the newspaper reader. He is the last editorial worker who has an opportunity to improve a story and to detect and correct errors.

It has been said that no matter what recondite bit of knowledge is tucked away in a copy reader's mind, a day will come when he will use it on a copy desk. By the same token, no matter what question may arise in the editing of the day's news, someone on the rim probably will know the answer. Perfection, therefore, would require that the copy reader knows everything about everything. At the least, he must have a wide range of information, general and specific.

He must know the city in which he works its history, its streets, its business and political leaders, its social, economy, and political problems. He must know his state, its geography, its sectional inters, and its politics. He must know Washington and the nation, the problems of Capitol Hill and the White House, legislation and legislators, and contemporary fiscal and social problems. In Indian context, the knowledge about President's office, Prime Minister's office, Lok Sabha, Rajya Sabha, State Legislature, Constitutional provisions, etc.

He must know the world at large-nations, statesmen, the conflicts of interests and ideologies—the reliability of news from various national capitals, and the probabilities of contemporary history in a shifting and ever-changing picture that appears as constant flow of news which daily comes under his pencil.

On all these fronts, factual knowledge is not enough. He must be able to understand the news. He must be able to judge, evaluate, and interpret local, National, and international news. Editing is a process of selection, and the choice of facts and emphasis is a matter of understanding.

Whatever nose for news may be, the copy reader should have it. He should know how the newspaper gathers news, how the reporter covers a story. The operation of the news beats, the flow of copy in the office, the practices and demands of the city desk and the news desk. He should be able to write a news story, because he is called upon to judge a story when he edits or recasts it. He not only discovers the flaws, ambiguities, and inconsistencies in a story, he ably remedies the defects by editing or rewriting. This demands the news judgment that enables him to take a story apart and reconstruct it so that it becomes a better story. In addition, he must have news judgment that enables him to reduce the salient facts of a story to five or six words that will form an arresting and accurate headline.

He must have a contemporary mind. He must be interested in the flow of current affairs. He must read widely in newspapers, magazines and books. He must know contemporary culture, the novels and plays, the latest song hits, the current slang and wisecracks.

He must have a critical faculty. A lazy or supine mind will permit errors to go unchallenged. Figure in a story, dates, spelling of names, ever assertion of fact or logical relationship puts the copy reader on guard against possible error. For this task, he must have an alert, logical and factual mind.

Words are the copy reader's tools. He must know grammar. He must have a ready command of language and be able to use words precisely. He must have an ear for words and be able to detect, while reading an awkward phrase or sentence that might confuse the reader.

He must be able to work quickly, frequently under the pressure of editing a story minutes before deadline. He must be able to make fast and accurate decisions about the emphasis and details of a story.

He must have zest for his job and a capacity for work. An eight hour stint on the copy desk is mentally and physically fatiguing, and no copy reader does his work well unless he finds it interesting and challenging. The best copy readers satisfy a personal pride in improving a story, in transforming cliché into a sparkling phrase, in writing a headline that summarizes a story dramatically. There are no 'by lines' for the copy reader, his only satisfaction is a job well done.

Given these traits of interest and personality, what does a copy reader do? He edits copy. He watches for factual errors and corrects them. Responsibility for everything in the story is his.

He guards against contradictions and edits the story to eliminate them.

He corrects errors in punctuation, grammar, spelling, figures, names, designations and addresses.

He makes the story conform to the paper's style. He condenses the story, making one word do the work of five, making one sentence express the facts contained in a paragraph. He trims the story to the space ordered by the slot man.

He guards against libel, double meaning, and bad taste. He dresses up the story with typographical devices, such as sub-heads, bold face, indent paragraphs, initial letters, and other forms used to add attractiveness to the newspaper. He writes the headline for the story.

On some newspapers, he writes the captions for pictures relating to the stories he has edited. After the edition has gone to press, he reads his stories in the paper as a further protection against error. The copy reader bears a large share of responsibility for the production of the newspaper. He is held accountable for each story he has handled, because he is the last editorial worker who sees the story before it appears in print.

If the reporter has misspelled the mayor's name and if it gets into the paper, the responsibility is the copy reader's. He should have caught the error. If the reporter caused two parallel stories to intersect, the copy reader is held responsible. If a wire service identifies a Republican stalwart as a member of the Democratic Party, the mistake is that of the copy reader; he should have detected it. The copy reader is eternally surrounded by traps and pitfalls.

The most satisfying pay-off is that the rewards are many. The pay is relatively high, judging by news room standards, because editors value good copy readers. The average copy reader receives a higher salary than the average reporter. On the whole, the copy reader with 15 years' experience will find his pay higher than that of a reporter with similar length of service. Hours are more regular, because the copy reader works a specific shift, while a reporter may work irregular hours. Job opportunities on copy desks are better than average. Time was when itinerant copy readers like itinerant printer, could journey from city to city, working when and where they wished. Such openings rarely were available to reporters. While the days of the so-called tramp copy reader are past, a copy reader still can find a job more readily than a reporter.

Moreover, copy desk training is invaluable for writing. A good writer is his own best editor. Many newspapers consider that copy desk work is the best preparation for young persons entering the newspaper business, because it teaches accuracy, conciseness, and attention to detail.

The copy desk generally is the road to advancement in the newspaper office. The copy reader is more familiar with the news room's problems and policies than is the average reporter. Thus, when an opening develops for a slot man, the managing editor turns to the other men on the copy desk to fill the job. When someone is needed as make-up editor, or news editor, or assistant managing editor, the choice usually is made from among the men who have proved themselves on the copy desk.

DESK WORK

The physical tools of the copy reader are pencils, scissors, eraser, ruler, and paste pot. There are other tools, too; the common procedures and the editing symbols used in editing copy and understood by the workers in the composing room.

The copy reader must have a system to keep track of stories he has handled. The sheet on which he does this book-keeping is the copy reader's schedule. In some offices, book-keeping methods are haphazard and the copy reader keeps his records by scribbling the slug, the headline order, and the length of the story on a sheet of copy paper. Other papers provide each copy reader with a form sheet on which to keep this daily record.

This schedule shows from left to right the headline written for the story, the slug of the story, its length in column inches, the name of the reporter, the time the story was handled on the copy desk, and additional remarks concerning the story.

Copy Reader's Schedule

Name : Sh. Kushagr Sharma
Date : September, 2010

Head	*Slug*	*Amount*	*Written*	*Time*	*Remarks*
# 4	Pal	5″	Shailendra	3:50	Nil
#1	U.N.	24″	AP	4:10	Nil
#5	Blast	11″	AP	4:20	Nil
#3	Rail	10″	Stringer	4:55	Nil
#5	Boy	5″	Latika	5:12	Nil
#8	NL. UN	+6″	AP	5:50	Nil
#4	Rome	9″	AP	6:30	Nil

Measuring the length of copy is necessary in planning the newspaper. The news editor and the make-up editor must know the length of each main story. Also, when the copy reader inserts new material and is required to hold the story to its original length, he must be able to determine how much type should be trimmed from the original story.

Length is estimated in percentage of a column on some newspapers. Thus, 100% represents a column, 75% three quarters of a column and 50% half a column.

On other newspapers, length is estimated in column inches. A certain number of lines of typewriter or teletype copy, on the average, will fill a given number of column inches, depending upon the size in which the type is set. The following table shows how to estimate type in relation to copy.

Point Size of Type	*Lines of Copy in Column Inch*
6	6
7	5
8	4
10	3
12	2

Most newspapers use 8-point body type. Forty-eight lines of copy will make 12 inches of 8-point type. If the copy reader is told to trim one-fourth from a 48 line story, he will rim 12 lines, leaving 36 lines or nine inches of type.

COPY READER'S SYMBOLS

Uniform methods of marking copy have been developed for the editing of stories, although minor practices vary from one newspaper to another. For example, #, and still others use three diagonal lines///. Some papers use I, as a paragraph mark, others use I__ and still others use ___I in editing copy.

These symbols are aids to the typesetter and must be used carefully. Copy that is carelessly marked invites typographical errors because it makes the typesetting difficult. Copy that is carefully marked speeds the job of getting to press.

The careful copy reader blots out or eradicates a word or a phrase. He draws a line through it. Perhaps, he will change his mind and wish to restore it. He can restore it by marking the deleted part stet (from the Latin for let it stand), or by placing dots under it. Most copy readers, however, use neither stet nor the dots. Art gum can be used to erase deletions when the copy reader decides to restore part of the story.

New copy readers should resist the temptation to transpose words, sentences or paragraphs vertically within the copy. Most copy is cut in the composing room by a copy cutter. If the copy reader tries to move a paragraph higher in case of a paragraph that is to be moved, the marking will be lost when the copy cutter cuts the story. Such transpositions should be made by cutting out the paragraph and pasting it into the story where it is intended to go. For the same reason, editing a story by writing vertically in the margins causes trouble.

Proof Reader's Symbols

Copy-reading symbols should not be confused with proof-reading symbols. Some of the marks are similar, but for the most part, the copy reader's marks are made internally in the copy and the proof reader's are both internal and in the margin.

Using of Symbols

We can see how copy reading symbols are used by examining a typical piece of copy.

Confusing Marks

Marks that are likely to confuse or delay the typesetter must be avoided in editing a story. The paragraph mark should be placed where the paragraph starts in the copy.

Dressing the Copy

A variety of typographical devices is used to dress copy to give stories emphasis and readability. The average newspaper column is two inches wide; a solid mass of type crammed into the column is gray and monotonous.

Among devices that lend variety are sub-heads, bold face indents, initial letters, asterisk, dashes and dingbats, multicolumn leads, boxes and freaks, boxed precedes, and indent cuts.

The Sub-head

The sub-head is a minor headline placed at relatively uniform interval in the body of the story. It dresses the type by relieving the monotony, and it summarizes subsidiary angles in the story. The common form is one line of body type set bold face and centred between the column rules. As the copy is edited, the sub-heads are checked, too.

These sub-heads are written between paragraphs at the points where they should appear in type. They are marked with brackets to indicate they should be centred in the column and are slugged sub for sub-head.

Style on sub-heads varies. Many newspapers use the bold face centred line, in caps and lower case. Others set sub-heads centred in caps. Still others, set them flush to the left side of the column in caps and lower case, or in caps. Also, they are marked in various ways, depending on office practice.

CHAPTER

21

Improving the Story

THE LEAD

Take it seriously that copy reading calls for the exercise of news judgment in all phases of the editing of a story. The lead is subjected to particular scrutiny, in part because it sets the tone of the story and in part because the copy reader usually extracts the headline angle from it.

An inverted pyramid form, which makes it possible to present the facts with their greatest impact, has been developed for the structure of the news story. This consists of a lead that summarizes or keys the story and a body of block paragraphs arranged in the order of their importance. The inverted pyramid form: (1) summarizes the story quickly, (2) facilitates the reading of the paper, and (3) in making up the paper, it makes it possible to trim the story from the bottom. Essential fact and detail, however, must be placed sufficiently high so that no important angles will be lost if the story is trimmed.

A good lead is as clear as a picture. It commands attention. It answers some or all of the five W's and the H—who, what, where, when, why and how.

THE BURIED LEAD

Interesting and important angles sometimes are buried in the story as a result of mistaken news judgment, and the lead is based on a perfunctory fact. An example is given below:

> Police today searched for chandroo satpute, 25, after two confessed robbers named him as their accomplice.

Some papers bar such a lead, because better material usually is buried in the story. Moreover, 'Police today searched' wastes words, because police search for many persons every day.

Another buried lead is given below:

> Technical pleas of innocence were entered today for two ex-convicts arraigned in criminal court in the slaying of austrian tourists. mr. justice shamsher singh continued the hearing. . .

Buried in the fourth paragraph is the sentence:

> Prosecutor balbir singh told judge shamsher singh that the state would seek the death penalty, he declared ....

That is a better news peg for the story, and the lead should be recast to emphasise it.

THE CROWDED LEAD

The old rule evolved by practice in the Print Media was that the lead must summarize all the facts of the story. This, however, often resulted in a long, complicated lead, difficult to read and difficult to assimilate.

Today's lead more often is a news peg lead, based on key facts or the essence of the story. Secondary elements such as authority, identification, and background often are relegated to the second and third paragraphs. A news peg lead is harder to write than a summary lead because it calls for refined news judgment and faculty for finding the precise words. Compare the following three leads:

> The country's rail roads and two operating unions today agreed to a pay increase of 30 rupees an hour for 175,000 employees.
>
> The raise, effective october 16, will add approximately inr 150 weekly to the pay checks of conductors, trainmen, yardmen, and dining car employees. it will cost the railroads an additional INR 5,56,65,000 a year.

The leads in the foregoing examples have refined the interesting and important elements of the story and accented them. Authority, identification, and background are introduced later when the lead is the news peg.

The News Peg Lead

Corn and cattle solid today at all time highs for the year.

The news peg lead here has reduced a complex set of facts to a simplified generalization. It has interpreted the news in terms with which every one is familiar. Against this background, understanding of the details, even though they are complicated, is not difficult, and the potential readership of the story is expected to increase immeasurably.

THE FEATURE LEAD

Some stories demand human interest treatment. They come alive with a lead that intrigues the reader. Feature treatment, however, can be overdone. A paper in which every lead is a summary lead lacks variety.

This story would be worth one paragraph at the bottom of an inside page.

The feature lead should be short and sharp. Compare these two leads below:

> What started out to be a routine check by two west Gujarat patrolmen of a parked van in apparent trouble in

front of a grocery turned out to be a nighmarish race with the stork to mercy hospital.

The copy reader edited it to read:

Two policemen investigated a parked van today and met the stork on his way to work.

Question and Quotation Leads

Question and quotation leads are frowned upon in many news rooms because, unless they are used sparingly, the paper will appear to be studded with them. It is easy for a reporter to lift a quote from a speech or a debate and use it as the lead. Unless the quote epitomizes the story better than a paraphrase, it usually is better to avoid the quote lead. When used properly, however, the quote lead is effective:

"She said she wanted to die', and i thought i would help her.

With this explanation, Jagdeep Prasad, 42, today confessed the poison slaying of his wife, Malini, 24, he said ". . . ."

That is more effective than a paraphrase, which would be:

Kanpur husband today confessed the poison slaying of his wife, asserting she said she wanted to die and that he thought he would help her.

The question lead usually is inappropriate for a first day story, because it fails to tell what happened. A lead reading like the one below is worth scrutiny:

Who killed little shamli?

That's what police were trying to determine today. . .

It is ineffective because the newspaper reader has not been informed that Little Shamli has been slain.

The Negative Lead

The negative lead must be avoided, even though at first glance, the story may appear to lack positive facts.

Negative Lead

Police said today that details of plans for handling traffic during the republic day celebrations have not yet been worked out. mr K.C. Angiras, senior superintendent of police, head of the traffic detail, said, however, that the Parliament Street and Minto Bridge will be closed to traffic to avoid a tie-up Tuesday during the parade.

Improved

The Parliament Street and Minto Bridge will be closed to vehicles to avoid a traffic tieup Tuesday during the republic day parade.

Backing into the Lead

Sometime, a story is written in periodic sentences that place the important element at the end, instead of the beginning of the lead. Leads beginning "there is, at a meeting of, or according to" put secondary element first.

Backed Into

With the declaration that "it looks as if the doors are closed on future industries coming to dera bassi", bakshi tota singh of the sixth ward today asked that a meeting of the mayor, the corporation counsel, and members of the city council be held in the near future to consider the city's going into the building business.

Improved

A proposal to put the city into the building business was made today by tota singh of the sixth ward.

"It looks as if the doors are closed on future industries coming here", he said.

The Time Element

The time element should be spotted as close as possible to

the principal verb in the lead, to prevent confusion and to add impact to the phrasing.

The following lead is confusing because the time element is misplaced:

> A salior who was drowned when a plane plunged into the sutlej river yesterday was identified by the sixth naval district as sham lal chauhan today.

Confusion arises from the sequence 'yesterday' was identified. Did the plane plunge into the river yesterday, or was the sailor identified yesterday? If the time element is spotted close to the verb that describes the action, 'the drowning', the point is clear at once. The lead, then reads:

> A sailor who drowned yesterday when a plane plunged into the Satluj river was identified today by the sixth naval district as Sham Lal Chauhan.

The sentence usually will flow easier if the identification element is placed near the verb.

Identification

Identification improperly used clutters a lead. If the 'what' is more important or more dramatic, then the 'who', identification should be subordinated.

CLUTTERED

Kamala Thakur, 24, daughter of Brij Bhushan, 1234, Sector 21, Panchkula, an accountant, was stabbed to death today by a masked man while she and her girl-friend were walking in topiry park.

Improved

A-24-year old girl was stabbed to death today by a masked man while she and her girl friend were walking in topiary park in panchkula (haryana).

In the foregoing story, the 'what' is more important to the lead than the 'who', because very few of the newspaper readers can be expected to be acquainted with the girl.

When the 'who' is more important, it should be the basis of the lead.

INADEQUATE

A wealthy mohali resident was killed today when his car struck a bridge parapet on national highway four km west of burail colony.

He was Joginder Lal, 68, of 420, Phase 3B, proprietor of Bulbul Press, Magazine Publishers, the accident .....

Improved

Joginder Lal, 68, proprieter of Bulbul Press, was killed today when his car struck a bridge parapet on national highway No. 22, four km. west of bapudham colony.

Qualification

Awkward use of a qualifier weakens a lead. The following is awkward:

> New Delhi—India will spend, foreign minister, Anand Sharma, told the Lok Sabha, $ 761,594 during the next year, to maintain her information service in the united states.

It has been seen how this lead can be improved by placing the qualifier at the natural break in the sentence, and while spotting the qualifier in the position will help to put across the idea more lucidly; there is a way to do it here that is still better.

Although Anand Sharma is widely known, the fact that it was he who made the statement is not as important as the statement itself. Therefore, part of the lead can be deleted and placed elsewhere. The lead then can read:

> New Delhi—India plans to spend $ 761m, 594 during the

> next year to maintain her information service in the united states.
>
> Anand Sharma, foreign minister, today informed the Lok Sabha.

Reference and Event

Detailed reference or elaborate description of the event also weakens a lead.

> Bonn, Germany: Secretary of State, Dean Acheson, paying a state visit to the capital and government of the western german federal government, today promised "every assistance" to the state and expressed his hope that the coming talks between the allied high commission and the germans "will contribute mightily to the development and recovery of germany".

Improved

Bonn, Germany: Secretary of State, West Germany, Dean Acheson, today promised eastern Germany "every assitance" and expressed hope the coming talks at Bonn will contribute to the nation's recovery.

Acheson, on a visit to the capital of the western german federal republic, said that ......

Figures in the story

There is an erroneous notion that figures repulse newspaper readers. If the meaning of the figures is clear, they are more likely to attract readers.

Standing alone in this lead, the figure means nothing:

> The community fund drive stood at $ 56,000 today.

When the significance is explained, the figure takes on meaning:

> The community fund drive stood at $ 56,000 today, 50 per cent of the goal.

Reworking the Story

Occasionally, it is necessary for the copy reader to rework a story from stem to stem. When possible, he does it by editing and by cutting up the story and rearranging it. Sometimes, when a story cannot be refashioned in the manner, the copy reader rewrites it.

Boiling or Sweating a Story

A story is boiled by eliminating every non-essential word. Boiling often turns a weak story into a strong one.

The copy reader sometimes dealt with story that would run 50 or 75 per cent of a column and required to trim it to three paragraphs. His ability to boil it to this size, yet preserving its main angles, is a true test of his ability.

It is rare when a copy reader cannot improve a story by sweating it for words. He deletes dead wood and the verbiage, but he preserves the flavour. Boiling starts with words, then sentences, and then paragraphs. That is, the copy reader deletes words, if he can, instead of sentences and sentences instead of paragraphs.

Hopscotch

Improved organization results in a story that is otherwise hopscotch. When a story is hopscotch, it goes from one angle to a second, then back to the first, then jumps to a third, and hops back to the first, then jumps to a third, and finally hops back to the second. Such a story is difficult to assimilate. The copy reader should reorganize it so that it disposes of the first angle, goes on to the second and disposes of that, then goes on to the third, and so on.

> Kolkata India, Nov., 11: ground parties fanned out over a wide area today seeking clues to the fate of ac-54 transport plane that disappeared yesterday with a crew of six.
>
> Capt. Ashok of the search and rescue unit from air force base, Adampur, said he sent one ground party at 4:30 a.m. to investigate a report of a fire or a ridge west of there.

> Other ground parties continued the search in the area of Doaba, Punjab Capt. Ashok had another party in readiness to move northeast, where a report came from an unidentified man who said he saw a transport plane flying low and then circle out of sight yesterday he said he heard what he thought was an explosion about 15 minutes later.
>
> The plane, from kolkata field was on a routine training flight.
>
> It was while the plane was over jalandhar that it sent its last radio message. the pilot said, "i am confused" then the planes radio went dead.

The first two paragraphs are in fair shape, the copy reader decides, but the second and fourth paragraphs belong together, as do the third and sixth paragraphs.

The copy reader cuts the story with his scissors and pastes it back together to eliminate the hopscotch.

The story emerges as follows:

> Kolkata, Nov. 11: ground parties fanned out over a wide area today, seeking ac-54 transport plane that disappeared yesterday with a crew of six.
>
> Capt. Ashok of the search and rescue unit from Adampur air force base, said he sent one ground party at 4:30 am to investigate a report of a fire on a ridge west of there. he had another party in readiness to move northeast, where an unidentified man reported he saw a transport plane flying low and then circle out of sight yesterday. he said he heard what he thought was an explosion 15 minutes later.
>
> Other ground parties continued the search in the area of Doaba. it was while the plane was over woodland that it sent its last radio message.
>
> The pilot said, "I am confused", then the plane's radio went dead.
>
> The plane, from kolkata field, was on a routine training flight.

Brightening the Story

A dull story often can be brightened with a deft touch here and there, by the use of significant detail and apt choice of words.

Rewrite

Sometimes, the copy reader finds it necessary to rewrite a story. Rewrite involves all the problems of copy reading—improving, condensing, rearranging, amplifying, localizing, and adapting the story to later developments.

Use of numbered paragraphs is a common practice in rewrite in papers where stories are boiled hard.

The Round-up Story

Several related events frequently are written into one story instead of being run as separate stories. Sometimes, the copy reader can edit the stories together, but often a round-up involves a complicated job of studying and assessing the separate stories and rewriting them into one story.

Testing the Story

Here is a checklist by which the copy reader can judge the effectiveness with which he has edited a piece of copy:

- Is the story clear, and are the facts so lucid and specific that the reader will absorb them quickly?
- Is it buttoned up?
- Do you understand the story? (If not, the reader will not).
- If controversial, is it fair to both sides?
- Is it free of libel?
- Is it in good taste?
- Have all the names been checked?
- Have all the figures been checked?
- Does the story conform to office style?
- Has it been trimmed for verbiage and deadwood?
- Is it free of hopscotch?
- Is it the prescribed length?
- Did your editing improve the story?

CHAPTER

22

What Makes a Story Newsworthy

There is a key concept that is surrounding the development of a "news philosophy" and that is of newsworthiness. Given the vast number of items that compete for limited news space, while some are sometimes newsworthy, the others are not, and relatively speaking, why are some items more newsworthy than others? Indeed, these questions are broad philosophical ones which seem to underline many specific points of criticism of individual editorial decisions and policies concerning news selection.

In the Chapter of the book, "A prolegomenon for a theory of News", Joshu Halberstam attempts to take some first steps towards a philosophical understanding of the concept of "newsworthiness". Beginning with a general characterization of "news" as the report of current events, he examines three theories of newsworthiness. According to the first, news may be analyzed on a *"speech act"* model, a relativistic conception of news according to which any report of a current event counts as news and is newsworthy by virtue of its being published. On this view, the news and the newsworthy are created, not discovered, by the press through its act of publication: they are "whatever the news people say they are". Second, newsworthiness my be analyzed in terms of the *degree of importance, or significance,* of the news item in question. Third, it may be analyzed in terms of people's interests.

Halberstam, himself, provides a partial defence of a version of the third approach. In his view, the concept of newsworthiness is linked to the satisfaction of actual interests, especially those interests that we share with others, and which mark us out as members of specific communities. However, this view can be interpreted quantitatively to imply that the amount of interest in an event determines its newsworthiness. For example, on this understanding, a sports event could be more newsworthy than the discovery of a cure for diabetes, provided that more people shared an interest in the former than in the latter. As Halberstam acknowledges, such a purely quantitative approach might be amended by construing newsworthiness not in terms of actual interests but rather in terms of those interests that people ought to have. But a major difficulty he notes with the latter view is that of providing an adequate standard for identifying those interests.

According to one such standard, the interests that people ought to have are those that are important for them to have. While Halberstam dismisses the latter notion of importance, Berny Morson takes it seriously. "The significant Fact", according to Morson, ("facts become meaningful only to the extent that we recognize some significance in them", and "facts are significant to the extent that they imply consequences for people's lives". For example, the facts surrounding the neglectful treatment of the patients at the Greenview home for the mentally retarded were "meaningful" or newsworthy because they had serious consequences for the lives of residents at homes like Greenview as well as for their families.

According to Morson, the reporting of the significant facts in a manner that conveys their significance, may be a "question of art" calling forth a literary presentation, especially in cases where the content of the purported facts are human emotions. In this regard, he discusses by example some literary techniques a reporter can use in promoting an empathetic understanding of different points of view. Quoting John Dewey, he contends that "artists have always been the real purveyors of news, for it is not the outward happening in itself which is new, but the kindling by it of emotion, perception and appreciation".

One major problem with Morson's view is that his concept of "significance" is ambiguous. Halberstam queries, "is this concept to be construed in terms of the moral significance of the facts?" If so, then a murder in Broklyn would appear to be more newsworthy than the destruction of the Mona Lisa. Second, "is it the significance of the facts themselves or the significance of reporting the facts (or some combination of both) that constitutes the standard of newsworthiness?" For example, a fact, say that of a covert government operation may have significance as such but it may also have further social consequences by virtue of being promulgated by the media. Third, "how many people must an event affect before it is newsworthy?" Indeed, "are events newsworthy only for those whose lives are significantly affected by them?"

Finally, it is arguable that a relatively insignificant fact may still be newsworthy provided there is some degree of interest in it. For example, the fact that The Prime Minister, Manmohan Singh was hospitalized for a heart ailment may be newsworthy despite that it has little impact upon the lives of most people.

On the one hand, relatively insignificant fact may still have newsworthiness such as the "speech act" conception or those in terms of actual interests may, upon reflection, suggest the need for a more "objective" ground of newsworthiness (such as one in terms of consequences for people's lives). On the other hand, the attempt to articulate a standard of the latter kind itself meets with further problems such as those noted above. Perhaps an adequate understanding of newsworthiness must incorporate all three theories discussed herein.

CHAPTER

23

A Theory of News

We are often bewildered at what passes for news in the daily media. Supposedly, we recognize "real" when we see it. Defining news, however, is far more complicated than one might initially have supposed and the wide range of definitions offered by sociologists, communication theorists; and the more speculative among journalists give one additional pause.

A comprehensive theory of news must address two basic questions:

(a) What is news? and
(b) What makes some piece of news newsworthy?

The present aim, then, is to offer some beginning steps in a theory of news and, *pari passu*, to indicate the philosophical interest in constructing such a theory.

Not everything in a newspaper is news: Advertisements are not news, nor are cultural review, obituaries, T.V. listing, recipes and letters to the editor. In fact, the greatest part of most newspapers or the "news" on TV and radio is not news.

Genuine news is distinguished by a number of features but I intend to lend focus here on three?

(a) News is about events, not states of affairs.
(b) News aims at current rather than past or future events.
(c) News is the report to fan event, not the experience of an event.

These features not only help distinguish news from that which surrounds it, but also explain a number of other characteristics of news, e.g. why news rapidly becomes obsolete, why single calamities are more newsworthy than a series of smaller calamities, why no news is good news.

(a) News is about *events.* A new development entails some change in the world and at least that much metaphysical similarity is captured in the etymological relationship between "new" and "news". News is about events and facts. The existence of an intact fifth century Mayan tomb is not news but its discovery is, as is the report that S died this morning but not the fact that she is dead.

This event orientation can be turned finer still: News is nominalistic. Trends, statistics, patterns and classes of events may be sturdy entities in the inventory of the social scientist but the basic furniture of the news world is the single event. How to identify an event; establish its duration and extension are troublesome issues in the determination of news as they are in describing all events.

This emphasis on single event also illuminates that old adage "no news is good news". If we insist on being grimly pedantic about it, the maxim must be dismissed as plainly false: no news is not any news, good or bad. However, in a more expansive spirit, we had noted that if no news is good news then good news is no news and it is certainly the case that bad news rather than good news dominates our news media. The standard explanation for this is that the press trades in the sensational and tragic because people enjoy reading and hearing about other people's misfortunes (as to why they enjoy it, we are free not out to have our favourite explanatory psychological insight). This may be true but a more straight forward explanation for this tendency is that good events are infrequently reported because good events infrequency occur.

(b) News is aimed at *current events*. News quickly becomes obsolete. Many would walk a mile for this morning's edition of a newspaper but not twenty feet for yesterday's. A report of an earthquake in this paper is of interest but the same piece of "news" two days later is no longer topical.

A number of *differences between history and news* are readily apparent. History for one thing, is only about people or events that directly "impinge on the lives of people". While news too is primarily concerned with the actions of people, motives are often immaterial to a news story. In fact, news need not concern people at all. It's news when a hen in India lays three purple or blue eggs even if this occurrence has no significant consequences for anyone.

Historical narrative requires some explanatory scheme, be it a cover law model, causal or other linking structure. News reports, on the other hand, need not be explanatory.

History is about *the past* while news aims at *the present*. When in early 1990's, Russian Satellite dropped to within twenty miles of the earth's atmosphere, it was the major news story of the day, though, in retrospect, the historical importance of the incident was negligible.

News aims at the present. We are attracted to news because we seek to satisfy our desire to be informed of what transpires beyond the limited range of our immediate experience. The "latest news" is tantamount to the fastest means of delivery at our disposal. One remarkable consequence of the electronic news medium is that it has an accelerated speed of news transmission to "live converge", simultaneous with the event itself.

News becomes obsolete when it is superseded by more current developments. But like an old joke which retains the formal structure of a joke, it has a punch line. Although no punch of old news report retains the former and formal characteristics of news, these reports become historical documents but not historical writings.

(c) An event becomes news only *when it is reported*. When I watch a fire in progress, attend the super brawl or observe a robbery, I am not witnessing news but what will become news is when I recount my experience to others. Anything that happens can become the subject of news but nothing that happens is itself news.

The essential purpose of the news is not to warn, instruct or amuse but *to inform*. We may be entertained by a news feature by the media notoriously, if often more interested in entertaining than informing, but insofar as a report does provide information, it counts as news. Therefore, film clips of the day's sports events or space shots are news even though these events are dressed in graphic adornments which are not part of the news report.

I now want to consider *three promising candidates for identifying newsworthiness*. News as speech acts, news as a matter of importance, and news as a matter of interest.

NEWS AS SPEECH ACTS

The term "speech act" is borrowed from the philosophy of language; the pertinent idea is that *"saying it's so, makes it so"*. The judge pronounces you married and you are, you utter the words "I promise" in an appropriate context and thereby place yourself under an obligation. Similarly, in this view, it is useless to posit a general, objective criterion for newsworthiness. None exists. While not everything published is news on no account would we describe a crossword puzzle as news. Any published item which meets the formal conditions stipulated above counts as news and is newsworthy. *So, "News is whatever news people say it is"*.

News reports certainly create news. No country can claim a psychological victory over its enemies without the media creating the impression that it has achieved such a victory. Studies indicate that voters believe that the important issues in an election are those that receive the most coverage on television. When a crime wave is declared by the media, the public perceives itself as in the midst of one, and its response generates additional news. *The news media can unify a society and solidify that unity when it warns of foreign threats to the nation and its reference to "national spirit"*. The broadcast of official announcements provides the publicity needed for rendering a decree authoritative and binding, and media gossip assures the renown without which celebrity status withers.

According to this speech act approach, there is no news "out there" waiting to be reported rather events are transformed into news only if they meet the specific demands and practices of the news making process." "Events become news by the news perspective and not because of their objective characteristics. The news process de-contextualizes an event in order to recontextualize it within the news format. Moreover, it is argued, not only does news do more than merely report events, it does not mirror values either. In reporting, say, *a deviant event* man bites dog the news media actively defines what is deviant and what is normative. As one proponent of this "interpretative" school of journalism writes, *"news is perpetually defining and redefining, constituting and reconstituting social phenomena"*.

The news media can create news and news coverage is certainly filtered through the special machinery of the news process. Nevertheless, these observations do not in themselves solve the question of newsworthiness.

The descriptive insight of this speech act approach does not address the evaluative component inherent in the notion of newsworthiness. Even if we allow that news is whatever the media says it is, we must still ask for the grounds on which the media decide which events to report and which to ignore, which to emphasize and which to note in passing. We still need a criterion for newsworthiness.

NEWS AS A MATTER OF IMPORTANCE

The declaration of a red alert by the joint chiefs of staff is more important than the result of last night's hockey game and, therefore, more newsworthy. *What is newsworthy is what makes a difference in our lives.*

The notion of importance, however, is complicated. Should we think of importance in terms of consequences without regard to the actual public interest in those consequences? But what sort of ramifications are we to consider? Moral implications? But surely the murder of an individual anywhere in the world is morally worse than the ruination of any painting, yet no newspaper would give priority of coverage to a killing in Australia.

What is newsworthy is information, which affects people's lives and decisions. This view of newsworthiness underlines the traditional emphasis on the role of a free press in a free society; only an enlightened citizenry can make the informed decisions required in an effective democracy.

This revised interpretation of importance is also inadequate. The adoption of this criterion of importance would result in a radical alteration in the way news is presented. The discovery of an event pointing to the destruction of the planet in seven billion years was especially unworthy, while in the present approach in which importance is a function of the consequences of the revelation of the event, this discovery would hardly be newsworthy at all. While the appeal to the utility of publicity might further democratic aims, it could also sanction censorship of any material deemed harmful to the general good. An appeal to the demands of national security would not only justify quashing provocative news report but, according to this criterion, *provocative reports would be rendered newsworthy.*

In focusing on the consequences of news and disregarding the actual interests of those to whom it is directed, the essential features of newsworthiness are ignored.

News as Interest

Any event can be news and anything that happens can be of interest to someone for some reason or other. If we identify newsworthiness with interest, then any news is potentially newsworthy.

Local or specialized news is not less newsworthy than global or national news but merely newsworthy to a smaller audience.

Can we define newsworthiness in purely quantitative terms without regard to the quality of the news? The fact that thirty per cent of Australians read only the sports pages while far fewer follow development in scientific research might seem insufficient grounds for deeming sports more newsworthy than science. To meet this objective, we might wish to base newsworthiness not on what satisfies those interests that people do have but on *what satisfies interest that people ought to have.*

Being newsworthy is *akin to being ship worthy,* a ship worthy vessel gets you where you want to go but where you want to go is your decision. Similarly, what is newsworthy is what satisfies your curiosity, but what you should be curious about is a different matter. The identification of newsworthiness with the satisfaction of interest becomes clearer when one considers why people followed the news in the first place.

Keeping up with the news serves to establish an ongoing sense of belonging to the community, and connecting to the world around us. To think of the news only as a source of needed information is to miss the crucial role that news plays in our lives.

Granted, what we learn from the news is of lesser consequences than what we learn from studying "deep theories of science" or great works of literature, but education is not the sole, nor even the main, purpose of news.

The news is the focus of much of our anger, hopes, curiosity and rumination. It also provides a common set of topics about which individuals can exchange ideas and engage in *social dialogue.* On yet another level, following the news reflects and affirms our membership in a community of shared interest.

The network of our membership is composed of many interesting strands. We belong to families, friendships, cities, countries, nations, political parties, unions, and professional association. But those who follow baseball belong to the sports public; those who play chess seriously are part of the chess world, and those who frequent the theatre are part of the theater communities and they put no emphasis on political developments.

We belong to various groupings with varying degrees of intensity; correspondingly, we seek out news concerning these different communities with varying degrees of interest.

This linkage to community also underlies our greater attachment to news about present development than to facts about past events. Suppose you have the choice of learning the details about one or two earthquakes. One earthquake occurred fifty years ago, the other this morning. Suppose, furthermore, that the two earthquakes are equal in scale and damage and, suppose too, that nothing you do will have more impact on this morning's earthquake than on the earthquake of fifty years ago. Other things being equal, we can assume that you would rather hear about *today's tragedy*. For while we do not know the victims of either earthquake, today's victims are *our contemporaries* with whom we share a history.

It is precisely in these quotient pursuits that one's interests, values, and social reality are manifested. The common-place attention paid to the news is, therefore, an important expression of our commitments and concerns.

CHAPTER

24

Press-service Copy

Almost every daily newspaper is served by at least one of the major press services. These services bring news of the world, the nation, the region, and the state over telegraph wires to teletype machines in the news rooms or via the Internet. News services are:

- The Associated Press (AP), a cooperative news gathering agency owned by member newspapers.
- The United Press Association (UPA) owned by the Scripps—Howard newspapers, which sell their services to clients.
- International News Service (INS) owned by the Hearst newspapers, which also sells its services to clients.
- Reuters (PTI), many other news and news feature services, some operated by metropolitan newspapers, are also available:

PRESS SERVICES

The operation of the principal press associations is

similar, and the Associated Press, which serves the largest number of newspapers, will be used here as an example of the functioning of a wire service. The nerve center is in New York City, and AP bureaux are located throughout the United States and the rest of the world. With some exceptions, most of the news from outside the nation is sent to New York from AP foreign bureaux. From there, it is relayed to domestic bureaux in the principal cities of the country and to newspapers throughout the nation. The domestic bureaux relay news to papers in their areas and originate news that breaks in their areas and transmit it to other bureaux.

THE WIRES

News is relayed from bureau to bureau and to papers by what is known as wires. Although bureaux and newspapers are connected by means of telegraph hook-ups, the world wire is used in a somewhat different sense than that of a cable connecting, for example, New York and Chicago. In news room parlance, wire describes the kind of news that is relayed on a press-service circuit.

Four wires the A-wire, the B-wire, the D-wire, and the Sports-wire provide papers with the main news of nationwide interest. In addition, there are state wires that transmit news of interest in relatively limited geographical area. Metropolitan papers, for the most part, are the only ones that subscribe for the services of all the main wires, and many of them use also the various wires of the two other principal press associations the UP and the INS.

The A-Wire

This is the *main trunk* that relays stories to every part of the United States. It carries news considered to be of interest in all areas of the country. All the big-stories, national and international; the first breaking spot news that explodes into eight column banners is carried on this wire.

News of the general interest, no matter where it originates, is carried on the A-wire. When a big story breaks in a small town or in a remote area, it is fed into the A-wire by a bureau located nearby and is transmitted throughout the nation.

The B-Wire

This wire, also called the *regional wire,* is another main trunk that carries stories to all parts of the country. It carries the most of the stories of comparatively restricted and regional interest. Other news, for which the demand is regional, also is filed on this wire.

The D-Wire

This wire, known also as the *business wire,* transmits the world's financial news. It caries stories of business, industry, banking, and labour, news of the securities and commodities markets, and market quotations, tables, and financial statistics. There is a wide variety of this news—industrial developments, government activities affecting business, Reserve Bank's rulings, orders issued by such agencies as the inter-state commerce authority and the Central trade authority, and stories about persons prominent in business. Like the B-wire, the D-wire thus also transmits news of special interest.

The Sports-Wire

This wire, also called the *SP-wire,* transmits sports news, as its name implies. Stories filed on it cover the entire realm of sports—results of games, box scores, news of boxing and wrestling, news of auto races and horse races, and stories about persons prominent in sports. An adjunct of the sports wire is the race-wire, a special service wire that carries detailed results from race tracks starting line-ups, odds, winners and other stories of interest in this specialized field.

State Wires

The operation of a state wire can be explained by describing the one that originates in Chicago and serves Illinois, Indiana, and Wisconsin. Most of the medium size dailies in the three states depend upon this wire for their AP news.

Except for the A-wire and the B-wire, hours of operation of the other wires vary. Most metropolitan papers receive all of the wires, which transmit a total of approximately 100,000 words a day.

THE TELETYPE-MACHINE

Wire copy is received in the news room on a teletype machine. The machine prints from a moving carriage, containing letters arranged as on a typewriter, on to a roll of paper. The teletype contains no lower case letters. It prints in capital letters and in figures or symbols. To strike a figure, the teletype cooperator presses a shift key, as the key of a typewriter is shifted when a typist strikes a capital letter. Occasionally, due to malfunctioning after shifting, the teletype prints a line or more of figures instead of letters, scrambling the story. The following shows the letters and figures that are paired on the teletype keyboard and enables a copy reader to decipher lines that have been scrambled.

Teletype Letters and Symbols

A	-	J	'	S	'
B	?	K	(	T	5
C	:	L	)	U	7
D	$	M	.	V	;
E	3	N	,	W	2
F	!	O	9	X	/
G	&	P	0	Y	6
H		Q	1	Z	"
I	8	R	4		

BUST IT

Stories in the process of being filed sometimes are interrupted when news of greater urgency breaks. This is called busting a story. A story that is busted is stopped dead on the wire to make way for the new story, which usually is filed in bulletin form.

The bulletin for which a story has been busted might be followed by an ad, or the wire might return to transmission of the story that was busted.

RUNNING STORIES

Except for the few, and when there is lull in news, very few long stories are filed in one complete take. Most of the news is transmitted as running stories, meaning that the stories are filed in the form of leads followed by ads. This is because a press service provides news for many newspapers, each with its own copy deadlines. When news is filed running, several stories, in various stages of being completed, are on the wire at all times, providing coverage of the top news and lending variety regardless of deadline time.

FIRST LEADS

Press associations designate new leads in a manner different from the practice of most newsrooms. In news rooms, a lead that supersedes the opening paragraphs of a story is called a new lead. The press service, however, calls it a first lead. A first lead, in turn, is superseded with a second lead, and so on.

EDITING TO CONFORM

An additional instruction—editing to conform—appears at the close of A140. This warns the copy reader that facts in A140 duplicate some facts in the pick-up material. Duplications cannot be avoided in the filing of fast breaking stories, but the copy reader must delete them from the story. When the copy is still in hand, it can be edited to conform before being sent to the composing room. If the original story is in type, the revisions are made on a proof.

CORRECTIONS

In addition to duplications and contradictions, errors in fact occasionally creep in. When an error occurs, it is corrected.

INSERTS

The insert explains specifically where the new material can be placed in the story, telling which paragraph precedes it and which paragraphs follows it.

HOLD FOR RELEASE

Wire services frequently transmit stories on a hold-for-release basis. Sometimes, these stories are handled on the copy desk and sent to the composing room and set into type, so they can be published quickly upon release.

MARKING WIRE COPY

In editing teletype copy, the copy reader marks the letters that are to be capitalized. He doesn't, as some beginners try to do, go through the story marking down all except the letter that should be capitalized. The standard marks for capitalization, paragraphs, connectors, and bridges are used.

CHAPTER

25

The Changing Story

Stories frequently change from edition to edition throughout the day, and new leads and inserts are necessary to keep them abreast of developments.

THE CORRECTION

Corrections in a story already in type are made on its proof or a tear. The proof or tear is marked cx and the correction is written on it.

KILL AND SUB

Developments frequently necessitate killing a story and subbing it with a new one. Assume that the original story, one paragraph long, tells of a woman leaping to her death in front of a train. The story runs through the first edition, and it is subbed in the second with a story containing additional details of the death leap.

THE TRIM-DOWN

A story that has run at some length in early editions sometimes is trimmed drastically in the final edition to make room for news of greater importance.

Using a tear or proof, the copy reader prepares a mark in which he kills the paragraphs he wishes to delete and edits the remainder so it reads smoothly. He puts the slug and cx on the mark and places an end mark at the termination of the story.

A-MATTER

A-matter (*The A is for Add*) is used in handling a story when the action extends over several hours and when the climax, on which a lead will be based, is expected shortly before deadline.

A sensational murder trial commanding extensive coverage lends itself to A-matter. Assume that the socially prominent, Mrs. Mariam Hawthorn is on trial, accused of killing her husband. Today is the day for selecting the jury. The reporter covering the session writes a chronological, running account of what happened in the courtroom. It is brought to the news room by telegraph or by messenger service. The copy reader slugs it A-matter trial.

CHAPTER

26

Writing Headlines

The Headline has four functions:

(1) It captures the reader's attention.
(2) It tells the story.
(3) It grades the news, and
(4) It helps make the newspaper attractive.

TYPOGRAPHICAL PATTERNS

There are six typographical patterns in vogue:

(1) Cross lines,
(2) Step lines,
(3) Inverted Pyramids,
(4) Hanging indentions,
(5) Flush lines, and
(6) Combinations.

Headlines usually consist of two or more elements. A typical form is one consisting of a top and deck (also called a bank).

The headline consists of a three-line step-line top and a three-line inverted pyramid deck. There are many other typographical patterns.

The Cross line

The cross line is the simplest headline. It is one line of type, centred between the column rules or set flush to each side. Because the crossline is short, copy readers sometimes have difficulty telling the story in it, especially when it is used on a major story. But when the cross line is used on a minor story, it serves the purpose well.

The Step line

This is one of the most common headline forms. When it consists of two lines, one is set flush to the left and the other flush to the right. When it consists of three lines, the top line is flush left, the middle line is centred, and the bottom line is flush to the right. The three-line step line is a common form; the one consisting of four lines is relatively rare.

The Inverted Pyramid

The inverted pyramid commonly is used as a deck. It may consist of two, three, or even four lines.

The Hanging Indention

The hanging indention, also called the hanging indent, likewise, is a deck. It usually consists of three lines; although sometimes, it is four lines. And occasionally, it is five lines. It consists of top line flush left and right, with the remaining lines indented from the left. Some papers require that the last line may end flush right.

Flush lines

One type of this pattern is the flush left headline, set flush to the left column rule. The other, the flush left and flush right headline, also known as the full-line head, is set flush to both column rules.

Hunt 2 *In bingo probe*	*Drifting snow stalls autos, slows trains*

Combination

The foregoing patterns are combined in many forms, one of which is shown in the following figure. In this combination, the top is a two column, three-line stepline. The first deck is a one-line crossing. The second deck is a three-line inverted pyramid. The third deck is another one-line crossline. The fourth deck is another three-line inverted pyramid.

RED CHARGES
BY M' CARTHY
RUYLED FALSE

SENATORS SPLIT, 3-2

Democratic majority of
Subcommittee Sees
Fraud on People

ACCUSER ACIDLY ATTACKED

Budenz Testimony Minimized
Personalities Cleared
Commission sought.

Another combination: here the top is a two-column, three-line stepline, the first deck is a five-line hanging indent, the second deck is a two-line step lines, and the third deck another five-lines handing indent. Pyramids and hanging indents rarely are combined in the same head.

ELDERS LAUNCH
CRIME INQUIRY IN
DELHI SUDDENLY

Investigator Arrives Secretly,
Hearing Gets
Under Way Swiftly in
Closely guarded
CBI Courtroom

CITY REGARDED AS
GANGSTER HAVEN

Woman Operator of Hotel is First witness
Indications Are Kefauver Group is
looking into Tax Evasions.

Variation in Pattern

In addition to these patterns, unusual combinations also are used.

The rocket-head consists of a one-word, centred crossline, a second crossline, a two-line inverted pyramid, and a three-line inverted pyramid. The first three elements read into one another to express a complete idea (whence the name rocket, although today, it might be described more precisely as a "Jet" headline). Here, the first three lines, completed, read Senator Calls for Return of Mac Arthur to US As arms Aid witness. The three-line inverted pyramid expresses at second complete idea.

Another variation is the combination of three cross lines and three inverted pyramids.

(a) Variant pattern
(b) Cross lines and inverted pyramids
(c) Rocket

SAVE TWO PLANS
Reorganization of Trade
and Power Commission Upheld
by Senators.

TAFT MAY HAVE TURNED TIDE

After Five Hoover Ideas Are
Killed, Ohioan Favours
Remaining Sixteen.

A VOTE SHIFT DOES IT
Unless Action is Taken Against
Others, they go into
Effect tonight.

500 Workers out
at Masell Plant
In Wage dispute

Workers at New Egerton (Lal Imli) Mill Road plant determined to work no longer without contract. 400 leave jobs in afternoon and 100 more on night shift refuse to enter plant. Only wages remained in dispute in negotiations during last two months.	SENATOR Calls For Return Of Mac Arthur To U.S. As Arms Aid Witness. Navy Forces Commander In China Area Also Is Wanted To Testify

The third pattern is another variation. The top is three lines flush left, and the deck is nine flush left lines, only slightly larger than body type. The form and the size of type permit use of complete sentences in the phrasing of the deck.

Two other variations are the spread head and the kicker head. The spread here is a one line head, three columns side. Any head exceeding one column in width technically is a spread head (also called a broken column head) and spread heads extend to various widths across the page. Here it encompasses the body type.

The kicker, also called the whiplash, the sparkler, or the read in, is still another variation. It is the line reading Jobs as tough. They Agree. The kicker is used to exploit a colourful or epitomizing angle of a story. It can be combined with any headline pattern.

The Banner

The headline that reaches across the top of Page 1 is known variously as the banner, the streamer, the ribbon, and the line. Its spread varies. Sometimes, the banner stretches over five, six, seven, or eight columns. Sometimes, it consists of one line, similar to a crossline, sometimes it is two lines, similar to a stepline.

Some newspapers also use a secondary banner, which is a spread in type smaller than main banner. The spread of the secondary banner also varies.

The main banner and a secondary banner:. The main banner here stretches across eight columns and the secondary banner across six.

A banner requires a transitional element to take the reader to the lead of the story. This element is the read out, so named because it reads out of the banner. The read out (abbreviated R.O.) of the main banner is the headline in column 8 and that of the secondary banner is the headline in column 3.

Jump Heads

A Jump head is used when a story continues from page 1 to an inside page. Various patterns are used.

Here, five page 1 heads are shown with their corresponding jump heads. When a story is jumped, a jump line (such as which reads continued on page 4, column 3) appears at the body type of the jump.

Simplicity in Pattern

The trend in headlines is towards simplicity. Historically, with some notable exceptions, newspapers have reduced the number of decks, and many newspapers with so-called modern make-up have eliminated them. A parallel modern development is heads in caps and lower case, set flush left, instead of heads in caps, set in step-lines. The consensus is that heads in caps and lower case enhance the readability of a page.

Writing Headlines

Advocates of simplified headline typography believe that the multiple deck head wastes time, both on the copy desk and in the composing room, that it wastes space, and that it delays the reader in his perusal of the newspaper. Critics of the single deck head, on the other hand, contend that the transition from a large bold face head to the body of the story is too abrupt. Aesthetics requires it an intermediate step, in the form of a deck, between the top and the body type.

The Headline Schedule

A headline schedule is a chart that shows the headlines used by the paper. This schedule combines Tempo Roman bold, Bodoni, italics, bold, and in the 96-point banner, gothic Roman. The heads are step-lines and combinations of step-line tops with inverted pyramid decks. The schedule designates each headline by number.

Counting the Headline

The headline must fit the space. Each letter and each space must be counted carefully. A head written too tightly or too loosely is unattractive.

With most type faces, headlines can be counted as follows:

Heads set in caps:

M and W	$2^1/_2$ units
I	$^1/_2$ units
Other letters	1 unit

Heads set in caps and lower case:

Cap M and W	2 units
Cap I	½ unit
Other caps	$1^1/_2$ units
Lower case m and w	$1^1/_2$ units
Lower case f, I, I, t	½ units
Other letters	1 unit

Other elements, in both caps and lower case:

Symbols ($ % #)	1 unit
Punctuation	½ unit
Quotes	½ unit
Numeral 1	½ unit
Other numerals	1 unit
Space between words	½ unit

TRUMAN WARNS NATION	($18^1/_2$)
OF 'HARD FIGHT' AHEAD	(18)
SLATE-Patching Jobs	($17^1/_2$)
Ahead for 2 Parties	(17)

How to count a head set in caps and one set in caps and lower case. This table provides a counting system that is adequate when applied to most type faces. Some papers use type faces that require a more precise count, particularly for one column heads. These papers use a point system. For example, a lower case f might count 3 under this system, a lower case e 5, lower case w 8, and cap W 11, an example of the point system follows:

Capital Letters

A, 9; B, 7; C, 7; D, 8; E,7; F, 7; G, 8 ; H, 9; I,4; 5, J, K; 9; L, 7; M,0, N, 8, O, 8, 7; Q, 8; S, 6; T, 8; U, 8, V; V, 8, W, 11, X, 8; Y, 8; Z, 7;

Lower Case Letters

a, 6; b, 6, c, 5; d, 6; e, 5; f, 3, g, 6;, h,6; I, 3; j, 3, k, 6, I, 3, m, 9, n, 6, o, 5, p, 6, q, 6, r, 4, s, 4, t, 3, u, 6, v, 6, w, 8, x, 6, y, 6, z, 5

Space between words, 3; punctuation, 3; figures, 7; except numeral 1, which counts 3.

Counting by the point system consumes more time than counting by the unit system, but the method is valuable when the count is tight.

Trim Orders

Stories are trimmed to fit the needs of the paper and the exigencies of the news. A small headline is used on a short, relatively unimportant story. A large headline is used on a long, important story. So that copy readers may trim the stories to prescribed lengths; some headlines call for mandatory trim orders.

THE LANGUAGE OF THE HEADLINE

Headline writing requires a facile vocabulary; if the maximum count of a line is 12, the copy reader cannot squeeze 13 units into it, even if by doing so he could write the most graphic head ever set in type.

The copy reader, handed a story calling for a three line head with a maximum count of 10 in each line which he is called upon to describe India's attitude toward China must be deft with synonyms. Even with an extensive vocabulary, the copy reader, headed in by the restrictions of typography, often is forced to make compromises between what he wants to say and what the limitation of space permits him to say. Thus he develops a headline vocabulary and puts a premium on short words.

Finding the Clues

The novice usually needs five steps to edit a story and write a headline. He (1) reads the story for general meaning, (2) goes through it a second time and edits it, (3) goes through it a third time and writes the sub-heads, (4) searches it for key words on which to base his headline, and (5) writes the headline.

The experienced copy reader does it in two steps. As he reads the story, he edits it and writes the sub-heads. While editing it, he makes mental note of the key words for the headline. When he has finished editing the copy, he is ready to write the headline.

Clues to the headline usually are in the lead. In his search for the clues, the copy reader asks himself, "What happened? Who did what? How did it happen? Why or in what way did it happen?

This simple, declarative subject-predicate relationship is the key to headline writing. A good start has been made if the first line of the head expresses vividly the main idea of the story—the who and what angle. The rest of the headline can express the how and the why.

Juggling the Words

It can be seen that one secret of headline writing is the

ability to juggle words and to switch lines as the headline takes form.

The Headline must be Specific

The headline must tell specifically the news of the story. It must not be a label, such as Council meeting or President's Message. A test is whether the headline could be used as well on some story other than the one in hand. If it could be, it is too general. Thus the copy reader avoids heads that say City Council Holds Meeting, which would be appropriate for all council meetings; or of Parliamentary Committees. Gets message from President, which fails to tell in what respect today's message is different from previous ones.

The stories of today's Council Meeting and today's Message tell specifically what happened. The headlines, likewise, must be based on specific angles—Council Votes Parking Curbs or P.M. asks Parliament to Raise Taxes.

Generally, but not always, the specific angle will be found in the lead. If the angle is not there, the story probably has been written improperly.

The Headline must be Positive

Negative heads must be avoided. The business of the newspaper is to tell what happened, not what didn't happen. Thus to be avoided is the head, Plane Crashes with 40 aboard, no one Hurt, Instead, it should say Plane Crashes with 40 Aboard, all Escape.

Verbs and Subjects

Part of the battle is won when the copy reader has found a vigorous, expressive verb vividly reflecting the flavour of the story with which to hoist the headline.

In writing a two-part headline consisting of a top and a deck, or a head with a top and several decks, care must be exercised that the verbs agree with the subjects. If the top contains the subject, the deck may be written without one, provided that the subject of the top also is clearly the subject of the deck.

Present Tense, Active Voice

Headlines are written in the present tense, although news stories usually are in the past tense. The present tense imparts immediacy and vividness to the headline. It enhances the impact of the language. It moves the reader closer to the story, in a measure making him a participant in it.

The is and the are

A headline is stronger, if the compound forms of is and are are omitted. Thus, 'Cashier found shot to death in bank branch' is crisper with the 'is' implied than 'cashier is found shot to death in bank office'. Likewise, '40 Accused Tax Cheaters indicated by India' tell the story better than '40 Accused Tax Cheaters are indicated by India'. Not only are the heads more effective, but space is saved by omitting the forms of the verb to be.

There are times, however, when a form of 'to be' must be included in the headline.

Names in Headlines

Whether to use a name in a headline often baffles a new copy reader. There are some general principles, however, that determine whether a name is good, and may be used, or whether it should be omitted.

A name should not be used in a headline on a straight news story unless most of the leaders will recognize it readily in general. The smaller the city the more local names are good, while the larger the city the fewer the names that are good.

Location in Headlines

Practices of locating the story in the headline telling the' where' vary widely. Some newspapers require that 'where' be made clear in all except local stories. Some in large cities go so far as to tell the part of the city in which the incident happened. Inclusion of the 'where' angle, however, consumes space that might otherwise be devoted to exploiting more interesting angles of the story. When carried to extreme, the following results.

ADMITS KILLING FOSTER MOTHER

Mumbai Fugitive is Captured Near Pondy

Unless news room rules dictate otherwise, the copy reader should ask himself whether inclusion of the 'where' contributes valuable information to the headline.

Punctuation in Headlines

Headline punctuations follow the general rules of writing but some exceptions have developed to meet the exigencies of telescoped expressions. Depending upon style, most of the conventional punctuation marks are used. Some papers, though not many, still use periods at the end of tops and decks of headlines.

The principal departure from ordinary usage is use of the comma as a substitute for the co-ordinate conjunction and the headline '30 Dead, 4 injured in air Crash' uses the comma in place of and to say 30 dead and 4 injured in Air Crash. The comma cannot be used in place of other co-ordinate conjunction, however, except 'where' and 'is' can be substituted for 'but is'. Thus, 'King Returns, Snubbed' could be read as 'King Returns and is Snubbed' or 'King Returns but is Snubbed', the meaning is the same in either case.

A semicolon generally is used to separate two complete thoughts in the top or the deck of a headline. Sometimes, a comma can be used for this purpose, but at other times, only a semicolon can be used for this purpose; at other times, only a semicolon can be used properly.

Abbreviations in Headlines

Most abbreviations are determined by style, although certain liberties are permitted in headlines.. Abbreviations widely known and readily recognized can be used freely.

Obscure abbreviations must be avoided. Whether an abbreviation is clear sometimes depends upon its use.

Numerals in Headlines

As with abbreviations, style determines the extent to which numerals may be used, although liberties are permitted in headlines. A common style practice is to spell out one digit figures in the body of the story and to use numerals for figures of two or more digits. Some papers extend this rule to headlines, but many permit use of numerals to express one digit figures.

Blind Heads, Humour and Taste

When a human interest story lends itself to whimsical treatment, the copy reader can forget many of the rules of headline writing and have fun with the story by writing a blind head, also called a teaser head.

The blind head does not attempt to tell the story. Indeed, telling it would spoil the story that is tailor-made for a teaser—the suspended interest feature—in which the point is driven home in the last sentence with a so-called snapper. The blind head also is effective when the 'who-what' headline would fail to do justice to the situation.

An effective blind head piques the interest of the reader. Although it must not give away the story yet the blind head must suggest the story by means of indirect, figurative language that reflects the flavour of the story and contains valid clues into it.

It is difficult to explain how to write a blind head. Some highly competent copy readers are unable to write one. Usually, there is no middle ground; the blind head is a work of art or it falls on its face.

The Neglected Sub-head

Sub-heads sometimes are looked upon mistakenly as minor details in copy reading. They should, however, be given their careful attention as any other headline. Sub-heads carelessly written and carelessly placed in the story mar the appearance of the story, of the column, and of the page.

A sub-head should be neither too long nor too short. Three average words look well. Two average words are unattractive typographically.

Biting out the Headline

The copy reader should build his headline on angles that are high in the story. If he can extract the entire head from the lead paragraph, so much the better. Going too deep into the story, except perhaps in a human interest story, is dangerous, and going to the last paragraph or the last sentence can be embarrassing, because the last paragraph or the last sentence may be trimmed from the story to make the story fit the page. Thus there is the danger that the headline angle taken from deep in the story may not be borne out by the story as it appears in the paper.

Tests for the Headline

After writing a headline, the copy reader ought to ask himself:

- Is the head accurate?
- Does it tell the story specifically, forcefully and crisply?
- Does it express the particular flavour of the story?
- Is it easy to read?

CHAPTER

27

Editing Today's News

The news room is quiet when we go to work, three hours before the first-edition deadline. The day assistant city editor has completed making his assignments and most of the reporters are out on stories, one rewrite man is taking notes over the phone. A second is reading a book of Spanish grammar. The telegraph editor, using a pencil as a spoon, is stirring coffee in a paper cup. The picture editor is leafing through a heap of wire service photos.

The copy desk is working on stories that are presumed to be static stories in which further developments are unlikely and on filler. Other prospective head stories, the bulk of the spot news, are in a state of flux; developments are to be expected in them. We do not know in what manner or to what extent those stories will develop, because spot news is never predictable. Some may grow to the extent of demanding other major position on page 1; developments may reduce others to inside pages. Some present filler items may grow into head stories. Some prospective head stories may wind up as pieces of filler.

THE ROTATION SHEET

Here, from the floor below, comes the man we have been expecting—the composing room foreman—bringing the dummies for today's paper. With the dummies is a rotation sheet, which shows how today's paper is laid out.

The rotation sheet shows that today's paper contains 52 pages and that the main news section runs through page 22. It shows that page 14 is the editorial page and that page 15 is the op (for "opposite") editorial page, where run the syndicated columns, the editorial features, the letters from readers, and the other opinion material. Page 20 is a full-page advertisement. Page 21 is the obit page.

Pages 23 through 28 are the features section not where human-interest stories are run but where news of society and other women's feature is carried. We do not make up the section. It is the province of the features editor, and we turn the dummies for it over to him.

The arrangement of the paper is such that we do not anticipate trouble in making it up. On the whole, the paper is open. Except for a few pages, there is room on each page for pictures and for an adequate representation of news. Several pages contain sufficient space to permit the grouping of classifieds. Unless the run of news is exceptionally heavy, we should be able to make up the paper so that it does not appear crowded.

THE NEWS POURS IN

The tempo of the news room has accelerated while we were sizing up the dummies. Stories have been coming in and the news is taking form. All the copy is routed through our hands on its way to the copy desk. We determine the amount of space to be allotted to each story, the headline it will carry, and the position in the paper that it will occupy. We determine the front-page play and we dummy the inside of the paper. The picture editor makes up his back page, but we dummy all news page pictures.

THE PICTURE SCHEDULE

The picture editor now comes over with his schedule of first-edition pictures.

There are the pictures for page 1 and for the inside pages for the first edition. The schedule shows the size of each picture available for the edition.

We enter the picture schedule in the master schedule. When a picture is accompanied by a text, we write the letter T after the slug of the picture, to remind us that a text runs with the picture. We do not know the exact length of the picture texts. Generally, they run approximately two or three inches. We have gentlemen's agreement with the picture editor under which he gives us warning when a text runs extraordinarily long.

The picture schedule does not contain the pictures that are being used on the back page, the editor page. The picture-editor draws his own dummy of the back page and sends it to the composing room.

Arrival of the picture schedule marks the time when specific plan for page 1 must be made.

Qualities of Sub-editor

Every person wants to excel in his assignments. So, to be a good reporter or a good sub-editor what one needs is *common sense and command over language.* These two requirements in fact summarize the qualities, which all newsmen should have as other qualities flow from these two, and the *basic human values.*

It is customary to describe desired qualities of a reporter and sub editor separately, but as both of them deal with the same commodity called news, and their basic job is to communicate effectively, many of these qualities have to be common.

News Sense

It is the basic quality of newsmen. Every reporter has to have news sense or nose for news to distinguish news from non-news. He should be able to compare various news values and decide where to begin his story and should not miss important details.

News sense is essential for a sub-editor also. He is the first reader of a reporter's copy, and if the reporter has made a mistake, he has to correct it. A bad copy may have the most important element of the story buried in the fourth paragraph. It will be left to the sub-editor's nose for news to bring that to the first paragraph.

Clarity

A reporter should have clarity of mind and expression. A person who is confused himself cannot tell a story to others. Only clarity of mind is not enough unless it is accompanied by clarity of expression. Without clarity of expression, clarity of mind has no meaning.

Sub-editor is the judge of clarity of the copy. A good sub-editor will never allow a copy escape him unless the meaning is crystal clear. He has every right to make life miserable for a reporter who is not clear and does not write in simple language.

Objectivity

Objectivity is the soul of journalism. Therefore, both reporter and sub-editor should aim at objectivity while dealing with a story. They should not allow their personal bias or ideas to creep into a story. They should not take sides but try to cover all the different viewpoints to achieve balance in the story.

Accuracy

As a matter of habit, a reporter should strive for accuracy. He should check and re-check his facts until he is satisfied that he has them accurate. In this respect, he should not take any chance as accuracy is directly proportional to the credibility of a reporter and his newspaper.

The main role of a sub-editor is to check for accuracy. It is particularly important when background is involved. In the case of dates and names, the reporter may rely on his memory but the sub-editor must check them from reference material available in the newspaper office. When there is a doubt, he should leave it out—this is the golden rule of journalism. It is better not to say a thing than to say it wrong.

Alertness

A reporter should always be alert while dealing with his subjects. Many major news breaks in the past were possible because of alertness of reporters. Scoops don't walk into newspaper offices; alert reporters catch them in the air and pursue.

A sub-editor has to be alert while working on news desk. Lack of alertness of a sub-editor can be seen by readers in the morning for he will be leaving mistakes uncorrected, for everybody to see.

Speed

In today's world, speed matters everywhere; people expect jet speed. A person who cannot work fast cannot be a good reporter. While maintaining all other desirable qualities, a reporter should strive to work faster. He should think fast, decide fast and write or type fast for he has to meet deadlines or may have to go for another assignment.

Speed is of great consequence in the profession. A sub-editor also has to work with speed. He cannot sit with a copy for long. He has to do swiftly whatever is required of him for a lot more copy is waiting for him.

Slow person at the desk is just unwanted because he/she halts the work of others, particularly of integration. Therefore, a slow sub-editor is a curse at the news desk and is treated with contempt. Such people are misfits in the profession.

Calmness

Maintaining balance, calm, sense of achievement, loyalty to the readers and organisation are the qualities, which must be imbibed, emulated and sustained. Reporters and sub-editors often work in trying situations and difficult circumstances. They have to remain calm and composed in most exciting and tragic circumstances. In many situations, they have to be calm devoid of hysterical actions or utterances and apply appropriate mental and physical effort to write or edit the story.

We all agree that reporters and sub-editors are human beings. They have emotions but they have to stifle them in the face of disturbing influences. They have to develop resistance to excitability. Being in the field, reporters face many such occasions when they have to control their emotions.

Adaptability is a necessary virtue in reporters and sub-editors. Therefore, the sub-editors should develop a temperament to work under pressure of deadlines. They should not lose their cool if they are behind the clock for calm mind can work faster.

Curiosity

Curiosity of a cat is invaluable possession of a sub-editor and reporter. It generates creativity and brings innovation to the job. Therefore, reporters and sub-editors should have an insatiable curiosity. For reporters, it is useful in developing lust for facts that may lead to better stories. This characteristic will keep on improving a sub-editor for with every passing day a curious sub-editor will have a better background to do his job the next day. Reporters and sub-editors should read as much as possible to constantly improve their awareness level.

Scepticism: Doubting Thomas who later became St. Thomas realized truth with acceptable facts. Like him, the sub-editor and reporter must develop the desirable attitude of brainstorming self to find answers and facts for each story. Therefore, it is another necessary quality, which a reporter and a sub-editor should cultivate. They should not take anything for granted. They should have an unwavering posture of doubt until faced with undeniable proof.

Vigilance is yet another virtue of reporter and sub-editor. Reporters should be more vigilant for many forces constantly try to use them, and through them their paper. Many people try to plant on reporters a wrong story for their own ends. Many a time, reporters fall into such traps in good faith. They should have enough scepticism to avoid such plots.

The world is full of selfish and crafty men and organisations. Sub-editors should, therefore, also be careful since some clever politicians, public relations men and product advertisers keep on trying to take them for a ride. They should not allow anything to go in news columns that should actually go as an advertisement. They should not fail to check even the reporters' copy for such foul play.

Punctuality

It is a good habit in personal life as well as in professional life. For reporters, it is a must. If they are not punctual, they may miss something for which they may have to depend on secondary sources. It is always better to be punctual and then wait than reach late and ask others. A rival may misinform you or hide some important information.

At the desk, too, punctuality pays. If a sub-editor is punctual, he will be treated with respect by his co-workers. If he happens to be late, he will irritate them and spoil the working atmosphere. Besides, he may have to face the problem of piled up backlog of copy, which he will have to clear under the pressure of the deadline.

Patience

It is the quality, which helps a reporter in a big way for many a time rather almost daily, he has to test his patience. It denotes the voluntary self-control or restraint that helps one to endure waiting, provocation, injustice, suffering or any of the unpleasant vicissitudes of time and life. It is not unusual that most of the time a reporter waits for someone or something and patience gives him the willingness to wait without becoming disgruntled or anxious. Many a time, he has to tolerate other people's shortcomings and remain unperturbed by someone else's tardy actions or other quirks.

Patience helps also the sub-editors as they work long hours in trying conditions. As things do not reach in the condition they want, they have unavoidably to put up with many annoying situations everyday *vis-à-vis* reporters, proofreaders or printers.

Imagination

It is the art and craft to add springs to the story for swings and uniqueness. This basic mental faculty helps reporters in writing better stories that retain the readers' interest. For a sub-editor, this creative faculty is very useful as he can add sparkle to somebody or subject-matter of someone else and make it lively and colourful like a butterfly. It is common knowledge that imaginative headlines attract the reader and improve the quality of a newspaper. After all, it is the age of packaging! News stories are also packaged to make them attractive, interesting and gripping.

Farsightedness

Looking into the future with imagination is the recipe, which adds flavour and unique or memorable taste to the mental palate. It is, therefore, but natural that an intelligent envisioning of the future helps newsmen in general. The quality helps them in identifying processes and people who will be important in future, reporters can watch such processes and cultivate people who may become important news sources in the future.

There is truth in the assertion that It helps reporters and sub-editors in determining the importance of an event. This significant quality of reporter with foresight can think ahead and prepare for eventualities. With a little forethought, sub-editors, too, can plan their work to avoid tension and it results in better functioning of the desk bringing in the desired efficiency.

Self-Discipline

All of us are aware of the importance of self-discipline. One can achieve a degree of proficiency in sub-editing or reporting by systematic effort and self-control. Judged from this angle, self-discipline suggests dedication and firm commitment, apart from other traits or qualities/attributes. Self-discipline helps in journalism as in any other field of activity.

Integrity

It is the core of one's character. It is a virtue in itself and implies undeviating honesty and strict adherence to a stern code of ethics. This human quality is important for journalists. It is more important for reporters for they are more likely to be exposed to temptations as compared to sub-editors.

Fearlessness and Frankness

Swami Vivekananda said, "fear not for fear is death and fearlessness is life". These qualities help reporters in asking unpleasant questions and taking professional risk to ferret out truth. No body gives the reporter a story on a platter. The reporter will have to probe, question, authenticate and exercise his skill of deduction to get a good story by separating the grain from the chaff.

Tactfulness

A reporter should be tactful. He should have the ability to handle sensitive people and situations gracefully without causing hurt or arousing angry feelings. He should be considerate of others and should be careful not to embarrass, upset or offend them. A Reporter should have flexible approach, dynamism and sociable personality and should have a nature that tastefully realizes variety of experiences. He should have an understanding of human nature, behaviour and emotions. This will help him in developing contacts that are very essential for news gathering.

Initiative

A reporter has necessarily to be self-starter. As he works in the field, he should have an outgoing nature with initiative and drive. These qualities will help him get acquainted with news sources and get stories from them. A meek, retiring or shy person is not fit for reporting. He may be good at his desk. Reporters need a fair amount of assertiveness and aggressiveness to be successful in their profession and go up the career path.

Mobility

A great amount of leg work is involved in journalistic work in the world of realm. A reporter should, therefore, be mobile. He should display an attitude to enjoy moving around and should not hesitate travelling distances to get stories when required. He should go to his news sources as often as possible for such constant contacts help him get news. A mobile reporter is seldom caught napping when a major story breaks.

Diligence

It is a necessary attribute of the personality of a journalist. Reporters and sub-editors should be diligent. Their jobs require painstaking exertion of intense care and effort, alertness and dedication to the task and wary watchfulness. They have to build capacity to be able to make extremely fine distinctions while writing or editing copy. A sub-editor should aim at and insist on perfection. He should love his job; he can make or mar the newspaper.

All the qualities described in the preceding paragraphs are basically qualities of good and efficient human beings. Those persons who possess these qualities make good and efficient sub-editors and reporters. All other things being equal, reporters need additional qualities to deal effectively with all sorts of people they meet in the field. Sub-editors should have better command over language as they improve what reporters write.

Reporters have a clear career path to go up the hierarchical ladder. They can become senior reporters, correspondents, senior correspondents, special correspondents and foreign correspondents. Sub-editors are promoted to the positions of senior sub-editor, chief sub-editor, deputy news editor and news editor. But the basic job of a reporter remains news gathering and filing the report or "copy" to the news desk. Similarly, the basic job of the sub-editor also remains the same to "sub" copy to make it fit to print which includes collecting, selecting, arranging, reducing, framing, translating and adapting for publication according to the importance of the story. Sub-editor is also called copy editor as what he edits is called copy. Whatever is filed by reporters, special correspondents, etc. is copy for him. Whatever comes to the news desk from wire services (news agencies like PTI and UNI) is also copy although it is technically called creed.

Although reporting and editing are separate and independent activities yet reporting and editing sides are not water-tight compartments. Reporters and sub-editors can swap places. In many newspapers, it is a routine. A sub-editor is sent on a reporting assignment many a time. He is also asked to write news items from the handouts that land up in the newspaper office from various government departments, business organisations and voluntary associations when the reporters are away on routine or special assignments.

Academic Push-up

The celebrated theorists and writers on Journalism had foreseen that there would probably always be exceptions to what has so far been discussed. The prophesy made by them is fast coming true. The current trends indicate that future journalists will be college trained. Most of the degree holders at present go to schools of journalism. Among them, the proportion of those with masters' and other higher degrees is also increasing. While those who are ambitious to specialize ultimately in particular fields should do so, but the majority should, in my humble opinion, strive for a thorough and well-rounded background in the social sciences: political science, sociology and economics in particular, and in literature, psychology, anthropology and philosophy in general. A student of Journalism should try to get in courses in public finance, criminology and labour problems among others as these are the areas fast emerging as affecting human life profoundly. The courses in History give him perspective and psychology enables him to come closer to understanding both individual and crowd behavior: behavior in fact response to environmental stimuli.

There are and should be advanced courses in journalism, in which the student should expect to learn how to utilize the background and theoretical knowledge acquired all over the rest of the campus, in reporting and interpreting the contemporary scene. On being placed on assignments, he observes to his surprise and pleasure "theory becoming action". Learning some philosophy, he will be better placed to comprehend and evaluate the immediate incident in terms of the general and eternal.

I strongly feel rather I am confident that the graduate of the school of journalism is fortunate where he learns practical side of his job. The first job enables him to write as well as report. I suggest thorough preliminary journalistic training, which should include some contact with politics and government as well as the fine run of general assignments—meetings, speeches, obituaries, accidents, interviews, routine business, society and similar news. My opinion is to get a stint of "under study" with an experienced Reporter for observing the nuances of the profession by self-study. After a few years of such varied experience, the beginner (pup-reporter as he/she is called) is able to start thinking about settling down to specialize.

CHAPTER

28

The Quotable Quotes

- I have no doubt that even if the government dislikes the liberties taken by the press and considers them dangerous, it is wrong to interfere with the freedom of the press. I would rather have a completely free press with all the dangers involved in the wrong use of that freedom than a suppressed or a regulated press.

  —Jawaharlal Nehru

- Freedom of the press, to appeal to reason, may always be construed as freedom of the press to appeal to public passion and ignorance, vulgarity and cynicism. And freedom of the press is always in danger, so is it always dangerous. The freedom of the press illustrates the commonplace that if we are to live progressively, we must live dangerously.

  —The Hutchins Commission's Report on Freedom of the Press in USA (1947)

- Were it left to me to decide whether we should have

a government without newspapers or newspapers without government, I shall not hesitate a moment to prefer the latter.

—Thomas Jefferson

- The purpose and duties of the two powers (the government and the press) are constantly separate, generally independent, sometimes diametrically opposite. The dignity and freedom of the press are trampled from the moment it accepts an ancillary position.

  —John Thaddeus Delane

- Somebody at the end of the day has to put a paper together and decide what it is going to do that day, whether in the last resort that somebody is the editor or the proprietor, has a power which he may misuse, but this is merely to say that power, wherever it resides, is capable of abuse.

  —Maurice Webb

- As with a ship, the proper running of a newspaper does not allow for dissentions in its command, and democracy here, if there is democracy, must be more strictly disciplined than elsewhere.

  —M. Hubert Beauve—Mery

- The democratic from of society demands of its members an active and intelligent participation in the affairs of their community whether local or national. It assumes that they are sufficiently well-informed about the issues of the day-to-day, to be able to form the broad judgement required by an election, and to maintain between elections the vigilance necessary in those whose governors are their servants and not their masters.

  —U.S. Royal Commission on the Press (1947-49)

- The views expressed by a newspaper should be

formulated by the person appearing to the public as the head of that newspaper (Editor)

—Herbert Ingsten

- Freedom of the press means freedom from and freedom for. The press must be free from the menace of external compulsions from whatever source. To demand that it be free from pressures which might warp its utterance would be to demand that society should be empty of contending forces and beliefs. But persisting and distorting pressures—financial, popular, clerical, and institutional—must be known and counter balanced.

  —Commission on Freedom of the Press, USA

- I ran the paper purely for the purpose of making propaganda and with no other object. I do not think a paper is any good for propaganda unless you run it as a commercial success. That is essential if you are to have a good propaganda instrument.

  —Lord Beaverbrook

- A US president tends to view attacks upon himself as attacks upon the country. LBJ could pull out a mental file drawer in which he had catalogued every major sin by any one who had ever held a pencil.

  — George E. Reedy

- The freedom of the press does not exist for the private enjoyment and self-esteem of journalists but to keep people, even presidents, informed. Watergate could be a turning point, after several years of government hostility and harassment towards a renewed national perception of why a fully independent press (with its abundant faults and excesses) is essential to the American system.

  —Times on Watergate

- The editorial columns are all too often taken up with ill-conceived, ill-informed, ill-digested expressions of opinion on matters that are of little real consequence to the people who buy the paper.

—Clifton Daniel

- Investigative journalism, which can be of great value exposing waste and corruption, is less held back by law than by laziness, the prevailing ethics, and dykes in the flow of information.

  —Harold Evans

- Give me but the liberty of the press and I will give to the minister a Venal House of peers and service House of Commons. I will give him all the power that place can confer upon him to purchase up submission and overawe resistance. And yet, armed with liberty of the press, I will attack the mighty fabric he has reared and bury it amidst the ruins of the abuses it was meant to shelter.

  —Richard Brinsley Sheridan

- The way to get at the nature of an institution, as if anything else that is alive, is to see how it has grown.

  —A.G. Keller

- They that can give up essential liberty to obtain a little temporary safety deserve neither liberty nor safety.

  —Benjamin Franklin

- The question before the court is not (just) the cause of the poor printer. Nor it may in its consequence affect every free man on the main of America. It is the best cause; it is the cause of liberty. The liberty both of exposing and opposing arbitrary power by speaking and writing truth.

  —Andrew Hamilton's defence in the Zenger Trial

- Should the liberty of the press be once destroyed,

farewell the remainder of our invaluable rights and privileges.

—Isaiah Thomas

- The press (is) the only true son of nation.

  —Jefferson

- I have lent myself willingly as the subject of a great experiment to demonstrate the falsehood of the pretext that freedom of the press is incompatible with orderly government.

  —Jefferson

- A country, like an individual, has dignity and power only in proportion as it is self-informed.

  —Willian Ellory Channing

- Journalism is literature in a hurry

  —Mathew Arnold

- Journalism is a first rough draft of history

  —Aroon Purie

- He who opposes the public liberty overthrows his own.

  —William Lloyd Garrison

- The newspaper has has history, but it has, likewise, a natural history. The press, as it exists, is not, as our moralists sometimes seem to assume, the wilful product of any little group of living men. On the contrary, it is the outcome of a history process.

  —Robert E. Park

- Every issue of the paper presents an opportunity and a duty to say something courageous and true, to rise above the mediocre and conventional, and to say something that will command the respect of the intelligent, the educated, the independent part of the community, to rise above fear of partisanship and fear of popular prejudice.

—Joseph Pulitzer

- The magnitude of financial operations of the newspaper is turning journalism upside down.

  —Lincoln Steffens (1897)

- The reason why such journals (yellow journalism) lie is that it pays to lie, or in other words, this is the very reason for which they are silly and scandalous and indecent; they supply a want of demoralized public.

  —E.I. Godkin

- It will be my earnest aim that the *New York Times* gives the news, all the news, in concise and attractive form, in language that is parliamentary in good society, and gives it as early, if not earlier, than it can be learned through any other reliable medium, to give the news impartially, without fear or favour, regardless of any party, sect or interest involved, to make the columns of *New York Times* a forum for the consideration of all questions of public importance, and to that end to invite intelligent discussion from all shades of opinion.

  —Adolph S. Ochs

- All who expect to become journalists must begin as reporters; the first requirement is knowledge of the language. You must know your language as musician knows his instrument. You must be able to detect the false word as readily as the musician does a false note. You must not invent, but you may imagine. If you possess the flight of imagination to any degree, you will be qualified to adorn your profession.
- The first test of good reporter is the collection of facts and impressions. He must be eager and curious about everything under the sun and beyond it. Next,

he must have industry and lastly, he must possess the ability to distinguish the true from the false, to differentiate the dull from the common place.

- Let me commend the copy reader to you. His work is no less essential to the paper than that of the reporter. A first rate copy reader can make a first rate newspaper out of the third rate copy. On the other hand, a poor copy reader can spoil the work of the best reporter. He must possess keen literary appreciation. If he cannot write brilliantly, he must write well enough to convert bad copy into good. He must be able to apply sandpaper to the bodily excrescence of an article, but not to its soul. His range of information must be wide and at instant command. He must know where to lay his hands on the fact he cannot draw from his memory. His chief joy is in the headlines. A two or three column story is told in a few words, luring the reader on if the subject interests him, warning him to pass on if it doesn't. In writing headlines, stick to honest nouns and verbs.

  —Carr V. Van Anda

- It is much easier to report a battle or a bombing than it is to do an honest and intelligible job on the Marshall plan, Taft-Hartlay law or the Atlantic Pact.

  —Edward R. Murray

- It is often made a matter of boasting, that the United States contains so many public journals. It were wiser to make a cause of mourning, since the quality, in this stance, diminishes in an inverse ratio to the quantity.

  —James Fenimore Cooper (1838)

- There can be no such thing as a free press and no such thing as the integrity of the news if the men and women who write the news live in fear of the insecurity of their jobs.

  —Heywood Brown.

- Partisanship in editorial comment which knowingly departs from the truth, does violence to the best spirit of American journalism; in the news columns it is subversive of a fundamental principle of the profession.

  —ASNE Canons of Journalism

- It is as difficult to apply objective standards to newspaper as it is to people, and the greatest newspaper is as difficult to identify as the greatest man. It all depends upon what you require.

  —Gerald W. Johnson

- The most useful man on a newspaper is one who can edit. Writers there are galore. Every profession offers them but the editor is of a profession apart.

  —Adolph S. Ochs

- Those who get the news have the responsibility to gather all the news. The editors will decide what part of the news cannot, for any reason (of taste), be put into print.

  —J. Russell Wiggins

- To edit is "to improve an essentially well-written piece or to turn a clumsily written one into, at the very least, a readable and literature article, and at the very most, beautifully shaped and effective essay which remains true to the author's intention, which realizes that intention more fully than he himself was able to do. He cares about the English language; he cares about clarity of thought and of grace of expression; he cares about the traditions of discourse and of argument.

  —Norman Podhoretza

- No man is qualified to be his own copy editor. No matter what his reputation; his writing will benefit from another's look.

  —L.R. Blanchard

- There are many elements that go into the making of a fine newspaper, but one of the least heralded and most important is an outstanding copy desk. It can make a good newspaper better. It can make better newspaper the best.

  —Stan Amisor

- Because copy editing is an art, the most important ingredient after training and talent, is strong motivation. The copy editor must care. Not only should he know his job, he must love it: every story, every edition, every day. No art yields to less than maximum effort. The copy editor must be motivated by a fierce professional pride in the high quality of editing.

  —J. Edward Murray

- The copy desk is the abiding place of curiosity, discretion, cynicism, sympathy—all those human instincts personified in men who give your paper its flavour; news hounds all, with noses in the air for the scent of human interest and for libel. I salute the copy desk, the sacrificial altar of the sacred cow.

  — Care Lindstron

- There are indications that stories which perform a service, telling people how to cope, are among the most popular and best read today.

  —H.L. Stevenson, Editor in Chief UPI (1975)

- Some news items, of course, can drive you up the wall because they have been garbled by typesetters or emasculated by copy editors or amputated up to pointlessness by robots who are concerned only with making lines of available space without bothering to read the remnants they cut out.

  —Leo Rosten

- All I know is what I see in the papers.

  —Will Rogers

- Get the news, get all the news, and nothing but the news.

  —Charles A. Dana

- No news is good news.

  —A proverb

- It is the newspaper's duty to print the news and raise hell.

  —Wilbur F. Storey

- If a man bites a dog, that is news.

  —John Bogart

- Newspapers are the schoolmasters of the common people.

  —Henry Ward Beecher

- Comment is free, facts are scared.

  —C.P. Scott

- News judgment is a skill long-time journalist use with the same pride with which weight lifters use their muscles.

  —Mitchell Stephens

- The subject of deepest interest to an average human being is himself, next to that he is most concerned with his neighbourers. Congo and Tongo Islands stand a long way off after these in this regard.

  —Horace Greenlay

- If there were a simple definition of news upon which all could agree, the failings of journalists as writers would be easier to diagnose and correct. But none exists.

  —John Hohenberg

- Actually, the concept of news varies among the media. To morning newspapers, it is what happened yesterday. To afternoon newspapers, it is what happened today. To news magazines, it is what happened last week. To wire service, radio and television, it is what happened a moment ago.

—John Hohenberg

- News is a living, growing, expanding entity, constantly changing direction, constantly producing the dramatic and the unexpected. In early years of this century, the notion of producing an atom bomb or landing men on moon was not news, indeed both were considered impossible. A generation ago, few thought there was news in the ecology, the consumer movement or the struggle for equal opportunity for women.

  —John Hohenberg

- When somebody says, "Gee whiz, I didn't know that", its news.

  —Keith Fuller

- News is anything you didn't know yesterday.

  —Turner Catledge

- The basic qualities of the news are accuracy, interest, and timeliness. To these must be added a fourth, explanation. Of what use is an accurate, interesting and timely report of a news event if people cannot understand it?"

  —John Hohensberg

- News is about the economic, political, social and cultural hierarchies we call nation and society. For the most part, news reports on those at or near the top of the hierarchies and on those particularly at the bottom who threaten them, to an audience most of whom are located in the vast middle range between top and bottom.

  —Herbert J. Gans

- It is hard news that catches readers.

  —Lord Northcliffe

- Any bloody fool can write. It needs a heaven born genius to edit.

  —H.W. Nevinson

- A good sub-editor is a creative artist.

  —F.J. Mansfield

- The facts we see depend on where we are placed and the habits of our eyes.

  —Walter Lippmann

- The only qualities essential for real success in journalism are rat like cunning, a plausible manner and literary ability. The rat like cunning is needed to ferret out and publish things that people don't want to be known (which is and always will be the best definition of news). The plausible manner is . . . helpful in the entertaining presentation of it and even more useful in later life when the successful journalist may have to become a successful executive on his newspaper. The literary ability is of obvious use.

  —Nicholas Tomlin

- Your (journalist's) biggest weakness is that too many of you want to believe in people and things you are too lazy to question. Every now and then you do go wrong and put a good man down and a bad man up—how is that different from anything else in life? Reporters, one should presume, are normal human beings with the same ambition, competitive fire, desire for status and affluence, fear, caution, ethics, honesty and guile, like any other human being. They can be, therefore, and are often, manipulated, threatened, rewarded and punished, cajoled and conned into doing what their news sources want them to do—sometimes, even without realizing that they have been any of the above.

—Tom Wicker

- The journalist's role in society is more like a dredging engineer whose job is to keep channels free and clear. A journalist watches the currents of society closely and acts when he sees the channel silting up or its course deflected. His concern is always with the now and with what comes next, he is not interested repeating what he has already been told, his delight is in discerning the new and then making it clear; discovery is his job.

  —Thomas Griffith

- I keep six honest serving men. (They taught me all I know). Their names are, what and why and when and how and where and who.

  —Rudyard Kipling

- American reporters worry about the dilemma between their obligation to the truth and their obligation to their country. They know that they often embarrass officials by reporting the facts and even interfere with the public policy occasionally but they go on doing it because somehow the tradition of reporting the facts, no matter how much they hurt, is stronger than any other.

  —James Reston.

- "Muckrakers"—(Reporters)

  —Theodore Roosevelt

- What is a journalist? Not any business manager or publisher, or even proprietor. A journalist is the lookout on the bridge of the ship of state. He notes the passing sail, little things of interest that dot the horizon on finè weather. He reports the drifting castaway whom the ship can save. He peers through fog and storm to give warning of dangers ahead. He is not thinking of his wages or the profits of his owners. He is there to watch over the safety and welfare of the people who trust him.

—Joseph Pulitzer

- Go with what you have got.

  —Old Deadline rule

- Where in doubt, leave out.

  —Old Newsroom Saying

- Get it right, or let it alone. The conclusion you may jump to may be your own.

  —James Thurber

- I don't know of any sure way to success but there is a recipe for certain failure. Just try to please everybody and you will surely fail.

  —Herbert Bayard Swope

- When I first went to work on a newspaper, which was after World War I, the generally accepted theory was that it was the duty of the news columns to report the "facts" uncoloured by "opinion" and it was the privilege of the editorial page to express opinions about what was reported in the news columns.

  —Walter Lippmann

- To this simple rule of the division of labour between reporters and editorial writers, we all subscribed. In practice, we all reporters and editorial writers, broker the rule and this led to many disputes, good-natured and some not so good-natured. The news columns would have opinions with which the editorial writers disagreed. The editorial pages would contain statement of fact that the news editor had not certified.

  —Walter Lippmann

- In the course of time, most of us have come to see that the old distinction between fact and opinion does not fit the reality of things—the modern world being so very complicated and hard to understand, it has become necessary not only to report the news but to explain and to interpret it.

—Walter Lippman

- Regardless of the advances of science and technology, however, the practice of journalism in the open societies of the western world will be based in the future, as it has been in the past, on four ideals that often seem utterly unattainable. The first is the never-ending search for the truth. The second is to push ahead to meet changing times instead of waiting to be overtaken by them. The third is to perform services of some consequences and significance to the public interest. The fourth and by all odds the most important is to maintain a steadfast independence.

—John Hohenberg

- Use short sentences. Use short paragraphs. Use vigorous English not forgetting to strive for smoothness. Be positive, not negative . . . those were the best rules I ever learned for the business of writing. I have never forgotten them. No man with any talent, who feels and writes truly about the thing he is trying to say, can fail to write well if he abides by them.

—Earnest Hemingway

- The function of an editor of a daily paper is largely, if not entirely, directional, political and administrative. Virtually, the only part of the paper on which an editor can impose his personal stamp is on the edit page. The rest is at the mercy of the news-editor who presides over the desk, the chief of bureau and the reporters. Very often, the editor only sees their handiwork when the paper is delivered to him in the early hours of the morning. Then all he can do is to perform a kind of post-mortem in the hope that improvement will follow.

—Khushwant Singh

- The trouble with the newspaper business is that it is becoming more and more just a business.

  —Thomas Griffith

- The press's lack of skepticism, its unwillingness to look behind official statements and claims, its too ready linkage of the powers of office with knowledge and ability, its assumption of official virtue where vigorous inquiry would have disclosed no virtue at all—these delinquencies could be charged to the press itself.

  —Tom Wicker

- The editor's task is to deal with spiritual values. Concentrating his attention on his professional work, he should at the same time keep his mind open to the outer world. His relationships are multilateral in a very wide sense and he should always take into consideration the consequences which his policy, known by every reader, will have even in the smaller matters. Just as in a person, the public expects a strong character in a newspaper.

  —Maarty Rooy

- There is no mid-way in Press Freedom is like virginity—either you have it or not have it.

  —Preetish Nandy

Glossary

A

ABC	Audit Bureau of Circulations; source of authoritative figures for newspapers' net sale over specified periods.
Ad	Advertisement; classified or display.
Ad alley	Section of composing room where advertisements are assembled.
Add	Written or copy to be added at and of story already set or subbed and sent to printer.
Ad dummy	Miniature set of pages marked with ad placing and size of advertisements. Sometimes called the 'the scheme'.
Ad rule	Rule separating ads from editorial matter.
Advertisement manger	Newspaper executive in charge of advertising in newspapers.
Advertising agency	Organizations preparing ads for clients and buying space in newspapers and magazines, and TV time.
AFP	Agence France Presse, French news agency.

Agate	Old name for $5^1/_2$ Pt. Type; Fourteen agate lines are 1 in. deep.
Agency	Organization supplying news but not publishing or printing newspapers; or advertising agency.
An insert	Copy to be inserted (according to marked accompanying proof) into matter already set.
All in	Proof reader's term meaning all copy and proofs are in the reading room.
All in hand	Printer has received and is setting all copy and heading for a particular story or page.
All out	Printer has dispersed all copy for setting.
All rights reserved	General copyright warning, usually to avoid lifting of exclusive material/ information.
All up	All copy has been set, but not necessarily read and corrected.
Alterations	Changes on proof that differ from original copy (i.e. not simply corrections.).
Angle	Aspects or points of approach in a story; 'play up this angle'.
AP	Associated press, US news agency.
Arabic numerals	Those we commonly use; 1, 2, 3, etc. (as distinct form roman numerals: I, II, III, etc.).
Arm	Horizontal stroke on T, diagonal lines of Y and K.
Art	Frequently means pictures and other illustrations plus layout and design; used is changing with increasing role of designer artist in newspapers.

Art editor	Picture editor, responsible for acquiring photographs and in change of photographer; or (more recent) design editor.
Art paper	Coated paper with high finish. Process department requires proof on art paper to make white-on-black handing strip type into illustrations, etc.
Ascender	Part of letter rising above x-height; I, g, f, h , k, all have ascenders.
Assignment	Reporter's specified task.
Author's marks	Corrections on proof made by author as distinct from those made by reader.
Author's proof	Proof altered, corrected or passed by author.

B

Back numbers	Previous issues of the paper kept for sale.
Back room, back shop	Mechanical department of a newspaper.
Back set	Section of a newspaper printed and folded separately at the end (back) of the first.
Bad break	Incorrect division of a word between the end of one line and start of the next; turning (from one column to next, or to another page) on a divided word.
Bad letter	Broken type, not printed fully.
Bad spacing	Irregular or over-spacing of a line of type; space not distributed correctly for sense and appearance.
Bank	(i) Part of a multiple headline; (ii) place where matter in type is assembled.
Banner	(i) Title of newspaper on front page or

	above editorials on leader page; (large headline across all or most of top of page).
Barker	Headline variant in which one line, usually one word, is set in large type over deck of smaller headline.
Bastard measure	Type set to a width different from the basic column width or multiples of it.
Beard	Projecting part of type mount or shank producing white space below character when printed; varies between typefaces but needs to be taken into account in page design and measurement.
Beat	Reporter's regular or special area (e.g. court, politics, crime, etc.).
Bed	Part of printing press that carries type form or plate to be printed.
Ben day	Mechanical tint for producing shading on blocks.
Bf	Abbreviation for *boldface.*
Bind binding	A type form that will not lock up squarely and evenly is 'binding'.
Bite off	To remove complete paragraphs at the end of a story to fit the space. The noun 'bit off' is what has been removed.
Black	(i) Carbon copy of reporter's story of feature; (ii) boldface type.
Black letter	Old black, angular, spiky typefaces based on hand-written books basis for modern types in this style.
Blanket	Newspaper page proof.
Blanket head	Headline covering all columns accepted by a story or combination of related stories.

Blind ad	In which the identity of the advertiser is not named.
Blind interview	One in which the source is quoted but not named.
Blobs	Black circles (properly, full face circles), useful for adding colour to a page by itemizing or setting out a series of points in a story without numbering (any can be held out without ruining sequence).
Block	Illustration in metal form, either half-tone or line or combination of both.
Block heading	Heading enlarged photographically from proof, useful for producing headlines in larger size than normally available.
Blow up	(Enlargement), applied to picture and other artwork, including headings photographically enlarged form proofs.
Blurb	Commonly a publisher's eulogy on the jacket of a book, but in newspaper, outside the literary department, is more frequently used to mean a preliminary paragraph set up distinctively to introduce a feature or news story.
Body	Type has thick, thin, medium, etc. body according to thickness of vertical strokes.
Body matter	Text set in newspaper's body type, or the text as distinct from headings, cross-heads, etc.
Body type	Typeface in which the main text of a newspaper is set, usually in sizes 4¾, 5½, 6, 7, 8, 9, 10, 12pt.
Bodoni	Type series in common use for

	headings, etc. distinguished by its clean lines, fine serifs and vertical stress.
Boiler plate	Editorial term for timeless raw 'filler' material.
Blood, Blood face	Type loss which varies from the standard (or regular) form by having thicker vertical strokes so that it prints blacker.
Bowl	Curved stroke of letter surrounding closed "white" area or counter as in letters o, b, a
Box	Type matter enclosed by rules on all four sides, also in some offices the stop press column.
Bracketed	Serifs are said to be bracketed to the stem when they are joined to it in a continuous curve rather than set at a sharp right angle. Old face types have bracketed serifs.
Break	(i) convenient or appropriate place in text to insert cross head or make a turn to another page, (ii) tear in web of newsprint feeding the presses.
Break up	Disperse type material from a page, either for melting down and recasting or to type cases.
Brevier	Old name for 8 pt. type.
Bridge	Proof reader's mark showing that words or characters are to be joined together.
Brief	Short cut news paragraph.
Broad sheet	A page the full size of a rotary press plate, approximately 22 in. deep by 15 in wide.
Broadside	(i) Full-size newspaper page as printed on a rotary press, (ii) old

	announcement or newspaper page printed as a single sheet irrespective of how it is to be folded.
Broken matter	Text, headings, etc. that have been taken out of a page and are probably disordered (pied).
Broken word	Word turned from one line to another, with a linking hyphen at the end of the fist line, words should be split to respect sense and etymology, vertical ranks of hyphens should be avoided.
Bromide	Piece of positive film—of either type of illustration used for sticking on to page in photo set newspaper.
Bucket	Rules below and on both sides of type matters.
Bulk	Bench or stone where assembled type is kept ready for use.
Bulletin	Short message giving new development of latest situation on running story.
Bump	Add extra spacing material to type matter to make it fill a given space.
Bureau	Editorial office separate from main publishing building, mostly in another city or country.
Buster	Headline with too many characters and spaces for the given measure.
By-line	Line of type indicating authorship.

C

Cabalese, Cablese	Set forms of words and abbreviations used in cabled copy to reduce expense of transmission.

Cancelled matter	Type material removed from stores by corrections, cuts, etc.
C & I c	Caps, and lower case, i.e. the normal mixture of capital and small letters, often written as u & i, c, (upper and lower case), m which is the same thing.
C & s, m, c	Caps and small caps, i.e. capital letters with the small capitals (the same height as lower case letters) belonging to the same size and type. The abbreviation is sometimes rendered c & sc
Canned copy	Publicity material sent to newspaper.
Caps	Capital letters, i.e. A, B, C etc.
Caption	Line (s) of type below a picture or other illustration.
Caret	Proof reader's mark (l) indicating something is to be inserted.
Carry-forward	Instruction to compositer to carry text matter to next page or to turn.
Case	Tray holding individual type characters of type matrices.
Case Rack	Cabinets for holding cases.
Case-room, case Department	Printers' workshop, composing room.
Carlson	Solid, serifed typeface often used for feature display.
Cast	Printing plate, produced by molten metal from a cast (matrix) of a form.
Catch	Notice an error, or make a last minute correction to a page (rectifying a bad error is called a good catch).
Catch line	Identifying word on copy or proofs enabling related material to be identified quickly and brought or kept together.

Centre spread	Two facing pages at middle of newspaper. A spread is any two facing pages.
Century	Made-of-all-work type series for modern newspaper, serifed, with vertical stress but robust rather than elegant like bodoni.
CGO	Short for 'can go over' Indicates that the copy may be held over until the following day or days.
Chart pack rules	Trade name for rules, dotted borders and other designs supplied on transparent sticky tape for use in make-up of photoset newspaper.
Chase	Metal frame in which type is assembled to make up newspaper page; when filled it is called a form.
Check	Confusingly for the layman, printer's readers use a tick (which elsewhere denotes that something is correct) to indicate the need for a check to determine accuracy.
Chimney	Grouping of pictures and/or headlines (or advertisements) so that they run in a narrow band from top to bottom of the page.
Chocked type	Type filled with ink or dirt, producing blotchy printer work.
Circled numbers	Instruction to printer to spell out, applies also to abbreviations.
Circulation	Number of copies sold, not to be confused with readership, which is usually about five times as high.
Circulation Manager	Newspaper executive in charge of paper's distribution to wholesale and retail outlets.

Classified	Small advertisements, set in single-columns and charged and measured by the line.
Classified Display	Advertisements in the classified columns given prominence by rules and use of boldface or larger type, at extra charge.
Clean copy	Copy that can be read easily and without ambiguity.
Clean proof	Proof of type matter after all alternations and corrections have been made.
Close quote(s)	Punctuation mark, indicating end of direct quotation.
Close-up	Reduce space between words, letters or lines of type.
Cock-up	(i) Initial letter rising above the line of smaller type on which it stands, (ii) incompetent confusion at any point of the newspaper making process.
Col	Short for column.
Cold type	Film set type.
Column, inch	An area one column wide and one inch deep, used as a unit of measurement of newspaper space, and as basis for advertisement charges.
Column rule	Thin type rule used to divide adjoining columns.
Columnist	Regular writer, either on a particular subject or in a special place in the paper.
Comp	Compositor, craftsman who assembles type.
Composing stick	Small, hand-held tray on which type is composed.

Condensed type	Narrower, thinner version of standard type, providing contact with it.
Copy	Written or typewritten material which the printer sets in type according to the instructions given.
Copydesk	Table where copy editors (sub-editors) work and over which all editorial copy passes.
Copy Desk	Sub-editor marks and prepares editorial copy for printer.
Copy Holder	Proof reader's assistant.
Copy Paper	Usually newsprint reel ends cut into blocks or pads of a convenient size for type writer and setting purposes.
Copyright	Ownership of original elements and form of words in written and printed material
Copy-taster	Sub-editor who reads all incoming copy and estimates its worth for publication.
Correct	Mark proofs so as to make them conform to copy.
Cover	(i) Report on event or situation, have responsibility for a particular area of news gathering, (ii) deputise for a colleague otherwise engaged.
Coverage	Extent of newspaper's attention to particular events or situations.
Credit	Photographer's or artist's by line, usually in small type below or next to block/cut.
Creed	Teleprinter machine, or copy.
Crop	Reduce limits or frame of picture to concentrate on required area, and/or to fit required shape.

Cross = head, cross line	Sub-heading placed in text, between paragraphs.
Cross-reference	Line of type directing attention to story or picture on another page.
Cursive	Flowing style of type, resembling handwriting but without joining up of letters.
Cut	Make deletions from copy or text in type.
Cut in	Make deletions from copy or type to reduce to a required length, or to get an add matter.
Cut line	Caption, line(s) of type below a picture or other illustration.
Cut-off rule	Rule separating one story or advertisement from another above or below.
Cut-out	Half-tone plate in which all background has been removed, leaving figure in silhouette.
Cuttings	Items cut from previous issues and other publications and filed for reference (US clippings).

D

Daily	Daily, usually morning, newspaper.
Dak edition	Up-country edition containing matter that has already appeared in a previous final edition.
Dateline	Place and date of origin of newspaper story; sometimes attached to by-line, sometime given separately.
De	Double-column.
Dead	Copy discarded (killed) and not used. Also text, headlines, etc. removed after

	being set or being run for an edition.
Deadline	Time by which copy must be delivered to appear in a particular edition; varies from page to page for each edition, and also according to whose deadline it is (on the same story, there will be progressively deadlines for copy to subs, copy to printer, set matter to page, and page to press).
Deck	One unit of a multiple headline, or one more line of a two-or-more-line heading.
Delete	Take out; proof reader's mark.
Descender	Part of letter producing below x-height (e.g., in g, j, y).
Design	(i) Selection of typefaces, illustrations, rules, determinations of spacing and general visual style of a newspaper; (ii) layout of individual pages or articles.
Desk	Sub-editors' table.
Diary	Daily list of jobs to be covered by the newsroom.
Dirty copy	Copy so heavily marked and corrected that it cannot be read easily or is ambiguous.
Dirty proof	(i) Proof so marked that changes cannot be easily followed; (ii) proof containing so many literal and other errors that it cannot be worked on until matter is corrected.
Dis	Break-up type from page for return to cases or melting for recasting; the word is short for 'distribute'.
Display	(i) Headline and illustrations for feature, (ii) Display ads department.

Display ads — Larger ads, frequently designed in ad agencies and supplied to newspapers as stereo plates, to be mounted for use in page.

Dot Leaders — Dotted lines (e.g. those relating one column of figures to another).

Dotted rule — Rule composed entirely of dots.

Double — (i) The same story, whether in identical or different form, appearing twice in the same edition, (ii) repetition of words in different headlines on the same page.

Down column — Across two columns, measure is not simply twice single-column, but also includes the space between columns.

Down style — Style with minimum of capital letters.

Drop cap — Initial capital covering more than one line, but hanging below the top line.

Drop head — Headline in which each line is set further to the right, stepped head.

Dummy — (i) 'Miniature' of paper showing where ads have been booked, (ii) mock-up of newspaper for design experiments, rearrangements, launching and promotional use, etc.

Dummy run — Producing a new newspaper or section up to any stage short of actual publication.

Dupe — Duplicate.

Duplex — Line-casting matrix which carries two characters, also make of newspaper press.

E

Ear pieces — Ads or ad spaces to left and right of page one banner.

Ears	Curved projections of letters such as r, g.
Edit	Prepare copy for printer.
Edition	One of several separate issues of a newspaper on the same day.
Editor	Chief journalistic executive of newspaper, responsible for all it contains, including advertisements.
Editorial	Leader, leading article, Expression of the newspaper's opinion.
Editorialize	Insert opinion in what is meant to be informative copy.
Egyptian	Type family distinguished by thick slab serifs and heavy main strokes, also known as "antique'.
Elrod	Machine which casts rules, borders, spacing.
Em	Unit of linear measurement, the square of any type size, but usually the 12 pt em (six to 1 in.) also called a 'mutton'.
Embargo	Request not to publish information supplied in advance until specified time or circumstances.
Em dash	Dash one em long.
Em quad	Spacing unit, below type height, one em wide.
En	Half an em.
English	Old name for 14 pt type. Double English is old name for 28 pt.
Engraving	Printing plate produced by engraver.
Exclusive	Newspaper word for material or information that no other newspaper has.
Extended, expanded	Type face with width greater than normal.

Extra — Extra or special edition.

Extra-condensed — Exceptionally narrow type face.

Eyebrow — Short line in smaller type, often underlined, above main deck of headline, also called teaser, highline, overlie, strap.

F

Face — Engraved image which carries the ink to be impressed on the paper.

Facsimile — Exact reproduction of the original. Also method of transmitting news pages by wire or radio waves for printing in second centre.

Fake — Falsified story.

Faking — Patching several photographs together for special effect.

Family — All the type of any one design, e.g. 12 pt. Bodoni Bold and 14 pt. Bodoni Bold Italic, and 72 pt Bodoni Black are all members of the Bodoni family.

File — To send a story by wire, one day's output by a news agency.

Files — Back issues, library clippings/cuttings are also 'on file'

Fillers — Short item used to fill out a column. Evening papers rushing to press need a good supply of fillers of varying lengths to suit the varying size of 'holes' in a page after the main stories and pictures have been placed.

First proof — First pull of a setting after line casting which is read from copy. It is then corrected and reproofed as 'clean'.

Flag — Title plate on the first page of a

	newspaper. Also, a piece of paper or slug kept in gallery of type of printers that correction, or insert, is required at that point.
Flash	Urgent, brief message on wire service announcing big story.
Flat bed press	Press which prints from a level surface.
Flong	Blank sheet of absorbent paper board used to make mould, or matrix, in stereotyping.
Flush	To set type even with the column rule or margin, on either left or right. A 'Flush left" head has all the lines ranging evenly on the left.
Fold	(n) Point at which the newspaper is folded horizontally/commonly. In newspaper display, 'below the fold' means, in a broad sheet 22 inches deep, any point below 11 inches.
Folio	Page or page number.
Folio line	Technically, line at top of page carrying page number, but generally now means inside page line carrying page number, name of newspaper, and date.
Fc	Follow copy.
Follow Copy	Instruction to printer to set copy exactly as written despite apparent errors.
Follow	Story that follows up a first day story
Follow-up	To seek new information on an earlier story, a story that takes an earlier story further.
Format	Strictly, the size and shape of a page, newspaper or book. More generally refers to the fixed elements in a newspaper design, shape and size of

	the page, plus the number and measure of columns to a page.
Forme	Combination of type, blocks, etc. locked up in a chase and ready to go to press or to the foundry for duplicating.
Foul copy	Copy so heavily corrected and marked it is difficult to follow.
Foul proof	Proof set aside by the compositor (usually spiked) after he has made the corrections marked on it, proof containing errors, so not to be used for sending corrections to printer.
Fount	All the characters of any one typeface in any one size needed for a piece of printing, pronounced 'font'.
Fourth Estate	The public press, the three original Estates was the Lords Temporal, the Lord Spiritual, and the Commons.
Freelance	Self-employed writer, artist, editor or advertising man.
Fudge	Small box-like device inserted into cylinder of newspaper to permit printing directly from slugs of type, the fudge box is used for printing late news on the run. The fudge or box is also the name for the place on the page where the late news, so printed, appears.
Full face	Old term for bold face. Contracting.
Full line	Line set 'flush' both to left and right.
Full measure	Type composed to the full width of the column (or page).
Full out	Type composed the full normal measure of page or column. Full left is type full to the left, but ranging freely

	on the right, full right is type full to the right, but ranging freely on the left.
Full point	Printer's term for full stop.
Furniture	Wood or metal, less than type high, used to fill in blank spaces in the chase.

G

Galley	Shallow, three-sided metal tray in which type is assembled and proofed. Also, about twenty column-inches of text matter.
Galley press	Press which produces printed image on proofing paper of type in gallery.
Galley Proof	Impression taken on a strip of paper by inking a galley of type, and 'pulling' a proof so that the type can be checked with the original copy for errors.
Galley slug	Slug with catch word, phrase, or number placed on galley of type to identify it, e.g. News 20.
Geraldo	British Standards Institution term for classifying what is popularly called old face roman type, such as Bembo, Garamond, Carlson.
Gate-fold	Wider or deeper page in magazine or book which has to be folded to fit the format. To be read properly, it has to be swung open like a gate. Usually sold to advertisers in a magazine.
Get in	Instruction to printer to make adjustments to spacing, etc. to accommodate extra letters, or words.
Ghost	Ghost writer is the author of stories that bear someone else's name.

Give it some air	Instruction to printer to add white space.
Glossy	A shiny finished photograph usually preferred for making half-tone engravings, a magazine printed on glossy paper.
Gone to bed, gone to press	Page or edition forme has left the composing room and is being, or about to be printed.
Gothic	Type family of monotone letter forms without serifs and with vertical emphasis. Gothic is US term, Europeans prefer to call these types grots (grotesques).
Great primer	Old name for 18pt type.
Green proof	Uncorrected proof.
Grid	Basic divisions and sub-divisions of a page which the designer uses as a skeleton for his layout. Also clear sheet of plastic used in making up photostat papers. It is a bit larger than page size and is graduated in lines, a blank sheet of paper is attached to the grid and bromides are assembled on it in the same way that type is put into a chase.
Grot	Abbreviation for grotesque, type family of moonstone letter forms without serifs. Modern types based on early nineteenth century forms and despite name, have subtle appeal which makes them best of sans serifs for newspaper display. US term for grots is gothic.
Gutter	Blank margins between two printed pages. Also a river of white caused by wide spacing or spacing occurring in awkward pattern.

H

Hairline	Thinnest stroke in letter form. Thinnest rule used in newspapers. Also unwanted wisps of metal which sometimes adhere between letters on a slug and so impair printing.
Hair space	Thinnest spaces in line casting, six to an em or thinner.
Half-tone	Engraved plate reproducing, by patter of dots, graduations of tone of photograph or drawing.
Hammer	One-or-two word heading set flush left over main heading of about half the size.
Handout	Copy supplied by speaker or publicity agent.
Hand-set	Type set by hand, newspapers try to avoid much hand setting, though Ludlow headline matrices are assembled by hand before casting.
Hanging-indent	Style for text and headline composition in which first line is set full measure and all succeeding lines are indented an equal amount at the left.
Hanging par	One paragraph set with a hanging indent.
Hdg, head	Abbreviation for headline.
Head to come	Notice to composing room that headline will be sent after the story.
Headline schedule	Sheet or booklet displaying all headline types used by a newspaper. Displays are grouped in column widths, or scored with pica rulings, unit count per column may be given.
Hold over	Instruction to keep, rather that discard,

	the type of all or part of a story which has not been published. As held over story that is one intended to publish at the next opportunity.
Hole	Gap in page chase or dummy where type and illustrations insufficient to fill.
Hood	Rules arranged around three sides of a headline, top, left and right.
Horizontal make-up	Style in which multi-column headlines are arranged across the page with text type running underneath in short legs.
Hot metal	All metal printing materials, composition by metal rather than by film-set type which is pasted up.
House rules	Style notes and procedures laid down by individual offices.

I

IENS	Indian and Eastern Newspaper Society. Organization of newspaper owners.
IFWJ	Indian Federation of Working Journalists.
ILNA	Indian Language Newspapers Association
Imposing stone	Full tile of the composing room 'stone'.
Imprint	Name and address of the publisher.
Indent	To set narrower than normal measure by having blank white space at either beginning or end. Pronounced indent.
Indention, indentation	White space at the beginning or end when a line is set short of full measure. The usual paragraph, indention is one em quad of the body size.
Inferior letters/figs	Small letters or figures cast on the lower part of typeface as in H_2O.

In hand	Copy is being set or a block is being made.
Insert	Copy or type to be inserted in the body of a story to interrupt the sequence already set or being set. Inserts are marked A, B, C, etc. and their placing is indicated on galley proof.
Inside columns	Columns on any page which are not either at extreme left or extreme right.
Inside page	Any page except the front or back.
Intaglio	Printing process from sunken images.
Inter type	Trade name of keyboarded line casting machine.
In the page	Type already transferred from galley to chase.
Intro	Introduction or opening paragraph of a story.
Inverted pyramid	Headline style of centred lines in which each successive line is shorter than the one above, also story structure, which arranges facts in descending order of importance.
Issue	All copies of one day's newspaper. An issue may consist of several editions.
Italic	Type with letters and characters that lean to the right.
Ital(s)	Abbreviation for italic.
ITU	International Typographical Union.

J

Jim dash	Small rule, usually three ems long to separate decks of headline or headline or headline from text.

Journalese	Offensive term for shoddier styles of newspapers writing.
Jump to	To continue a story from one page to another.
Jump head	Headline on continued part of story
Jump line	Continued from page I.
Jump story	Story continued from a previous page.
Justify	To space out a line of type so that it fills the column measure, to space out a column of type so that it fills the page measure.
Justowriter	Trade name of typewriter which sets cold type from perforated tape.

K

Keep down	Instruction to printer to set in lower case.
Keep in	Instruction to compositor to use thinnest spacing possible to keep all words in a line or section.
Keep standing	Instruction to hold type available for use.
Keep up	Instruction to printer to set in capitals.
Kicker	(US) Small headline, usually underscored, placed above and to left of main headline. Also eyebrow, teaser, over line.
Kill	Do not publish. The instruction may refer to part or all of a story. Copy marked 'kill' is spiked, type is killed by discarding in the hellox.
Klischograph	Trade name for electronic engraving machine.
Knifing corrections	Corrections made in photo-composed

	newspapers by chopping up printed images and superimposing on photoset material in the page grid.

L

Label	News headline with no force or life, or standing features headline such as Women, Sport, etc.
Late man	Deskman who stays behind to fudge or replete for late news when last edition has gone to press.
Layout	Plan showing how type matter is to be fitted into space available.
Lead	Pronounced lead. First paragraph of a news story.
Lead	Pronounced lead. Strip of metal less than type high, used for increasing the space between lines of type.
Lead all	A lead or intro containing a general summary of a long news story.
Leader	Leading article or editorial carrying newspaper's opinion. Leader page carries the leader and other opinion.
Leaders	Dots to lead the eye across the page.
Lead story	Story supporting the main display headlines of a page.
Lead to come	Signal to printer that the opening paragraphs lead, or intro will come later.
Legend	Obsolete word for caption or cut line.
Legman	Reporter who collects facts but does not write the story.
Letterpress	Printing from a relief, or raised surface. The raised type and blocks are inked and come in direct contact with the paper.

Letter spacing	Thin spacing inserted between letters of a word, as in this e x a m p l e, usually to justify a line.
Lift	To carry type forward from one edition to another, either all or part of a story or illustration. Also, to steal a story from another publication.
Light box	Back-lighted work surface for viewing transparencies, negatives, and for marking on back of photo prints.
Light face	Type with lighter appearance, compared with bold.
Light table	Back-lighted work surface used in photo-composed newspapers. The compositor places the page on it to assemble the elements of the page.
Line	Single line of headline or text type.
Lineage, linage	Measure of printed material based on the number of lines printed. Freelance copy is lineage copy because it is normally paid so much a line. In US, term more commonly used for amount of advertising printed in specific period.
Line-and-tone	Process-engraved printing blocks combining both screen and line-etching techniques.
Line block	An engraving which prints only black and white without the shades of a half-tone.
Line-casters	Typesetting machines such as linotype and Inter type, which cast text type in lines. Also, operator who uses keyboard of a line-casting machine.
Line Drawing	Brush or pen drawing consisting of black and white element.

Line up	To arrange evenly flush left or right.
Lino	Abbreviation for Linotype.
Linofilm	Trade name of photo-setting machine.
Linotron	Trade name for photo-setting machine using cathode ray tube.
Linotype	Trade name for keyboarded line casting machine.
Lithography	Paleographic method of printing from ink impressed on a sheet.
Live copy	Copy yet to be set into type.
Lock up (a page)	The process of placing the type and illustrations in a chase, and adjusting the furniture and quoins so that the type is firmly held and the forme can be sent to foundry or presses.
Logo	Abbreviation for logotype.
Logotype	Nameplate for a newspaper or identification of a section, business, family, etc. cast on one block of type.
Long primer	Old name for 10pt type.
Long run	When a printing press is not interrupted for a long time by a new edition, or when a page similarly remains unchanged, or greater than usual space given to a single story or feature.
Loose	Too much letter or word spacing in composition.
Lower case	Letters which are not capitals, thus c, d, e. also the name given to the composing case which holds these letters.
Ludlow	Trade name for machine which casts larger sizes of headline on a slug from hand assembled matrices.

M

Machine border	Border cast on such machines as Elrod, Linotype, inter type, Mono type.
Machine-set	Type which can be set mechanically on a keyboarded line-casting machine, as distinct from hand assembled type or matrices. Newspapers prefer machine set text, captions and small headlines for speed.
Magazine	Container which holds matrices on a line casting machine.
Make over	Process of rearranging a page of type or series of pages to accommodate later news, improve appearance or make corrections.
Make-ready	The process of preparing a page form or stereo plate for the presses. Sheets of paper trimmed and laid beneath areas, especially blocks, to assure an even impression on every part of the printing area.
Make up	To take type from a galley and arrange in pages with illustrations, the physical appearance of the paper and, sometimes, the dummy page plan for the disposition of stories and pictures.
Make up editor	Journalist who supervises the make up of the paper in the composing room.
Mangle	Stereotype's molding machine which takes a papier-mâché impression of the type.
Margins	The un-printed surround of the area occupied by reading matter
Masking	Technique of obscuring part of a photograph (e.g. by paper overlay) to indicate the session to be printed.

Master proofs	Set of proofs, galley or page incorporating all writer's and editor's corrections.
Masthead	Strictly, heading on editorial or leader page which gives paper's name and the paper's ownership and management. Often confused with nameplate or flag.
Mat	Abbreviation of matrix.
Matrix, matrices (pl.)	A die or mould from which type is cast. Also the papier-mâché mould from which a stereo plate is made.
Matter	Any type or blocks, it may be body matter (the text setting), standing matter (not intended for immediate use), straight matter (simple setting), solid matter (without leads), open matter (loaded), live matter, dead matter, and so on.
Matt finish	Dull finish to photograph or printing paper, contrast glossy.
Measure	The width of a line, column, or page of type, usually expressed in pica ems.
Medium	The weight of type the maker puts forward, under the name of the family, as representing the design in normal weight from which variants have been derived.
Mf	Abbreviation for "more follow".
Mickey Mouse	A linotype line casting machine stripped down to its casting mechanism so that headlines can be cast from hand assembled Linotype matrices.
Middle leads	2 pt. leads (leads) called middle because they come between thin and thick leads.

Middle space	A space of four ems.
Minion	Old name for 7 pt. type.
Minionette	Old name for 6½ pt type.
Minuscule	Lower case letters of the alphabet.
Misprint	Inaccurate setting, a typographical error.
Mitre	Corner piece of rule or border cut at angle of 45 degrees to form a perfect joint, to level a rule or border so that there is a neat fit at the right angle.
Mitred rule	Angle corner rule used to make perfect joints.
Modern	Term for typefaces having abrupt contrast between thin and thick strokes, the axis of the curves is vertical, and there are often no brackets on the serifs.
Mofussil	Indian newspaper term for district or tehsil news, also mofussil desk, etc.
Monotype	Composing machine which casts each character on a separate type body.
Montage	Arrangement or mounting in one composition of pictorial elements from several sources.
More	Written at foot of copy or proof to show that more is to follow.
Morgue	File of prepared obituaries.
Mte	Abbreviation for 'more to come'.
Multiple rules	Three or more type rules of the same or differing point sizes cast on a single body and running parallel.
Must	An instruction, from a senior newspaper executive, that the copy or proof on which it is written must be followed and published without fail.

Mutton	Printers' slang for the em.

N

Nebitype	Trade name for Italian machine which casts metal slugs from hand-assembled matrices, its own or Ludlow/ Intertype/Linotype.
Negative working	Process used in production of photo set web offset newspaper. Most pictures are inserted as negative. On the paste up, an opaque patch is placed where a picture is to go when the page is photographed; the patch, being reversed, becomes a window and shows clear on the page negative. The screen negative of the illustration is then placed in the window.
News hole	Total editorial space in a newspaper after the ads have been placed.
Newsprint	Generic term to describe the pulp paper widely used for newspaper production.
Nonp	Abbreviation for nonpareil. Commonly used to indicate spacing 'add a nonp' means add half a pica (12 pt) em of spacing, or about one-twelfth of an inch.
Nonpareil	Pronounced nonprul. Old name for 6 pt.
Notch	Opening cut out of corner of engraving to accommodate type: an external mortise, q.v.
NUJ	National Union of Journalists, trade union.
Nut	Printer's term for an en, the unit of measurement half as wide as an em of the same type.

O

OANA	Organization of Asian News Agencies.
Obit	Obituary, biography of person who has died.
Oblique stroke	One sloping to left or right, diverging from vertical or horizontal.
Odd folio	First, third, and all unevenly numbered pages. The odd folio is always a right hand page.
Office style	House style: standard system of spellings and punctuation laid down for a newspaper so that continuity is recognizable, depending on style.
Off print	Reprint of an article or illustration specially run off after publication in a newspaper or magazine.
Off set	Strong candidate for most misused term in history of newspaper production. It is not a description of setting, but of printing. Papers set by photographic method are often printed off set; papers are transferred from a lithographic plate to a rubber roller, and then set off this on to paper. Off set has become a synonym for lithography.
Off set blanket	Blanket made of rubber which takes designs from the lithographic plate and impresses them on the paper
Off set gravure	Fine printing process giving wide range of tonal expression. Printing is by plates and impression rollers as in off-set, but here the image is in intaglio or beneath the surface of the plates.

Off set paper	Absorptive, non-curling paper suitable for off-set printing process, or the newspaper produced by off-set printing.
Off set press	Press which prints by the indirect method of lithography.
Ok	Proof-reader's sign to indicate that there is no error on the proof.
On the hook	Edited copy awaiting setting in the composing room.
Op-ed	American expression to describe page facing the editorial or leader page.
Open format	Style of newspaper page with white space dividing columns.
Open matter	Type which is either well leaded or has lots of short lines.
Open quotes	Begin with quotation marks ( ), the beginning of a quotation set-off by quotation marks.
Open spacing	Wide spacing of type, whether by white between letters, words, or lines.
Out of sorts	Shortage of some characters in a font of type
Over banner	Banner headline running higher than the nameplate of the newspaper. Also called sky liner (r) and over the proof in US.
Over lay	To place a transparent covering over an illustration, or a film set over a film set page, to indicate colour separation or alterations or corrections.
Over line	Display type over a picture, also sometimes called a title. Also a line of smaller type over the main headline, which in turn, may be called a strap or an eyebrow.

Over matter, over set	Type set too wide for space allocated.
Overnight pages	Pages scheduled to go to press early, late p.m. or early a.m. before work begins on the pages of the day's newspaper.
Oxford rule	Heavy and light rules running close together in parallel, not to be confused with simple parallel or double rules.

P

P	Abbreviation for page, hence p 1 : p 2, etc. its plural is pp.
Padding	Portions of copy not necessary for the narrative.
Pagination	The numbering of pages; the pagination budget for a newspaper is the number of pages it is budgeted to achieve.
Panel	Short item indented either side and with a strong rule on top and bottom. Some offices still call it a panel when it has rules on four sides, but box is the preferred term.
Paragraph indent	Beginning the first line of a paragraph with a white space, usually one pica em quad.
Paragraph mark	Signal to a line caster to begin the line with an indention.
Parallel rule	Rule with two lines in parallel and of equal weight.
Parenthesis	(Brackets)
Paste-on	Cold type pasted on to page plan for the plate maker.
Paste-up	To arrange cold type on a page plan

	(or 'mechanical', as it is sometimes called) for the plate maker.
Pearl	Old name for 5 pt. type.
Perforator	Machine which punches holes in tape to a pattern which, when fed into a line casting machine, produces lines of type. Also, the operator of a perforator or tape-punching machine.
Period	Another name for full point, full stop.
Photo-chase	Film bromides pasted n to thin strips of polystyrene for easier movement. Often used to collate columns of classified advertising.
Photo engraving	See process engraving.
Photogravure	Fine printing method. The paper sheet passes between a rubber-covered impression cylinder and an intaglio plate, photographically prepared, and in so doing takes the ink from the finely etched recesses in the plate.
Photo-Lathe	Trade name for mechanical engraving machine.
Photon	Trade name for photo type setting machine.
Photoset	Abbreviation for photo-composition the reproduction photographically on film or paper of lines of type characters. Photo-set newspapers are called cold type papers in contrast to hot metal papers composed from lines of metal type.
Photostat	A misused a general term for photo-copy. It is a trade name for the machine and the photo-copies it produces.
PIB	Press Information Bureau.

Pica	Printer's unit of measurement, there being 12 points in a pica. Also old name for 12 pt type.
Pica em	Standard unit of square measurement, pica em being 12 x 12.
Pick up	Proof instruction from editorial section/desk to pick up type already set, and incorporate with new material.
Pics, pix	Abbreviation for pictures, usually half tone illustrations.
Pie, pie line	Disarranged type, freak line cast when a Linotype operator has made a mistake and fills out a line at random.
Plain rule	Rule with plain straight lines, in variety of sizes but without decoration.
Planer	Flat wooden block which comps place over the type in the chase and hammer to ensure type surface is even.
Plate	Semi-cylindrical metal printing sheet cast from a flong for attachment to rotary press, or photographically engraved metal.
Platen	Surface which holds paper and presses it against an inked relief surface, roll holding paper in typewriter.
Play	Editorial term indicating emphasis to be given to a story. Points in a story can be played up or down or played lightly. If the story itself is played up it is given a big display.
Plug	To push the popularity of a show, book, or song by publicity. Also a wedge of wood used in some printing and engraving.
Point	Unit of measurement in type. It is about one seventy second of an inch,

	actually 0.01383 in. The European Didot point (q.v.) is slightly larger.
Point size	The measurement of a type from the front of the base to the back. Also called the body size.
Point system	System of casting type and measuring areas in multiples of the point (q.v.)
Points	Punctuation marks. A full point is what follows the last letter of this sentence.
Pool	Non-aligned news agencies pool.
Pork-chop	Tiny half-column engraving of some one's face also called thumbnail.
Poster make-up	Format which uses the front page as a poster headline and pictures, with little or no text, designed to attract the reader insider.
Poster type	Big sizes of type, upwards of 72 pt., commonly made of wood.
Pot	Holds the molten type metal in a line caster.
PR	Public or press relations.
Precede	Pronounced precede. A new lead or story which takes precedence over an earlier story. Or a preliminary paragraph or two set up in different type to introduce, summarize or explain a succeeding story.
Preferred position	Advertiser's request for position on a page.
Prelim	Introductory material.
Primary letters	Lower case letters without either ascender or descended primer, i.e. x, o, a, etc.

Primer	Old name for 18 pt. type, long primer (LP) is old name for 10 pt.
Print	Total number of newspapers printed, or the positive picture taken from a photographic negative.
Printer	Sometimes means the printer, the man in charge of the composing room. Strictly, a craftsman who makes up forms or operates the presses, but loosely used to describe comps. Line casters, proof readers, and all those engaged in the making of print. Also abbreviation for teleprinter.
Process engraving	General term for producing an image on a sensitized metal plate.
Proof	Inked impression type, or engraving, or page for study of accuracy or appearance before sending to press.
Proof hook	Assembly point of galley or page proofs.
Proof press	Machine for printing a galley or page proof. Proofs are said to be 'pulled' rather than printed.
Proof reader	Person who reads the proof to make sure it follows copy accurately.
Proof reader's marks	Standardized system of marks for correcting errors on proof.
Proof-slip	A long galley proof. Also called slip proof.
PTI	Press Trust of India, a national news agency.
Pull	Synonymous with proof. A proof is said to be pulled, so a pull of a galley or page is a proof of a galley or page.
Pull-out	Section of a newspaper or magazine that can be extracted easily and read separately.

Punch-tape head	The signal from the keyboard or computer drives the punch-head to produce punch-tape for feeding into phototypesetting machine or line caster for hot metal.
Put to bed	To put the form or stereo plate on the press. When a page has gone to bed, it is too late to make corrections.

Q

Q and A	Question and answer copy, as in formal interview or court badinage.
Quad, quadrate	A pace. A piece of blank type of equal body size but less than type high used to fill spaces in a line of type. Quads are made six to a fount so that their widths are multiples of the em of the size of type used. Thus the em quad is the square of the body type, the en quad is half the body, and the smallest, the hair space, is about one-twelfth the body.
Query	Question raised on copy or on proof, or in a message to a news agency. Also a freelancer's inquiry whether a newspaper is interested in such and such a story.
Quoin	Wedge-shaped metal device for locking type and plates in chases.
Quoin key	Iron key to tighten quoins in locking up chase.
Quotation marks, quotes	Punctuation marks to indicate that words are those actually used by a speaker or in report. Can be double (" ") or single (' ') , "If double quotes begin, single quotes are used for

	'quotes within quotes' and vice-versa". Headlines should have single quotes; books usually have single quotes in text, newspapers double quotes.
Quote	Quotation, in newspapers, often means a sentence or paragraph of a speaker's words.

R

Random	Composing room table, divided into galley widths, where galleys are assembled before make-up
Rate card	Schedule of advertising spaces available and the cost of each.
Readability	A story is said to be readable and have readability if it has a compelling narrative easy to grasp. Readability in type graph means the ease with which the eye skims the type.
Reader	Man who checks proofs for consistency with copy and corrects errors in setting, punctuation, etc. The 'readers' is the department where proof readers and their assistants, copy-holder, do their work as correctors of the press.
Readership	Not the same as circulation of a newspaper. Something like five people read a single copy.
Recast	To cast a new plate for a page whose content, usually editorial but sometime advertising, has been changed; re-plate.
Reel	Roll of newsprint fed into the presses, the revolving drum or core which receives and winds the paper.
Reel-end	Part of the paper machine where the web is reeled up, the last few yards of a reel of newsprint.

Reglet	Narrow strip of wood 12 or 6 point wide, for spacing type in the form.
Regular type	Standard width of a typeface, as distinct from extended or condensed versions. The preferred term is medium type.
Rejig	Editorial alterations to a story in type, usually involving a change in the sequence of paragraphs in type, deletions, and the insertion of new matter. When a story is rejigged, the type standing in the page will be taken out and the new arrangement assembled on the random.
Release	A press note or a handout, to 'okay' for publication
Repro proofs	Proofs of high quality on art paper usually, to be made into engravings.
Re-punch	Repetition of a telegraphed message by the sending station, usually for the correction of an error in transmission.
Retouching	Improving a photograph by painting in certain tones, most useful in painting out any streaks on photographs received by wire, before engraving, most questionable when photographic content is altered or inserted.
Reuters	British news agency.
Revamp	Altering a story by changing the sequence of paragraphs, but not by rewriting.
Reverse indent	The first line of type is full measure and the remainder of the paragraph lines are indented one or more ems at the beginning. This is the reverse of normal indentation where it is the first

	line only which is indented. Also called a hanging indent.
Revise	Second or subsequent proof incorporating corrections made from previous proof.
Rewrite	To write a story again, rather than simply edit the copy. American newspapers have a rewrite man to put telephoned facts into prose.
Rivers	Ugly streaks of white space in a page caused by over spacing between letters and words.
RO	"Run on", instruction on copy to set two written paragraphs as one, or treat set out matter as a single paragraph.
Rotary press	Conventional newspaper printing press in which both printing surface and impression cylinder rotate at high speed.
Round up	Collection of separate items into one story or under one headline, a common one is a weather round-up.
Ruby	Old name for 5½ pt. English equivalent of US agate.
Rule	Type-high metal strip that prints as line or lines.
Run	Duration of printing an edition, or number of copies printed.
Run in full	Senior editorial instruction that copy must not be cut.
Running story	A story which changes rapidly between editions, as in a plane crash. Or a story which develops over several days.
Roman	Group of alphabets in the printer's fount which is distinguished from italic

	by verticality and the shape of certain lowercase letters.
Roman numerals	I, II, III, IV, V or i, ii, iii, iv or v instead of 1, 2, 3, 4, 5.
Routing	Cutting away unwanted metal from any part of an engraving plate.
Rush	Urgent news agency summary of news break. Or a direction on copy asking the composing room to give it priority.

S

Sandwich	Panel inset in text type cross referring to associated material elsewhere, or, a reference to a side less box.
Sans, sans serif	Type without serifs on the ends of the strokes.
Scan-A-Graver	Trade name for mechanical engraver producing plastic half-tone relief plates.
Schedule	There is the time schedule, or sheet, listing deadlines for pages, the chief sub's or city editor's schedule recording stories processed, and the headline schedule which categorises all headlines used in the paper, often to a code.
Scoop	A story or picture of some importance nobody else has an exclusive.
Screamer	Crude, sensational headline, exclamation mark.
Screen	Given number of dots to a square inch (of a process of engraving) which make up the light and shade of the picture. Fine screen engraving is suitable only for the finer quality paper.

Seal	Wording or symbol at the top of the front page indicating the edition, i.e. city edition, late edition, etc.
See copy	Direction to readers or composing room to check proof against the copy.
See other proof	Indication that two or more proofs need to be combined to make all the necessary changes.
See Scheme	Direction to composing room to check page proof againt the page scheme or layout, or to set a piece of copy according to a scheme sent to the composing room
Self-contained	Any item which stands by itself, a self-contained caption or picture is one without an accompanying story; a self-contained story is one without any cross references or sidebars.
Send (a page)	Dispatch a page form to the stereo department.
Send (copy)	Usually the instruction is to 'send it out' or 'sent it down' or 'send it up' and they all mean the same thing, send the copy to be set.
Separation	Use of colour filters so that single colour negatives can be made of multi-coloured illustration.
Sequence	Picture strip showing consecutive action in a number of pictures taken shortly after one another.
Serial	Of, in forming a series of articles published in instalments. Generally used for fictional or biographical feature material or investigative stories.
Series	Size range of any design of typeface. Also, number of articles pursuing some

	theme but in different issues of the paper.
Serif	Line or stroke projecting from the end of a main stroke. Serifs are of different form and join the strokes in different ways, and some types have no serifs (sans serifs).
Set	To compose in type, also the width of a piece of type from side to side.
Set and hold	Set in type but do not publish without a release.
Set close	Instruction to printer that minimum spacing should be used.
Set flush	To set matter 'full-out' or without indenting.
Set off	Desirable and deliberate in off set printing, being the transfer of image from rubber blanket to newsprint, but accidental and undesirable in letter press printing, being the transfer of ink from one printed page to the facing page.
Set open	Instruction to printer that type is to be well spaced.
Set out	Instruction to printer to tabulate the matter, setting up letters from a case of type so that wrong founts can be picked out.
Set solid	Instruction to printers to dispense with leads and to set type on body of same size—8 or 8pt., rather than, say, 8 on 9.
Set up	To compose in type, or instruction to set in capital letters.
Shadow	Typeface in which a three dimensional effect is created, such as cameo, Graphique, Gill shadow.

Shank	Rectangular main body of a piece of type, also called the stem.
Sheet	Slang for newspaper.
Shirt-tail	Brief addition to a long story,
Shooting a page	Term in photo set newspapers. When the bromides of type are assembled in position on the page, the page goes to the camera room for 'shooting'—it goes into negative form ready for plate making.
Short measure	Type set narrower than the standard width of a column in a newspaper.
Shorts	Stories of a few paragraphs with smallish headlines (up to, say, two lines of 24 pt) intended for use down the page.
Short takes	Sheets of copy of only a paragraph or two, to 'send in short takes' means to send copy urgently to the composing room, a sheet or two at a time.
Shotgun head	Multi-deck headline—two or more decks of heading on the same story, each deck consisting of one or more lines.
Shoulder	That part of the upper surface of a type which carries no relief image itself and on which the relief image stands.
Shrinkage	Narrowing of the stereotype flung during molding process, producing page fractionally smaller than original typeset page.
Sidebar	Story related to main story and run next to it.
Side-head	Small subsidiary heading in the body of a story, set left instead of centred (cross head).

Sidelight	Similar to sidebar but with emphasis on personalities.
Side stick, foot stick	Pieces of wedge shaped metal or wood used to tighten type in a galley.
Single leaded	Lines of body type separated by the insertion of a thin lead between each line.
Single quotes	'These'/Better for headlines.
Single rules	Rule printing one light line.
Situational	News feature usually giving background information, as distinct from urgent, 'spot' news, and so will properly hold until space is available or events make it topical.
Size down	Instruction to printer to decrease the size of type to the next size down unless specified.
Size up	Instruction to printer to increase the size of type to the next size up unless specified.
Sked	Slang for schedule.
Sky-line	Headline running above the name plate across the top of the page, also called over-the-roof.
Slab serif	Typefaces with heavy, square ended serifs with or without brackets (i.e., gentle curve) at the junction. Faces such as rock-well, clarendon, playbill.
Slot	The centre of the inner side of the copy desk, traditionally horseshoe-shaped; the slot man or slot is the copy editor who sits here and instructs copy editors who sit on the rim.
Slug	Line of type cast on a line casting machine, spacing material six points thick, the identifying words or phrase

given to each story which is set in one line at the top of the story and discarded when the story is complete and 'clean'.

Small caps — Capital letters smaller than regular capitals of a particular type face; they are much the same size as the lowercase letters of the same fount.

Solid — Type lines without any space between them.

Space band — Metal wedge which automatically provides spaces, words or letters.

Spactacolour — Form of preprinted colour advertising.

Spike — Basic tool of sub-editor and especially copy-taster, being a metal spindle on which unwanted copy is thrust/spiked. 'Spike it' means 'kill it, but keep the body available'.

Splash — The main story on the front page, the front page itself.

Spot colour — Non-process colour. No special plate is prepared but colour is applied during the run to selective parts of the page, usually one place and one small amount of colour, as in a coloured seal or coloured fudge.

Spot news — Unexpected news such as accidents or fires, as distinct from scheduled news (court cases, speeches).

Spread — Two facing pages, or a major display which covers part of two faces in pages, also an advertisement that covers full page or almost full.

Staggered head — Headline in which each line is set with an indention on the previous line, opposite effect of a centred headline.

Standing type	Type composed and stored awaiting use.
Stars	Common symbol for edition: one star, two star, etc.; often apparent only to the trained eye.
Stereotype	Plate cast in metal from a papier-mâché mould of type and/or blocks. A sign on copy that a correction or deletion has been made in error and should be ignored. The words affected are underlined with dots and the word 'stet' written in the margin.
Stick	Metal tray used to hold type being set by hand. Its size provides a rough common measurement; a stick of type is about twenty lines of 8pt type, two inches or so.
Stone	The imposing surface on which pages are made up; it is now steel, not stone.
Stone hand	Print worker who arranges type in page form often called comp (compositor).
Stone sub	Editorial man who works at the stone in the composing room, seeing that the make up is followed, cutting stories which run too long in type, and ensuring that deadlines are kept.
Story	Any news item, editorial item in a newspaper other than letter and illustrations.
Straight matter	Ordinary editorial setting in regular column width without illustrations.
Straight news	Story without colour or interpretation of any kind.
Strap	Subsidiary headline in smaller type over main headline.

Streamer	Headline running across top of all or most of the columns.
Stringer	Non-staff reporter who is paid on the basis of what is published, plus perhaps, a small retaining fee.
Strip in	To combine line and half tone negatives before making off set plates; to arrange for a headline to be superimposed on a half-tone block.
Strip the form	Take type and furniture out of the chase.
Style	System of spellings, punctuation, capitulation, etc. followed in an office.
Style sheet	Pages listing office or house style.
Sub	Sub-editor, to edit a story and write the headline.
Sub-editor	The editorial craftsman who edits copy for sense and length and legal safety and writes the headlines.
Sub-head	Small subsidiary heading in the body of story, usually centred.
Subst	Substitute, meaning story so marked is to run in place of another.
Supercaster	Trade name of monotype machine, which casts large sizes of type for headlines, borders, rules and leads.
Swelled rule	A rule that is thicker in the centre and tapers to each end.
Symmetrical make-up	Attempting to balance display elements in a page on either side of a given central axis.
Syndicate	Organisation selling and buying feature or news material; group of newspapers, to sell editorial material or circulate widely.

T

Tab, tabloid	Newspaper, half the size of broad sheet, approximately 11 inches wide by 16 inches deep.
Tag line	Smaller line attached to a headline to attribute source of statement there.
Tailpiece	Short addition to a story, separately displayed, usually of only a paragraph or two and of a light nature.
Take	Each sheet of copy for a story, Unit of news agency transmission.
Take in	Instruction to typesetter to thin-space a line or lines to get in an extra syllable or words; direction to incorporate or insert matter at that point.
Tape	Strictly, ribbon of paper with perforation which instructs a teleprinter to type copy or a line caster to set copy in metal. Also, loosely used to refer to news agency or wire copy.
Tass	News agency of the erstwhile Soviet Union (now Russia).
Taste	To skim a story or stories in copy and assess their editorial value.
Taster	Abbreviation for copy taster.
Teaser	Headline or caption to picture which rather than informing the reader intrigues him to read further: e.g. 'Why the soprano blushed'.
Telephoto	Photograph transmitted telegraphically. To send a picture by wire, or a photograph taken with a telescopic lens.
Teletype	Machine that types out news coming from a news agency—too often in capital letters that hinders readability.

	Also called a tele-printer or ticker or just "the wire".
Tele-type setting	System in which line casting machines are operated from code in perforated tape. Tape may be punched at the local plant but in US it is commonly supplied to newspapers all over the country by central news agency.
Text	Body matter, as distinct from illustrations, headlines and white space.
Text type	Type in which the body of the paper is set, as distinct from headline or display type.
Text type	Old English or black letter type style with bold thick body stroke and sharp thin serifs.
Thick lead	3 pt. lead (led).
Thick space	Space of 3 points.
Think piece	Article of opinion or interpretation rather than straight news report.
Thin lead	1 or 8½ lead (led).
Thirty	30, 30-dash. Sign at the end of a story, either in type or copy. It is written '30', in metal it is a dash of about six picas.
Thumbnail	Half-column portrait block, also called pork-chop, or rough small dummy for advertisement, also single quotation mark or apostrophe.
Tight story	One written so concisely that it cannot be cut without damage.
Tight sub	Sub-editor who is expert at slicing the fat from a story.
Time copy	"Anytime" copy, meaning copy or type matter which is timeless and can be run at any time.

Tint block	Block or surface used for printing flat background colour.
Tinted headline	One in which the block of the type has been softened to a grey.
Tip	Hint or information worth checking for a story.
Tomb stoning	Old-fashioned newspaper display in which a page was made up of single column headlines in identical type side by side.
Tone	The amount of reflected light; the difference of the areas of light and dark on a printed page.
Top deck	The fist deck or bank/block of a headline of several decks.
Tramlines	Unsightly effect of two rules running close and parallel.
Transitional	Type-face mid-way between old style and modern, or Garalde and Didone in the British Standard, and there defined as typefaces in which the axis of the curves is vertical or inclined slightly to the left, the serifs are bracketed, and those of the ascenders in the lowercase are oblique.
Transpose	Mark trim.
Trim	To shorten copy by small amounts nibbling at it rather than cutting severally.
Trs	Abbreviation for transpose.
TTS	Tele-typesetter, the trade name for machine which does tele-typesetting
Turn head	Headline on inside page identifying resumption of story continued from another page.

Turn line	Line of type, in bold or itallic usually, directing reader to continuation of story on another page ('continued page …'), also the line on the inside page identifying the beginning of the continuation ('continued from page ….').
Turtle	Steel trolley with a flat surface used to move a single page form from the stone, just large enough to hold a single page, the turtle is also used sometimes as a make-up stone.
Two-decker, three-decker	Headline composed of two or three decks, i.e. self-contained units which may each have several lines.
Two-line cap	Capital letter, usually at the beginning of text as a rising initial having the depth of two lines of accompanying text.
Two-line double pica	Old name for 44 pt. type.
Two-line English	Old name for 28 pt. type.
Two-line pica	Old name for 24 pt. type
2 pt. lead	Lead (led) which is two points thick, the commonest.
Type	A piece of metal or wood bearing a relief image of a letter or character for printing.
Type area	The amount of space on a page to be filled with type.
Typeface	Any individual type, its appearance when printed. Usually defined by name of type family (e.g. Bodoni, Century, etc.) style (roman, italic, etc.) and point size.
Type high	Of the same height as type, English type is 0.918 of an inch high.

Typographical error	Mistake in setting the copy (as distinct from editorial error).
Typo setter	Trade name for photographic machine producing cold display type.

U

Uc	Upper case, or capitals.
Undated story	A pull-together or round up in which material from several sources is presented in one story, copy to be used when convenient.
Underline	Wording, call it legend or caption or underline, beneath an illustration.
Under measure	Setting which falls short of the standard column measure.
Underscore	To underline a word or letters in copy or in type.
Uneven folios	Page numbers of the right hand pages 3, 5, 7, 9, 11, etc.
Units	Standards of measurement, the point being the unit of measurement for type size, the pica (12 points) or area of type lines, white spaces, pages, etc.
UNI	United Press International, a US agency.
Upper case	The capital letters of a fount type.

V

Varitype	Trade name for electric automatic justifying machine producing strike on material and with great facility for changing type faces.
Venetians	Type faces classified as Humanist in the British Standard in which the cross stroke of the lower case is oblique, the

axis of the curves is inclined to the left, there is no great contrast between thin and thick strokes, and the serifs are bracketed, e.g. Verona, Centaur, Kennelly.

Vertical make-up — Once the standard, now the rarity; page make-up in which no display element is allowed to cross a column rule, i.e. all single column headlines or pictures, or an emphasis in that direction.

Vignette — Small illustration or decoration not squared up or enclosed by a border.

W

Wash drawing — A sketch made with a brush in washes with more tonal scale than simple black and white, and hence suitable for half-tone reproduction.

Waste copied — Copies of a newspaper run off at the beginning of a run when ink, etc. are being adjusted.

Wavy rule — Rule that prints undulating line.

Waxing — Process in photo set newspapers. Each bromide of type is fed into a heated roller machine which coats the reverse side of the bromide with an adhesive so that the film can be stuck down on paper.

Web — Roll of paper which is treaded through the printing presses.

Web off-set — Web-fed lithography, in which printing is done not directly from the plate but from a rubber blanket that has picked up the images from the inked plate. See off set, 'Webb', who does not exist,

	is often credited with this invention through an error in spelling.
Web press	Printing press in which a continuously running web of paper is fed in between an impression cylinder and another cylinder carrying the printing plate. See rotary press.
Weight	The degree of blackness of a type face.
Wf	Abbreviation for wrong fount.
White	Any part of the page which does not carry ink spaces around headlines, in and around words and letters, margins, etc.
White out	To put more spacing material in the page where indicated.
Wide leaded	Lines of type separated by more than one thickness of lead.
Windy line	Line with excessive white space.
Wire photo	Telephonic photo transmission system operated by Associated Press.
Wire room	Department which receives tele-printed copy and photographs from the news agencies and correspondents on distant assignments.
Wrong Fount	A mistake in composition by using a letter of the wrong size or not of the same design as the rest.

X

X-height	The height of all the primary lower case letters, which, size for size, are almost identical, and omitting those letters of the alphabet with ascenders or descenders.
X-ref	Cross-reference.

Y

Yellow journalism — The motto is 'never let the facts stand in the way of a good story. It is sensational, exploiting chauvinism.

Z

Zinco — Strictly, half-tone plate engraved on zinc, but commonly used for all photo-engravings, whatever the metal.

Zip-A-Tone — Trade name for tinted sheet added to line drawings or headlines.

Bibliography

Agrawal, Sushila, Press, Public Opinion and Government in India, (Asia Publishing House: Jaipur), 1970.

Alva, Joachim, Men and Supermen of Hindustan, (Mackeray & Co. : Mumbai), 1943.

Amal Home (ed.), All India Exhibition, Kolkata, 1948— Descriptive catalogue of exhibits in the Historical Section of the Newspapers and Periodicals Court, All India Exhibition, Kolkata, 1948.

Azad, Abdul Kalam, India Wins Freedom, (Orient Longmans: Mumbai),1958.

Ball, U.N., Ram Mohan Roy, U. Ray and Sons, Kolkata, 1933.

Englishman Press, Kolkata, 1878.

Banerjea, Sir Surendra Nath, A Nation in the making, Oxford University Press, Kolkata, 1946.

Banerji, Branjendra Nath, Ram Mohan Roy as Journalist, *Modern Review*, April, May and August, 1931.

Baistow, T., Fourth, Rate Estate: An anatomy of Fleet Street, London, U.K. Comedia Publishing Group, 1985.

Bannerjee, D.N., India's Nation Builders, (Headley Brothers: London), 1919.

Banerjee, Rajni, Romance of Journalism, Kolkata, India: Industry Publishers, 1947.

Barns, Margarita, The Indian Press, (George Allen & Unwin Ltd., London), 1940.

Bharatiya Vidya Bhavan, Rajaji's Speeches, Vol. I, (Bharatiya Vidya Bhavan: Mumbai), 1978.

Bhattacharje, Arun, Indian Press—Profession to Industry, (Vikas Publications: New Delhi), 1972.

Bose, Nirmal Kumar, Selection from Gandhi, Navjivan Publishing House, Kolkata, 1947.

Boyer, J.H., 'How Editors view Objectively?', *Journalism Quarterly*, 58(1): 24-28, 1981.

Bryce, George, *et. al.*, Newspaper History: From the 17th century to the Present Day, (Constable: London), 1978.

Budd, R., Thorpe, K.R. and Donohew, L., Content Analysis of Communication, New York, USA : Macmillan 1967.

Busteed, H.E., Echoes from old Kolkata, Thaker Spink and Co., Kolkata, 1888.

C.L.R., Journalism, (Thacker and Co. Ltd., Mumbai), 1944.

Campbell, Laurence Randolph, How to Report and Write the News, Prentice Hall, 1961.

Chakravarti, Satish Chandra, The Father of Modern India, Ram Mohan Roy Centenary Committee, Kolkata, 1935.

Chalapath Rau, M., The Press in India, (Allied Publishers: New Delhi), 1968.

Chalapathi Rao, M., The Press, Land and Peoples Series, (National Book Trust: New Delhi), 1974.

Chalapathi Rau, M., The Romance of the Newspaper, (National Council of Eductional Research and Training: New Delhi), 1975.

Chatterjee, R.K., Mass Communication, New Delhi, National Book Trust, 1973.

Chaturvedi, J.P., The Indian Press at Crossroads, New Delhi: Media Research Foundation, 1991.

Chirol, Valentine, India, (Ernest Benn Ltd. : London), 1926.

Chirol, Valentine, Indian Unrest, (Macmilln: London), 1910.

Cooper, Kent, Barriers Down, (Farrer and Rinehard Inc., New York), 1942.

Copple, Neale, Depth Reporting: An Approach to Journalism, Prentice Hall, 1969.

Dasgupta, Hemendranath, Desabandu Chitranjan Das, (Publications Division, Government of India: New Delhi), 1960.

Desai, Ashok V., Economic Aspects of the Indian Press, (Press Institute of India: New Delhi), 1971.

Desai, Mahadev, Day to Day with Gandhi, (Servo Seva Sangh: Varanasi), 1968.

Desai, Mahadev, Maulana Abul Kalam Azad, George Alien & Unwin Ltd., London, 1940.

Desmond, Robert W., Professional Training of Journalists, UNESCO, Paris, 1949.

Dhara, R., Journalism, (Industry Publishers Ltd., Calcútta), 1945.

Dutt, Paramananda, Memories of Motilal Ghose, Amrita Bazar Patrika, Kolkata, 1935.

Eapen, K.E. ,Journalism as a Profession in India: A study of two states (Bihar and Kerala) and cities (Mumbai and Delhi), Ph.D. Thesis, University of Winconsin, USA, 1969.

Edwards, Michael, History of British India, (Sidgwick & Jackson: London), 1967.

Emery, Edwin and Michael Emery, The Press and America, (Prentice Hall: Eaglewood Ciffs, N.J.), 1978.

Gandhi, Indira, My Faith, (Vision Books: New Delhi), 1982.

Gandhi, M.K., Young India (1919-27), (Tagore & Co., Chennai), 1922.

Gandhi, M.K., Autobiography, Navjivan Publishing House, Ahmedabad, 1940.

Ganguli, Deena Nath, Memories of Raja Ram Mohan Roy, The People's Press, Kolkata, 1884.

Garst, R.E. and Bernstein, T.M., Headlines and Deadlines, Columbia, USA. : Columbia University Press, 1963.

Ghose, Hamendra Prasad, The Newspapers in India, University of Kolkata, 1852.

Ghosh, Kedar, Freedom or Fraud of the Press, (Pupa: Kolkata), 1973.

Gokhale, Indian Moderates and British Raj, (Oxford University Press: London), 1977.

Government of India, Publications Divison, Facts about India, Ministry of I&B, New Delhi, 1952.

Grey, Elizabeth, The Story of Journalism, (Longmans Young Books: London), 1968.

Gross, Gerald (Ed.), The Responsibility of the Press, New York, USA : Fleet Publishing Corporation, 1966.

Gundappa, D.V., The Press in Mysore, (Karnataka Publishing House, Bangalore), 1940.

Hamlin, Bruce, 'Owners, Editors and Journalists': Ethical Issues in Journalism and Media (Eds.), Belsay, Andrew and Chadwick, Ruth, London, UK.: Routledge, 1992.

Haque, M., 'Is Development news more Salient than Human Interest stories in India's elite Press' ? *Gazette* 38(3): 83-99, 1986.

Heimrath, Charls, H., Indian Nationalism and Hindu Social Reforms, (Oxford University Press.

Herd, Harlod, The march of Journalism, (George Allen and Unwin Ltd., London), 1952.

History of Early Printing in Western India, The Indian Library Association : Proceedings of the 5th All India Library Conference held in Mumbai (1942).

Indian Statesmen (Dewans and Prime Ministers), G.A. Natesan and Co., Chennai.

Intelligence Unit "Economist", The Problem of Newsprint and other printing papers, The UNESCO (Paris), 1949.

International Labour Office, Conditions of work and life of Journalist, Geneva, 1926.

Iyengar, Srinivasa, K.R., S. Srinavasa Iyengar, Basel Mission Press (Canara) Ltd., Managalore, 1939.

Iyengar, Srinivasa, K.R., Sri Aurobindo, Arya Publishing House, Kolkata, 1950.

Iyer, Vishwanath, The Indian Press, (Padma Publications Ltd., Mumbai), 1945.

Jagadisan, T.N., Letters of Rt. Hon. Srinivasa Sastri, Rochouse and Sons Ltd., Chennai, 1944.

Jagadisan, T.N., The other Harmony (Selection from the writings and speeches of V.S. Sastri), S. Viswanathan, Chennai, 1949.

Jagadisan, T.N., Thumb Nail Sketch T.N. from the writings and speeches of the Rt. Hon. V.S. Srinivasa Sastri, S. Viswanathan, Chennai, 1946, Biography of Bhola Chunder.

Jagdisan, T.N., The Wisdom of a Modern Rishi (Writings and speeches of Mahadev Govind Ranade), Rochouse & Sons Ltd., Chennai.

Jambhekar, G.G., Memories and Writings of Acharya Balk Shashtri Jambhekar, Lokashikshana Karyalaya, Poona, 1950.

Jamnadas Dwarkadas, Political Memoirs, (United India Publications: Mumbai)

Jayakar, M.R., The Story of My Life, Vol. I, (Asia Publishing House: Mumbai), 1958.

Karunakaran, K.P., Continuiy and Change in Indian Politics, (People's Publishing House: New Delhi), 1964.

Kaye, J.W., Selection from the papers of Lord Metcalfe, (Smith Elder & Co. London), 1855.

Kaye, John William, Life of Indian Officers, A., Strahan & Co., Bell and Daldy, London, 1867.

Kipling, Rudyard, *et. al.*, Realist and Fabulist, (Oxford University Press: London), 1967.

Klaidman, S. and Beauchamp, T.L., The Virtuous Journalist, New York, USA.: Oxford University Press, 1987.

Krishnamurthi, Nadig, Indian Journalism, (University of Mysore: Mysore), 1966.

Krishnamurthy, Nadig, Indian Journalism: Origin, Growth and Development of Indian Journalism from Ashoka to Nehru, (University of Mysore: Mysore), 1966.

Krishnamurthy, N., Indian Journalism, Mysore, India: Mysore University Press, 1966.

Krishnamurthy, D., 'Media and Social Responsibility', Paper presented at Seminar held from February 3 to 5, 1996 at Osmania University, Hyderabad, 1966.

Krishnamurthy, D., 'News Values, Freedom and Accountability', *Communicator,* XXIII (3): 28-34, 1988.

Lovett, Verney, A History of the Indian National Movement, (John Murray: London), 1920.

Majumdar, Ambika Charan, Indian National Evolution, (G.A. Natesan & Co. : Chennai), 1915.

Mankekar, D.R., Press under Pressure, (Indian Book Co. : New Delhi), 1973.

Mankekar, D.R., Press *vs.* The Government—Before and During Emergency, (Clarion Boobs : Delhi), 1978.

Marin, Gilbert, Servant of India : Diaries of Sir James Dunlop Smith, (Longmans: London), 1966.

Martin, Kingsley, The Press the Public wants, (Hogarth Press, London) 1947.

Masani, R.P., Dadabhai Naoroji, (Publications Division, Government of India: New Delhi), 1960.

Masani, Zaheer, Indira Gandhi—A biography, (Hamilton: London), 1975.

Meherally, Yusuf, Price of Liberty, National Information and Publication Ltd., Mumbai, 1948.

Mehta, Ved, Portrait of India, (Weidenfield and Nicholson: London), 1968.

Mehta, Vinod, 'Mr. Editor, How Close are you to the Prime Minister?—25 Years of selected Writings, New Delhi: Konark Publications, 1999.

Menon, P.K., 'Effective Media and Mass Communication', Jaipur, India: Pointer Publishers, 2004.

Mid Century Issue, The Indian Press Year, (Indian Press Publications, Chennai), 1951-52.

Mody, H.P., Sir Pherozeshah Mehta, Times Press Bombay 1921

Moraes, Frank, Witness to an Era, (Vikas Publihing House: Delhi), 1977.

Moramkar, R.A., Kashinath Trimbak Telang, Telang Centenary Celerbation Committee, Mumbai, 1951.

Motivala, B.N., Karsondas Mulji, Karosondas Mulji Centenary Celerbration Committee, Mumbai, 1935.

Mudholkar, J.R., Press Law: Tagore Law Lectures, (Eastern Law House: Kolkata), 1975.

Muggeridge, Malcolm, Chronicles of Wasted Time, (Collins: London), 1981. Durga Das (ed.),

Muller, F.Max., Ram Mohan to Ramkrishna, Susil Gupta (India Ltd.), Kolkata, 1952.

Murthy, D.V.R., 'Indian Press: The Path Forgotten', Ringside View, 2001.

Murthy, D.V.R., 'Developmental Journalism', New Delhi, India: Dominant Publishers and Distributors, 2000.

Murthy, D.V.R., 'Mass Communication: Concepts and Issues', Kochy, India: Olive Green Publishers, 2002.

Naipaul, V.S., India—A Wounded Civilisation, (Andre Deusch : London).

Narasimhan, V.K., Kasturi Srinivasan, (Populr Prakasan: Mumbi), 1969. Rajendra Prasad.

Narayani, Gupta, Between Two Empires, (Oxford University Press: Delhi).

Natarajan, S., A History of the Press in India, (Asia Publishing House: Mumbai), 1962.

Nation, The Indian Builders Part-I, Ganesh and Co., Chennai.

Nation, The Indian Builders Part-II, Ganesh and Co., Chennai.

Natrajan, K., Gopal Krishna Gokhale, Indian Social Reformer, 1930.

Nehru, Jawahar Lal, Autobiography, John Lane, The Bodley Head, London, 1936.

Nehru, Jawahar Lal, Discovery of India, (Asia Publishing House: Mumbai), 1961.

Pal, Bepin Chandra, Memories of my life and Time, Modern Book Agency, Kolkata, 1932.

Palit, R., Life of Arvindo Ghose, 1911.

Palit, Ram Chandra, The Great Contempt Case, B.C. Mazumdar, Kolkata, 1883.

Panickkar, K.M., The Foundation of New India, (George Allen & Unwin: London), 1963.

Parthasarathy, Rangaswami, Hundred Years of The Hindu, (Kasturi & Sons: Chennai), 1978.

Parthasarathy, Rangaswami, Hundred Years of The Hindu, (Kasturi & Sons: Chennai), 1975.

Parthasarathy, Ramaswami, History of Journalism in India, New Delhi, India: Sterling Publishers, 1991.

Parvate, T.V., Mahadev Govind Ranade, (Asia Publishing House: Mumbai), 1963.

Pat, Lovett, Journalism in India, Banna Publishing Co., Calcutta.

Payne, Robert, The Life and Death of Mahatma Gndhi, (The Bodley Head: London), 1969.

Pillay, G. Paramaswaram, "Keraliyan", The father of political agitation in Travancore, Radh-Ind, Publications, Thiruvananthpuram, 1928.

Primrose, Rev. J.B., The First Press in India and its Printers, (The Bibliographic Society, London), 1940.

Publication Division, Government of India, Report of the Second Press Commission, Vol. I, (Publications Division, Government of India: New Delhi), 1984.

Raja Ram Mohan Roy (1 anna pamphlet series), Ramulu & Co., Chennai.

Rajendra Prasad, An Autobiography, (Asia Publishing House: Mumbai), 1957.

Rama Rao, K., The Pen as my Sword, (Bharatiya Vidya Bhavan: Mumbai), 1965.

Ramasamy Aiyer, C.P., Biographical Vistas, (Asia Publishing House: Mumbai).

Ranade, Mahadev Govind (1 anna Pamphlets series), M.S. Ramulu and Co., Chennai.

Ranade, Mrs. Ramaba, Miscellaneous writings of the late Hon. Mr. Justice Ranade, Manoranjan Press, Mumbai, 1915.

Rao, P.G., Famous Indian Journalists & Journalism, (Kanara Book and News Agency), Mumbai.

Ray, R.C., Life and times of C.R. Das, Oxford University Press, Kolkata, 1928.

Romeo, Captain Francies, Letters to the Marquis of Hastings on the Indian Press in British India, (J.M. Richardson, London): 1884.

Sabari, Amdad, Tarikhe-Sahafat-I-Urdu (History of Urdu Journalism), Subash Book Depot Delhi, 1952.

Sahni, J.N., Rogues Gallery and Indian Politics, (Allied Publishers: New Delhi), 1982.

Sahni, J.N., The Lid Off, (Deep Publications: Agra), 1977.

Sahni, J.N., Truth about the Indian Press, (Allied Publishers: New Delhi), 1974.

Samuel Hebich of India, Basel Mission Book and Depository, Tract, Mangalore.

Sardar Patel's Correspondence, Vols. I to 10, (Navjivan Publishing House: Ahmedabad), 1972-74.

Sawant, P.B., 'Accountability in Journalism', *Journal of Mass Media Ethics*, 18(1): 16-28, 2003.

Sarkar, Chanchal, Newspaper and Community, (Press Institute of India: New Delhi), 1966.

Scott, C.P., The making of the Manchester Guardian, (Fredrick Muller Ltd., London): 1946.

Sen, N.B., Punjab's eminent Hindus, New Book Society, Lahore, 1944.

Setalvad, Chrimanlal, H., Recollections, Padma Publication, Mumbai, 1946.

Sethi, Patanjali, Professional Journalism, (Orient Longman: Mumbai), 1974. Sommerlad, E.L., Press in Developing Countries, (Atma Ram: Delhi), 1966.

Sharma, M.N., The Spirit of the Anglo Bengali Magazine, (Thacker Spink & Co., Kolkata), 1873.

Sharma, R.K., Journalism as a profession in India, Mumbai, India: Media Promoters and Publishers, 1990.

Smith, Anthony, The Newspaper—An International History, (Thames and Hudson: London), 1979.

Soloski, J., 'News reporting and professionalism', Media Culture and Society, 1989.

Sorabjee, Soli, J., Law of Press Censorship in India, (Tripathi: Mumbai), 1976.

Southern India Journalists Federation, The South Indian Journalists (Nov. 1952 Issue), Chennai.

Speeches and writings of Dr. Sir Rash Behari Ghosh, G.S. Natesan & Co., Chennai.

Speeches of Gopal Krishna Gokhale, G.A. Natesan & Co., Chennai, 1920

Srinivasa Sastri, The Rt., Hon. V.S., Life and times of Sir Pherozeshah Mehta, *Madras Law Journal Press,* Chennai, 1945.

Srinivasa Sastry, V.S., Life and Times of Sir Phirozeshah Mehta, (Bharatiya Vidya Bhavan: Mumbai), 1975.

Srinivasan, C.R., Press and Public, University of Travancore.

Stanhope, Leicester, Sketch of the History and Influence of the Press in British India, (C. Chapple Royal Library, London), 1823.

Stephens, Ian, Unmade Journey, (Stacey International: London), 1977.

Tahmankar, D.V., Lokmanya Tilak, (John Murray: London), 1956.

Tendulkar, D.G., Mahatma, *Times of India,* Mumbai, 1951-53.

Testament of Subash Bose, Rajkamal Publications, Delhi, 1946.

The English Works of Raja Ram Mohan Roy (Centenary Edition), Sadharan Brahma Samaj, Kolkata, 1934.

The Granada Guildhall Lectures, 1974: The Half-Free Press by Harold Evans.

The Statesman, 100 Years of The Statesman, (Statesman Printing Press: Kolkata), 1975.

Tinker, Hugh, The Ordeal of Love, C.F. Andrews in India, (Oxford Universith Press), 1979.

U.N. Department of Public Information, *Punjabi Journalism,* These Rights and Freedoms, 1950.

Universal Declaration of Human Rights, 1948. Freedom of the Press—A Framework of Principles (Report of the Commission on the Freedom of the Press in the United States of America).

Vigneshwara, Our New Rulers, (B.G. Paul & Co., Chennai), 1961.

———, The Avadi Socialists, (B.G. Paul & Co., Chennai), 1964.

Wayfarer, Life of Shishir Kumar Ghose, *Amrita Bazar Patrika,* Kolkata, 1946.

Yadava, S., 'The Changing Role of the Indian Press', Media Asia 12(3): 111-19, 1985.

Index